Journalist **Kate Aronoff's** writing has appeared in *The Guardian*, *Rolling Stone*, *Dissent*, *The Intercept*, and the *New York Times*. She is a fellow at the Type Media Center, the co-author of *A Planet to Win*, and the author of *The New Denialism*. She lives in Brooklyn.

Peter Dreier is E.P. Clapp Distinguished Professor of Politics at Occidental College. He is the author of *The 100 Greatest Americans of the 20th Century: A Social Justice Hall of Fame* and co-author (with Robert Elias) of the forthcoming *Rebels of the Diamond: The Baseball Reformers and Radicals Who Shook Up the Game On and Off the Field*. He is a contributor to *The Nation*, *American Prospect*, *Dissent*, *Jacobin*, and the *Los Angeles Times* and lives in Pasadena, California.

Michael Kazin is a professor of history at Georgetown University and co-editor of *Dissent*. He is the author of *War Against War: The American Fight for Peace, 1914–1918*, *American Dreamers: How the Left Changed a Nation*, *The Populist Persuasion: An American History*, and other books. He contributes regularly to the *New York Times*, *The Nation*, the *New Republic*, and other periodicals. He lives in Washington, DC.

We Own the Future

Democratic Socialism— American Style

Edited by Kate Aronoff,
Peter Dreier, and Michael Kazin

THE
NEW
PRESS

NEW YORK
LONDON

Compilation and introduction © 2020 by Kate Aronoff, Peter Dreier, and Michael Kazin
Individual essays © 2020 by each author

Published in the United States by The New Press, New York, 2020
Distributed by Two Rivers Distribution

ISBN 978-1-62097-521-3 (pb)
ISBN 978-1-62097-522-0 (ebook)
CIP data is available

The New Press publishes books that promote and enrich public discussion and understanding of the issues vital to our democracy and to a more equitable world. These books are made possible by the enthusiasm of our readers; the support of a committed group of donors, large and small; the collaboration of our many partners in the independent media and the not-for-profit sector; booksellers, who often hand-sell New Press books; librarians; and above all by our authors.

www.thenewpress.com

Book design and composition by Bookbright Media
This book was set in Fournier and Avenir

Printed in the United States of America

10 9 8 7 6 5 4 3 2 1

Contents

We Own the Future

Part I

Is a New America Possible?

Introduction

Kate Aronoff, Peter Dreier, and Michael Kazin

"AMERICA WILL NEVER BE A SOCIALIST COUNTRY," PRESIDENT DONALD Trump declared in his 2019 State of the Union address. "The American left is on the cusp of a great victory," wrote an apprehensive David Brooks, the conservative *New York Times* columnist, in 2018.

More than at any time since World War I, over one hundred years ago, Americans are talking about socialism. Conservatives fear it. Liberals question it. Many progressives and radicals embrace it. Why is that word, and the egalitarian vision it defines, enjoying a resurgence in the United States? And does it mean, as Trump warned and Brooks predicted, that socialism is on the American horizon?

In 2016, Senator Bernie Sanders, a democratic socialist, captured the nation's attention—and more than 13 million votes—in his campaign for the Democratic nomination for president. Two years later, voters elected democratic socialists Alexandria Ocasio-Cortez of New York and Rashida Tlaib of Detroit to Congress, while dozens of their counterparts won races for city council, state legislative, school board, and other seats around the country. According to a 2019 Gallup poll, 43 percent of all Americans, and 58 percent of Americans between 18 and 34 years old, believe that socialism would be a good thing for the country.[1]

Democratic socialists have played key roles in the upsurge of activism during the twenty-first century, in social movements like Occupy Wall Street, Black Lives Matter, the Fight for $15 minimum wage, #MeToo, the anti-Trump resistance, and the battle for a Green New Deal. The Democratic Socialists of America (DSA)—which long languished with just a few thousand members—has exploded. By mid-2019, the organization counted more than 60,000 people among its ranks, with more than two hundred chapters in red and blue states alike; Iowa has the highest density of DSA members per capita. Almost all of those new members are millennials or younger still, without the Cold War–era hang-ups of their baby boomer and Gen X parents.

Americans seems to be holding their breath, trying to decide what kind of country we want to be. An overwhelming majority of Americans are frustrated and fed up with the economic and political status quo. Ideas considered radical only a few years ago—universal health care, tuition-free college, a $15 federal minimum wage, same-sex marriage, requiring big corporations to put workers and union members on their boards, a Green New Deal, and many others—enjoy popular support, and have been embraced by some of the Democratic Party's biggest names.

Is it possible that, within a generation, we might turn this troubled plutocracy into a socialist democracy?

It's hardly radical to say that the United States could be run a lot better and more decently than it is now. There's much we can learn from other countries. We could cobble together the best parts of what other cities and countries have to offer to make the United States a much fairer and more caring place: Sweden's generous family leave policy; Vienna's luxurious public housing, which still accounts for about a third of the city's housing stock (another third is cooperatively owned); Britain's comprehensive National Health Service; Spain's financial support for coal miners who'll lose their jobs as the country shutters its last mines.

But we don't just have to look abroad for successful ideas. We should also look to our own nation's history to find examples of progressive, even radical, programs that raised standards of living, tamed the greed of big corporations, made our cities and rural areas more livable, and expanded rights to previously disenfranchised groups. During the 1930s, federal programs created not just magisterial infrastructure and conservation projects, but also murals, national parks, and avant-garde theater productions. Back in the 1950s, before decades of wage stagnation and outrageous corporate profits, the top marginal tax rate in the United States reached 91 percent, and young people graduating from college weren't burdened with five-, six-, and even seven-figure debt. More than a third of wage earners belonged to unions, compared to just over 10 percent today.

This period from the mid-1930s to the mid-1970s—which historians call the New Deal Order—was far from a wonderland of equality and economic security. People of color and their white allies waged epic battles for survival, civil rights, and a measure of political power; women and LGBTQ people had to fight for respect and the right to live and love as they pleased. Many were excluded from the redistributive policies that built the white middle class. In the name of anti-communism, the U.S. government tried to crush popular revolutions in the third world and, under Presidents Lyndon Johnson and Richard Nixon, waged a near genocidal war in Indochina. It's hardly an era worth returning to. But the gap between the rich and everyone else was far smaller than it is now, and liberal presidents, facing pressure from below, were confident enough in the powers of government and continued economic prosperity that they actually vowed to do away with poverty. A bestselling 1962 book about the poor by America's leading socialist, Michael Harrington, *The Other America*, did much to inspire that ambition.

Today, in what is still the richest nation that has ever existed, a few things should be as nonnegotiable as they are elsewhere. Everyone should enjoy quality health care that stretches from cradle to grave, including preventative care, mental health services, and prescription drugs. No one should go hungry. Anyone who wants a job should have one. What zip code you live in shouldn't determine the quality of the education you receive, and the color of your skin shouldn't dictate how you're treated by banks, landlords, police officers, or district attorneys. The country you were born in shouldn't predict how many rights you have once you leave it. And no one should live in fear that their world—or that of their children or grandchildren—will be made unlivable by global warming. And that's just the bread, to crib a phrase coined by the labor organizer Rose Schneiderman a century ago. We can have our roses, too: paid vacations, public parks and beaches to spend them on, and expansive public transit networks within cities and high-speed rail between them.

For residents of today's actually existing social democracies, most of which are in Northern and Western Europe, these ideas might all seem run-of-the-mill. Their citizens live in what the UN has called some of the "happiest countries in the world," with Finland taking the number one slot. And while these models are not without their limitations, residents of these places enjoy all or most of the benefits one needs to live a dignified life. For many Americans, that probably sounds downright utopian—even, dare we say, socialist.

Trump's warning about America's socialist future—echoed by Fox News and the Republican Party—was intended to rile up the conservative base. For sure, some Americans still identify socialism with totalitarian communism, or just with "big government." But for most Americans—especially those under forty—socialism is no longer the authoritarian red menace it was for generations past, nor the province of an out-of-touch and isolated left-wing fringe peddling newspapers and ideology. Magazines like *New York* publish trend pieces about how young socialists spend their Friday nights. Elected officials are asked to explain democratic socialism on late-night talk shows. More consequentially, proposals that have long wallowed in left-wing backwaters—from Medicare for All to a federal job guarantee—are now decidedly mainstream. Many leading Democrats, including those eyeing the Oval Office, have adopted ideas once considered "radical." Politicians who once fashioned themselves as business-friendly centrists have embraced policies long championed by socialists past and present. Their reasoning is entirely pragmatic; these proposals are popular with large swaths of the voting public because most Americans realize they would go a long way toward meeting today's most pressing challenges, from climate breakdown to wealth inequality, at the scale those crises demand.

Even former Clinton-era Treasury official Brad DeLong recently admitted that the approach he and his colleagues adopted in Washington—pursuing compromise with the GOP and economic growth above all else—has run its course.[2] If they ever did, Republicans are no longer operating in good faith and "there is no political path to a coalition built from the [center] out. Instead," he suggests, "we accommodate ourselves to those on our left. . . . The world appears to be more like what lefties thought it was than what I thought it was for the last 10 or 15 years."

The gap between what's needed and what establishment types consider pragmatic might be clearest when it comes to the climate crisis. As the world's leading scientists urge that "rapid, far-reaching and unprecedented changes in all aspects of society" are needed to avert catastrophe, elites in both parties have joined the fossil fuel industry in casting large-scale public investments to mitigate this existential threat as a pipe dream.[3] As climate scientist Will Steffen observed, getting greenhouse gas emissions down as soon as possible "has to be the *primary target of policy and economics.* You have got to get away from the so-called neoliberal economics." The main constraints on climate action, he added, aren't physical or chemical, but tied up in "our value systems, politics, and legal systems." In the context of massive racial and economic inequality, rising temperatures will distribute their worst destruction to those already worst off.

We still have time to prevent the most apocalyptic of climate scenarios from playing out, and it's been the young people flocking toward socialism who grasp that fact and the need for a clear alternative most firmly. Unlike environmentalists past, they don't see any trade-off between a decarbonized world and a more equal and prosperous one. As Naomi Klein writes in her chapter in this book ("Democratic Socialism for a Climate-Changed Century"), the Green New Deal—embraced by DSA and 81 percent of Americans, as of February 2019—is a chance to build both.

There is no alternative but to build an alternative. And more and more Americans think democratic socialism might be the best option.

Still, what those who embrace the label mean by socialism is subject to much debate. On the right, everything from the Green New Deal to an increase in the minimum wage has been decried as a step toward Stalinism. But conservatives have been making such charges since the 1928 presidential campaign, when Herbert Hoover branded Al Smith, his Democratic opponent, a socialist for wanting to raise taxes on the rich and favoring an eight-hour workday. For some on the radical left, social democratic policies are merely compromises to preserve capitalism, preferring a society where all productive enterprises are held in common and administered by workers.

If you're looking for an authoritative definition of democratic socialism, you won't find it in this anthology. What we do believe is this: any socialist society worth struggling for should be fiercely democratic, ensure that human rights will flourish, and hold free elections open to all kinds of candidates and parties—including those who oppose socialism itself. We hold no brief for the one-party dictatorships that still exist in North Korea, China, and Cuba—or for the failed states of the old USSR and its allies in Eastern Europe, which gave socialism a bad name.

At the same time, there is plenty of daylight between democratic socialism and social democracy and left-liberalism. The biggest fault lines break down around questions of who owns what—be that corporations, the public, or the workers directly—and how many of society's key institutions are democratically controlled. Do we simply take some services like health care out of private hands to be run in the public interest? Or try to nationalize key sectors like the fossil fuel industry through a public buyout? What role does the government play in guiding economic activity, and what matters should be left to the market?

Our contributors answer these questions differently. They run the gamut from social democrats to democratic socialists and points right and left, and define each in different terms. So do the three of us. But we also see diversity of outlooks as a strength in this messy, growing, and ever-evolving movement of people who have profound criticisms of the system in which we live.

Uniquely, democratic socialists set their sights on moving beyond capitalism as society's operating system, not simply to make it more tolerable. They strive to build an economy and society that prioritizes the well-being of people and planet above all else, replacing capitalism's endless thirst for hoarded profits with a quest for widespread prosperity.

The pressing question isn't how precisely to define democratic socialism, but what we need it to do when its alternatives have so clearly failed. Fleshing that out and building toward it will mean much more than just importing best practices from history or abroad, although we have much to learn from both.

In Scandinavia's social democracies, health care is free and state-of-the-art. A far higher proportion of workers are in labor unions; in tiny Iceland, 92 percent of residents are unionized. As a result, wages are higher and more evenly distributed across professions and skill sets. That—combined with excellent public education—makes upward mobility a far more realistic prospect than it is in the United States. A proliferation of "red-green" parties have also made gender equality and mitigating climate change top priorities; the Nordic countries are consistently world leaders on both.

Existing social democracies offer many lessons, but they are by no means a blueprint for building a sustainable and multiracial democracy in today's United States. Norway's generous social democracy has been furnished largely by oil wealth, and xenophobic politicians have gained clout across Europe on promises to defend their countries' generous welfare states from mostly nonwhite foreigners. Amid rising anti-immigrant sentiment, Denmark, for instance, sorts predominantly Muslim new arrivals into official "ghettos" to be surveilled and assimilated; in hardening these laws, the country's Social Democrats have found common cause with its far right.[4] "Danes," the *New York Times* wrote in an extensive report on such policies, have become "so desensitized to harsh rhetoric about immigrants that they no longer register the negative connotation of the word 'ghetto' and its echoes of Nazi Germany's separation of Jews."

Of course, racism and xenophobia are no lesser threats to prospects for an egalitarian America. "We don't look like Denmark in terms of our social policies because we don't look like Denmark demographically," Ian Haney López and Heather McGhee have observed. "In our diverse society, racism has been the plutocrats' scythe, cutting down social solidarity to harvest obscene wealth and power." Right-wing politicians and their corporate patrons have ripped apart vital social programs and divided social movements on the false grounds that they only serve people of color, whom they paint as lazy and undeserving, and that a generous welfare state somehow deprives industrious whites their fair share of America's pie. Amid the labor militancy of the 1970s—when one in six union members went on strike—that strategy was corporate America's antidote to sever the bonds built on picket lines, and to unraveling the New Deal Order.[5] It was a quick jump from right-wing lies about "welfare queens" defrauding the dole to the nineties' destructive War on Drugs and the mass incarceration it brought with it—a war battled by Republicans and Democrats both.

White supremacy isn't just another issue for socialists to take seriously. It's a major barrier to building the world we need. Moving toward a more equal future—as several contributors contend in the pages to come—will require public policies that grapple squarely with our past and its burden on the present. There is nothing short of a world to lose.

The chapters that follow propose ways to build a kinder, more humane, and altogether freer society—and suggest how to overcome the barriers to that future. We've asked a group of talented writers, academics, and organizers from across the American left to lay out their visions for this better world, how to get there, and what stands in the way.

As has always been true in the history of the left, there are contradictions and disagreements, as well as plenty of common ground. This collection is meant, above all, to spark a conversation about what an American democratic socialism might look like, which (we think) is the best way of defining it.

To ground the discussion, Peter Dreier and Michael Kazin first trace the history of socialism in the United States through its successes and failures and through the lives of some of its most important figures—well-known and otherwise. Andrea Flynn, Susan Holmberg, Dorian Warren, and Felicia Wong then lay out how deeply racism shapes American society and public policy, making the case for a Third Reconstruction to address rampant racial and economic inequality that could begin to right historical wrongs. Diving in further, economist Darrick Hamilton proposes what he calls a three-legged stool of policies to mend our unequal economy, comprised of a federal job guarantee, baby bonds, and reparations. Naomi Klein describes how the logic of extraction has defined socialist and capitalist governments, and how—learning from resistance to both—the Green New Deal can help repair the disastrous results in time to save the planet.

Kicking off a section on expanding and freeing up democracy, Bill Fletcher Jr. offers some tough lessons for a new generation of socialists eager to take power, unpacking the many things that word can mean to the left. J. Mijin Cha reviews how our electoral system—and the way we vote, in particular—serves elite interests and keeps millions out of the democratic process, then offers commonsense reforms to correct the imbalance. Robert Kuttner explains how corporate power took over our government—and how to wrest it back. David Dayen sears our bloated financial sector in his plan to remake the banking system and root out the greed that created the last recession and continues to leave Americans worse off. Sarita Gupta, Stephen Lerner and Joseph A. McCartin consider the future of work, and how a more militant labor movement could play a key role in making the American economy and our politics more democratic. Aviva Stahl calls for dismantling our destructive criminal justice system by challenging our understanding of safety and the role of police and prisons. In her chapter on immigration, Michelle Chen spells out the case for open borders and prioritizing human rights above citizenship. Tejasvi Nagaraja explores what a democratic socialist approach to foreign policy would entail, abroad and in our own backyard.

Thomas J. Sugrue then maps out how corporate America, the real estate industry, and government policy fostered racial and economic segregation in our metropolitan areas, and outlines a set of housing, transportation, and other policies to make cities and suburbs both more livable. Dorothy Roberts makes the case for universal health care—and why Medicare for All alone won't go nearly far enough in correcting the many ways our medical system mistreats patients of color. Sarah Leonard reimagines the family freed from capitalism, and the many forms it can take on when reproductive justice is front and center. Pedro Noguera charts a path to defending, improving, and expanding one of America's oldest public goods: education. From Little League to stadiums to players' unions, David Zirin envisions sports under democratic socialism (spoiler: they're more fun). Francesca Fiorentini looks forward to a world where artists of all sorts are supported to do what they love, and make societies more resilient in the process.

Finally, Harold Meyerson points us toward the world we need, drawing lessons from the past about how to get from here to there. And we revive Michael Walzer's 1968 essay, "A Day in the Life of a Socialist Citizen," which details how pleasantly mundane a radically egalitarian world could be.

As these chapters underscore, the scale of work required to build the United States envisioned here is daunting but not impossible. It will require going toe-to-toe with some of the most powerful industries the world has ever known, from finance to fossil fuels. And given the accelerating climate crisis, we're working against the clock. But socialists have never been keen to back down from a fight. Today's democratic socialists are bringing both big ideas back to American politics and a willingness to go to bat for them, from inside and outside the halls of power. Insurgent left politicians have been shaped and inspired by the social movement uprisings of the last decade. They know full well that transformative change in the United States—whether the abolition of slavery, universal suffrage, the eight-hour workday, or civil rights—has always been the result of pressure from below that forced officeholders to change their policies, if not their minds. Those victories also required naming enemies and, in the case of slavery, battling the defenders of an economic and political order that had been core to the growth of American capitalism.

The opportunity waiting on the other side of these fights is tremendous: to salvage humanity's prospects for a livable future from the jaws of the 1 percent; to finally reckon with our nation's racist past and present; to wrest true democratic control over the institutions that shape our world; and to create a society of joy and contentment instead of anxiety and insecurity. As the socialist poet Langston Hughes once put it,

> *O, let America be America again—*
> *The land that never has been yet—*
> *And yet must be—the land where every man is free.*

How Socialists Changed America

Peter Dreier and Michael Kazin

WOMEN'S RIGHT TO VOTE, SOCIAL SECURITY, THE MINIMUM WAGE, WORK-place safety laws, universal health insurance, and civil rights for all races and genders were once considered radical ideas. Today, a vast majority of Americans consider these to be commonsense ideas, among the corner-stones of a decent society. They also favor government-run police depart-ments, fire departments, national parks, municipally owned utilities, local subway systems, and public universities. They think that the super-rich should pay much higher taxes than the middle-class. They believe that businesses should be subject to rules that require them to act responsibly. Banks shouldn't engage in reckless predatory lending. Energy corporations shouldn't endanger the planet and public health by emitting too much pol-lution. Companies should be required to guarantee that consumer products (like cars, food, and toys) are safe and that companies pay decent wages and provide safe workplaces.

How did these and other radical ideas move from the margins to the mainstream of our culture?

Socialists played a major role in bringing about all these changes—in the parties they founded, the social movements they helped to form and lead, and the ideas they expressed.

America has had a socialist movement since the late 1800s. For most of that time, socialists had a respected political party that ran candidates for office, popular newspapers and magazines, and well-known, even beloved, public figures. But even when the party itself was marginal, there have always been individuals who espoused socialist ideas with vigor and eloquence. Helen Keller, W.E.B. Du Bois, Upton Sinclair, Charlie Chaplin, Albert Einstein, Walter Reuther, A. Philip Randolph, Gloria Steinem, Martin Luther King Jr., and Michael Moore were among the most famous Americans of the twentieth century, although most of their fellow citizens did not know that they embraced socialism.

Socialism has always been both an idea and a movement. As an idea, it is about advancing human progress by creating laws and institutions that give people the chance to reach their full potential and to tame the forces of greed, racism, inequality, and exploitation inherent in capitalism. As a movement, socialism is about promoting those ideas through education, grassroots activism, and elections. During the past half century, activists and thinkers have embraced the phrase "democratic socialism" to emphasize the importance of such democratic ideals as free speech and voting rights, and in part to distinguish their movement from authoritarian communism.

Has American socialism been successful? If success means that the United States has become a democratic socialist country, then the movement has certainly failed. But if success means that many Americans now accept ideas that were once considered radical, even socialist, and made the United States a more egalitarian and humane society, then it has accomplished a great deal.

The left—and the socialist movement within it—has always included three kinds of people. Organizers built grassroots organizations that pushed for reforms such as women's equality, civil rights, workers' rights, environmental justice, and peace. Politicians used election campaigns to educate the public and, if they won, push for changes that translated radical ideas into legislation. Artists and thinkers—novelists, painters, poets, theologians, journalists, actors, playwrights, academics, and singers—used their talents to inspire people to dream, hope, and struggle for social justice, often under difficult circumstances.

Origins

In the early 1800s, Europe began a new phase of human civilization. Historians call it the "Industrial Revolution," or "capitalism," but for most people, it was simply a momentous change in everyday life. People who once lived as farmers and peasants were pushed off their land and pulled into the burgeoning cities and towns, where they worked in factories, mines, and warehouses under brutal conditions and for long hours, lived in overcrowded and unhealthy slums, and suffered indignities that squeezed their humanity from them. In most countries, the owners of the factories and the slums used their political influence to ensure that the laws protected their property and profits, not workers' lives. Few workers had the right to vote, so they had no voice in establishing the rules and laws that shaped their lives.

In response, people rebelled. Workers challenged the crushing oppression of the factory by refusing to work, destroying machines, or demanding better conditions, higher pay, and fewer hours. Journalists, theologians, and other thinkers documented these conditions, called for immediate improvements, and imagined a different world where the "means of production"— the tools and machines—could be used to liberate people and make life easier rather than oppress and exploit them. They called this better world "socialism" and began forming organizations—unions, political parties, social clubs, and others—to demand the right to vote, the right to organize, and the right to decent pay, working conditions, and housing.

These ideas spread from Europe to America. In the early 1800s, women and men who called themselves socialists formed small "utopian" communities designed to demonstrate that people could live in egalitarian ways that avoided vast differences of power and income and that emphasized sharing and cooperation. They located most of these experiments in rural areas and engaged in farming and crafts work, such as making furniture.

Most of these communities were inspired by religious beliefs as well as secular social and political ideas. For example, in 1825, Robert Owen, a wealthy Welsh industrialist who became a socialist, founded a communitarian colony called New Harmony in rural Indiana. Writers Nathaniel Hawthorne and Ralph Waldo Emerson briefly lived at Brook Farm, a community founded in 1841 in Massachusetts by transcendental utopians based on the ideas of French writer Charles Fourier. These and similar groups often faced financial and other practical difficulties. Few lasted for more than a decade. But their ideas continued to influence American culture.

Edward Bellamy's utopian novel *Looking Backward*, published in 1888, described a socialist America in the year 2000. It inspired a network of

Bellamy Clubs around the country and influenced the thinking of many leading figures in America's reform and radical movements, including labor leader Eugene Debs and feminist writer Charlotte Perkins Gilman.

But for most Americans, utopian socialism was neither practical nor desirable. By the late 1800s, America had become a nation of immigrants, primarily from Germany, Ireland, Scandinavia, Italy, Greece, Poland, Russia, and China. Some became farmers, but most arrived in the growing cities and got poorly paid and dangerous jobs in factories and on the docks.

Some of these immigrants brought radical and socialist ideas with them to the United States. Some were already familiar with the writings of Karl Marx, particularly his *Communist Manifesto*, a pamphlet written with Friedrich Engels and published in 1848, that not only encouraged the "workers of the world" to unite to bring about a new world, but also called for the eight-hour workday and other reforms. A German immigrant named Joseph Weydemeyer, who was close to Marx, came to the United States in 1851 and established the first Marxist journal in the United States (*Die Revolution*) and the first Marxist political organization, the American Workers League. Marx was only one of a number of radical thinkers—including American Josiah Warren, Frenchman Pierre Proudhon, and German Ferdinand Lasalle—whose ideas became part of America's growing socialist ferment.

A large part of that ferment was channeled into organizing workers into the first labor unions. Most union activists were not socialists, but many socialists devoted themselves to building the labor movement, which they viewed as the foundation of a broader movement to transform America into a society based on economic, political, and social equality rather than what they called "wage slavery."

In the 1870s, socialists formed the Social Democratic Party of North America and the Workingmen's Party of the United States, which changed its name to the Socialist Labor Party, led by Daniel De Leon. A onetime socialist, Samuel Gompers, formed the American Federation of Labor in 1886 to unite the various unions in particular industries and crafts. These two ideas—worker-oriented political parties and labor unions—became the dominant form of socialist activism from the late 1800s through the mid-1900s.

The Gilded Age and Progressive Era

The emergence of the Gilded Age at the end of the 1800s catalyzed a broad progressive movement in which socialists played a prominent role. The era was characterized by an increasing concentration of wealth, a widening gap between the rich and the poor, and the growing political influence of corporate power brokers known as "robber barons," like banker J.P. Morgan and steel magnate Andrew Carnegie, who were exploiting workers, gouging consumers, and corrupting politics with their money.

In foreign affairs, Americans were battling over the nation's role in the world. America was beginning to act like an imperial power, justifying its expansion with a combination of white supremacy, manifest destiny, and the hubris of making the world "safe for democracy." At the time, nativist groups in the North and Midwest as well as the South were pushing for restrictions on immigrants—Catholics, Jews, and Asians—who they believed "polluted" Protestant America. In the South, the outcome of the Civil War still inflamed regional passions. Many Southerners, including Civil War veterans, still swore allegiance to the Confederate flag.

Out of the poverty, slums, child labor, epidemics, sweatshops, and ethnic conflict that afflicted America during that period emerged a coalition of immigrants, unionists, radicalized farmers, middle-class suffragists, clergy, and upper-class philanthropists. Workers organized unions. Farmers joined forces in the Populist movement to challenge the power of banks, railroads, and utility companies. Progressive reformers fought alongside radical socialists for child labor laws, against slum housing, and in favor of women's suffrage. Journalists, sometimes called "muckrakers," investigated and publicized the problems of the poor. Progressive middle- and upper-class Americans joined with working-class activists through groups such as the Women's Trade Union League, the National Consumers League, the International Ladies' Garment Workers' Union, the National Child Labor Committee, and a growing network of settlement houses such as Chicago's Hull House and New York's Henry Street Settlement.

Among America's leading socialists of the period were public health pioneer Alice Hamilton, workingwomen's rights activist Florence Kelley, crusading attorney Clarence Darrow, novelist Jack London, feminist writer

Charlotte Perkins Gilman, "Big Bill" Haywood (leader of the Industrial Workers of the World [IWW]), Helen Keller, dancer Isadora Duncan, Roger Baldwin (founder of the American Civil Liberties Union), Margaret Sanger (founder of Planned Parenthood and a pioneer crusader for birth control), and W.E.B. DuBois (the nation's leading black intellectual and a founder of the National Association for the Advancement of Colored People [NAACP] in 1909).

The socialist Charlotte Perkins Gilman was, at the time, one of the most prominent feminist thinkers in the country. She wrote economic and social treatises, as well as short stories (including "The Yellow Wallpaper," a feminist classic), which gave her work broad appeal. Such books as *Women and Economics: A Study of the Economic Relation Between Men and Women as a Factor in Social Evolution* (1898) challenged the dominant ideas about women's role in society. In her novel *Herland* (1915), the fictional author visits an island community of women organized around the principle of New Motherhood, where cooperation in all spheres of life has replaced male domination, competition, and war.

Gilman believed that women would be equal to men only when they were economically independent. The unpaid labor that women perform in the home—child rearing, cooking, cleaning, and other activities—was, she wrote, a form of oppression. Society had to accept the idea of women, even married women, having careers. She encouraged women to work outside the home and maintained that men and women should share housework.

But she went further, arguing that marriage itself had to be modernized to meet new realities. As much as possible, she believed, housekeeping, cooking, and child care should be done by professionals, not by biological parents. To Gilman, the very idea of "motherhood" was outdated in a modern society. Children, she believed, should be raised in communal nurseries and fed in communal kitchens rather than in individual homes. Girls and boys, she thought, should be raised with the same clothes, toys, and expectations.

Some of Gilman's fellow feminists tried to put her ideas into action. In 1915, after a lobbying campaign by the Feminist Alliance, New York City's school system changed its policies and permitted women to continue teaching after they married and even after they had children.

Socialists were also influential in the garment workers unions, formed and led primarily by Jewish immigrants. One of them was Rose Schneiderman, an immigrant from Russia. By the age of twenty-one, she had already organized her first union shop and had led a successful strike. In 1908, a philanthropist offered Schneiderman money to complete her education. The organizer refused the scholarship, explaining that she could not accept a privilege that was not available to most workingwomen. She did, however, accept the philanthropist's offer to pay her salary as chief organizer of the Women's Trade Union League (WTUL). Schneiderman's efforts to build the labor movement paved the way for a strike of twenty thousand garment workers in 1909—the largest such uprising by women to that point in U.S. history.

On March 25, 1911, a fire at the Triangle Shirtwaist Factory in New York City killed 146 workers, mostly female immigrants and teenagers. One week later, activists held a meeting at the Metropolitan Opera House to memorialize the victims. Schneiderman rose to speak: "I would be a traitor to these poor burned bodies if I came here to talk good fellowship. We have tried you good people of the public, and we have found you wanting," Schneiderman told 3,500 listeners, a mix of workers and the city's wealthy and middle-class reformers. "This is not the first time girls have been burned alive in the city. Every week, I must learn of the untimely death of one of my sister workers. Every year, thousands of us are maimed. There are so many of us for one job, it matters little if 146 of us are burned to death."

Her speech fired up the garment workers in the balcony and the wealthy women in the front rows. They forged a crusade that led to the nation's first state factory safety laws.

Socialists and other radicals also played key roles in the Industrial Workers of the World, founded in 1905. The IWW pioneered in the organization of unions among immigrant workers in mass-production industries in cities like Lawrence, Massachusetts, and Paterson, New Jersey, and among migrant workers in the lumber camps and mining towns of the Far West.

Socialist ideas also attracted a growing following in Christian churches—where they helped inspire the Social Gospel—as well as in the feminist movement and on college campuses. Many leading radicals were first exposed to these ideas through the Intercollegiate Socialist Society, founded in 1905, which became the student wing of the Socialist Party. Socialists, black and white alike, were also among the founders of the NAACP in 1909, which waged campaigns against lynching and against discrimination in housing and jobs.

Francis Bellamy, a Christian minister who was fired from his Boston church for his sermons depicting Jesus as a socialist, wrote the Pledge of Allegiance in 1892 for *Youth's Companion*, a magazine for young people published in Boston with a circulation of about five hundred thousand. He hoped the pledge would promote a moral vision to counter the individualism embodied in capitalism and expressed in the ruthless climate of the Gilded Age, with its robber barons and exploitation of workers. Bellamy intended the line "One nation indivisible with liberty and justice for all" to express a more collective and egalitarian vision of America.

The words to "America the Beautiful" were written in 1893 by Katharine Lee Bates, a socialist and professor of English at Wellesley College. She was part of progressive reform circles in the Boston area concerned about labor rights, urban slums, and women's suffrage. "America the Beautiful" not only speaks to the beauty of the American continent but also reflects her view that American imperialism was undermining the nation's core values of freedom and liberty. The poem's final words—"and crown thy good with brotherhood, from sea to shining sea"—are an appeal for social justice rather than the unbridled pursuit of wealth.

Eugene Debs and the Socialist Party of America

For the first two decades of the twentieth century, Eugene Debs was America's most prominent socialist. Born in 1855, Debs had come rather late to the cause. Until he was almost forty, the Indiana native had traced the arc of a self-made man, albeit one making his way largely within the humble orbit of organized labor. As a teenager, Debs dropped out of school to work on the railroads. At the age of twenty-five, he was elected leader of the Brotherhood of Locomotive Firemen, a conservative union that represented some of the most highly skilled and well-paid tradesmen in America. "The mission of the Brotherhood . . . ," Debs wrote in 1884, "is not to antagonize capital. Strikes do that; hence we oppose strikes as a remedy for the ills of which labor complains."

In 1888, however, he began to change his mind. Firemen on the Burlington Railroad stopped work in sympathy with a strike begun by employees who belonged to a different union. Debs tried to convince the railroad bosses to bargain with their employees, but the company secured court injunctions against the unions and fired most of the strikers. To his alarm, Debs learned that capital was not interested in bargaining and compromise. He now declared, "The strike is the weapon of the oppressed, of men capable of appreciating justice and having the courage to resist wrong and contend for principle."

Class-conscious anger led Debs to take actions that completed his ideological transformation. In the early 1890s, he assumed the helm of the new American Railway Union (ARU), a brave attempt to transcend the complex differences of craft and region (although not race), which frequently had workers in the nation's most important industry fighting more with one another than with their anti-union employers. In 1894, the ARU undertook a boycott of trains that carried Pullman sleeping cars, in sympathy with a strike by the workers who produced those vehicles. The U.S. attorney general, a former railroad lawyer, got a court injunction that clapped Debs in jail. Then President Grover Cleveland dispatched federal troops to smash the boycott.

Soon after he got out of jail, Debs announced that he had become a socialist. "We have been cursed with the reign of gold long enough," he wrote. "Money constitutes no proper basis of civilization. The time has come to regenerate society—we are on the eve of universal change."

Debs, who lived until 1926, became the most popular messenger American socialism has ever known. He crisscrossed the nation for more than twenty years, stretching out his long arms as if to touch the crowds, urging them to use their votes to destroy "the foul and decaying system" and erect a free, cooperative order in its place. Often, Debs would pace back and forth on the stage, sweat pouring down from his balding head. His inspirations were eclectic: he praised Christ as "a pure communist" and described socialism as the fulfillment of shared American ideals instead of an alien creed.

"He was a tall shamblefooted man," wrote the novelist John Dos Passos, who "had a sort of gusty rhetoric that set on fire the railroad workers in their pine-boarded halls . . . made them want the world he wanted, a world brothers might own where everybody would split even."

Debs was a tireless campaigner but could not expect sympathetic coverage in the mainstream press. He could, however, depend on a vibrant socialist press, led by the *Appeal to Reason* in the Midwest and the *Jewish Daily Forward* in New York—which each reached at least a quarter of a million readers around the country—as well as many socialist newspapers and magazines in different cities.

Like many other socialists—in fact, like many white progressives at the time—Debs sometimes repeated racial and ethnic stereotypes. During his days with the firemen's union, he told jokes in black dialect, supported keeping blacks out of good jobs, and favored segregation on trains. He also had bigoted opinions about Jews, Italians, and Chinese immigrants. But his views evolved. As the leader of the Socialist Party, he challenged his members and white unionists alike to shed their racist prejudices, in part because capitalists would be able to pit black and white workers against each other, weakening both.

Debs ran for president five times on the Socialist ticket. He did best in 1912, when he won 6 percent of the national vote but more than 10 percent of the vote in the western states, most of whose residents were small farmers or wage earners who felt exploited by big corporations and Wall Street. His campaign also helped fellow Socialists win local campaigns. That year, about twelve hundred Socialist Party members held public office in 340 cities, including the mayors of Milwaukee, Buffalo, and Minneapolis.

In 1917, Congress declared war on imperial Germany and its allies. The Socialist Party opposed that decision and suffered for it. The Woodrow Wilson administration banned some of its newspapers and magazines from the mails. Congress passed the Espionage and Sedition Acts, which made it illegal to incite active opposition to U.S. involvement in the war, leading to the arrest, and even deportation, of socialists, Wobblies, and other dissidents. Though ill, Debs delivered a series of anti-war speeches. After one, which he gave at a socialist picnic in Canton, Ohio, he was arrested, charged with impeding the war effort, convicted, and sentenced to ten years in a federal penitentiary.

On September 18, Debs delivered a famous oration in a Cleveland courtroom after learning of his sentence. He began, "Your Honor, years ago I recognized my kinship with all living beings, and I made up my mind that I was not one bit better than the meanest on earth. I said then, and I say now, that while there is a lower class, I am in it, and while there is a criminal element I am of it, and while there is a soul in prison, I am not free."

In 1920, Debs ran for president one final time from his cell in the Atlanta federal penitentiary. A popular campaign button showed Debs in prison garb, with the caption "For President, Convict No. 9653." He received nearly a million votes—3.4 percent of the total. It was a tribute to Debs, a beloved figure in many parts of America. But the fact that he sat in prison underscored the brutal repression that radicals like him faced for opposing a war that, according to President Wilson, was allegedly fought to create a world "made safe for democracy."

During the war and then during a Red Scare that followed, some radicals challenged the egregious abuses of basic civil rights. In 1917, they formed the National Civil Liberties Bureau, which three years later changed its name to the American Civil Liberties Union (ACLU). The group's sixty-four founders included such prominent socialists as Helen Keller, Rose Schneiderman, Norman Thomas, Morris Hillquit, and Roger Baldwin, who led the ACLU for the next three decades.

Municipal Socialism

During the early twentieth century, both progressives and socialists earned reputations for running clean, efficient, and well-managed local governments. With votes from immigrants, workers, and a rising professional middle class, progressives and socialists won elections in many cities, where they fought for fair taxes and better social services, and against high streetcar fares and utility rates. Socialists recognized that they could not bring socialism to one city, but they pushed for public ownership of utilities and transportation facilities; the expansion of parks, libraries, playgrounds, and other services; and living-wage laws (which paved the way for state laws in the early 1900s and the adoption of the federal minimum wage in 1938). They were especially successful in promoting public health, including clean water, to help reduce dangerous diseases. During strikes, the progressive and socialist mayors stopped the local police from protecting strikebreaking scabs. A decade after muckraking journalist Jacob Riis published his 1890 classic, *How the Other Half Lives*, exposing the awful conditions in New York City's slums, reformers and socialists successfully pushed for state laws requiring fire escapes, windows in every room, interior bathrooms, and courtyards designed for garbage removal. Muckraking journalist Lincoln Steffens, a socialist, exposed municipal corruption in his articles in *McClure's Magazine*, collected in *The Shame of the Cities*. Socialist Lewis Hine's photographs exposed the brutal conditions facing children living in slums and working in sweatshops.

In Milwaukee, where Socialists led the city government for several decades, this attention to good management and infrastructure earned them the label "sewer socialists."

Dominated by the brewery industry, the city was home to many Polish, German, and other immigrant workers who made up the movement's rank and file. In 1910, Milwaukee voters elected Emil Seidel, a former patternmaker, as their mayor, gave Socialists a majority of the seats on the city council and the county board, and selected Socialists for the school board and as city treasurer, as city attorney, as comptroller, and for two civil judgeships.

In office, Milwaukee's Socialists turned the city into a laboratory for progressive change. They expanded the city's parks and library system and improved the public schools. They paid city employees union-level wages and granted municipal employees an eight-hour workday. They adopted tough factory and building regulations. They reined in police brutality against striking workers and improved working conditions for rank-and-file cops. They improved the harbor, built municipal housing, and sponsored public markets. The Socialists had their own newspaper and sponsored carnivals, picnics, singing societies, and even Sunday schools. Under pressure from city officials, the local railway and electricity companies—which operated with municipal licenses—reduced their rates. Grateful for these programs, Milwaukee voters kept electing Socialist mayors, with one brief interruption, until 1960.

Socialists' strength in Milwaukee and New York City catapulted two of their ranks to Congress. In 1910, Victor Berger, an immigrant from Austria-Hungary and founding member of the Socialist Party, was elected to Congress by Milwaukee's immigrant workers. He was defeated for reelection in 1912, but in 1918 Milwaukee voters sent him back to Congress, even though he had been indicted for violation of the Espionage Act. But the House of Representatives refused to seat him. Finally, in 1922, after his Espionage Act conviction was overturned by the U.S. Supreme Court, Berger was once again elected to Congress and allowed to take his seat. He was reelected twice more before retiring.

In Congress, Berger sponsored bills providing for government ownership of the radio industry and the railroads, women's suffrage, abolition of child labor, self-government for the District of Columbia, and a system of public works for relief of the unemployed. He put forward resolutions for the withdrawal of federal troops from the Mexican border and for the abolition of the Senate (which was then not yet elected directly by the voters and was called the "millionaires' club"). He introduced the first bill in Congress to provide old-age pensions—an idea that was eventually adopted in 1935 when President Franklin Roosevelt created Social Security.

The other socialist congressman in the early decades of the twentieth century was Meyer London, a Jewish immigrant from Lithuania. After attending law school at night, he provided legal services for working-class immigrants and their unions. London was elected to Congress from the heavily Jewish Lower East Side of Manhattan in 1914 and was reelected three more times.

Like Berger, London sponsored bills that had no chance to pass but later became pillars of the New Deal: minimum wage, unemployment insurance, and increased taxes on the wealthy. He also proposed then radical ideas like anti-lynching laws and paid maternity leave. In 1917, London cast one of the few votes in Congress against American entry into World War I, viewing it as a capitalist struggle at the expense of working people on both sides. But after Congress approved American participation, London angered many fellow Socialists by voting to fund it. He explained, "I owe a duty to every man who has been called to the service of his country . . . to provide him with everything he needs [and] to get this fight over as soon as possible."

Norman Thomas, Upton Sinclair, and the New Deal

After the stock market crashed in October 1929, triggering the Great Depression, many Americans lost faith in themselves; a growing number also lost faith in the capitalist order. More than 13 million Americans were jobless, and most banks had to close. Right-wing demagogues competed with a flourishing radical movement of angry farmers, veterans, workers, and others for the loyalty of the American people and politicians. As the Depression deepened, more and more Americans became radicalized, questioning the basics of capitalism. They became open to radical ideas, including socialism and communism, although most put their faith in a more modest revolution, President Franklin D. Roosevelt's New Deal.

In 1932, in the depths of the Depression, the Socialist Party platform called for old-age pensions, public works projects, a more progressive income tax, unemployment insurance, relief for farmers, slum clearance and subsidized housing for the poor, a shorter workweek, and the nationalization of banks and basic industries. Socialists helped lead the struggles of the unemployed to win adequate relief and in the dramatic expansion of unionism through the Congress of Industrial Organizations (CIO), which founded or expanded unions in the steel, coal, electrical, garment, auto, longshoring, and retail industries. Socialists also helped organize southern sharecroppers, trying to build an interracial union movement in the Deep South.

Norman Thomas was the nation's most visible Socialist from the 1930s until his death in 1968. He was a constant and effective presence in battles for workers' rights, civil liberties, civil rights, peace, and feminism. He was influential because of his great moral authority, his spellbinding oratory, and his leadership of broad coalitions of radicals and reformers, who put aside ideological differences to win progressive victories.

Thomas hailed from a family of conservative Presbyterian pastors. After attending Princeton University, he followed in their footsteps and was ordained in 1911. But by then he had been inspired by the emerging Christian Social Gospel movement, which saw religion as a way to help working people and the poor. He turned down an offer to be the minister of a wealthy congregation on Fifth Avenue in Manhattan to serve a largely immigrant parish in East Harlem for several years.

Thomas considered socialism an extension of liberal democracy and the Christian Gospels, and he viewed communism as the opposite of his basic values. He joined the Socialist Party during World War I when it was facing repression and its foreign-born members were threatened with deportation. Party membership fell from more than one hundred thousand in 1917 to barely twelve thousand by 1923.

By the 1930s, the Communist Party had eclipsed the Socialist Party as the most influential organization on the American left. The two groups were bitter rivals, primarily because of their different views about the Soviet

Union, which Socialists viewed as undemocratic, and which Communists considered the vanguard of the struggle against world capitalism. The two organizations competed for members. Aided by financial support from the Soviet Union, the Communist Party siphoned off some of the Socialist Party's more left-wing activists.

Thomas refused to let the Socialist Party die. He ran for president six consecutive times, beginning in 1928. He did best in 1932, during the Depression, when he won just under nine hundred thousand votes (2 percent of the vote). Many voters who may have agreed with Thomas's views did not want to "waste" their vote on a Socialist who had no chance to win and who might even take enough votes away from FDR to keep Republican Herbert Hoover in office.

FDR had not run for president as a progressive, and he took office with no bold plan to lift America out of the Depression. But he was willing to try new ideas and recognized that his ability to push progressive legislation through Congress depended on the pressure generated by protesters—workers, World War I veterans, the jobless, the homeless, and farmers—even though he did not always welcome working closely with these constituencies.

When friends of Thomas expressed delight that FDR was carrying out some of the Socialist platform, he responded that it was being carried out "on a stretcher." He viewed the New Deal as patching, rather than fixing, a broken system. He wanted FDR and Congress to socialize the banks and expand credit for job-creating businesses, including public and cooperative enterprises. Instead, FDR bailed out the financial system with some modest regulations, and, Thomas said, "gave it back to the bankers to see if they could ruin it again."

Like Thomas, Upton Sinclair was a perennial candidate on the Socialist Party ticket. His bestselling 1906 book, *The Jungle*, had made him a household name, and he went on to write a series of novels and nonfiction books exposing the corruption of the rich and the evils of capitalism. In 1920, having moved to California, he ran for a variety of offices on the Socialist ticket, never winning many votes but using the campaigns to promote his left-wing views.

After Roosevelt was elected president in 1932, Sinclair figured he might have more success running for office as a Democrat. Like most Socialists, he supported the New Deal but thought it did not go far enough, allowing business to undermine its more ambitious goals. Sinclair joined the Democratic Party, wrote a sixty-four-page pamphlet outlining his economic plan—*I, Governor of California and How I Ended Poverty*, which he published himself—and declared his intention of running in the Democratic primary for California governor in 1934. His campaign slogan was "End Poverty in California" (EPIC).

Sinclair's plan focused on the idea of "production for use." The thousands of factories that were either idle or working at half capacity would be offered the opportunity to rent their plants to the state of California, hire back their workers, and run their machinery "under the supervision of the state." The workers would turn out goods and would own what they produced. Similarly, farmers, who were producing huge quantities of unsold foodstuffs, would be invited by the state to bring their produce "to [state] warehouses," where they would "receive in return receipts which will be good for taxes." The farmers' food would be "shipped to the cities and made available to the factory workers in exchange for the products of their labor."

Much to Sinclair's surprise, his pamphlet became a bestseller, and his campaign turned into a grassroots movement. Thousands of people organized EPIC clubs across the state. The campaign's weekly newspaper, the *EPIC News*, reached a circulation of nearly 1 million by primary day in August 1934.

Sinclair shocked California's political establishment (and himself) by winning the primary. Dozens of other progressive candidates, running on the EPIC platform, also won nominations for seats in the state legislature. Sinclair seemed to have a good chance to beat the sitting Republican governor, Frank Merriam, a colorless politician trying to defend the GOP's pro-business views at a time of massive unemployment and misery.

FDR's progressive advisers, including his wife, Eleanor Roosevelt, and Harry Hopkins, who ran the New Deal's jobs programs, urged the president to endorse Sinclair, but his more conservative aides feared that Sinclair was too radical and would hurt the Democrats' chances of winning a big victory in the midterm elections around the nation that fall. So the president made no endorsement. On Election Day, Merriam beat Sinclair by 9 percent of the vote. Although he lost the election, Sinclair's campaign helped nudge the New Deal to the left and laid the groundwork for an upsurge of progressive activism in California. After the Democrats won a landslide in the midterm elections, FDR launched the so-called Second New Deal, which produced Social Security, major public works programs, and the National Labor Relations Act.

World War II and the Cold War

In 1939, concerned that big business and FDR were preparing the nation for another world war, Norman Thomas joined the America First Committee, which included anti-Semites and racists whose views he strongly opposed. It was Thomas's most serious political and moral mistake.

However, three days after the Japanese bombed Pearl Harbor on December 7, 1941, Thomas reluctantly announced his support for America's war effort. During the war, he was one of the few public figures to oppose the internment of Japanese Americans. He also pleaded with FDR to allow Jewish refugees into the country to escape the Nazi Holocaust. He worked closely with fellow socialist A. Philip Randolph, an African American union leader, pushing FDR to integrate the nation's defense factories and abolish discrimination in the nation's armed forces.

Americans entered the post–World War II era with considerable anxiety. Now that the war was over, would the U.S. economy revert to Depression-era conditions, or would there be prosperity? Would the postwar world be the start of an "American Century" (as *Time* magazine publisher Henry Luce claimed), in which the United States would engage in a struggle among superpowers for economic, military, political, and cultural domination? Or would it be, as former vice president Henry Wallace proclaimed, the "Century of the Common Man," featuring world peace, cooperation between the United States and Russia, and greater social and economic equality at home?

Business groups and conservative politicians and journalists helped create two cold wars. One was a foreign cold war against Soviet expansion. The other was a domestic cold war against unions, an expanded welfare state, civil rights, and other progressive ideas that were viewed as being part of the communist menace. Big business was particularly worried about the growth of the labor movement, which between 1933 and 1945 had increased fivefold to more than 14 million members, about 30 percent of American workers.

During the next five years, as part of the Red Scare purges of the domestic cold war, many of labor's more radical leaders were expelled or defeated. Although the labor movement was still able to mobilize its members to influence legislation, it was now divided, confused, and on the defensive, its leaders more willing to compromise with management and less willing to listen to the more progressive wing. Business's cold war political agenda was aided by a variety of extreme right-wing groups and veterans organizations such as the American Legion. If anything, they helped make mainstream business's views seem moderate.

Big business and political conservatives used the words "socialism" and "communism" interchangeably to attack anyone, or any organization, that espoused progressive views—such as urging an end to nuclear testing, calling for workers' rights, demanding laws against racial discrimination in housing and employment, or supporting the free-speech rights of dissenters.

From 1937 to 1948, when asking Americans about their party preferences, the Gallup poll routinely included "socialist" as an option alongside "Republican" and "Democrat." It typically found that only about 1 percent identified as socialists. In 1949, at the start of the Cold War, Gallup asked survey respondents to explain what they thought socialism was. In that political moment, about one-third (34 percent) of Americans described socialism as government ownership of business and utilities. Another 12 percent said that socialism stood for equality, including equal rights and equal distribution of wealth. More broadly, about half of Americans associated socialism with progressive policies, while 7 percent said it was "modified communism" or a "restriction of freedom." A little over a third had no answer at all. Only 15 percent of Americans said they wanted to see the country "go more in the direction of socialism."

The Red Scare—sometimes known as McCarthyism after one of its most influential architects, Republican senator Joseph McCarthy of Wisconsin—shaped American culture in many ways. Hollywood changed the kind of films it made. Schools and universities not only fired radical teachers but also revised their curricula to wash out traces of "radical" ideas. The Cincinnati baseball team changed its name from the "Reds" to the "Redlegs" to avoid the taint of communism. Public opinion polls found that Americans became increasingly willing to abridge First Amendment rights of free speech and assembly for those who had been labeled as "radical," "communist," or "socialist." Many Americans became fearful of speaking out, signing petitions, attending meetings, and joining liberal organizations.

Postwar America was experiencing unprecedented prosperity that lifted tens of millions of people into the middle class. Although the Red Scare demonized liberals and "big government," most Americans from the late 1940s through the early 1970s did not see any contradiction as the nation pursued major and costly government spending projects, such as the interstate highway program, a dramatic expansion of public colleges and universities, large subsidies to promote homeownership and suburbanization (primarily for white families and businesses), and significant spending for military bases, equipment, and aid to other countries as part of the Cold War arms race against the Soviet Union. In 1960, even President Dwight Eisenhower, a World War II military hero, warned about the growing influence of America's "military industrial complex." Thanks to government spending, the American economy prospered and most Americans experienced an improvement in their standard of living during this period.

Out from the Cold

The combination of the Red Scare and postwar prosperity limited socialism's appeal. Many Americans believed, as President John Kennedy said, that a "rising tide lifts all boats"—a booming economy would reduce poverty and raise the standard of living for almost everyone. Americans viewed socialism as either irrelevant or a dangerous foreign ideology. In this climate, socialists sought to distinguish themselves from communists, but most Americans didn't bother to make such distinctions.

Even so, socialists persisted. One way was to publish their ideas in journals with small circulations, which, they hoped, would influence intellectuals, activists, and college students. In 1954, for example, literary critic Irving Howe and sociologist Lewis Coser co-founded *Dissent* magazine, which—unlike existing left-wing publications like *The Progressive*, *The Nation*, *I.F. Stone's Weekly*, and the *New Republic*—explicitly identified itself as both socialist and anti-communist. It quickly became a forum for independent radicalism and tough-minded political analysis and debate.

Other forms of radical dissent emerged during the Cold War, including the bohemian and beatnik culture of writers like Allen Ginsberg and Jack Kerouac, the upsurge of protest music led by folk singers Pete Seeger and Odetta, and the stinging political satire of comics like Lenny Bruce and youth-oriented publications like *Mad* magazine.

In 1957 Norman Thomas co-founded the Committee for a SANE Nuclear Policy (known as SANE) to halt the escalating arms race between the United States and the Soviet Union. In 1960 he addressed a SANE rally in Madison Square Garden, along with Randolph, Eleanor Roosevelt, Walter Reuther (president of the auto workers union), and popular singer Harry Belafonte. The rally attracted twenty thousand people. SANE led a growing movement in the United States—with counterparts around the world—against nuclear weapons and testing, which they viewed as both a waste of money and scientific talent and a likely trigger for a global nuclear war.

The most dramatic sign of a new opening for radical change was the emergence of the modern civil rights movement. It began in dramatic fashion with the yearlong Montgomery bus boycott in 1955 and accelerated with the sit-ins, Freedom Rides, and voter registration drives of the early 1960s. The Montgomery protest was led by a little-known twenty-six-year-old minister, Martin Luther King Jr., who had just moved to the city to start his career. He initially declined the efforts by more experienced activists to recruit him as the movement's spokesperson and public face, but eventually agreed, despite his lack of activist experience.

King began his activism in Montgomery as a crusader against racial segregation, but the struggle for civil rights radicalized him into a fighter for social justice and peace, and into a self-declared democratic socialist.

King was born in Atlanta, Georgia, in 1929, the son of a prominent black minister. He saw the widespread human suffering caused by the Depression, particularly in Atlanta's black community. During his first year at Morehouse College, King heard a speech by prominent civil rights and labor activist A. Philip Randolph, a socialist. Randolph predicted that the near future would witness a global struggle that would end white supremacy and capitalism. He urged the students to link up with "the people in the shacks and the hovels," who, although "poor in property," were "rich in spirit."

The Montgomery bus boycott transformed King into a national figure. Between 1957 and 1968, King traveled more than 6 million miles, spoke more than 2,500 times, and was arrested at least twenty times, always preaching the gospel of nonviolence. Opponents of the civil rights movement tried to tarnish his reputation by calling him a communist. So he rarely talked publicly about his socialist ideas. But occasionally he made his radical views known. In a 1961 speech to the Negro American Labor Council, for example, King proclaimed, "Call it democracy, or call it democratic socialism, but there must be a better distribution of wealth within this country for all God's children."

King's most famous moment, when he became a nationally recognized public figure, was his "I Have a Dream" speech at the August 1963 protest rally at the Lincoln Memorial, called the March on Washington for Jobs and Freedom. As historian William Jones has pointed out, the protest march was "organized by a coalition of trade unionists, civil rights activists, and feminists—most of them African American and nearly all of them socialists." It was spearheaded by King's two political mentors, both veteran organizers and socialists—A. Philip Randolph and Bayard Rustin. The funding came primarily from labor unions led by socialists—the United Auto Workers, the Amalgamated Clothing Workers of America, and the International Ladies' Garment Workers' Union. It was, at the time, the largest demonstration in American history. Although it is known primarily as a civil rights rally, it was also a protest for economic justice and jobs. It included a demand to pass a Civil Rights Act as well as an increase in the federal minimum wage.

King was proud of the civil rights movement's success in winning the passage of the Civil Rights Act in 1964 and, spurred by the march from Selma to Montgomery in March 1965, the Voting Rights Act the following year. But he realized that neither law did much to provide better jobs or housing for the masses of black poor in either the urban cities or the rural South.

In 1966, King confided to his staff: "You can't talk about solving the economic problem of the Negro without talking about billions of dollars. You can't talk about ending the slums without first saying profit must be taken out of slums. . . . Now this means that we are treading in difficult water, because it really means that we are saying that something is wrong with capitalism. There must be a better distribution of wealth, and maybe America must move toward a democratic socialism."

Many Americans, particularly college students born as part of the swelling postwar baby boom, were radicalized by the civil rights movement. A few traveled to the South to participate in the sit-ins and voter registration drives. Most participated in civil rights activism in their hometowns or college campuses by pushing for colleges and local businesses to desegregate and hire more African Americans, and to revise the college curriculum to incorporate the black history and culture that had been ignored by most colleges. Their experiences opened their ideas to some of the problems of American society—racism, poverty and income equality, sexism, and militarism and imperialism.

Many activists in the growing black freedom movement were strongly influenced by socialist ideas. Ella Baker, a skilled organizer who had formed consumer cooperatives in Harlem during the Depression and traveled throughout the South building NAACP chapters, became a mentor to the young people who participated in the sit-in protests and then formed the Student Nonviolent Coordinating Committee (SNCC) in 1960. She declared that African Americans could not "be free in America or anywhere else where there is capitalism and imperialism." Stokely Carmichael, a charismatic leader of the SNCC who popularized the demand for "black power," wanted African Americans to emulate revolutionaries who held power in Cuba, Ghana, and other developing nations. The Black Panther Party, formed in Oakland, California, but which quickly spread to other cities, argued that unless American businesses guaranteed a job to every American who needed one, "the community" should own and operate them.

In 1960, a small and mostly white group of campus radicals formed a new organization, Students for a Democratic Society (SDS), which became a main organizational vehicle for what came to be called the "new left." SDS was actually a new name for an old organization—the Student League for Industrial Democracy, the youth branch of a socialist group called the League for Industrial Democracy, which, in turn, descended from the Intercollegiate Socialist Society, which had been founded in 1905. In 1961, Tom Hayden, a University of Michigan student and the key SDS leader, wrote that his generation trusted only three people over thirty: sociologist C. Wright Mills (author of *The Power Elite*, an indictment of America's corporate class), Norman Thomas, and socialist writer-activist Michael Harrington. These three leaders helped build bridges between older radicals and the baby-boom generation of student activists.

In December 1964, two thousand people gathered at New York's Hotel Astor to celebrate Thomas's eightieth birthday. Martin Luther King Jr., on his way to Oslo to accept the Nobel Peace Prize, recorded a message to Thomas and later published it as an article entitled "The Bravest Man I Ever Met."

In October 1967, the eighty-two-year-old Thomas—blind and crippled by arthritis and a recent automobile accident—took the podium to address a meeting of college students in Washington, DC. Many of them were angry at the U.S. government for conducting what they considered an immoral and imperialist war in Vietnam. Over the previous few years of escalating demonstrations, protesters would occasionally burn the American flag. That symbolic act, inevitably highlighted on TV news and featured in the next day's newspapers, led many Americans to conclude that people who opposed the war also hated the United States. Thomas, the lifelong pacifist and Socialist, as stalwart a foe of the Vietnam folly as anyone, raised the moral stakes by proclaiming, "I don't like the sight of young people burning the flag of my country, the country I love. A symbol? If they want an appropriate symbol, they should be washing the flag, not burning it."

Thomas's statement was a warning to the younger radicals that despite their disillusionment with American leaders, they should embrace American ideals of patriotism, dissent, and inclusion. Many heeded Thomas's warning, but some others did not, becoming increasingly alienated, affecting a "revolutionary" stance that conservatives and the media used to brand the left broadly as un-American.

Michael Harrington and the War on Poverty

Michael Harrington inherited Thomas's position as the leader of America's socialist movement, but he was realistic about what that meant. Being the country's foremost socialist, he often joked, "was like being the tallest building in Topeka, Kansas."

Harrington was raised in a middle-class Irish Catholic family in St. Louis and graduated from Holy Cross College. After a short sojourn at Yale Law School and then earning a master's degree in English at the University of

Chicago, he moved to New York in 1949, only twenty-one years old, and soon joined the Catholic Worker movement—a group of religious pacifists and anarchists who devoted their lives to working with and for the poor.

While living in New York City's Skid Row in the 1950s, he wrote for left-wing magazines like *Dissent*, *New Leader*, and *Commonweal* about political issues as well as about movies and novels. With his mentor, Dorothy Day, he joined and helped organize protests against the Korean War and nuclear arms and for civil rights.

After two years, Harrington decided that instead of ministering to the poor he wanted to work to abolish the system that produced so much misery, so he left the Catholic Worker. Several old-left socialists tutored him in Marxism and groomed him for a public role, recognizing that his midwestern boyish charm and his fiery speaking style made him a natural leader.

In the late 1950s and early 1960s, Harrington traveled by bus and thumb across the country to college campuses, giving speeches about peace, civil rights, civil liberties, and other topics, meeting with small groups of activists, hoping to sign up recruits for the Young People's Socialist League (YPSL) but finding little enthusiasm for the group.

Harrington's book *The Other America*, published in 1962, became a bestseller and catapulted him to national prominence. It challenged the conventional wisdom that the nation had become an overwhelmingly middle-class society as a result of postwar prosperity. Harrington revealed that almost one-third of all Americans lived "below those standards which we have been taught to regard as the decent minimums for food, housing, clothing and health." He told stories that humanized the poor as people trapped in difficult conditions not of their own making. He described them living in slum housing, suffering with chronic pain because they could not afford to see a doctor, and often going without enough food for themselves or their children.

"The fate of the poor," he concluded, "hangs upon the decision of the better-off. If this anger and shame are not forthcoming, someone can write a book about the other America a generation from now and it will be the same or worse." He added, "Until these facts shame us, until they stir us to action, the other America will continue to exist, a monstrous example of needless suffering in the most advanced society in the world." Harrington was soon in great demand as a speaker on college campuses, at union halls, and before religious congregations. He appeared often on television.

But the word "socialism" did not appear in *The Other America*. Harrington wanted the book to tug at people's consciences, to outrage them, and to push them to action. He wrote that poverty was caused and perpetuated by institutions and public policies, not by individuals' personal pathologies. But he did not argue that it was caused by capitalism or that the solution was socialism. The solution, he wrote, was full employment, more funding for housing and health care, and better schools and job training.

The book gave Harrington a national platform to talk about democratic socialism as well as poverty. He mesmerized audiences, especially on college campuses, with eloquent, funny, and morally uplifting lectures. He was also a talent scout, recruiting young activists and plugging them into different movement activities. When he talked about democratic socialism, he made it sound like common sense—rational, practical, and moral at the same time.

In 1964, Sargent Shriver, one of President Lyndon Johnson's close advisers, invited Harrington to help design a new initiative called the War on Poverty. Harrington co-authored a background paper in which he argued, "If there is any single dominant problem of poverty in the U.S., it is that of unemployment." The remedy, it said, was a massive public works initiative similar to the New Deal's Works Progress Administration (WPA) and Civilian Conservation Corps (CCC) programs. On this point Harrington disagreed with Johnson, who did not want to spend the money that such a program would cost, especially as he was escalating the war in Vietnam. Harrington's stint as a government adviser lasted about a month.

In his speeches and writings during that period, Harrington warned that campaigns for civil rights, union drives, and calls to withdraw U.S. troops from Vietnam were not enough. They were necessary stepping-stones toward a better world, but they were not sufficient to end poverty, expand happiness, or stop imperialism. He told audiences, "You must recognize that the social vision to which you are committing yourself will never be fulfilled in your lifetime." In the meantime, though, socialists, radicals, progressives, and liberals had to fight today for what he called the "left wing of the possible."

Unlike Debs and Thomas—his predecessors as the nation's leading socialist—Harrington never thought it was possible to create a radical third party that could succeed in electing candidates and gaining power. The task of socialists was not to run Socialist Party candidates for office but to keep the flame of socialism alive while building coalitions among labor, civil rights, and religious groups as well as liberal intellectuals to form a left flank within the Democratic Party. He worked closely with the leaders of major unions, wrote speeches for Senator Ted Kennedy and Martin Luther King Jr., and drafted a Poor People's Manifesto for King in 1968.

In 1973, in the aftermath of the 1960s and the decline of the anti-war movement, Harrington recruited students, professors, clergy, writers, community organizers, and union activists to join the Democratic Social-ist Organizing Committee (DSOC). In 1982, Harrington led a merger of DSOC and the New American Movement, which became Democratic Socialists of America (DSA). Many DSA members became key activists within unions, environmental groups, and other progressive organizations. During the last two decades of his life, Harrington was actively involved in the day-to-day activities of these organizations—a distraction from his writing and speaking, but a commitment he had made to himself years earlier. If he was to help keep socialism alive in the world's most capitalist country, he had to help maintain socialism's fragile infrastructure.

A key component of Harrington's "left wing of the possible" approach was to remind Americans that the United States fell far behind other democratic countries when it came to issues like poverty and inequal-ity, women's and workers' rights, education, housing, and foreign aid to developing nations. He often talked about Tommy Douglas, the founder of Canada's socialist movement (and its New Democratic Party), pointing out that America's northern neighbor had better health care, less poverty, and stronger unions. Harrington developed close friendships with leaders of Europe's socialist parties, including the prime ministers of France (Fran-çois Mitterrand), Sweden (Olaf Palme), and Germany (Willy Brandt), and invited them to speak to American audiences. DSA became the American affiliate of the Socialist International, the organization of socialist parties in the world's democracies.

From the 1970s through the 1990s, Harrington's vision of democratic socialism attracted a significant following among intellectuals and activists, community and labor organizers, feminists, and environmentalists. They sought to transform the academic world, the women's and environmental movements, and labor unions, pushing them to be more progressive and to build bridges across their organizations and issues. A number of well-known public figures—such as sociologist Frances Fox Piven, theologian Cornel West, San Francisco supervisor Harry Britt, Congressman Ron Dellums, William Winpisinger (president of the International Association of Machinists and Aerospace Workers), Doug Fraser (president of the United Auto Workers), and feminist writers Barbara Ehrenreich and Gloria Steinem—joined DSA and helped promote the organization.

Steinem was one of the best-known leaders of the feminist movement that emerged in the late 1960s. She appeared on many college campuses, in union halls, business meetings, and protests, on TV talk shows, and in magazines.

Her grandmother, Pauline Steinem, had been a prominent suffragist in the early 1900s. She was the first woman elected to the Toledo, Ohio, school board, on a coalition ticket with the city's socialists. Working as a journalist, Gloria Steinem made a big splash in 1963 with "A Bunny's Tale," an article written about the unglamorous working conditions (including sexual harassment) faced by waitresses—called "bunnies"—at the Playboy Club. Her 1970 essay in *Time* magazine, "What It Would Be Like if Women Win," Steinem predicted that feminism would liberate men as well as women. If women could have equal power, she argued, if homosexuals had the right to marry and women could refuse to have sex, then men would no longer be "the only ones to support the family, get drafted, bear the strain of power and responsibility."

Steinem was an early advocate of what today's activists call "intersectionality"—viewing race and class and gender as linked in a common structure of oppression. She built bridges between feminism's radical and liberal wings and between the women's and labor movements. She pushed middle-class white feminists to embrace the concerns of working-class women and women of color. She was also a co-founder of the Coalition of Labor Union Women, the National Women's Political Caucus, and *Ms.* magazine.

Ms. pioneered investigative stories about overseas sweatshops, sex trafficking, the wage gap, the glass ceiling, women's health (and the medical establishment's sexism), sexual harassment, and date rape. It explained and advocated for the Equal Rights Amendment, rated presidential candidates on women's issues, reported on feminist protests against pornography, and exposed the influence of sexist advertising on women's self-images. Even more, *Ms.* injected these issues into the political debate at a time when they were considered too radical for the mainstream media to cover—or at least to cover fairly.

In 2010, Steinem and immigrant rights activist Pramila Jayapal (now a member of Congress) co-authored an article linking women's and immigrant rights issues. In 2015 Steinem joined a delegation of thirty female peace activists from fifteen countries who made a rare crossing of the dangerous demilitarized zone between North and South Korea. In 2013 President Barack Obama awarded Steinem the Presidential Medal of Freedom. "She awakened a vast and often skeptical public [to] problems like domestic violence, the lack of affordable child care, and unfair hiring practices," Obama said at the White House ceremony. "She also changed how women thought about themselves."

Despite the support of public figures like Steinem, Harrington remained DSA's chief spokesperson, intellectual, and fund-raiser. A socialist movement so dependent on one person is obviously fragile, and when Harrington died of throat cancer in 1989, DSA fell on hard times. By 2000, DSA membership had declined to about five thousand members.

The Left Wing of the Possible

Twenty years later, its membership tops sixty thousand. Once again, the idea of socialism is exciting millions of Americans and bewildering, or scaring, many others.

Since the 1970s, many progressives and socialists have been elected to office, primarily in local and state government. Like their "sewer socialist" predecessors in the early 1900s, they've actually had to govern, not simply protest. In the 1970s and 1980s, when cities were reeling from drastic federal cutbacks and white flight to the suburbs, voters in Boston; Cleveland; Chicago; Madison, Wisconsin; Santa Monica; Berkeley; and Burlington, Vermont, elected progressives and leftists as mayors. In the past decade, a period of both stagnating wages and skyrocketing housing prices, progressive coalitions in Jackson, Mississippi; Seattle; Portland, Oregon; Minneapolis; New York City; South Bend, Indiana; Philadelphia; Los Angeles; and Richmond, California, have catapulted radicals into positions as mayor, city council member, and district attorney. Hundreds of their counterparts have won elections to state legislatures and statewide offices including secretary of state (such as Miles Rapoport's election in Connecticut from 1995 to 1999) and attorney general (such as Keith Ellison's election in Minnesota in 2018). By 2019, at least sixty members of DSA were serving in elected office, including six members of the Chicago Board of Alderman and Congress members Alexandria Ocasio-Cortez of New York City and Rashida Tlaib of Detroit.

The network Local Progress, founded in 2012, was created to bring together progressive and radical local officials in more than five hundred cities and forty-six states. To challenge progressives and leftists who win governing power, the business class typically threatens to go on strike. When activists propose policies to regulate business practices, corporate lobbyists and their consultants for hire, often with support from the media, warn that these policies will scare away private capital, increase unemployment, and undermine a city's tax base. When progressive movements and elected officials seek to raise the national, state, or local minimum wage, business lobby groups warn that it will "kill jobs." They use the same mantra when faced with efforts to enact rent control, inclusionary zoning laws (requiring developers to include low-income housing in otherwise market-rate developments), laws to strengthen oversight of banks' predatory lending and racial redlining, and efforts to require companies to reduce spewing of dangerous toxics into the environment or improve workplace safety.

Progressive and leftist public officials have tested the limits of government's authority to challenge corporate priorities. Corporations are often bluffing when they threaten to move, reduce jobs, and demand tax breaks or regulatory relief. Unlike most state and city officials, progressives have learned when to call their bluffs. When they do, they typically discover that the threats were empty.

In 2013, Seattle voters elected progressive Democrat Ed Murray as mayor and socialist Kshama Sawant to the city council. Both pledged to adopt the city's first municipal minimum wage. Despite business warnings that it would cause great harm to the local economy, including the loss of jobs, Murray and Sawant worked with unions and community activists to pass a minimum-wage ordinance that would reach $16 by 2019. Seattle's economy did not suffer. In fact, the number of restaurants in the city increased. After Seattle's victory, the idea spread quickly, and none of the many other cities that adopted local minimum-wage laws experienced the negative consequences predicted by local business groups.

In Cleveland, a progressive mayor and city council partnered with universities, hospitals, and community groups to promote community-owned or worker-owned cooperative businesses. Boston, Oakland, and other cities have enacted "linked deposit" laws to push banks to invest in underserved areas as a condition for receiving municipal business. Some cities have divested their pension funds from fossil fuel companies and gun manufacturers. A rising tide of tenant activism starting around 2015 has led to growing support for rent control in blue cities and red states; in March 2019, Oregon passed the nation's first statewide rent control law. With support of progressives in local and state government, the Los Angeles Alliance for a New Economy (a coalition of labor, community, and environmental groups) successfully pushed the city government to adopt a $15 minimum-wage law and the nation's first community-benefit agreements, improve working and environmental conditions at the city's port and in its sanitation and recycling industry, thwart the invasion of low-wage big-box stores like Walmart, and train inner-city residents for well-paying union jobs on government infrastructure projects.

Richmond, California, with 103,000 residents in the Bay Area, is perhaps the nation's most progressive local government. In November 2012, the *New York Times* reported that this "small, blue-collar city best known for its Chevron refinery has become the unlikely vanguard for anticorporate, left-wing activism." The Richmond Progressive Alliance (RPA), a union-community coalition, elected a majority slate of progressives and socialists to the city council. They improved city services, reined in police abuses, adopted rent control, and challenged the power of Chevron, the city's biggest private employer, by raising its property taxes and opposing its plan to expand its refinery in order to handle dirtier crude oil. In November 2014, Chevron poured more than $3 million into the municipal elections to unseat the RPA slate with conservatives. Despite being outspent by 20 to 1, the progressive coalition consolidated its control of the local government. All of its candidates for mayor and city council won.

Even in a global economy, state and local governments have considerable leverage over business practices, job creation, and workplace quality. Many cities and states have adopted progressive laws and policies that improve the lives of working-class people and challenge business groups' definition of a "healthy business climate" without triggering a flight of private investment, as described in Gar Alperovitz's 2013 book, *What Then Must We Do? Straight Talk About the Next American Revolution*, and in *Unmasking the Hidden Power of Cities*, a 2018 report by the Partnership for Working Families.

Most jobs and industries are relatively immobile. Private hospitals, universities, hotels, utilities, and other "sticky" industries—as well as public enterprises such as airports, ports, transit systems, and government-run utilities—aren't about to flee to Mexico or China if government policy requires them to raise wages, pay higher taxes, or reduce pollution. This makes threats to pull up stakes less compelling and gives progressive and radical public officials more leverage.

Growing support for socialism has provided progressives with more room to maneuver in local and state government and, increasingly, at the federal level, too. In his chapter in this book, "How Socialism Surged, and How It Can Go Further," Harold Meyerson explains the social and political forces and the significance of individuals like Bernie Sanders and Alexandria Ocasio-Cortez who have led the resurgence of democratic socialism that has conservatives nervous and radicals hopeful. We are at a moment when those who believe in the vision of a democratic socialism—what Michael Harrington called "the left wing of the possible"—are more creative and confident, and more in sync with American attitudes than they have been in nearly a century. What happens next depends on them—and on you.

Toward a Third Reconstruction

Andrea Flynn, Susan Holmberg,
Dorian Warren, and Felicia Wong

RACISM IS AMERICA'S ORIGINAL SIN. IT PERVADES EVERY ASPECT OF OUR history, politics, economy, and culture. The structure of American racial capitalism has changed dramatically since the nation's founding, but two essential features, the thirst for profit and the exploitation of black bodies—whether through slave labor or mass incarceration—have persisted. "To understand why the United States seems so resistant to racial equality," historian Keeanga-Yamahtta Taylor has written, "we have to look beyond the actions of elected officials or even those who prosper from racial discrimination in the private sector. We have to look at the way American society is organized under capitalism."

Throughout the nation's history, activists—from abolitionist organizers and anti-lynching campaigners to civil rights crusaders and Black Lives Matter protesters—have adapted their strategies to challenge the class and race obstacles to equality and full citizenship.

Even though civil rights activists have made considerable progress in "repairing the breach," in the words of Rev. William Barber II, a leader with the Poor People's Campaign, the historical legacy of racial bigotry, racial discrimination, and exclusionary racial rules, and their persistence today, remains a central part of America's unfinished business. Creating an egalitarian society requires us to move beyond "color-blind" politics, exposing and addressing head-on the often hidden rules and unconscious biases that shape how our institutions perpetuate racial injustice. Economic inequality and racial injustices are driving the public debate in America today. We see a growing consensus about a broken economic system; middle- and working-class families are working harder but enjoy less economic security, while extractive corporations and the superwealthy have amassed an ever-growing share of power and capital. And we also see growing concern about the country's 350-year-old racial divide, and the racial and gendered divisions that animate our politics.

But we have, for years, thought about these problems separately—a massive flaw that stands in the way of equitable opportunities and outcomes for all. Leaders on both the left and the right have pitted solutions to racial inequality and economic inequality against one another, but political leaders and policymakers are beginning to recognize that these problems are intertwined and cannot be solved in isolation. Our system of racial capitalism is built on a bedrock of racial rules that need to be acknowledged and rewritten in order for people of color—those who have shouldered the greatest burden of our broken economy—to achieve economic security and racial justice. For progress makers of the past, this is not a new realization. Nearly sixty years ago, the March on Washington for Jobs and Freedom carried forward a long legacy of racial justice advocates arguing that civil and economic rights could not be won independent of each other.

Today's push for progress is a stark contrast to the explicit brand of racialized and white identity politics embraced by Donald Trump and many of those who support him. Trump's nativist calls to return to the days of exclusion and isolation continue a long legacy. For centuries, politicians in the United States have used racism as a tool to divide voters along racial lines and within class categories and to enact policies that have had a devastating impact on communities of color, but in many cases also hurt white communities and our economic and democratic health more broadly. The Trump era hasn't, as some have argued, brought racism back. The Trump presidency has, instead, brought racism out of the shadows of "race-neutral" and dog-whistle politics. For decades it had been strategically hidden. It is now in plain sight.

Before describing the challenges facing us and outlining a political strategy and policy agenda to address racism in its many forms, it is vital to distinguish between the commonsense understanding of racism as individual prejudice by racist individuals and forms of structural racism. We can have, as political sociologist Eduardo Bonilla-Silva reminds us, "racism without racists." The "racial rules" framework we offer more accurately illustrates the complexity of the American system of racial capitalism. We must also be deeply historical and remember that the struggle against racism has had many significant accomplishments, although that history has occurred in fits and starts, with periods of both progress and retreat.

The Racial Rules Framework

The dominant economic frameworks of the last fifty years have failed us. Our neoliberal economic system has delivered us greater inequality than any time since the first Gilded Age and the Great Depression, and in response has used the state to encase and protect markets and market transactions and has left the majority of American families behind, with devastating consequences. Neoliberalism has diverted blame away from the rules that are driving inequality and shifted risks and costs to individuals, their families, and their communities. We've returned to punitive solutions (e.g., work requirements to access social welfare programs, the policing of communities of color) for those unable to find work. Neoliberalism has also focused on developing "human capital," teaching us that failure to thrive in this economic system is an individual failure, the solution to which is more education, more training, more work, and more ambition—and when that fails, punishment by the state. We now encourage individuals to invest in higher education as a way to increase their own earning potential, but we have failed to develop public systems of higher education and higher education financing to support students and families. The result: pushing millions of families further and further into debt as they strive to achieve something they've been told is their ticket to economic mobility and security.

As we described previously, even a more progressive economic framework has largely begun and ended with a focus on class: asking how best to improve the economy for the least wealthy and powerful, but rarely considering race or gender or any other ways that identity intersects with the economy. Additionally, most accounts of democratic socialism fail to grapple with an empirical truth since the founding of the country: America's political economy is one of *racial capitalism*, not simply capitalism. If the hopes and dreams of democratic socialists are to be realized, we argue that race must be central to that vision in the U.S. context.

In contrast to both neoliberal economic as well as democratic socialist economic paradigms, our framework argues that rules matter, as does the power to write them. Building on the work of john powell, Joseph Stiglitz, Mariko Chang, and Sandy Darity and Darrick Hamilton, among others, we present an alternative way to understand and address racialized economic inequality. Our framework considers both formal rules (the regulatory and legal frameworks that make up the economy and society) and informal rules (normative practices, behaviors, and standard operating procedures that also result in unequal racial outcomes). Especially on matters of race, formal and informal rules interact, and both have very clear effects on economic outcomes and overall well-being. These racial rules fuel and perpetuate racism in many different forms.

In this chapter, as in our *Hidden Rules of Race*, we focus specifically on the experiences of black Americans for a number of reasons. First, the United States' history and enduring legacy of black slavery is built into our current institutions, policies, programs, and practices and has multigenerational impacts on the life chances and outcomes of black Americans. Second, black Americans face among the worst social and economic outcomes of all ethnic and racial groups, and the factors that drive those outcomes are often unique to the historic experience of black Americans and deserve an in-depth analysis. Third, the marginalization of black Americans also generates unequal outcomes for other racially marginalized groups, particularly Latinxs and Asians, as well as poor and working-class whites. To paraphrase legal scholars Lani Guinier and Gerald Torres, issues of race are the "miner's canary," warning of conditions in American democracy and the economy that pose a threat to us all.[1] Finally, the focus on black Americans is a response to the proliferation of and increased attention to police violence and mass incarceration, and to the demand from grassroots movements for leaders at all levels to acknowledge our nation's long history of devaluing blackness and fostering black inequality in virtually every segment of American political, economic, and social life.

The First Reconstruction

The first Reconstruction, bookended between the 1863 Emancipation Proclamation and the 1877 end of federal oversight in the South, was an era of far-reaching ambition in its attempts to reverse the social and economic effects of enslavement on newly freed black Americans. The rules of this era brought newly freed slaves into the real economy and the labor market, expanded black social and political power, and opened educational opportunities to black Americans from which they had long been prohibited.

The core legal achievements of Reconstruction are the Thirteenth, Fourteenth, and Fifteenth Amendments to the U.S. Constitution: the abolition of slavery except as punishment for a crime, the guarantee of equal protection under the law and birthright citizenship for the formerly enslaved, and the prohibition of racially discriminatory voting laws. The Civil Rights Acts of 1866, 1870, and 1875, as well as the Reconstruction Act of 1867, enabled federal supervision and enforcement against voter suppression, permitted blacks to serve on juries, guaranteed equal access to public accommodations, and more. These acts also expanded federal power and federal enforcement while curbing southern states' rights (which southern Redeemers sought to use to reassert white dominance).

These legal and legislative successes altered the nineteenth-century system of racial capitalism and did lead to real gains for newly freed black Americans. Across the South, black families were reunited, and they built schools and churches and other benevolent associations that became core social and political institutions in black communities. Public school funding was equally distributed to black and white children, and black Americans had moderate access to legal protections. Indeed, it was the Reconstruction-era legislatures that introduced free public schooling in the South. Freed blacks organized to increase political participation and representation; black leaders used the Declaration of Independence to argue for full equality before the law and for black suffrage. In the decades after the war, black leaders held political control at the local and state level, albeit briefly. Black elected representation in Congress in the late 1870s was among the highest it has been in American history.

In the end, the early successes of post–Civil War racial inclusion were short-lived. The mass mobilization of free blacks was met with extreme violence, as many southern whites attempted to preserve their social and economic domination through racial terror: convict leasing, lynchings, and the rise of the Ku Klux Klan.

By the 1890s, both major political parties had given up on the promise of racial equality, and states throughout the South and some in the North enacted Jim Crow laws that relegated African Americans to separate and manifestly unequal schools, jobs, and neighborhoods—and disenfranchised most black voters with laws that subverted the intent of the Fifteenth Amendment. Southern states adopted poll taxes, literacy tests, and other restrictions to wipe out blacks' voting rights. In 1896, in its *Plessy v. Ferguson* ruling, the Supreme Court upheld the constitutionality of state racial segregation laws under the "separate but equal" doctrine.

A legalized caste system emerged that made any kind of racial mixing—in public places, schools, or workplaces—illegal. Political elites used white supremacy to justify an agricultural economy that exploited African Americans as low-cost agricultural and domestic labor and divided white and black farmers and workers from joining forces against the South's landed aristocracy. In *Black Reconstruction in America*, published in 1935, W.E.B. DuBois addressed the question of why poor and working-class whites failed to join black citizens to challenge the white elite. In the immediate aftermath of Reconstruction, DuBois wrote that poor and working-class whites received a sheer "psychic benefit" from their racial status: "The white laborers, while they received a low wage, were compensated in part by a sort of public and psychological wage." This psychological wage for white workers would shape American politics throughout the twentieth and well into the twenty-first century.

At the same time, in a series of high-profile cases, the Supreme Court systematically undermined the radical inclusionary reach of new racial rules—the civil rights legislation of the 1880s and of the Reconstruction amendments themselves. The effect was immediate, with states across the South implementing laws aimed at overturning newly won rights for former slaves and their families, and leading to the Jim Crow era that lasted into the mid-twentieth century.

The Civil Rights Movement:
A Second Reconstruction

The Second Reconstruction began during World War II and essentially ended in the early 1970s. In 1941, civil rights organizers scored their biggest victory since the end of the first Reconstruction when President Franklin D. Roosevelt issued an executive order banning racial discrimination in defense plants. He took that step only after socialist A. Philip Randolph, aided by his young protégé Bayard Rustin, threatened to organize a mass march on Washington of one hundred thousand African Americans.

Black Americans hoped that postwar America, victorious in defeating the racist Nazi regime, would be ready to treat them as first-class citizens. But Jim Crow still prevailed in the South and parts of the North. Most black citizens were still confined to the lowest-paying jobs and worst slums. Jackie Robinson's feat of breaking baseball's color line in 1947 was a sign of hope and progress but hardly compensation for the ongoing system of apartheid in every part of the country.

By the mid-1950s, after decades of assiduous political organizing and intellectual ferment, the United States entered the most recent era of inclusion, and the one that bears most heavily on our contemporary consciousness: the civil rights era.

One way to understand the levers and impact of the twentieth-century civil rights movement is through a legal lens. The NAACP Legal Defense Fund innovated a bold litigation strategy to win legal reforms around racial inclusion in a context where national political reforms were stymied. Led by the Warren court's landmark 1954 decision in *Brown v. Board of Education*, and then solidified by a range of subsequent legal decisions for the next several decades, the American legal system declared various forms of segregation—in schools and in housing—unconstitutional. In 1967's *Loving v. Virginia*, the court declared racial intermarriage legal. The impact of these laws was further strengthened by a series of hard-fought local, state, and especially national legislative actions, most importantly the Civil Rights Act, the Voting Rights Act, and the Fair Housing Act, which collectively outlawed racial segregation of public spaces as well as discrimination in employment, voting, and housing.

These legal and legislative victories would not have occurred without a dramatic rise of grassroots organizing by thousands of ordinary people who took extraordinary collective action, beginning with the 1955 Montgomery bus boycott, the courage of Little Rock high school students to integrate their school in 1957, the militancy of college students and other activists who sat in at lunch counters and risked their lives on the Freedom Rides. Activists and organizers working with diverse groups—including the NAACP, the Congress of Racial Equality, the Southern Christian Leadership Conference, and the Student Nonviolent Coordinating Committee—faced physical and economic threats by participating in voter registration drives and engaging in civil disobedience while battling racist police and sheriffs' billy clubs and fire hoses to challenge segregation.

These legal changes had at least three lasting consequences. The first was the decreased social acceptability of explicit discrimination and racial intolerance. The second was the ending of formal legal segregation in public accommodations, including public schools. School desegregation, although incomplete, was especially important, leading to material gains in years of education, income, employment, and health for black Americans.

The third was the move from protest to politics. By some measures, African Americans have gained significant political power since the middle of the twentieth century. As journalist Alan Flippen has written, in the wake of the March on Washington, nearly 59 percent of the black electorate went to the polls in 1964 (and outside of the South, which saw vicious voter suppression the year before the Voting Rights Act of 1965, the rate was 72 percent).[2] Although black Americans remained underrepresented as governors and members of Congress, more black Americans also held elected local offices beginning in the late 1960s. In 1970 there were only 1,469 black elected officials in the entire country. By 2000, that number had reached 9,040. In 1967, voters in Cleveland, Ohio (Carl Stokes), and Gary, Indiana (Richard Hatcher), elected the first black mayors in a major American city. By 2000, many major cities, including many with relatively few African Americans, had elected black chief executives, including New York City, Chicago, Los Angeles, Atlanta, Dallas, San Francisco, Denver, Seattle, and Philadelphia. In 1950, only two African Americans (William Dawson of Chicago's South Side and Adam Clayton Powell of Harlem) served in the U.S. House of Representatives. By 2019, there were fifty-five black members of the House, about the same percentage (12 percent) of African Americans in the nation. A growing number were sent to Congress by voters in predominantly white and suburban districts. And of course, by 2008, the voters elected the country's first black president in Barack Obama.

These victories form the backbone of the civil rights era's accomplishments, and in many ways continue to shape the legal norms around race in American politics. Of course, these gains were far from complete. Each time, a politics of resentment and retrenchment tapped into racial and economic anxieties and built support for recycled exclusionary policies that preserve white power and privilege at the great expense of people of color. But the successes of Reconstruction and the civil rights movement demonstrate that when we systematically account for race and gender we can begin to level the playing field for people of color and women.

We must not accept inequality as inevitable. We believe we are at an inflection point, and thanks to the organizing, advocacy, bravery, and protest of those who will not accept the status quo, there is hope for a "Third Reconstruction" that radically rewrites the rules of racialized and gendered American capitalism.

Ongoing Racial Inequities

Despite the midcentury victories for greater racial equality, a lack of political representation and economic inequalities for black Americans have persisted. At every level of education, black Americans are paid less than their white counterparts. At every level of income, black Americans have fewer assets than their white counterparts. Compared to white Americans, black Americans have higher rates of unemployment, accrue less wealth, and have lower rates of homeownership.

The black unemployment rate has consistently been at least twice the rate of white unemployment since the 1960s. Research by social scientist Algernon Austin shows that black poverty (and poverty overall) did see real improvements in the 1960s, but since then the rate has mostly held steady at around 30 percent, approximately three times the recent white poverty rate.[3] Staggering racial wealth inequities are rooted in the history of slavery and Jim Crow and also New Deal–era policies that locked black families out of benefits that boosted so many white families into the middle class. These racial rules have prevented numerous generations of black families from accumulating assets, a disadvantage that seeps into every sphere of life in the United States. Furthermore, as we describe in *The Hidden Rules of Race*, neither education nor income seems able to ensure that black Americans have the wealth, homeownership, or health outcomes—or the freedom from discrimination by the criminal justice system—that similarly situated white Americans enjoy.

The ongoing and deep racial inequities across a range of domains are evidence both of the incomplete victories of the periods of progress and of the need for a third Reconstruction and a meaningful commitment to rewrite the racial rules.

Toward a Third Reconstruction

We need a Third Reconstruction to finally ensure that African Americans and other people of color will be able to enjoy and depend on the same rights, economic opportunities, and access to high-quality public resources as any other American. It is our moral duty to change the system.

Removing the barriers that people of color face—for example, higher interest rates on business loans or higher incarceration rates—would unleash economic potential that would be important not only for them and their families but for all Americans and the broader economy as well. As we said earlier, by focusing on the "miner's canary" of race in our system of racial capitalism, we alert the entire country to the dangers of the system and forge a path forward toward freedom and inclusive prosperity for all.

The chaos and ideological vacuum of today's politics can be confusing and dispiriting. But freedom fighters and reformers of previous generations, in the face of significant obstacles, imagined a different kind of democracy. Now we must summon our strategic imagination and do the same.

Below, we articulate a truly effective agenda that takes on racial inequality and tackles the structures that shape unequal outcomes. That agenda must be broad and should be shaped by a clear set of guiding principles:

1. Reckon with our shared history. Our nation has not fully reckoned with its fraught racial history, whether by acknowledging the truth of our often horrific and undemocratic history of racial apartheid or by recognizing and celebrating the times that we have made progress. In all policy-making processes and political discourse, an acknowledgment of the complex reasons for our unequal starting places is critical.

2. Tackle race and other identity inequities affirmatively. Prima facie "race-neutral" policies are often not race-neutral in intent, and rarely have race-neutral outcomes. From 1990s welfare reform to mandatory minimum sentencing, prima facie race-neutral or color-blind

policies have most often led to racially unequal outcomes. We must now call out the race, class, and gender injustices that helped shape these policies, illustrate the extraordinary harm they have done to black families (and also point out how they have harmed many white families), and design new rules that will address these historic wrongs and prevent them from being replicated in the future. One path forward is through targeted universalism, wherein policies benefit all but are crafted to address the needs of the least privileged, such as wealth-building policies like baby bonds, guaranteed income with a racial justice dimension, or policies to curb environmental degradation.

3. Move away from market fundamentalism and toward an economics whose success is measured in security and stability for all people, as well as growth and investment. The rise of market-centric economic policies has led to disinvestment in public provisioning and broad safety-net policies, deregulation that has enabled the growth of extractive corporate power, and the erosion of labor unions and other forms of worker power. We must adopt policies that curb the extraction and hoarding of wealth by corporations and oligarchs, and increasing public provisioning, in order to increase economic security and life outcomes for all Americans, including especially people of color and low- and middle-income Americans of all races who have not benefited from neoliberal economics.

4. Reclaim political power. It is critical that people in power represent the full diversity of the United States. Black disenfranchisement and political exclusion throughout the majority of American history have resulted in a power imbalance in who gets to write the rules. In periods of greater racial political inclusion, representation, and power, we rewrote the racial rules to become more inclusive. We must again rewrite our electoral rules to ensure full political inclusion of marginalized communities who have been on the losing end of economic and racial rules written by a small, powerful elite over the last forty years.

These principles should guide a policy framework that is broad, ambitious, and structural. Rewriting the rules of our racially exclusionary economy will require a bold progressive agenda—and the political will and power—that comprehensively addresses each of the domains described in the following sections. These categories are not all encompassing. But, together, they can significantly address racial disparities in our economy and society.

Democracy

Much like the massive disenfranchisement of blacks following Recon-struction, the voting rights of black Americans—and all communities of color—continue to be targeted, and the events in the 2000s and 2010s have demonstrated the vulnerabilities of civil rights–era progress. Three sets of racial rules continue to create structural barriers to civic participation: the growth of the prison industry and mass incarceration, leading to increased disenfranchisement of those with a criminal record; the Supreme Court's 2013 curtailment of the key provisions of the Voting Rights Act; and, since 2010, the passage of ostensibly race-neutral but in fact by design racially exclusionary voter suppression laws. The current rules of our democracy result in the lowest rates of participation among wealthy democracies.

Rewriting the rules of our democracy is a critical first step in creating a more just and inclusive economy. We have expanded the franchise by amending our Constitution half a dozen times throughout our history, and now is the time to do so again. New rules must aim to guarantee the right to vote for all, implement a fully national system of universal voter registra-tion, prohibit voting restrictions in all forms (including the racially insidi-ous permanent disenfranchisement of those with a criminal record), and move toward a system of proportional representation that would guarantee fuller representation at all tables of power. Lastly, we must get money out of politics and ensure that our democracy is fueled by the majority, not the few who have written the rules that have allowed them to hoard wealth and power.

Criminal Justice

The radical scope and impact of the U.S. penal system is not an accident of history but rather a direct result of the increasingly harsh incarceration policies implemented over the last four decades. The contemporary racial rules around criminal justice and mass incarceration have deep roots in slav-ery and the Jim Crow era and as such have exclusionary effects similar to those of the rules from which they have evolved. As legal scholar Sharon

Dolovich explains, they predictably and effectively resulted in the permanent social and economic exclusion of black Americans, their families, and their communities.[4]

A progressive economic agenda must explicitly acknowledge the inextricable link between our criminal justice system and economic inequality. It must dismantle the complex web of rules of that system, including reducing investments in policing that resulted from the War on Drugs and in the wake of 9/11, and eliminating fines, fees, cash bail, and other economic penalties that criminalize racialized poverty. It must also confront the injustice of for-profit prisons, propose ways to decriminalize drugs and provide treatment for individuals suffering from substance abuse, and bring sentencing practices more in line with those of other nations. As the Movement for Black Lives calls for, the funds that are divested in the criminal justice system should be invested in rebuilding communities that have been hollowed out by decades of unjust policies.

Jobs

In recent decades, major shifts in the structure of the economy have taken a significant toll on all U.S. workers, but given the way these structural shifts have intersected with a host of racial rules, they have had a unique impact on black workers. The U.S. economy today is characterized by persistent racial and gender wage gaps, continued discrimination in hiring, low and stagnant wages, and jobs that are increasingly precarious and offer fewer and fewer benefits. These are trends that are hurting all workers across the country, but we must acknowledge they have represented the experiences of people of color in the labor market for centuries, and interventions must account for the racialized nature of wages and work in the United States. Deep cuts to public sector employment along continued political and legal challenges to public sector unions have disproportionately impacted black workers and eroded a critical pathway to economic security.

Progressive efforts to rewrite the rules of labor must combat the legacy of black Americans' exclusion from the labor market with a bold investment in jobs. This should include a deep public jobs program in fields ranging from infrastructure to caring-economy jobs—a kind of Marshall Plan for twenty-first-century America—and could also include a federal jobs guarantee. The jobs we invest in must promise equitable and decent wages, dependable schedules, and protections for workers. Additionally, efforts to improve jobs must once and for all remedy race and gender wage gaps.

Wealth

A progressive economic agenda must tackle not only wages and work, but also wealth. As economists Darrick Hamilton and William A. Darity and their colleagues have written, wealth itself may be one of the main mechanisms for perpetuating racial economic inequality by facilitating a lock-step "intergenerational transmission of socioeconomic status.[5] Wealth matters, in that it takes wealth to build wealth—to invest in homes, education, new businesses, and future generations, and to provide a buffer in times of economic strife. Wealth disparities are at the root of many other inequities, and unless they are addressed, other policy prescriptions will fall flat.

Effectively addressing racial wealth inequities will require a multi-pronged effort that will simultaneously expand asset-building opportunities for those who have historically been locked out of them by correcting for the runaway wealth of those at the top of the economy. This should include a consideration of child trust accounts, or baby bonds, which would provide every American at birth with a wealth grant to be accessed at age eighteen. It must also address the wealth-stripping mechanisms of our current economy: economic penalties of the criminal justice system; costs of health care, child care, and elder care; educational debt; and predatory lending of all kinds, which has by design extracted wealth and driven up levels of debt for families of color, particularly leading up to and in the wake of the Great Recession. These efforts must reform the tax code, which increasingly favors asset holdings over income earned, dramatically favoring those at the top at the expense of the rest of us.

Corporate Power, Market Power

Creating a just and inclusive economy depends on dramatically reforming our current system of extractive corporate power. Over the last four decades, policymakers have slashed regulations, reformed the tax code, and rewritten laws so that corporations are more consolidated, with fewer companies across various economic sectors controlling more markets, which are increasingly uncompetitive. This has allowed corporations more control over workers' wages and schedules; enabled the outsourcing of work and the "fissuring" of workplaces; and led to fewer new business starts and less investment in research and development. Much corporate power, especially in increasingly privatized areas of the economy like higher education and criminal justice, explicitly exploits people of color.

Making our economy, society, and democracy more equitable and inclusive necessitates rebalancing the scales of economic power. This will require curbing companies' market power through changes in corporate governance—encouraging longer-term investment and discouraging increased executive compensation, including through manipulative and unproductive stock buybacks, at the expense of worker compensation. It will also require a change in our approach to antitrust policy, moving away from the narrow and narrowly applied consumer welfare standard to a broader understanding of the harms of both vertical and horizontal integration—and to an investment in antitrust enforcement. The increasing financialization of our economy—the domination of finance and finance-dependent firms—also leads to a hollowing out. A range of novel policy proposals, including greater and more effective corporate taxation, is required.

Worker Power, Worker Voice

All social democracies have strong labor movements. Simply put, without a strong labor movement there cannot be a strong democracy. And without a strong labor movement there cannot be a thriving middle class. Rewriting the rules of racial capitalism to empower workers is a necessary condition to forge racial and economic justice. Approximately one in ten U.S. workers today is unionized, compared to one in three fifty years ago. The declines in unionization are directly related to the increasing rates of economic inequality.

Unions have traditionally been a springboard to economic security for black workers, and a site where race and gender wage gaps have been smaller. Among other factors, when hiring and promotions are more rules-based, as in unionized and public sectors, rather than subject to personal discretion, legal protections can blunt the role of institutional or individual racial and gender bias. Unsurprisingly, the neoliberal attack on collective bargaining, public employment, and labor standards has been particularly destabilizing for the black middle class. Of course, the destruction of middle-class work and the associated ladders to opportunity has decimated the white middle class as well. Research from economist Suresh Naidu and colleagues has shown that for decades unions served as a critical barrier to economic inequality by benefiting not only union members but also other workers.[6] Therefore, recent trends in de-unionization not only hurt workers who would have been in unions, but are having a negative impact on *all* workers.

This decline in labor standards and bargaining rights has not been an inevitable outcome of globalization and technology, but rather a choice. There is no silver bullet for building middle-class jobs in the new economy, but a strong start would include protecting existing bargaining rights and promoting new rules that support worker power in the fissured workplace. Elected officials can move toward these goals by moving beyond the traditional twentieth-century industrial economy framework of labor relations (with outdated National Labor Relations Act definitions of "bargaining unit," "employer," and "secondary action"). Instead, they can enact a broad range of new rules enabling the economic power of workers to increase their scope and power for bargaining in the new—and future—economy. Elected officials can set the standard for fair pay and benefits and overall fair labor practices through government employment and government contracts. Further, we should rewrite the rules around a robust package of labor standards including raising the floor (i.e., the minimum wage), portable benefits, and especially increasing funding and innovation for new models of enforcement and penalties for violation of existing labor law.

In addition to protecting labor rights, we must also consider ways to increase the power of workers' voices, including guaranteeing workers' representation on company boards; providing robust rights to all workers in all sectors, especially sectors excluded from protection like the care economy; protecting workers' voices by safeguarding their fundamental rights to strike, picket, and engage in other collective action; and ensuring that benefits of technological change are shared with employees.

Public Investments

Over the last four decades, neoliberal economics has led to the weakening of public programs that have long been the bedrock of economic security for millions of low-income families. We are currently faced with levels of inequality that prompted FDR to envision an expanded role for the government and ultimately enact the New Deal. It is again time for us to reimagine the role of government and remind one another that bold government solutions are, at their heart, American ideas that we should embrace. We must consider what is required for all families not only to achieve a basic floor of well-being, but to flourish and live in dignity as well. This will require proposals for broad and significant public investments in housing, infrastructure (including communications infrastructure, like broadband), health care, education, and social insurance programs that ensure all workers access to paid sick leave, paid family leave, and retirement. These proposals must account for the ways communities of color have historically been prevented from benefiting from such programs.

Constitutional Legal Change

We must recognize that as long as our reading of the Constitution is biased against race-conscious policies, we will be prevented from making structural change that affirmatively tackles the exclusions that have been baked into our system since before America's founding.

To make racially explicit rules a possibility, we need a significant shift in the current state of constitutional jurisprudence on issues of racial inequality, discrimination, and affirmative action. Racially explicit rules, even when geared toward remedying past structural discrimination, are, under current Supreme Court precedent, subject to a standard of "strict scrutiny" in judicial review. This means that such policies will be upheld only if they meet a "compelling government interest" and are "narrowly tailored" to that end. This, in itself, is not fatal to such proposals: as suggested in this chapter, achieving racial equity and inclusion and overcoming the deep legacy of racial segregation and inequality should be understood as a compelling governmental interest that justifies targeted policies of the kind proposed here.

Enduring racial inequities and the durability of racism as a driver and feature of our socioeconomic system demand that progressives recommit to, reimagine, and rebuild our policies and politics of inclusion and true social justice. A radical rewriting of our political economic rules in a color-blind way is not enough. This era demands an economic narrative and agenda that comprehensively addresses the obstacles and opportunities facing black Americans—and all people of color, women, immigrants, the LGBTQ community, and beyond—such as those put forth by gender and racial justice leaders in the policy platforms for the Women's March on Washington and the Movement for Black Lives. This agenda must acknowledge the ways in which politicians have strategically used racism to ratchet up fear and resentment of these communities in white Americans in service of a neoliberal economic agenda that is bad for the majority of Americans but disproportionately so for people of color. A democratic socialist agenda that fails to do this will fail—as it has before—on the American Achilles' heel of race.

For too long, progressives have talked about the symptoms of inequality without naming the rules that drive it, the people who wrote those rules, or the processes by which they were made. They have not connected the dots between the neoliberal economic agenda—one that strips investments and financial promise away from hardworking Americans and funnels it into the pockets of the few at the top—and an agenda that advocates for slashing the safety net, curbing health coverage and health access, expanding the criminal justice enterprise, and erecting barriers to voting. But these phenomena are two sides of the same coin. The challenge for progressives in the twenty-first century will be to hold on to the truth that the racial rules of the last 50—indeed, 140—years have not worked for any Americans, neither black nor white. Racial and economic justice is not a zero-sum game. Achieving equity for black Americans would benefit all Americans, and to do so, we must tackle the hidden rules of race and racism head-on.

A Three-Legged Stool for Racial and Economic Justice

Darrick Hamilton

FULL EMPLOYMENT, WHERE ALL WHO DESIRE TO WORK AT A JOB WITH decent wages and benefits are afforded a job, is a core foundation of any decent society. But it has long been clear that the private sector alone cannot achieve this goal. Nor can the capitalist markets deal with wealth, income, and racial inequalities and offer both protection against worker exploitation and opportunities for social mobility. These things require public policy. Any gains that the United States has made on these fronts have been due to government policy, spurred by social movements demanding racial, economic, and social justice.

Wealth and income disparities will continue to widen even during periods of economic growth unless the government establishes rules to create shared prosperity. Over the last half century, essentially all of the economic gains from America's increasing productivity have gone to the elite and upper-middle class, while workers' real wages have remained roughly flat. These inequalities are particularly pronounced for women, blacks, and other people of color. Their education, employment, earnings, and assets are more precarious, and they tend to have more caregiving and financial responsibilities.

Full employment has been part of the policy discourse in the United States since the early twentieth century. Among the most notable proponents of true full employment—defined as an economy in which any person who seeks a job can secure one—was President Franklin D. Roosevelt. His vision of "economic security" for all is a touchstone for full-employment advocates. For Roosevelt, direct hiring programs such as the Works Progress Administration (WPA) and the Civilian Conservation Corps (CCC) were great successes during the Great Depression. While they provided much-needed—albeit temporary—relief during the economic catastrophe, their size and transient nature were insufficient to achieve the long-term impact on employment that Roosevelt and the full-employment supporters who came before and after him sought.[1]

In his 1944 State of the Union address, Roosevelt went further. He called for an expansion of the Bill of Rights to recognize economic rights as well. "Necessitous men," Roosevelt observed, "are not free men." Those "who are hungry and out of a job are the stuff of which dictatorships are made." Moreover, real freedom, freedom to "pursue happiness," he said, required a "second Bill of Rights under which a new basis of security and prosperity can be established for all." For Roosevelt, full citizenship demanded more than the political rights designated in the nation's original Bill of Rights: it required economic rights—first and foremost, the right to a "useful and remunerative job." [2]

This chapter will make the case that reducing inequality and despair demands a shift away from *neoliberal and poverty governance frames*, a term derived from Joe Soss, Richard Fording, and Sanford Schram's aptly titled book *Disciplining the Poor*. Such frames attempt to address structural problems in the economy by managing the seemingly bad behavior and work ethic of the poor and black and brown people. What's needed instead is an *economic rights frame* in the spirit of FDR's Economic Bill of Rights, administered in a *race-conscious* way. Policies designed under such a framework would work to eradicate the structural factors that preserve existing inequalities, including the transfer of wealth from generation to generation and exclusionary practices in the job market that leave workers of color inordinately worse off.

In a social democratic or democratic socialist America, public policy should empower all people to live a dignified life and should shield vulnerable populations from predatory private employers, whose single-minded focus on generating profits drives them to exploit people and the planet. I will focus on three such policies. The first two are universal but race-conscious: a federal job guarantee and a substantial child trust program, widely known as baby bonds. The third, reparations, is a race-specific program in which benefits account for government policies and for outright predation—stretching back to chattel slavery—which have decimated black communities, particularly in the economic domain of building and retaining wealth. Together, these three policies would establish a firm three-legged stool for racial economic justice specifically, and economic justice in the United States more broadly.

As Andrea Flynn, Susan Holmberg, Dorian Warren, and Felicia Wong explained in the previous chapter, the historic links between racial and economic inequality in the United States suggest that policies can't simply address one or the other as separate issues. From different angles—and in tandem with their proposal for a Third Reconstruction—the three complementary policies that follow would go a long way toward eroding what keeps our economy so starkly unequal.

How Did We Get Here?

When the U.S. Census began collecting wage and earnings data in 1940, the typical black male earned less than 45 percent of the typical earnings of a white male. By 1980, black men earned on average a little over 70 percent of average white men's wages.[3] As early as the mid-1970s, though, this progress seemed to cease.[4] Prevailing explanations for this reversal have focused on education and individual attitudes as the key drivers of upward mobility. The presumption is that if black people were more responsible, made better financial decisions, and focused on education, they could get good jobs and achieve economic security. But studying and working hard aren't enough for black Americans.[5]

Since the United States started tracking unemployment by race, the unemployment rate for blacks has remained roughly twice as high as the white rate, regardless of education. Moreover, even for highly educated blacks a college degree does not guarantee job security.[6] Janelle Jones and John Schmitt estimate that the unemployment rate for black recent college graduates exceeds 12 percent.[7] Wealth disparities persist with high levels of education, too. Black households in which the head graduated from college have less wealth than white households in which the head dropped out of high school.[8] Overall, race is an even stronger predictor of wealth than class itself. The 2016 Survey of Consumer Finances indicates that the typical black family has about $17,500 in wealth; in contrast, the typical white family has about $171,000. This stark racial wealth gap is an inheritance from chattel slavery, when blacks were quite literally capital assets for a white landowning plantation class.[9] In the South, entrepreneurs and slave owners took loans out against the collateral value of their property in the form of people to fund new businesses.[10]

Focusing on personal responsibility instead of these structural barriers and material resource deprivation flows from a neoliberal perspective, where the "free market"—given the proper incentives—is supposed to be the solution to all our problems, economic or otherwise. After all, if the real problem is that poor people simply aren't investing enough in themselves, then why fund government agencies and programs, which at best misallocate resources to irresponsible individuals, and—at worst—create dependencies that fuel more irresponsible behavior? What is *glaringly* absent from this framework is how those with resources, corporations, and the wealthy actively shape supposedly free markets to suit their own interests. Without government intervention, inequality and stratification will persist.[11]

The remedy is a race-conscious economic bill of rights that looks beyond individual behavior and works to break down the structural factors that preserve inequality throughout the economy. Such policies should work to address both *intergenerational resource hoarding*—the ease with which the already rich and upper-middle class keep getting richer—and other exclusionary practices that foreclose on upward mobility for everyone else. We need to prioritize a federal job guarantee and baby bonds as economic rights that will promote economic inclusion, social equity, and fairness, providing a robust "public option" for jobs, and income and wealth generation to all Americans. To achieve racial justice we will need to acknowledge our country's racist past and reconcile these wrongs through a system of reparations.

A Federal Job Guarantee

Today, economists and policymakers, including the governors of the Federal Reserve System, tend to associate "full employment" with a 4 to 6 percent unemployment rate, using the standard measure of unemployment.[12] This measure counts workers who do not have a job, have actively looked for work in the previous four weeks, and are currently available for work. It does not count the millions who have stopped actively seeking employment, or those inadequately employed in temporary, seasonal, or other precarious work. This 4 to 6 percent unemployment rate target is based on a conception defined by economists as the non-accelerating inflation rate of unemployment (NAIRU), which says that an unemployment rate that is *too low* will trigger inflation. It is noteworthy that this "target" has changed over time. Moreover, an economy with these unemployment rates needlessly condemns millions of U.S. workers, who are disproportionately black, to unemployment and underemployment, often resulting in severe economic hardship for those left behind by decision-makers' policy choices.[13]

Even during periods of relatively low unemployment rates, millions of workers remain unemployed and millions more are working part-time, though they would prefer full-time work. The number of job seekers still substantially outnumbers job openings, especially when broadening the definition to include underemployment.[14] Moreover, this aggregate picture masks the fact that unemployment does not affect all workers equally. Historical unemployment data highlight the persistent trend of discriminatory labor market practices that result in substantially higher unemployment rates for some social groups. There is recent evidence that narrowing of the racial unemployment gap occurs as the labor market tightens, but these gaps may be exacerbated during economic downturns.[15] Moreover, the 2-to-1 ratio of black to white unemployment remains pretty robust regardless of business cycle.

The impact of joblessness extends well beyond financial and human costs. Having so many Americans out of work does immense damage to the human spirit and imposes extensive costs to individuals, families, communities, and society as a whole—costs born doubly by black households.

Dr. Harvey Brenner, a sociologist and public health expert at Johns Hopkins University, has studied the link between economic fluctuations and the nation's physical and mental health. He calculated that for every 1 percent increase in the unemployment rate (an additional 1.5 million people out of work), we can expect an additional 47,000 deaths, including 26,000 deaths from heart attacks, about 1,200 from suicide, 831 murders, and 635 deaths related to alcohol consumption.

When the economy goes south, the hardships in people's lives get translated into increased stress, anxiety, and frustration. According to Brenner's studies, recessions are accompanied by a significant increase in admissions to mental hospitals. But many people don't seek counseling, therapy, or other forms of medical help when they are under stress. In fact, Brenner says, layoffs typically result in people losing their health insurance, making it even harder to get the help they need.

Other social scientists and mental health experts have documented a spike in child abuse and domestic violence during economic downturns. A 2004 study by the National Institute of Justice found that the rate of violence against women increases as male unemployment increases. When a woman's male partner is employed, the rate of violence is 4.7 percent. It is 7.5 percent when the male partner experiences one period of unemployment. It increases to 12.3 percent when the male experiences two or more periods of unemployment.

Alleviating these hardships with a truly full employment economy is not a new idea. Neither did the country's quest to eliminate unemployment through a federal job guarantee end with Roosevelt's Economic Bill of Rights. That was just the beginning. Full employment was a cornerstone of the famed 1963 March on Washington, and civil rights leaders including Bayard Rustin, Dr. Martin Luther King Jr., and Coretta Scott King publicly endorsed the universal right to a job at nonpoverty wages for all Americans.[16] Although their work in the 1960s resulted in significant strides with regard to civil rights, economic rights were largely left unrealized. After Dr. King's assassination, Coretta Scott King doubled down on the pursuit of authentic full employment legislation. Her work was instrumental in shaping an early version of the 1978 Full Employment and Balanced Growth Act, better known as the Humphrey-Hawkins Act. Early versions of the bill established a federal Job Guarantee Office, signaling the government's direct involvement in ending unemployment through direct employment.[17]

While the Humphrey-Hawkins Act has never fully lived up to the transformative potential King and other organizers hoped for, other countries have employed job guarantee programs to promote full employment and alleviate poverty. Perhaps the best-known examples are India's National Rural Employment Guarantee Act and Argentina's Jefes y Jefas. India's program, the largest direct employment scheme in the world, with more than 600 million workers eligible for employment, provides up to one hundred days of guaranteed paid employment per year for rural households. Recent research indicates that the program increased earnings for low-income households and increased employment in the private sector. Income for the low-income households increased 13.3 percent, with the vast majority (90 percent) of the increase coming from higher wages in private employment rather than wages earned through program employment.[18] In Argentina, the government successfully provided guaranteed employment to a head of household for at least four hours a day to engage largely in community development projects.[19]

Recent momentum in the United States behind the Fight for $15—pushed by the labor movement, and already won and implemented in cities and states around the country—shows a revived interest in breaking from neoliberal norms by having the government play a more active role in the labor market. Given that a greater share of black and Latinx workers make less than $15 an hour, this may also be an example of a universal program that disproportionately benefits communities of color.

But it is not nearly bold enough. It still leaves many workers, and disproportionately black, brown, and other workers with stigmatized identities, unemployed or out of the workforce altogether. It does not address the volatility of work hours and job security in our increasingly precarious labor economy. The job guarantee would build on both the unfulfilled economic demands of the civil rights campaigns and those to raise the minimum wage by functioning as a de facto wage floor in the labor market, greatly increasing the bargaining position of workers throughout the economy. With a federal job guarantee in place, that is, private employers would have to offer jobs at least as good as those offered by the government in order to attract employees.

In this, a federal job guarantee provides a viable alternative to jobs that offer low pay, few (if any) benefits, and poor working conditions.[20] In changing the U.S. economy toward more high-wage jobs, a full employment program would also provide a buffer against employment transitions due to automation, technical change, and the United States' urgently needed transition away from fossil fuels. It would function, too, as a robust automatic stabilizer in the economy, expanding employment during economic downturns through direct hiring, and contracting during economic boom times when the private sector demand for workers heats up. While workers may see some decrease in their purchasing power during an economic contraction, the job guarantee will automatically expand as demand for employment in the private sector contracts, thereby dampening the macroeconomic volatility of business cycles more generally. These are all attributes that—while universal—would disproportionately benefit black and brown workers especially given their vulnerability to labor market discrimination.

In determining which projects would be included as part of a full employment program, priority would be given to those that aid the most distressed communities. Priority would also be given to those projects that address our twenty-first-century infrastructure needs, including "human infrastructure" like child care and elder care. Care workers would receive decent wages, benefits, and working conditions, while communities would have universal, quality, affordable child and elder care. Consistent with a Green New Deal, jobs would be designed to transform our nation into a green and sustainable economy through substantial public investment. Economist Pavlina Tcherneva has suggested that federal job guarantee projects, managed at the local level, could be divided into three broad categories: care for the environment (i.e., tree planting, fire- and other disaster-prevention measures, home weatherization), care for the community (i.e., cleanup of vacant properties, restoration of public spaces, oral histories projects), and care for people (i.e., elder care, after-school programs, and health awareness). Program participants could also obtain new skills through the program by shadowing teachers, hospice workers, and librarians, among others.[21] Under a job guarantee, the increased provision of these public and socially desirable goods and services would benefit us all.

It's important as well to clarify what a job guarantee is *not*. Stimulus and job-creation programs that offer temporary publicly subsidized jobs that are administered through the for-profit or nonprofit sector are often better than unemployment but do little to enhance the bargaining power of those already employed since they are designed to complement rather than compete with the private sector.

What's more, any job-creation program that relies on funding from state governments will see comparatively fewer benefits flow to black and low-income Americans, who are overrepresented in states that collect less tax revenue and are more hostile to public programs. In contrast, a *federal* job guarantee—reliant on national rather than state funds—would prioritize areas with the greatest employment needs, plus areas with the greatest human and physical infrastructure needs. By increasing overall employment, a federal job guarantee would bring the added benefit of raising tax revenues for cash-strapped local and state governments. So although the job guarantee is designed as a universal program, more resources would flow to communities that currently have the highest rates of unemployment and underemployment, where more workers would presumably take advantage of a full employment program, and where the benefits from public works are needed most. This will result in increased government resources to better serve constituents.

In addition, a federal job guarantee program would mitigate the personal and familial costs of damaged mental health and other stressors faced by the unemployed. Expanding an economic bill of rights into the twenty-first century means that everyone should have a right to work with the dignity of decent wages, benefits, and work conditions. Not only would a federal job guarantee restore psychological balance to the millions of unemployed individuals who want to work but cannot. It would also address long-standing discriminatory barriers that keep large segments of stigmatized populations—including the disabled and the formerly incarcerated—out of the labor force, and reverse the rising tide of inequality for all workers by strengthening their bargaining power in the labor market and eliminating the threat of unemployment for all.

Baby Bonds

Critical as a federal job guarantee is for tackling income inequality and discrimination in the labor market, other policies are needed to address the nation's dramatic wealth disparity. Baby bonds, or more accurately baby trusts, would establish a substantial child trust account program that is set up by the government for every child, providing all newborns with an opportunity to purchase an asset that will appreciate in value as they age. This would establish a birthright to capital for all young adults—a privilege today reserved mainly for those born into wealth.

These accounts would endow American newborns with an average account of $25,000 that gradually rises to $60,000 for babies born into the poorest families. These funds would be federally managed and would grow at a guaranteed annual rate of about 2 percent to curtail inflation. When the child reaches adulthood, released assets could be used for any number of wealth-generating activities: a debt-free university education, a down payment to purchase a home, or seed capital to start a new business.[22] The program would further complement the nation's existing right to old-age pensions (Social Security), providing every American with access to capital financing from cradle to grave.[23]

In short, baby bonds would form the foundation of an economically secure life, allowing all Americans to build assets regardless of either what family they were born into or how those families choose to spend their money. Given how little wealth is held by people of color compared to whites, the program's focus on wealth as both a policy criterion and an outcome makes it both race-conscious and universal.[24]

With approximately 4 million babies born each year in the United States, if the average endowment of a baby bond account is set at $25,000, the program would cost about $100 billion per year—about 2 percent of annual federal expenditures. That's far less than the more than $500 billion already being spent each year on "asset promotion" (tax breaks, mostly), let alone Republicans' regressive $1.3 trillion Tax Cuts and Jobs Act of 2018.

At issue is not how much the U.S. government spends on these asset promotion programs, but who benefits from that spending. Currently the top 1 percent of earners—those typically making more than $1 million a year—receive about one-third of this entire allocation; the bottom 60 percent of earners receive only 5 percent.[25] Simply put, our existing tax policies favor existing wealth over creating new wealth. A federal policy to reallocate wealth-building assets in a more progressive manner would dramatically transform the nation's income and wealth inequalities.

Baby trusts, then, represent a substantive break from the false narrative that inequality is owing to individuals' personal faults—a narrative that largely ignores the advantages of inherited wealth. Instead, the public provision of a birthright to capital could go a long way toward establishing a more moral and decent economy that facilitates economic security and social mobility for all its citizens, whatever race and class they are born into.

Reparations

Baby bonds and a federal job guarantee are pillars for establishing an economic bill of rights that ensures universal access to wealth and the economic security of asset ownership, as well as a job with decent wages, benefits, and working conditions. These rights would have a dramatic impact on reducing the 10-to-1 racial wealth gap and the 2-to-1 white-black unemployment rate difference.

However, the most direct and just approach to address racial inequality in America—and to right the wrongs of the nation's racist past—is a comprehensive reparations program. Concretely, this would include two key tenets. The first is a well-documented acknowledgment and account of the grievances extending from slavery through sharecropping, "whitecapping" (unpunished white vigilante violence to steal black property), Jim Crow laws, and the state-facilitated exclusion of people of color from several of the New Deal and postwar polices that built the white middle class. Flowing from that would be a compensatory restitution of lost capital that includes the ownership of land and other means of production, as well as accompanying structural reforms to facilitate additional wealth accumulation and intergenerational wealth building.[26]

The first component of a reparations program—a well-documented acknowledgment and account of our racial history—is a necessary but not sufficient condition for racial justice. Acknowledging state-sanctioned terror against black bodies, the seizure of black wealth, and the widespread exclusion of blacks from government policy that promotes wealth and social mobility is critical for the American psyche. An honest and sobering confession of our historical sins would pave the way for a new narrative and accurate understanding of inequality and poverty, with benefits for working people of all races.

As described earlier, inequality and poverty are fiercely racialized in the United States, and this racialization is applied to blacks, Latinxs, Asians, and poor whites alike. Markets, whether they're product markets, labor markets, or financial markets, are presumed to be "self-regulating"—the most astute, most valued, and hardest workers are believed to prosper and endure, while the least astute, least valued, and laziest are presumed to receive their just rewards and simply fade away. Those so-called undeserving poor are stigmatized under the umbrella of anti-blackness, whether they are actually black or not. And state interventions to promote their social mobility are seen as unnecessary market distortions that will only incentivize bad behavior. With a comprehensive reparations program, this narrative loses saliency, directly taking on the idea that markets are a natural, and a neutral, level playing field.

However, acknowledgment and apology alone will be empty if not accompanied by some form of material redress; it is only with both these factors that America can have racial justice. There are multiple ways that reparations could be paid, including a direct cash advance. Included in that payment, however, must be some ownership of land or the means of production, or both.

The racial wealth gap itself is an implicit measure of our racist past. That past began with blacks serving as capital and evolved into a system in which black bodies and whatever capital blacks may have established were always vulnerable to confiscation when state policy and law enforcement, in some cases, looked the other way, failing to offer protection from theft, destruction, and fraud, and, in other cases, actively facilitated theft, destruction, and fraud. It was also never the case that a white, asset-based middle class simply emerged naturally. Rather, it was government policy—and in some cases literal government giveaways—that provided many whites the finance, education, land, and infrastructure to accumulate and pass down wealth. In contrast, blacks were largely excluded from these wealth-generating benefits.[77]

As a result, blacks as a group have very little ownership in America's land or means of production. Without ownership, the stimulus of reparations could generate economic gains mainly for the owners of land and the means of production—a ripple effect that would further enhance racial inequality. Hence, a reparations program should include compensatory resources for blacks whose ancestors were the victims of racist U.S. policy and state-sanctioned vigilante violence. This resource distribution should include land, ownership, or both in the means of production, through payment means such as direct government purchase and corporate stock transfers.

A decent first step toward creating such a program would be for Congress to pass some version of H.R. 40, which calls for a commission to study proposals for reparations. This would at least introduce the first phase, a well-documented acknowledgment and account of the grievances. Though first introduced by Representative John Conyers of Michigan in 1989, the bill has never come to the floor for a vote.

Given the demographic size of the U.S. slave descendant population, getting anywhere close to a comprehensive reparations program would require a broad-based social movement and multiracial coalition. Meanwhile, the wealthy and corporations flood money into the political system, giving them disproportionate influence over our politics. This state of affairs continues, to a large extent, because of race. A predominantly white and wealthy owning class has throughout U.S. history worked to divide the working class against itself through racism, pitting white workers against a reserve army of disproportionately black labor. Elites consistently encourage whites to sacrifice the economic gains that could be attained through multiracial solidarity in order to preserve the social status that whiteness confers, along with the tangible material benefits that stem from this privilege, like having an unemployment rate that is half that of their equally educated black counterparts and benefiting from a 10-to-1 racial wealth gap. Critical race theorists have dubbed this phenomenon the "wages" or, more accurately, "property right of whiteness."[28]

It's not hard to see how this theory could play out. Take the 2016 presidential election, which caught most pundits and political scientists off guard. Viewed from the perspective of stratification economics or critical race theory, the results are less surprising. President Donald Trump's divisive appeal toward "whiteness" was loud, boisterous, and clear—and all about codifying the property rights in whiteness. His campaign slogan to "Make America Great Again" gestured toward a fictional time in which white dominance was unquestioned and unchallenged. His other not-so-subtle dog whistles broadcast the idea that "I am your last chance"—with clear overtures to a pending demographic shift in which whites will no longer be a numerical majority.

Even as pundits attributed Trump's stunning victory to economic populism, exit polls showed that the majority of households earning less than $50,000—the most racially diverse income bracket—voted for Hillary Clinton. This raises key questions about racial divisions among the working class, and the need for and difficulty of cross-racial coalition building to address economic conditions that are worsening for all working people.

Racial stratification unambiguously leaves black workers worse off and the overwhelmingly white capitalist class better off. What's far more ambiguous is the economic positioning of the white working class, as "white privilege" offers both psychological and material benefits. In an economic downturn, for instance, blacks are generally the first fired and last hired. Black expectant mothers with a college degree have a greater likelihood of infant mortality than white expectant mothers who dropped out of high school, and a black man with a college degree is nearly three times more likely to die from a stroke than a white man who dropped out of high school.[29] All of these examples illustrate "property rights in whiteness."

An authentic multiracial coalition to address the obscene concentration of economic and political power in America thus means whites rejecting the narrow self-interest embodied in the property rights of whiteness to pursue a widespread prosperity grounded in morality. With calls for policies like a federal job guarantee, younger generations and social movements are spurring a shift in this direction and beginning to redefine economic good to incorporate sustainability and humanity—not just GDP growth.

Rev. William Barber II describes economic justice as a moral imperative.[30] It is time to translate that idea into a public policy framework fit for the twenty-first century, one that builds an economy that—for the first time in its history—works for all its people.

Democratic Socialism for a Climate-Changed Century

Naomi Klein

AT THE CONSERVATIVE POLITICAL ACTION CONFERENCE IN 2019, RIGHT-wing luminaries set their sights tightly focused on two targets: the Green New Deal and democratic socialism—for them, one and the same. "It's a watermelon," ousted Trump White House adviser Sebastian Gorka summarized with his usual theatrics. "Green on the outside, deep, deep communist red on the inside. . . . They want to take your pickup truck, they want to rebuild your home, they want to take away your hamburgers. This is what Stalin dreamt about but never achieved."

Like climate change deniers' claims that global warming is a Marxist plot to steal American freedom, the idea of a Green New Deal is nothing new. And both are experiencing a revival.

In late 2018, the Intergovernmental Panel on Climate Change published a landmark report informing us that global emissions need to be slashed roughly in half in less than twelve years, a target that simply cannot be met without the world's largest economy playing a game-changing leadership role. Once Democrats took back the House that year, House Speaker Nancy Pelosi let it be known that her plan for meeting this historic moment was to convene a toothless committee to further study the endlessly studied crisis. Shortly after the midterm election, but before the swearing in, young climate activists with the Sunrise Movement let it be known that they weren't having any of it. Demanding a Green New Deal, Sunrise invited two hundred people to protest on Capitol Hill, where they were supported by several incoming members of Congress, including Ayanna Pressley, Ilhan Omar, Rashida Tlaib (who spoke at one of the Sunrise rallies), and Alexandria Ocasio-Cortez— like Tlaib, a member of the Democratic Socialists of America (who famously visited their sit-in of Pelosi's office).

Riding the tide of momentum, and working with Sunrise, Ocasio-Cortez's office made Pelosi a counteroffer for how to meet the climate challenge in 2019: rather than expending all their political energy on a carbon pricing scheme that was sure to be politically unpopular while failing to bring down emissions with anything like the speed required, the new Congress should have a select committee on the Green New Deal that would, over the course of a year, create a detailed plan to get off fossil fuels in the United States by 2030, taking full advantage of what the proposal called the "historic opportunity to virtually eliminate poverty in the United States."

That select committee was not created. Yet within four months, more than one hundred members of Congress and virtually every 2020 Democratic presidential hopeful had joined the call for a Green New Deal, an economy-wide mobilization for decarbonization along a science-based timeline. After decades of either silence or cautious moderation on climate change from Democrats, young activists and lawmakers had rewritten the rules of the possible in a matter of days.

To those outside the climate justice movement, the speed seemed dizzying. Yet the ground for this momentum has been prepared for decades— with models for community-owned and community-controlled renewable energy; with justice-based labor market transitions that make sure no worker is left behind; with a deepening analysis of the intersections between systemic racism, armed conflict, and climate disruption; with improved green tech and breakthroughs in clean public transit; with the thriving fossil fuel divestment movement; with model legislation driven at the state and city level that shows how carbon pricing—if progressively designed—can fight racial and gender exclusion; and much more.

What had been missing until 2019 was only the top-level political power to roll out the best of these models all at once, with the focus and velocity that both science and justice demand. That is the great promise of a comprehensive Green New Deal in the largest economy on earth.

Which is why the CPAC crowd is right to worry—Ocasio-Cortez wasn't actually coming for their hamburgers, but the Green New Deal was a true threat to their half-century-long ideological project. No wonder Gorka's speech came with a full-throated call to arms: "You are on the front lines of the war against communism coming back to America under the guise of democratic socialism."

The climate change denial movement that spawned these talking points is a creature of the very ideological network that deserves the bulk of the credit for redrawing the global ideological map over the last four decades. A 2013 study by sociologist Riley Dunlap and political scientist Peter Jacques found that a striking 72 percent of climate change denial books, mostly published since the 1990s, were linked to right-wing think tanks like the Heritage Foundation and the Cato Institute, a figure that rises to 87 percent if self-published books are excluded.

Many of these institutions were created in the late 1960s and early 1970s, when U.S. business elites feared that public opinion was turning dangerously against capitalism and toward, if not socialism, then an aggressive Keynesianism. In response, they launched a counterrevolution, a richly funded intellectual movement that argued that greed and the limitless pursuit of profit were nothing to apologize for and offered the greatest hope for human emancipation that the world had ever known. Under this liberationist banner, they fought for such policies as tax cuts and free trade deals and for the auctioning off of core state assets from phones to energy to water—the package known in most of the world as "neoliberalism."

At the end of the 1980s, after a decade of Margaret Thatcher at the helm in the United Kingdom and Ronald Reagan in the United States, and with communism collapsing, these ideological warriors were ready to declare victory: history was officially over and there was, in Thatcher's often repeated words, "no alternative" to their market fundamentalism. Filled with confidence, the neoliberals' next task was to systematically lock in the corporate liberation project in every country that had previously held out, which was usually best accomplished in the midst of political turmoil and large-scale economic crises, and further entrenched through free trade agreements and membership in the World Trade Organization.

It had all been going so well. The project had even managed to survive, more or less, the 2008 financial collapse directly caused by a banking sector that had been liberated of so much burdensome regulation and oversight. But to those gathered at CPAC and similar confabs, climate change is a threat of a different sort. It isn't about the political preferences of Republicans versus Democrats; it's about the physical boundaries of the atmosphere and the ocean. If the dire projections coming out of the Intergovernmental Panel on Climate Change are left unchallenged, and business as usual is indeed driving us straight toward civilization-threatening tipping points, then the implications are obvious: the ideological crusade incubated in think tanks like Cato and Heritage will have to come to a screeching halt. Nor have the various attempts to soft-pedal climate action as compatible with market logic (carbon trading, carbon offsets, monetizing nature's "services") fooled these true believers one bit. They know very well that ours is a global economy created by, and fully reliant upon, the burning of fossil fuels and that a dependency that foundational cannot be changed with a few gentle market mechanisms. It requires heavy-duty interventions: sweeping bans on polluting activities, deep subsidies for green alternatives, pricey penalties for violations, new taxes, new public works programs, reversals of privatizations—the list of ideological outrages goes on and on. Everything, in short, that these think tanks—which have always been public proxies for far more powerful corporate interests—have been busily attacking for decades.

If the free-market system really has set in motion physical and chemical processes that, if allowed to continue even for one more decade, threaten large parts of humanity at an existential level, then their entire crusade to morally redeem capitalism has been for naught. With stakes like these, clearly greed is not so very good after all. And that is what is behind the surge in climate change denial among hard-core conservatives: no, they have not lost their minds. They simply understand that as soon as they admit that climate change is real, they will lose the central ideological battle of our time—whether we need to plan and manage our societies to reflect our goals and values, or whether that task can be left to the magic of markets.

Here's my inconvenient truth: I think these hard-core ideologues understand the real significance of climate change better than most of the moderates in the so-called center, the ones who are still insisting that the response can be gradual and painless and that we don't need to go to war with anybody, including the fossil fuel companies. The deniers get plenty of the details wrong (no, it's not a communist plot; authoritarian state socialism, as we will see, was terrible for the environment and brutally extractivist), but when it comes to the scope and depth of change required to avert catastrophe, they are right on the money.

Fossil fuels, and the deeper extractivist mind-set that they represent, built the modern world. If we are part of industrial or postindustrial societies, we are still living inside a story written in coal.

Ever since the French Revolution, there have been pitched ideological battles within the confines of this story: communists, socialists, and trade unions have fought for more equal distribution of the spoils of extraction, winning major victories for the poor and working classes. The human rights and emancipation movements of this period have also fought valiantly against industrial capitalism's treatment of whole categories of our species as human sacrifice zones, no more deserving of rights than raw commodities are. These struggles have also won major victories against the dominance-based paradigm—against slavery, for universal suffrage, for equality under the law. And there have been voices in all of these movements, moreover, that identified the parallels between the economic model's abuse of the natural world and its abuse of human beings deemed worthy of being sacrificed, or at least uncounted. Karl Marx, for instance, recognized capitalism's "irreparable rift" with "the natural laws of life itself," while feminist scholars have long recognized that patriarchy's dual war against women's bodies and against the body of the earth was connected to that essential, corrosive separation between mind and body—and between body and earth—from which both the Scientific Revolution and Industrial Revolution sprang.

These challenges, however, were mainly in the intellectual realm; Francis Bacon's original, biblically inspired framework for the extractive economy remained largely intact—the right of humans to place ourselves above the ecosystems that support us and to abuse the earth as if it were an inanimate machine. The strongest challenges to this worldview have always come from outside its logic, in those historical junctures when the extractive project clashes directly with a different, older way of relating to the earth—and that older way fights back. This has been true from the earliest days of industrialization, when English and Irish peasants, for instance, revolted against the first attempts to enclose communal lands, and it has continued in clashes between colonizers and indigenous peoples through the centuries, right up to the indigenous-led resistance to new fossil fuel projects (pipelines, coal mines, export facilities) that have delivered the climate movement's most significant victories in recent years.

But for those of us born and raised inside this system, though we may well see the dead-end flaw of its central logic, it can remain intensely difficult to see a way out. And how could it be otherwise? Post-Enlightenment Western culture does not offer a road map for how to live that is not based on an extractivist, nonreciprocal relationship with nature.

This is where the right-wing climate change deniers have overstated their conspiracy theories about what a cosmic gift global warming is to the left. It is true that many climate responses reinforce progressive support for government intervention in the market, for greater equality, and for a more robust public sphere. But the deeper message carried by the ecological crisis—that humanity has to go a whole lot easier on the living systems that sustain us, acting regeneratively rather than extractively—is a profound challenge to large parts of the left as well as the right. It's a challenge to some trade unions, those trying to freeze in place the dirtiest jobs, instead of fighting for the good clean jobs their members deserve. And it's a challenge to the overwhelming majority of center-left Keynesians, who still define economic success in terms of traditional measures of GDP growth, regardless of whether that growth comes from low-carbon sectors or rampant resource extraction.

It's a challenge, too, to those parts of the left that equated socialism with the authoritarian rule of the Soviet Union and its satellites (though there was always a rich tradition, particularly among anarchists, that considered Stalin's project an abomination of core social justice and collectivist principles). Because the fact is that those self-described socialist states devoured resources with as much enthusiasm as did their capitalist counterparts, and spewed waste just as recklessly. Before the fall of the Berlin Wall, for instance, Czechs and Russians had even higher carbon footprints per capita than Canadians and Australians. Which is why one of the only times the industrialized world has seen a precipitous emissions drop was after the economic collapse of the former Soviet Union in the early 1990s. Mao Zedong, for his part, openly declared that "man must conquer nature," setting loose a devastating onslaught on the natural world that transitioned seamlessly from clear-cuts under communism to mega-dams under capitalism. Russia's oil and gas companies, meanwhile, were as reckless and accident-prone under state socialist control as they are today in the hands of the oligarchs and Russia's corporatist state.

And as I wrote in *This Changes Everything*, too many recent left governments in Latin America failed to diversify their economies away from fossil fuel and other raw commodity extraction when prices were high, leaving them intensely vulnerable to right-wing attacks when commodity prices collapsed, putting their laudable poverty-alleviation programs in dire jeopardy. From Brazil to Venezuela to Ecuador to Argentina, these left governments claimed they had no choice—that they needed to pursue extractive policies in order to pay for programs that fought dire poverty and inequality. And they have a point: the transition to postcarbon diversified economies should have been radically subsidized by wealthy economies in the Global North, as part of our collective climate debt. Forced to choose between poverty and pollution, these governments chose pollution, but those should never have been their only options.

Let's acknowledge these difficult facts, while also pointing out that countries with a strong democratic socialist tradition—like Denmark, Sweden, Costa Rica, and Uruguay—have some of the most visionary environmental policies in the world. Scandinavian-style social democracy has undoubtedly produced some of the most significant green breakthroughs in the world, from the visionary urban design of Stockholm, where roughly 74 percent of residents walk, bike, or take public transit to work, to Denmark's community-controlled wind-power revolution. From all this we can conclude that socialism isn't necessarily ecological, but that a new form of democratic ecosocialism, with the humility to learn from indigenous teachings about the duties to future generations and the interconnection of all of life, appears to be humanity's best shot at collective survival.

These are the stakes in the surge of movements and movement-grounded political candidates who are advancing a democratic ecosocialist vision for the United States, connecting the dots between the economic depredations caused by decades of neoliberal ascendency and the ravaged state of our natural world. These movements and candidates, whether or not they identify explicitly as democratic socialist, are rejecting the neoliberal centrism of the establishment Democratic Party, with its tepid "market-based solutions" to the ecological crisis, as well as the Trumpian all-out war on nature. And they are also presenting a concrete alternative to the undemocratic extrac-tivist socialists of both the past and present.

The Sunrise Movement and its supporters in Congress chose to model the Green New Deal after President Franklin D. Roosevelt's historic raft of programs, understanding full well that a central task is to make sure that this mobilization does not repeat the ways in which its namesake exclud-ed and further marginalized many vulnerable groups. For instance, New Deal–era programs and protections left out agricultural and domestic workers (many of them black), Mexican immigrants (some 1 million of whom faced deportation in the 1930s), and indigenous people (who won some gains in the New Deal era but whose land rights were also violated by both massive infrastructure projects and some conservation efforts). That is why "frontline" groups are mentioned repeatedly in the original Green New Deal resolution: this mobilization has to right the wrongs of the last one or it has no chance of catching fire.

Some deeper challenges about New Deal logic remain to be tackled. For instance, so far much of the emphasis has rightly been on industrial trans-formation and job creation. Not nearly enough has been on the outsize role that consumption plays in what used to be called "the American way of life," or the way that a culture of overwork fuels cycles of disposable consumption (stressed and overworked people need fast and easy everything). Our lead-ing emission-reduction experts tell us that if we are going to hit the targets demanded by science, we in wealthy countries don't just need to consume green stuff; we need to consume less stuff, with a higher premium placed on activities, like caregiving and the arts, that are inherently low carbon.

Despite these challenges, I have written before about why the old New Deal remains a useful touchstone for the kind of sweeping climate mobiliza-tion that is our only hope of lowering emissions in time. In large part, this is because there are so few historical precedents we can look to (other than top-down military mobilizations) that show how every sector of life, from forestry to education to the arts to housing to electrification, can be trans-formed under the umbrella of a single, society-wide mission.

Which is why it is so critical to remember that none of it would have happened without massive pressure from social movements. FDR rolled out the New Deal in the midst of a historic wave of labor unrest: there was the Teamsters' rebellion and Minneapolis general strike in 1934, the eighty-three-day shutdown of the West Coast by longshore workers that same year, and the Flint autoworkers' sit-down strikes in 1936 and 1937. During this same period, mass movements, responding to the suffering of the Great Depression, demanded sweeping social programs, such as Social Security and unemployment insurance, while socialists argued that abandoned factories should be handed over to their workers and turned into cooperatives. Upton Sinclair, the muckraking author of *The Jungle*, ran for governor of California in 1934 on a platform arguing that the key to ending poverty was full state funding of workers' cooperatives. He received nearly nine hundred thousand votes, but having been viciously attacked by the right and undercut by the Democratic establishment, he fell just short of winning the governor's office.

All of this is a reminder that the New Deal was adopted by Roosevelt at a time of such progressive and left militancy that its programs—which seem radical by today's standards—appeared at the time to be the only way to hold back a full-scale revolution.

It's also a reminder that the New Deal was a process as much as a project, one that was constantly changing and expanding in response to social pressure from both the right and the left. For example, a program like the Civilian Conservation Corps started with two hundred thousand workers, but when it proved popular eventually expanded to 2 million. There is plenty of time to improve and correct a Green New Deal once it starts rolling out (it needs to be more explicit about keeping carbon in the ground; about nuclear and coal never being "clean"; and about the connections between fossil fuels, foreign wars, and migration). But we have only one chance to get this thing charged up and moving forward.

The more sobering lesson is that the kind of mass power that delivered the victories of the New Deal era is far beyond anything possessed by current progressive movements, even if they all combined their efforts. That's why it is so urgent to use the Green New Deal framework as a potent tool to build that power—a vision to both unite movements and dramatically expand them.

Part of that involves turning what is being derided as a left-wing "laundry list" or "wish list" into an irresistible story of the future, connecting the dots between the many parts of daily life that stand to be transformed—

from health care to employment, day care to jail cell, clean air to leisure time. The Green New Deal has been characterized as an unrelated grab bag because most of us have been trained to avoid a systemic and historical analysis of capitalism and to divide pretty much every crisis our system produces—from economic inequality to violence against women to white supremacy to unending wars to ecological unraveling—in walled-off silos. From within that rigid mind-set, it's easy to dismiss a sweeping and intersectional vision like the Green New Deal as a green-tinted "laundry list" of everything the left has ever wanted.

Now that the call for a Green New Deal is out there, however, the onus is on all of us who support it to help make the case for how our overlapping crises are indeed inextricably linked—and can only be overcome with a holistic vision for social and economic transformation. This is already beginning to happen. For example, Rhiana Gunn-Wright, one of the leading architects of the Green New Deal, has pointed out that just as thousands of people moved for jobs during the World War II–era economic mobilization, we should expect a great many to move again to be part of a renewables revolution. And when they do, "unlinking employment from health care means people can move for better jobs, to escape the worst effects of climate, and re-enter the labor market without losing."

Investing big in public health care is also critical in light of the fact that no matter how fast we move to lower emissions, it is going to get hotter and storms are going to get fiercer. When those storms bash up against health care systems and electricity grids that have been starved by decades of austerity, thousands pay the price with their lives, as they so tragically did in post-Maria Puerto Rico.

And there are many more connections to be drawn. Those complaining about climate policy being weighed down by supposedly unrelated demands for access to health care and education would do well to remember that the caring professions—most of them dominated by women—are relatively low carbon and can be made even more so. In other words, they deserve to be seen as "green jobs," with the same protections, the same investments, and the same living wages as male-dominated workforces in the renewables, efficiency, and public-transit sectors. Meanwhile, as Gunn-Wright points out, to make those sectors less male dominated, family leave and pay equity are musts, which is part of the reason both are included in the resolution.

Drawing out these connections in ways that capture the public imagination will take a massive exercise in popular education and participatory democracy. A first step is for every sector touched by the Green New
Deal—hospitals, schools, universities, and more—to make their own plans
for how to rapidly decarbonize while furthering the Green New Deal's mission to eliminate poverty, create good jobs, and close the racial and gender
wealth divides.

My favorite example of what this could look like comes from the Canadian Union of Postal Workers, which has developed a bold plan to turn
every post office in Canada into a hub for a just green transition. Think
solar panels on the roof, charging stations out front, a fleet of domestically
manufactured electric vehicles from which union members not only deliver
mail, as well as local produce and medicine, but also check in on seniors—
all supported by the proceeds of postal banking.

To make the case for a Green New Deal—which explicitly calls for this
kind of democratic, decentralized leadership—every sector in the United
States should be developing similar visionary plans for their workplaces
right now.

We have been trained to see our issues in silos; they never belonged
there. In fact, the impact of climate change on every part of our lives is far
too expansive and extensive to begin to cover here. But I do need to mention
a few more glaring links that many are missing.

A job guarantee, far from an opportunistic socialist addendum, is a critical part of achieving a rapid and just transition. It would immediately lower
the intense pressure on workers to take the kinds of jobs that destabilize our
planet, because all would be free to take the time needed to retrain and find
work in one of the many sectors that will be dramatically expanding.

This in turn will reduce the power of bad actors like the Laborers' International Union of North America, who are determined to split the labor
movement and sabotage the prospects for this historic effort. Right out of
the gate, LIUNA came out swinging against the Green New Deal. Never
mind that it contains stronger protections for trade unions and the right to
organize than anything we have seen out of Washington in three decades,
including the right of workers in high-carbon sectors to democratically participate in their transition and to have jobs in clean sectors at the same salary
and benefits levels as before.

There is absolutely no rational reason for a union representing construction workers to oppose what would be the biggest infrastructure project in a century, unless LIUNA actually is what it appears to be: a fossil fuel astroturf group disguised as a trade union, or at best a company union. These are the same labor leaders, let us recall, who sided with the tanks and attack dogs at Standing Rock; who fought relentlessly for the construction of the planet-destabilizing Keystone XL pipeline; and who (along with several other building trade union heads) aligned themselves with Trump on his first day in office, smiling for a White House photo op and declaring his inauguration "a great moment for working men and women."

LIUNA's leaders have loudly demanded unquestioning "solidarity" from the rest of the trade union movement. But again and again, they have offered nothing but the narrowest self-interest in return, indifferent to the suffering of immigrant workers whose lives are being torn apart under Trump and to the indigenous workers who saw their homeland turned into a war zone. The time has come for the rest of the labor movement to confront and isolate them before they can do more damage. That could take the form of LIUNA members, confident that the Green New Deal will not leave them behind, voting out their pro-boss leaders. Or it could end with LIUNA being tossed out of the AFL-CIO for planetary malpractice.

The more unionized sectors, like teaching, nursing, and manufacturing, make the Green New Deal their own by showing how it can transform their workplaces for the better, and the more all union leaders embrace the growth in membership they would see under the Green New Deal, the stronger they will be for this unavoidable confrontation.

One last connection I will mention has to do with the concept of "repair." Ocasio-Cortez and Senator Ed Markey's Green New Deal resolution, introduced in the House and Senate in February 2019, called for creating well-paying jobs "restoring and protecting threatened, endangered, and fragile ecosystems," as well as "cleaning up existing hazardous waste and abandoned sites, ensuring economic development and sustainability on those sites."

There are many such sites across the United States, entire landscapes that have been left to waste after they were no longer useful to frackers, miners, and drillers. It's a lot like how this culture treats people. It's what has been done to so many workers in the neoliberal period, using them up and

then abandoning them to addiction and despair. It's what the entire carceral state is about: locking up huge sectors of the population who are more
economically useful as prison laborers and numbers on the spreadsheet of
a private prison than they are as free workers. And the old New Deal did
it too, by choosing to exclude and discard so many black and brown and
women workers.

There is a grand story to be told here about the duty to repair—to repair
our relationship with the earth and with one another, to heal the deep
wounds dating back to the founding of the country. Because while it is true
that climate change is a crisis produced by an excess of greenhouse gases
in the atmosphere, it is also, in a more profound sense, a crisis produced by
an extractive mind-set—a way of viewing both the natural world and the
majority of its inhabitants as resources to use up and then discard. I call it
the "gig and dig" economy and firmly believe that we will not emerge from
this crisis without a shift in worldview, a transformation from "gig and dig"
to an ethos of care and repair.

If these kinds of deeper connections between fractured people and a
fast-warming planet seem far beyond the scope of policymakers, it's worth
thinking back to the absolutely central role of artists during the New Deal
era. Playwrights, photographers, muralists, and novelists were all part of
a renaissance of both realist and utopian art. Some held up a mirror to the
wrenching misery that the New Deal sought to alleviate. Others opened
up spaces for Depression-ravaged people to imagine a world beyond that
misery. Both helped get the job done in ways that are impossible to quantify.

In a similar vein, there is much to learn from indigenous-led movements
in Bolivia and Ecuador that have placed at the center of their calls for ecological transformation the concept of *buen vivir*, a focus on the right to a
good life as opposed to a life of endless consumption.

The Green New Deal will need to be subject to constant vigilance and
pressure from experts who understand exactly what it will take to lower
our emissions as rapidly as science demands, and from social movements
that have decades of experience bearing the brunt of false climate solutions,
whether nuclear power, the chimera of carbon capture and storage, or carbon offsets.

But in remaining vigilant, we also have to be careful not to bury the over-
arching message: that this is a potential lifeline that we all have a sacred and
moral responsibility to reach for.

Part II

Expanding Democracy

Governing Socialism

Bill Fletcher Jr.

BERNIE SANDERS'S PRESIDENTIAL PRIMARY RUN SAW 13 MILLION PEOPLE vote for a democratic socialist, and tens of thousands of volunteers knock on doors. Two years later, Alexandria Ocasio-Cortez's underdog, grassroots-driven victory against one of Congress's most powerful Democrats shook the political establishment. Combined with the election of Donald Trump, these two campaigns reignited interest in something many on the left had shied away from for the better part of a century: electoral power.

But what would that look like? Leftists tend to use the term "power" in frequently confusing ways, referring to everything from a sudden seizure of the means of production to electing middle-of-the-road Democrats. As a new generation of leftists look to take it, it's worth understanding what power actually means, why so many have shied away from it, and what the risks are once we get it.

So what is power? The late Chilean theorist Marta Harnecker and U.S. theorists Manuel Pastor and Richard Healey distinguish between "state power" and "governing power." The "state"—as described here—is not simply a series of apparatuses but instead the representation of the balance of class forces, to borrow from global studies theorist William Robinson, with a hegemonic bloc looking out for the long-term interests of the dominant class—in our case, the "1 percent." Importantly, the capitalist state looks out for the long-term interests of capital rather than the particular interests of any one capitalist, never missing the forest for the trees. And the state has within itself institutions through which power is exercised, like Congress or the Federal Reserve.

"Seizing state power" is therefore a process of fundamentally altering the balance of class forces and creating a new hegemonic bloc that moves us away from capitalism, instead of just changing who controls the institutions that keep it running. Winning state power involves the domination and, over time, deconstruction and replacement of capitalist institutions.

"Governing power" is something altogether different from state power, though not unimportant—effectively, progressives or leftists winning political office within the context of a capitalist state. They may win office electorally and positions of leadership, but they do not control the state apparatuses and do not have the mandate or strength to carry out a full and thoroughgoing process of social transformation in which the capitalist state is dismantled and a new state is created in order to advance the process of socialism.

This might look like winning a mayor's or governor's office. This is also the situation Bernie Sanders or any other left-leaning candidate is likely to walk into should they make it to the White House. More crucially, this is the situation that has faced countless left-leaning politicians in the United States and abroad who have tried to make inroads toward a consistent democracy, let alone democratic socialism, at the local, state, and even federal level.

That governing power has been so difficult to achieve and exercise has led many on the left in the United States to fear it, and not without reason. Domestically and internationally there have been many examples of significant challenges faced by a left that has gained governing power only to become corrupted or checkmated. Convinced either that the left is simply a pressure group to push for a better liberalism or that electoral politics is a sham that can only "manage capitalism," leftists as a result have spent much of the last several decades instead mounting resistance battles and struggles for reform, including some laudable structural reforms. Beyond that, though, many have fallen back on rhetoric to articulate a path to power: first, delineate a list of capitalism's atrocities; second, socialism will resolve said atrocities—no intermediary steps required.

In such a context, recent optimism among socialists about the prospects for governing power is a welcome development, and sorely needed given the rise of neoliberal authoritarianism and right-wing populism. Yet there needs to be some middle ground between cynicism and naive optimism. Below are a few observations gleaned from history of what the left can expect should it attain governing power.

Don't Underestimate Backlash

In his last book, *State, Power, Socialism*, Greek theorist Nicos Poulantzas argued that power in capitalist society is not contained forever and ever in specific apparatuses of the capitalist state. Rather, he suggests that power is fluid, and any institution that had historically seemed to contain a specific amount of power can almost magically appear to lose it under different political conditions. Take the experience of the late, progressive black mayor of Chicago, Harold Washington.

Then congressman Harold Washington, from Chicago, was approached by representatives of a movement in the city that wanted a black progressive to run for mayor. He ran to break the stranglehold of the machine over Chicago politics and as a representative of black progressive power. His election was important nationally as illustrative of the black-led electoral upsurge underway, but it was also critical in the Chicago context as laying a foundation for a new coalition in city politics. Once he was elected, the office of the mayor, which—prior to Washington—had appeared to be nothing short of all-powerful, was suddenly usurped by the city council. Power seemed to drain from the mayor's office and appear within the city council, undermining many of Washington's initial reform efforts. A bloc of city council members (aldermen) blocked Washington on legislation and appointments, leading to a situation of near war between the pro-Washington forces and their reactionary opponents.

Power can shift in other ways, too. GOP efforts to shift decision-making authority away from cities and counties and rest it within state legislatures began during the rise of black mayors in the 1970s—most notably in the early efforts by Republican state legislators to undermine the efforts of Detroit mayor Coleman Young—but have now taken on greater scope and urgency. State legislative preemption is no longer a matter only targeted at municipalities and counties led by people of color.

Republicans have deployed their bases in rural areas in order to surround

municipalities and introduce legislation that blocks the ability of municipalities and counties to introduce certain reforms (read: state preemption).
As far back as the 1970s, upstate Republicans refused to approve legislation
that would have allowed New York City—which has limited authority to
raise taxes and revenue—to alleviate its dire fiscal crisis, paving the way for
a series of painful austerity measures as if to discipline the pro-Democratic
city. In the more recent past, Republican-controlled state legislatures have
blocked the ability of municipalities and counties to introduce living-wage
increases and environmental reforms without approval from the state
legislature.

The right, though, has no shortage of other tools for undermining
its enemies on the left. The slow-moving coup in Brazil that led to the
impeachment and removal of Workers Party president Dilma Rousseff, the
imprisonment of former Workers Party president Lula da Silva, and, ultimately, the election of a fascist in the person of former military officer Jair
Bolsonaro is among the most blatant of examples. There can, of course, be
open coups, with which the world and the United States in particular is very
familiar. The United States has supported countless coups abroad, particularly in Latin American countries that flirted too openly with socialism
or simply national sovereignty. Yet this has happened on smaller scales as
well. In the Wilmington, North Carolina, uprising of 1898, white supremacist forces carried out an armed uprising against a progressive, elected, and
multiracial government. They succeeded and suffered no consequences.
Uprisings of this sort—along with pogroms—are far from uncommon in
U.S. history and represent a dangerous precedent about which leftists must
be aware.

Not all backlash against left and progressive power is necessarily well
planned, though. A strange example was the rise of a movement during the
1970s to overturn the mandatory usage of helmets by motorcycle riders.
Despite well-documented evidence on the importance of helmets in saving
lives, reactionary mass movements have fought to overturn such legislation on the grounds of their alleged infringement on personal space and
individual rights. In other words, not all reactionary mass movements are
generated directly by capital or its allies on the right.

The combination of both Republican obstructionism and the sheer
breadth of the Democratic coalition and its establishment's deep ties to

capital further means that radical—using that term loosely—efforts at alternative forms of governance and economics will be challenged as being inappropriate, reckless, and doomed to fail. An administration lacking in self-confidence and an energized base may cave to such pressures.

Always Expand the Base

The election of a left leader or a left-led governing coalition (a "left-led bloc" as I call it throughout this chapter) always raises questions as to the expectation and mandate of the base that supported them. Was this leadership supported because of their left politics, or despite them? Or did they win because of the policies they promised to enact?

Any left, democratic socialist, or even progressive administration that is elected to office will have to make an immediate assessment as to why it is in office; in other words, what is its mandate? Using that as a starting point, the administration can construct a program of action but must always be working to expand its base of support for that mandate, both among the public and within governing institutions. This will involve broad-based education as well as winning over key leaders and organizations from among the so-called middle or center, which may have been, at best, ambivalent about the left's rise to power (more on that later).

A left or progressive government must be well rooted in its constituency and understand the issues that are on the minds of the people, taking up policy pushes that range from economic development to the environment to law enforcement. If that government is actually a coalition, it must recognize the existence of contradictions within the coalition itself and create a mechanism within that coalition to resolve disputes through democratic processes.

Both the left-led bloc and its base should prepare for a protracted battle. That necessitates having "marking posts," so to speak: incremental targets to work toward in service of fulfilling its overall agenda. For morale alone, there must be quick and demonstrable action on certain key projects that are central to the mandate on which the governing coalition was elected. At the same time, the base must be educated to understand that the larger problems, crises, and so on—climate change, for instance—will not be resolved all at once.

Relatedly, constituencies of the coalition partners must see themselves in the operation and public manifestation of the coalition itself. This is especially important in situations where there are constituency differences based on matters such as race, gender, religion, and ethnicity. A left or left-led coalition can never afford to make the assumption that their collective, redistributive politics will automatically endear them to all base members of a coalition. In situations where populations have been taken for granted—for example, African Americans, Latinxs, Native Americans, Asians—the mere fact of representation in a coalition government is insufficient to build trust and support. There must be a sense of partnership reflected in terms of who is in what positions of power. David Dinkins's tenure as mayor of New York City from 1990 to 1993, for instance, was possible because of a critical alliance between African American and Puerto Rican communities. Once Dinkins was elected, however, a perception developed within the Puerto Rican community that Dinkins, a longtime Harlem Democrat, was looking out for "his" constituency and not for the coalition that elected him. Accordingly, the promise of the administration began to evaporate.

A second example can be found in the 2016 Bernie Sanders campaign. Though Sanders advanced the most progressive platform of the candidates, and despite the fact that Sanders had "surrogates" of color who spoke on his behalf, he faced two major challenges. First, his platform and oratory evidenced little understanding of the centrality of race in the construction and operationalizing of U.S. capitalism. Sanders spoke about the injustices of the system but generally stayed away from analyzing and explaining the interconnections of race, class, and gender. This had a special impact on older voters of color, who constitute a sizable portion of Democratic primary voters. The second challenge was that there is a difference between having spokespersons supporting one's campaign and having real diversity among the strategists. The Sanders campaign lacked that diversity at its highest levels, instead relying mainly on the small team of advisers with whom the senator felt most comfortable.

Win the Middle

It's no secret that the self-described left, however successful, has always been far too small to control a country or even a state or city on its own. Fast as the Democratic Socialists of America's membership might grow, or that of any other left formation for that matter, democratic socialists specifically and the left more generally are not a plurality in any electoral precinct in the country. As a consequence, they'll need to make friends—both to win office and, critically, to stay there.

The success of any movement almost always hinges on its ability to win over the so-called middle forces that may have been ambivalent or in some degree of opposition to a left-led bloc.

To clarify, the notion of a "middle," as with "left" and "right," is relational; while there are forces that identify themselves as "left" and others that define themselves as "right," the actual politics of such forces varies over time. What is a left position today may have been considered wishy-washy centrism ten years ago. Much of the domestic agenda of President Richard Nixon, for instance, was to the left of President Bill Clinton. The middle vacillates in context, generally uncomfortable with whatever the status quo is but unprepared to make a significant break with it. In the case of today's United States, the middle tends to be comprised of people and organizations that see holes or dysfunction in the system but have not concluded that it is the system itself that is toxic, like those dissatisfied with Trump and the GOP and eager for the FBI and the U.S. national security apparatus to weed him out. They believe in the reform struggle from the standpoint that reforms are not simply necessary, but are all that is necessary in order to make the system operate as it should. A left or democratic socialist government will have to assume that the middle forces will be diverse by their very nature and not anti-capitalist, though potentially anti-corporate. They'll hold contradictory views on the relative importance of fighting various forms of non-class-specific oppressions, such as race, ethnicity, gender, and religion.

The first task is to identify those organizations and representatives of the middle forces and find means to embrace them. Assume as well that there will be protest and opposition, but not that such protests, regardless of militancy, are necessarily antagonistic to the program and existence of the left-led project. Middle forces will tend to assume that the left will move to repress dissent and will as a result use anything that approaches that as grounds to jump ship and join the outright opposition; we shouldn't give them the excuse to do so. The "tent," as it were, must be broad enough to keep the middle forces engaged.

Move Fast and Decisively

There's a lot to be learned from the first two years of Donald Trump's administration. After his election, Republicans seized every opportunity to advance their agenda at lightning speed. When it came up against opposition, it tended to either dismiss and steamroll or simply go around it, as with the GOP's tax bill and its appointment of Brett Kavanaugh to the Supreme Court. Regularly, the White House called upon its base to support its actions, holding massive rallies and corralling them to the polls.

Liberals and progressives rarely perform in such a manner. One need only look at the first few months of the Obama administration. Despite the electoral mandate he received in the 2008 elections, he moved cautiously, demobilizing his base (e.g., officially turning "Obama for America" over to the Democratic Party), continuously trying to prove to Republicans that he was prepared to be a great compromiser and unifier, apparently wanting to appear to be acting like an adult amid claims of inexperience, and fearing any perceptions of him as an "angry black man." He refused to accept that the Republicans sought to destroy him as quickly as possible. Even as they controlled all three branches of government, Democrats failed to pass climate policy and the Employee Free Choice Act, leaving the Affordable Care Act—a perilously watered-down compromise with the GOP—as the party's sole legislative achievement before losing control of Congress to Tea Party Republicans.

What the left can do with governing power depends on a combination of timing; the level of organization and mobilization of our base; and objective constraints. As detailed earlier, it should also be clear that whatever the left-led bloc does, it will be met with opposition from the right, and quite possibly the center, as it looks to achieve anything. It's worth breaking these factors down.

Timing

New leadership has a limited window in which to introduce major changes, which is why Jeremy Corbyn's Labour Party in the United Kingdom was hard at work crafting a plan for its "radical" first one hundred days, per Shadow Chancellor John McDonnell, soon after it won party leadership.

It is not that leadership cannot introduce change later in an administration. Rather, speedy action taken at the beginning of an administration both appeals to the base and frequently catches the opposition off guard. Caution in the early days can be dangerous, which is not an argument for being reckless and stupid. But there must be both quick and bold steps.

Level of Organization

Does the left-led bloc have the capacity to turn an electoral win into an ongoing source of pressure and support? Is there a level of organization that can be mobilized to fend against political opponents?

Though Barack Obama was not on the left, his decision to abandon "Obama for America" was fateful and holds invaluable lessons for the left. When he won, his base was far greater than just African Americans. He had achieved a broad cross section of support, particularly in the context of the financial collapse of 2008 and the start of the Great Recession. He had a base that was sick of the Bush era and saw in Obama a vehicle to bring about dramatic change. Leaving aside the problem that too many people saw in Obama what they wanted to believe, on its own merits and in his own interests, Obama made a crucial mistake in decommissioning "Obama for America." Abandoning it meant eliminating an independent base of activists. "Obama for America" had developed as a very sophisticated and broad opposition to Republican rule. It was not democratically operated; it was a campaign organization of committed believers. And many of those who joined the campaign were quite explicitly looking for marching orders after Obama had succeeded in his run for office. "Obama for America" perfected online organizing and expert voter identification, techniques that would transform electoral organizing for years to come. Its skills could have been put to work across the United States in 2009, laying the foundation for progressive races at the local level, but also as a means of advancing the policy priorities articulated by the Obama campaign. Rather than being able to draw on this broad and talented coalition, Obama effectively retired them and became entirely dependent on the Democratic Party establishment. He gave his base little to nothing to do in the process, leaving what had once been a dynamic campaign organization to fester. This weakened the ability of progressive forces within his base to keep pressure on him to fulfill his mandate, and helped ensure that he never did.

The upshot? An elected left-led bloc must have an organized mass base. This might be in the form of a united front organization or a loose collection of existing organizations that make up the bloc—that is, political parties and mass organizations. Trump's mass rallies, for instance, may seem over-the-top. But they give his supporters a sense that they are part of a movement, even a sense that they are part of history. For the left the challenge will be one not simply of governing, but of engaging the base and finding means for all parts of it to be directly involved in the process of governing. This means, among other things, the need to create new institutions that allow many more people to actively participate in democratic processes in ways that go well beyond voting, and certainly well beyond attending rallies.

Objective Constraints

At the municipal and county levels, left and progressive governments will be constrained by liberal and conservative forces at the state level. At the state level, left and progressive governments will be constrained by forces at the national level. At the national level, left and progressive organizations will be constrained by forces at the level of the transnational capitalist class, state and local (subnational) resistance, and the organized political right.

One of the biggest constraints on a left-led bloc—particularly at the state and local level, where deficit spending is all but impossible—will be the resources available to introduce changes. Any left-led bloc must further anticipate a blockade by capital. This may take any number of forms. The experience of Gary, Indiana, during the administration of Mayor Richard Hatcher, is one case in point. Edward Greer's *Big Steel: Black Politics and Corporate Power in Gary, Indiana* describes how the social democratic administration of Hatcher—an African American civil rights activist and attorney—overcame the Democratic Party machine backing his white Republican opponent to win the mayor's office in 1967. He was just thirty-four years old. White flight followed soon afterward, and businesses like Sears, Roebuck began to flee as well, decamping to predominantly white enclaves outside of city limits. Perhaps most damaging was the backlash by U.S. Steel, the major employer in the area, which had founded Gary as a company town in 1906. A combination of political calculations, automation, and broader economic circumstances caused the industrial giant to shed thousands of jobs over the course of Hatcher's four terms. The disinvestment and plummeting property values that ensued devastated the local economy and hollowed out the city's downtown business district. Hatcher worked tirelessly to obtain federal grants to build housing and job-training programs to redress the damage, but was severely constrained in what the municipality alone could do to build anything like the kind of social democracy he envisioned.

At a national level, any left government should consider placing controls on capital to prevent the sort of business and industrial flight that encumbered Hatcher's administration at a much smaller scale. Should a left-leaning government take governing power federally, industry and finance may well try to undermine it through a capital blockade or divestment—moving their money elsewhere. If there are no capital controls, they can succeed.

The Twenty-First-Century Resource Curse

Ten years from now, twenty years from now, you will see, oil will bring us ruin. . . . It is the devil's excrement.

—OPEC creator Juan Pablo Pérez Alfonzo

Social democratic experiments in Western Europe and the so-called welfare state in the United States and Canada were able to accommodate broader segments of the population in large part due to cheap energy costs. The welfare state was able to exist under exceptional conditions, one of the most important being colonialism in the Global South and the semicolonial domination of key markets by the major capitalist powers in the North. Cheap energy costs there made it easier for capital to grant concessions to social movements and the left. That this wealth had its limits became clear in the 1970s, as several factors came into play. For one, national independence and liberation efforts drastically changed the relationship of Western Europe and the United States to their former colonies. In some cases—particularly where national populist regimes came to power in the South—newly independent governments limited or set conditions on the availability of cheap and accessible resources to the North. Around the same time, the rise of OPEC and other resource cartels, formed by formerly colonized states, created additional pressure on former colonial powers that had grown accustomed to an easy flow of oil and other commodities. Even though this effort did not go anywhere near as far as many proponents of this fledgling new international order had hoped, it did place some constraints on capital in the Global North.

There was an ironic reversal of this trend a few decades later. The so-called Pink Tide regimes of Latin America (e.g., Hugo Chávez in Venezuela; Lula in Brazil; Rafael Correa in Ecuador) were in part able to succeed in at least some of their goals by relying on the profits from the extractive industries and the "resource sovereignty" embraced by several Pink Tide governments looking to liberate themselves from U.S. capital. The financial resources for many of the major welfare state expansions of that period, as in the case of Venezuela, came from the funds earned through pumping and exporting oil. When the prices for commodities started to drop and, in the case of oil, plummet, so, too, did the fortunes of the regimes that relied on them. Insofar as these regimes failed to carry out steps to reorganize their respective economies away from volatile commodities markets, they were vulnerable to attacks from the right and foreign opposition.

Resources can be, therefore, a double-edged sword. Capital uses possession of them to blockade the left. But, as witnessed in the case of the Pink Tide regimes, abundance of certain resources can be a means of seducing the left away from taking more fundamental steps in order to reorganize the economy. Even if oil prices could remain high forever, the looming threat of climate change means that leftists the world over should take seriously the challenge of expanding welfare states and building toward a democratic socialism while transitioning off of fossil fuels. This need is especially pressing in the United States, one of the world's most prolific producers and consumers of fossil fuels.

But What About Socialism?

Here it's worth introducing one last definition. The term "democratic capitalism" is in many ways a contradiction in terms. Capitalism can only be so democratic, acting in more cases than not in contradiction to democracy. Its most fervent adherents have understood this well. Defending Pinochet's coup in the *New York Times*, Friedrich Hayek—the godfather of neoliberalism—reasoned, "In modern times there have of course been many instances of authoritarian governments under which personal liberty was safer than under democracies." The term "democratic capitalism," rather, distinguishes that specific form of rule from these kinds of openly authoritarian variants of capitalism, whether military dictatorships or fascism.

Historically, the embrace of "social democracy" came from the belief that leftists occupying the heights of political power could lead, over time, to the construction of a new socialist society. The evolution would be slow and would not require the clear and unadulterated gaining of state power by the working class and their allies. This strategy—along with social democratic parties' widespread embrace of warmed-over neoliberalism, particularly in the wake of the global financial crisis—proved to be a cul-de-sac.

"Governing power," as discussed earlier, is what the left faces within the context of democratic capitalism. That is not to demean it but to state a fact. Can "governing power" under democratic capitalism lead to socialism?

No one knows. We can, however, make certain assumptions based on history regarding this fundamental question. To summarize:

The forces of capitalism will not voluntarily walk away from the stage simply because the masses demand it, or because the political representatives of capitalism lose at the polls. There is no example of such a thing happening. We should assume that the forces on the political right will use legal and extralegal means in order to retain power, disrupt efforts at social transformation, or both.

Embarking on a process of social transformation will necessitate a political alignment that embraces changes more ambitious than simple reforms. To borrow from the Marxist "classics," there will need to be a critical mass of the population that has concluded that the capitalist system is toxic and must be rooted out. Further, they must be organized. To borrow again from Marta Harnecker, there must be a "political instrument," be it a party or some other organizational vehicle, that can bring collective self-awareness to the dispossessed. Reliance on spontaneous consciousness-raising is yet another dead end. This political instrument must be a means of building a

revolutionary democratic bloc that can lead the process of social transformation, including at the stage of winning governing power with a "ruling
coalition" capable of bringing about real change.

In occupying governing power, the left must anticipate backlash—and
plenty of it, from all sides. There will be pressure from those on the left who
want to push farther and faster, and from the right attempts to halt or stall
transformational efforts. How any left-led government chooses to respond
will depend on the context of the moment and the balance of forces.

The great numbers of people newly excited about the prospects of the left
winning real power in the United States are boldly going where no movement has gone before—at least not successfully. What we can say with great
assurance, however, is that any decision by the left to avoid the struggle for
governing power condemns it to the margins, if not to history's dustbin.
Such a choice would see the left exist only as a force useful in defense of
popular reforms, but not one that can lead a process of social transformation
and emancipation.

Regardless of how many victories leftists rack up in the struggle for governing power (namely, elections), they'll forget to continue the class struggle alongside those victories at their own peril. In simpler terms, the forces
grouped around capital and other forces on the political right will relentlessly try to undermine left and progressive political power. Simply holding
an office is a poor guard against that. What's more, reaching beyond governing power to make democratic socialism a reality will mean changing the
balance of class forces.

In fighting for governing power, the left and its allies can begin to demonstrate a different set of assumptions regarding governance, political power, and the role of massive numbers of people as agents of change. Doing
so can and must push the limits on democratic capitalism under the banner
of fighting for consistent democracy—which, in the long run, must be one
without capitalism.

We the People: Voting Rights, Campaign Finance, and Election Reform

J. Mijin Cha

IN A COUNTRY THAT TOUTS ITSELF AS AN EXEMPLAR OF DEMOCRACY, THE electoral and political systems are dominated by a few wealthy voices. Citizen voting is fundamental to a democratic system, yet states have legally created obstacles and barriers to voting that disproportionately impact low-income voters and voters of color, often with the support of the Supreme Court. Ever-increasing amounts of money flood into the electoral system, dominating electoral narratives and supporting candidates that advance the priorities of special interest groups and the wealthy, which are overwhelmingly not aligned with the priorities of working Americans. The result is political, economic, and societal structures that help further and protect elite interests.[1]

America's democratic practices and policies are fundamentally flawed, with policies implemented to reflect the priorities of the richest Americans. The minimum wage remains stagnant while wealthy households continually see their taxes cut. Wealth is becoming more and more concentrated among the few: the top 0.01 percent of households, just sixteen thousand families, own 11 percent of the wealth in the country and have at least $111 million in net worth.[2] In contrast, the average household worth was $97,300 in 2016; the figure was even lower for black households ($17,100) and Latinx households ($20,600).[3] In order to build a more equitable country, we need to remove the toxic influence of money in politics and protect and advance the right of every eligible citizen to vote.

Commonsense solutions can ensure that every eligible citizen in the United States can participate in the democratic process, and make elected officials and government policies each more responsive to the will of the voters. Moreover, creating an electoral system dependent on getting out the vote rather than on fund-raising from moneyed donors will encourage more women, people of color, and working-class candidates to run for office. As a result, elected officials would better reflect the actual demographics of our country, with more diverse candidates bringing different perspectives and priorities into legislatures. Ending the capture of our politics by the wealthy is an essential building block to enacting any policies that might be described as democratic socialist, and would greatly help bring about a society that is finally of, and for, the people rather than a wealthy few.

A System by the Wealthy, for the Wealthy

Substantial research reveals the outsize influence that affluent and corporate interests have over policy decisions.[4] Benjamin Page and his colleagues found that, compared to the average American, the wealthy were far more likely to contact their elected representatives, donate to political campaigns, and vote. In 2008, nearly 99 percent of their sample voted, compared to average voter turnout that year across incomes of 59.7 percent. Those making between $20,000 and $29,000 annually voted at a rate of just 48 percent; voter turnout for people making less than $10,000 was 41.3 percent.[5]

The priorities of the electorally active 1 percent are very different from the priorities of the average American, and they are far less supportive of state-run welfare programs compared to the general public. As shown in Figure 1, there are stark differences between how the affluent view the role of government in providing economic security and how the general public view the role of government.

The minimum wage is particularly popular with the general public, and particularly unpopular with the affluent. Accordingly, Congress has not raised the federal minimum wage since 2009, and it remains stuck at just $7.25—far too low to support a family.[6] Wealthy Americans' influence and hostility toward active government have resulted in limited federal action on issues that are important to the general population. For instance,

Figure 1: Job and Income Programs

	% of Wealthy in Favor	% of General Public in Favor
The government must see that no one is without food, clothing, or shelter	43	68
Minimum wage must be high enough so that no family with a full-time worker falls below the poverty line	40	78
The government should provide a decent standard of living for the unemployed	23	50
The government in Washington ought to see to it that everyone who wants to work can find a job	19	68
The earned income tax credit should be increased rather than decreased or kept the same	13	49
The federal government should provide jobs for everyone able and willing to work who cannot find a job in private employment	8	53

DKs excluded. All public percentages are calculated from the 6/07 Inequality Survey conducted by CSRA, University of Connecticut, for Page and Jacobs 2009.

62 percent of people think Congress should do more on climate change, yet there has been no meaningful national climate action.[7] The Environmental Protection Agency (EPA) is instead under constant attack as regulations are continually rolled back, particularly by the Trump administration.[8] The strong preference of the wealthy to limit the role of government hinders many other policy priorities, such as gun control and health care reform. Many members of Congress are also themselves part of the 1 percent. The vast majority of congresspeople and senators are in the top 10 percent of wealth distribution, with a substantial portion in the top 1 percent. In this case, the priorities of the affluent *are* the priorities of the elected officials.

Figure 2: Financial Wealth Distribution in the United
States as a Percentage of Congress and Senate

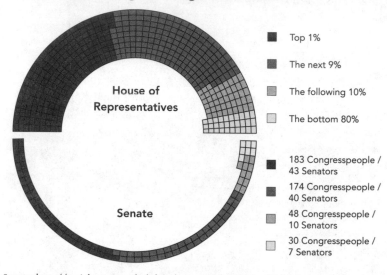

Source: http://sociology.ucsc.edu/whorulesamerica/power/wealth.html.

Elected Officials Are Out of Touch with Their Constituents

By almost any measure, political elites are out of touch with what is important to average Americans. Both parties, David Broockman and Christopher Skovron discovered, overestimate how conservative their constituents are, but "Republicans overestimate support for the conservative position on every issue by over ten percentage points and often by over 20 percentage points."[9] Just 9 percent of Americans support abolishing all federal welfare programs, "but politicians perceive it to be many times that, at almost 32 percent."[10] Researchers have found similarly skewed perceptions among legislative staffers.[11]

Because elected officials and their staffs are hearing more from conservative viewpoints—and conservative lobbyists—they may think that those viewpoints are representative of their constituents in general.[12] Conservatives, corporations, and far-right interest groups invest substantial amounts of money in think tanks, policy organizations, and lobbying elected officials to push their agendas, which rarely align with public opinion. The American Legislative Exchange Council (ALEC), for example, writes model legislation that many right-wing state legislators introduce verbatim, including right-to-work statutes and stand-your-ground laws.[13] Almost all of ALEC's funding (nearly 98 percent) comes from corporations, right-wing foundations, such as the Charles G. Koch Charitable Foundation, and trade associations, including PhRMA, the drug industry lobbying group.[14] Not surprisingly, Hill staffers who relied heavily on such groups for policy information were more out of touch with their constituents' preferences.[15] Staffers who had greater contact with liberal groups, membership-based groups, and unions had more accurate perceptions of constituent opinions.[16]

Moreover, the revolving door between Capitol Hill and K Street lobbying firms gives even more access to lawmakers for special interest groups.[17] Out of sixty-one members who left Congress after the 2016 election, twenty-six landed in lobbying firms.[18]

An Electoral System Dominated by Money

The Supreme Court's 2010 ruling in *Citizens United v. FEC* opened the door for unlimited funding from outside groups not aligned with a candidate, such as corporations, political action committees (PACs), and unions. Yet the root of the problem with money in the electoral system began with *Buckley v. Valeo* in 1976, when the Supreme Court ruled, in essence, that political money equaled speech. As such, any attempts to curb spending in elections are akin to attempts to curb free speech.[19] In the *Buckley* ruling, the court struck down spending limits and a mandate that presidential candidates participate in public financing of elections, while upholding limits on the amount that can be contributed directly to a candidate.[20] And although direct contributions are still limited, the post–*Citizens United* electoral landscape is dominated by outside spending through PACs.

In such a context, elections will only keep getting more expensive (see Figure 3). When adding in the "independent expenditures" of outside individuals and groups, the 2018 midterm election cycle cost more than $5 billion, making 2018 the most expensive congressional election cycle ever.[21] While staggering, this amount is still less than the $6.5 billion spent in the 2016 presidential election cycle.[22]

The sheer amount of money involved in political campaigns creates tremendous barriers to entry for people who are not independently wealthy.[23]

Fund-raising does not stop after Election Day, either. As one House member detailed, members of Congress must raise some $18,000 a day for their next election and have schedules that are "arranged, in some ways, around fund-raising. . . . You never see a committee working through lunch because those are your fundraising times."[24] In other words, rather than focusing on their constituents' needs and policy making, the electoral system requires elected officials to constantly prioritize fund-raising. Freed from that, elected officials could have more time to study legislation, meet with constituents, and engage in actual governing instead of continually chasing donors and their money.

It's worth noting that the United States is an outlier among democracies for how much money is spent during elections and the length of our election season, which can stretch on for years in presidential cycles; most countries' election seasons last for only several weeks or months.[25] In the United Kingdom, candidates can spend around $64,500 starting roughly five months before Election Day, and parties can spend up to $24.4 million

Figure 3: Election Costs

Cycle	Total Cost of Election	Congressional Races	Presidential Race
2018 (proj.)	$5,190,063,790	$5,190,063,790	N/A
2016*	$6,511,181,587	$4,124,304,874	$2,386,876,712
2014	$3,845,393,700	$3,845,393,700	N/A
2012*	$6,285,557,223	$3,664,141,430	$2,621,415,792
2010	$3,631,712,836	$3,631,712,836	N/A
2008*	$5,285,680,883	$2,485,952,737	$2,799,728,146
2006	$2,852,658,140	$2,852,658,140	N/A
2004*	$4,147,304,003	$2,237,073,141	$1,910,230,862
2002	$2,181,682,066	$2,181,682,066	N/A
2000*	$3,082,340,937	$1,669,224,553	$1,413,116,384
1998*	$1,618,936,265	$1,618,936,265	N/A

*Presidential election cycle.

Source: Center for Responsive Politics, "Cost of Election," www.opensecrets.org.

if they are contesting all 650 parliamentary seats.[26] Candidate spending in Canada depends on the size of the constituency but ranges from $55,945 to $85,782.[27] India comes closest to the United States in election spending, with $5 billion spent in 2014, but India has three times the population of the United States.[28]

A system that relies on this level of spending can only cater to its main constituent: money.

"Voting Is a Privilege, Not a Right"

The right to vote is one of the fundamental pillars of American democracy. But states put huge obstacles in the ways of Americans exercising that right. Voter suppression is woven into the nation's history. Initially, only land-owning white men could vote, with every state expanding the vote to white men without property in 1856 after widespread protests; women could not vote in most states until 1920. After the Fifteenth Amendment granted freed male slaves and African American men the right to vote in 1870, states adopted poll taxes and literacy tests to disenfranchise the newly franchised.

Modern voter disenfranchisement begins with the burden of voter registration. Whereas in most democracies the government is responsible for voter registration, that process in the United States is plagued by myriad issues: arbitrary deadlines for registration, nonuniform requirements for reregistration when a voter moves, and heavy reliance on paper registrations rather than upgrading to online voter registration.[29] These administrative hurdles create confusion for voters and contribute to low voter registration rates.

Yet barriers to registration are not the only hindrance potential voters face. There is a committed effort at the state level to prevent eligible voters—particularly voters of color—from voting by making it difficult, and to chip away at some of the civil rights movement's most important victories. For instance, the Voting Rights Act of 1965 once prohibited states that had a history of discriminating against voters of color from changing their election rules unless those changes were specifically cleared by the federal government before implementation, a process known as "preclearance."[30] In 2013, the Supreme Court gutted this provision in *Shelby County v. Holder*. In his majority opinion, Chief Justice John Roberts reasoned that, when the Voting Rights Act was passed, "racial disparity . . . was compelling evidence justifying [preclearance]. . . . There is no longer such a disparity."

As if to prove him wrong, states that previously required preclearance immediately moved to enact restrictive voting practices.[31] Research by the Brennan Center for Justice shows that states previously covered by preclearance are now purging voters from rolls at a rate significantly higher than jurisdictions that were not required to undergo preclearance.[32] Texas announced a strict photo ID law within twenty-four hours of the *Shelby v. Holder* ruling, and Mississippi and Alabama began to enforce their photo ID laws, which had been struck down under preclearance and which disproportionately impact voters of color, who are more likely to lack a government-issued ID and be made to show one than white voters.[33] In 2000, the majority of states had no ID requirements. By 2016, the majority of states—both clearance and preclearance states—had adopted some form of ID requirement.[34]

Figure 4: Voter ID Enhancements, 2000–2016

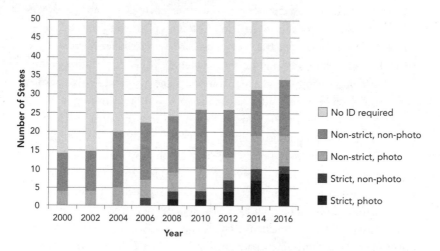

Source: National Council of State Legislatures, "Voter ID History."

Conservative politicians justify restrictive voting measures as protections against "voter fraud," a phenomenon multiple studies have debunked.[35] The truth is that you are more likely to be struck by lightning than discover a valid case of voter fraud.[36] Still, this lie is used to create fearmongering and to implement overly restrictive voter protections that disenfranchise thousands of eligible voters.

Gerrymandering

In one of the greatest distortions of democracy, even when people do vote, partisan politicians have drawn congressional, state legislative, and even city council districts to distort the will of the people. The number of House members a state can elect is based on its population. Once a state determines how many congressional representatives it can elect, the state is divided into districts.[37] Most states are divided into districts by the state legislature, which opens the door for partisan politics. Gerrymandering occurs when the electoral map is manipulated, either to benefit one party or to break up areas with high populations of people of color to dilute their voting bloc.[38]

In the 2012 election, Pennsylvania—then heavily gerrymandered—sent five Democrats and thirteen Republicans to Washington, the latter accounting for 72 percent of the state's congressional delegation.[39] Democratic candidates, meanwhile, had won 51 percent of the votes, compared to Republicans' 49 percent.[40] The League of Women Voters of Pennsylvania filed a lawsuit in response, alleging that the district boundaries constituted an unconstitutional partisan gerrymander.[41] The Pennsylvania Supreme Court ruled that the congressional districts violated the state constitution in January 2018. The court then drew a fairer map for that year's congressional elections after the state legislature and the governor failed to reach an agreement on one.[42] The outcome of that year's midterms in Pennsylvania was more balanced, with each party receiving around half of the vote and half of the congressional delegates.[43]

Gerrymandered districts are entrenching an undemocratic advantage for Republicans. To be clear, gerrymandering is a concern regardless of which party is in power because it distorts democracy, and gerrymandering done by Democrats—although more rare—is equally undemocratic.

Limiting the Influence of Money
Through Public Financing

Voter suppression combined with an electoral system dominated by money has left our democracy in dire straits and in need of immediate reform. Though this state of affairs is distressing, it is not inevitable. There are solutions that can limit the flood of money in our electoral system, protect the right to vote, and place the priorities of the people, not corporations and the wealthy, at the heart of policy priorities. With these reforms in place, progressives will have a far better chance to advance meaningful action on climate change, gun control, health care reform, and minimum-wage increases, among other issues. All of these policies are both popular with majorities of the electorate and realistic solutions to rising inequality and the threat of climate change. The following section details steps that can be taken to reduce the amount of money in the electoral system and ensure that every vote is counted.

Fairer Election Financing

In our current system, money talks and elected officials listen. The first step to amplifying the voices of nonwealthy, noncorporate voters is to equalize election spending through public financing of elections, which can include small-donor matching, full funding for candidates, and individual vouchers that voters can use to donate to candidates.[44]

Connecticut has a robust public financing election system that had a record number of participants in 2018.[45] As a result, instead of just a few big donors, candidates must interact with more constituents and have a bigger donor pool.[46] Under Connecticut's system, candidates must receive a minimum number of donors within their district before qualifying to receive public funds.[47] Once qualified, candidates for governor, for example, receive $1.4 million for their primary races and up to $6.5 million for a major-party candidate facing opposition; candidates with limited to no opposition receive substantially less funding.[48] While there may be opposition to spending public money on elections, those funds are an investment that pays back in spades through a stronger democracy that limits the influence of lobbyists and outside money, and passes legislation that aligns more closely with the priorities of working people than with the affluent.

An analysis of Connecticut's program shows that more people were able to run for office, as the high price tag of elections was not a concern. More women and people of color were elected after public financing was implemented, and the policies adopted post–public financing were more in line with the preferences of the public, rather than those of the affluent and big business.[49] In the first election after public financing took hold, the state legislature passed a slew of bills that helped working families, including mandatory paid sick days, an increased minimum wage, and an earned income tax credit.[50]

Not all candidates and elected officials partake in the big donor, corporate, and PAC money, though. The 2018 midterm election had two very-high-profile congressional candidates, Beto O'Rourke in Texas and Alexandria Ocasio-Cortez in New York, turn down special interest, corporate, and PAC money. O'Rourke raised $38 million in just one quarter from more than eight hundred thousand small donors.[51] Ocasio-Cortez raised 62 percent of her campaign money through donations of $200 or less.[52] In his 2016 presidential primary run, Senator Bernie Sanders received more than 70 percent of his campaign funds through small donations.[53] Prioritizing small donors over big ones means public servants have more contact with regular people, those who can only afford to give $200 or less, and fellow elected officials who are not beholden to big-money interests for reelection.

Without a change in the composition of the Supreme Court, the only way to overturn its ruling that money is speech is through a constitutional amendment. Progressive advocates have proposed the Restore Democracy Amendment, which would ban corporations and unions from giving money to candidates or PACs.[54] While ambitious, this effort seems unlikely to make much headway in the short term given how difficult it is to amend the Constitution. H.R. 1, which House Democrats passed through that body as their first piece of legislation after taking the majority in the 2018 election, introduced more disclosure requirements and expanded the ban on foreign money in elections, as well as voter registration reform to make voting easier.[55] So long as Democrats lack control of the Senate and White House, supporting candidates who refuse corporate and PAC money may be an easier way to get money out of the electoral system and to make more ambitious pro-democracy reforms more possible. Once candidates see they can be successful without the big money, it may pave the way for more small-donor candidates, who, once elected, can push for campaign finance reform on a broader scale.

Counting Every Vote

Voter turnout rates in the United States are some of the lowest among all developed countries in the world.[56] In the 2016 election, only 55.7 percent of eligible voters cast their ballot.[57] Even in the historic election of President Barack Obama, which saw the highest level of voter turnout since 1968, fewer than 60 percent of eligible voters voted.[58] While the overall turnout rate is low, levels of voter turnout among African Americans are just below rates among white Americans, and other nonwhite populations have voter turnout rates that are far lower.[59] Systematic efforts to disenfranchise voters of color, combined with registration barriers, may contribute to the lower rate of both registration and voting among voters of color. Making matters worse is that Election Day is on a workday, a practice that no longer has relevance or justification. It is time to modernize the electoral system. The more people who participate, the stronger our democracy.

Same-Day and Automatic Voter Registration

Demos, a progressive think tank, has proposed a set of policies to increase voter turnout called Millions to the Polls, with measures ranging from registration reforms to Election Day reforms.[60] For example, same-day registration would allow voters to register at the same time they vote.[61] The seventeen states that have already adopted same-day registration generally have significantly higher levels of voter turnout than those states that have not.[62] Some states have gone one step further to take the registration burden off the voter and enacted automatic registration, where eligible voters are automatically registered to vote with a provision to allow individuals to opt out.[63] Under automatic registration, individuals are registered to vote when they engage with a select government agency, most commonly the motor vehicle agency, unless they opt out.[64]

Automatic voter registration is the logical extension of existing registration efforts, particularly the National Voter Registration Act (NVRA). The NVRA increased voter registration rates, particularly among lower-income voters, by providing individuals with the opportunity to register when they interact with certain government offices, including motor vehicle departments and public assistance and disability offices.[65] The NVRA applies to all states, except for those that either had no voter-registration requirements or allowed for same-day registration when the NVRA was enacted.[66]

Making Voting Accessible to All

Restoring voting rights to formerly incarcerated individuals would have an outsize impact on increasing the right to vote among African Americans due to the disproportionately high rate of incarceration of African Americans. In November 2018, Florida voters amended their state constitution via a ballot initiative to allow citizens with past felony convictions to vote, a change that could add as many as 1.4 million new voters to the state's rolls. Many states still have similar restrictions on the books, likely keeping millions more from accessing their basic democratic rights.

In addition to same-day voter registration, no-excuse, permanent absentee ballots, making Election Day a national holiday, and ending voter ID laws would help remove barriers at the ballot box and remove arbitrary barriers to voting that disproportionately impact voters of color; in a 2018 survey, black and Hispanic voters were three times as likely as white voters to be told they did not have the correct identification.[67] Nonpartisan congressional districting would further eliminate partisan gerrymandering and ensure that the will of the people is reflected.

Compulsory Voting

Another avenue to increase voting is to make it compulsory. In addition to increasing voter turnout, compulsory voting would make voter suppression tactics, such as strict ID requirements and closing polling places, more difficult to implement because states would have the mandate to make voting more, not less, accessible. Twenty-seven countries have some form of a compulsory voting system.[68] Some countries, including Austria and Switzerland, have compulsory voting only in certain regions. Others, including Australia, have compulsory voting for all elections within the country.[69] In the 2016 election, voter turnout in Australia was 91 percent, which was the lowest voter turnout rate since compulsory voting was introduced in 1925.[70] Since 1925, the highest U.S. voter turnout rate was 63.3 percent.[71]

To ensure voter participation, a small fine could be imposed for not voting. Australia's fine is Aus$20 (less than U.S.$15), which is imposed only if there is not a "valid and sufficient reason"—ranging from illness to accidents—for not voting.[72] Any fine should be small enough not to cause economic distress, particularly for low-income populations, but large enough to act as an incentive.

With Australia's near-universal voter turnout, turnout increased significantly among working-class individuals. In turn, government policies shifted toward those more favorable to working-class populations, such as increased pension spending.[73] Given that many voter suppression efforts are targeted toward disenfranchising low-income voters and voters of color, compulsory voting could boost participation among these communities and shift the priorities of elected officials. While some progressive policies have been implemented since compulsory voting, it is worth noting that Australia has enacted regressive policies that oppressed the aboriginal population and repealed a carbon tax,[74] indicating that compulsory voting is necessary but not sufficient for passing progressive policies.

Americans concerned that compulsory voting restricts our freedom might be reassured if the law included a "none of the above" option on any ballot or a process by which voters can opt out of the compulsory system. Australia's law allows voters to abstain from voting for several reasons, including not having enough time to understand the candidates and issues, sickness, accident.[75]

In the United States, there could also be a provision for opting out based on constitutionally protected grounds, such as freedom of religion and the freedom to not participate. A "none of the above," option, though, would assuage most concerns. The benefits of near-universal voting outweigh any small inconvenience to individuals who do not want to exercise their right to vote. Under compulsory voting, the burden is placed on those who want to opt out of voting. Too often in our current system, the burden is placed on those trying to exercise their right to vote.

Compulsory voting will take time to adopt and implement. In the meantime, there are several immediate reforms that would help boost voter turnout, including increasing early voting periods, where voters can cast their vote before Election Day; removing restrictive voter ID requirements: permitting no-excuse, permanent absentee voting; allowing voting by mail, where ballots are mailed to eligible voters who return completed ballots either by mail or to a designated drop-off center; and restoring voting rights to formerly incarcerated people. These would all make voting more accessible, particularly for low-income voters and voters of color.

Voting is so powerful that thousands have died fighting for the right to vote, and millions of dollars have been spent to trying to suppress it. The future of democracy stands on whether that right can be not only protected, but allowed to thrive as well. Implementing systematic reforms to the electoral system and pushing for bolder ones, such as compulsory voting, can honor the sacrifice of those before us and protect the fundamental right to vote.

Confronting Corporate Power

Robert Kuttner

AT THE HEART OF THE CRISIS IN OUR POLITICS THAT BROUGHT US DONALD Trump is a rigged system that concentrates too much wealth and power at the top. The instrument of this reversal has to be democratic politics and government. But paradoxically, one consequence of this tilt has been a broad disaffection of the citizenry from politics itself, since politics seems to be—*is*—the province of the rich. Even though Trump epitomizes the swamp that he proposed to drain, in classic demagogue fashion he succeeded in displacing grievances about wealth and power onto grievances about race and identity. To turn that vicious circle back into a virtuous one, we need to restore the primacy of pocketbook issues to the center of American politics, and to rebuild public institutions, public regulation, public taxation, and public investment.

The good news is that this transformation has already begun. Popular politics, as epitomized by the 2018 midterm victories and continuing in the run-up to the 2020 presidential election, has already provided a tailwind. The anti-Trump backlash began almost immediately after his election, with the women's marches and groups such as the Indivisible movement, and has only grown. Policies that once seemed utopian are being offered and debated as mainstream. But the stance of recent Democratic presidents, and of corporate Democrats proposing centrism as a remedy, creates a continuing undertow. The debate over the future of American democracy and our economic system should be a clean contest between Republicans as conservatives and Democrats as progressives. Much of it, sadly, is still *within* the Democratic Party. That reality itself is testament to the continuing power of big money.

A Lost Social Compact

The social bargain that began with Franklin Roosevelt's Depression-era New Deal stopped short of social democracy, much less democratic socialism. But it was the most effective and salutary set of constraints on capitalism that we've ever seen in America, before or since. It included a good deal of public capital, such as the Tennessee Valley Authority and the Reconstruction Finance Corporation, various forms of social housing, and the massive public investments that came with the war. Labor was empowered via the Wagner Act (National Labor Relations Act), the Fair Labor Standards Act, and several emergency wartime measures that made unions social partners. Finance was heavily regulated so that it would be the economy's servant rather than its master.

This unusual social compact was the result of the disgrace of laissez-faire economics and the Republican Party in the Great Crash, and Roosevelt's increasing radicalism in the New Deal, prodded by the growing strength of labor, farmers, and other social movements, and strengthening them in turn. World War II served to further empower labor and enhance both the power and the prestige of public institutions. Taxes were steeply progressive; the top marginal tax rate in 1944 was 94 percent.[1] The Bretton Woods Agreement provided an international counterpart, to prevent a global race to the bottom. The result was an unprecedented era that combined high rates of economic growth and increasing equality of income and wealth. A mixed economy, it turned out, worked far better than raw capitalism, in terms of both average economic performance and its distribution.

Yet this mixed economy was both incomplete and vulnerable. The New Deal deliberately excluded African Americans from its protections, as the price of southern political support. For the most part, women benefited only as widows or as wives. Progress on race and gender had to await the movements of the 1960s. Understood as an entente between labor and capital, brokered by the state, and anchored in popular politics, the New Deal system was a major step forward. Yet, as subsequent events proved, it was neither radical enough nor durable enough. The political power of private capital was suppressed—but only temporarily.

This bargain, on both sides of the Atlantic, lasted only until the turbulence of the 1970s gave conservative politicians, big business, and free-market ideology another turn at bat. The result was a gradual but intensifying rewriting and rigging of the rules to serve economic elites and to weaken the countervailing power of unions, citizens, and the democratic state.

This reversal, first engineered by Ronald Reagan and Margaret Thatcher, and then partially absorbed by corporate Democrats (and their counterparts in Britain and Germany), dismantled much of the New Deal system, weakened the power of unions, gutted progressive taxation, and reversed constructive forms of regulation. Global trade rules were used to create a race to the bottom—a competition to cut wages, reduce taxes, and liberate corporate power. Public institutions and assets were increasingly privatized. The right created a fiscal politics in which conservative governments cut taxes; then when growth did not make up the promised revenues, conservatives rediscovered the perils of deficits and cut public spending.

Centrist Democratic presidents—Jimmy Carter and Bill Clinton—played into this trap by equating austerity economics with fiscal virtue. Even Barack Obama became a partisan of budget balance. For elites, there was a convenient bipartisan division of labor: Reagan and George H.W. Bush cut taxes and spending; Clinton restored budget balance. George W. Bush then took Clinton's surplus and cut taxes again. Obama raised taxes and cut spending and brought the budget back under control, and then Trump and the Republicans delivered the biggest tax cut ever, virtually all of it for corporations and the rich.

Inequality of Wealth, Income, and Power to Rig the Rules

An iconic chart, regularly updated by the Economic Policy Institute, shows median income and productivity growth rising in lockstep throughout the early postwar period, and then suddenly diverging in the mid-1970s, with that divergence continuing right through to our own day.[2] Though orthodox economists have tried to tell a story attributing that divergence to technology, or to changing demands for skills, the reality is much simpler. The divergence of income mainly reflects a widening divergence of power to make the rules.

Research by Lawrence Mishel and others at the Economic Policy Institute, and by labor economists such as David Weil and David Howell, has demolished the story of increasing demands for skills resulting in widening pay disparities. As Weil and others have shown, failure to enforce labor laws on the books has resulted in what is antiseptically known as "misclassification," and which is more accurately described as payroll theft—in which regular employees are disguised as contract workers and thus stripped of a variety of legislated rights (including the right to organize a union), as well as underpaid.

The new labor market creates a long-standing right-wing fantasy (and Marxian prediction) in which labor is a "spot market" in which all workers are competing against one another to see who will work for the lowest wage. This has little to do with technology or skills and everything to do with shifting power to make the rules. Adjunct college professors have some of the highest skills in the economy, yet they are subject to the same insecure spot market as Uber drivers. (Indeed, many work part-time as Uber drivers to supplement their dismal university pay.) The cure for this pattern is not a second PhD but a union and a set of tougher wage regulations.

What's true of adjuncts is true of the entire service economy. For instance, home care workers and prekindergarten teachers could be paid a living wage as professionals, rather than the minimum wage they tend to receive—if a national policy were set to pay all human service workers decently. Since most such workers are ultimately paid one way or another by the government, the choice of what they are worth is a social choice, not a market choice. In France, pre-K teachers must have more certification in early child development than regular public school teachers, as a matter of national policy, and are paid accordingly.

The flip side of deregulated labor markets, depressed income and dwindling security for the middle and the bottom is the impact of deregulation on income and wealth at the top. Until the 1980s, finance was well regulated; though executive incomes were high, they were not astronomical. With the hyperconcentration of finance and the rise of (largely unregulated) leveraged buyouts, hedge funds, and private equity firms, annual incomes in the billions of dollars became normal, and ordinary salaried financial executives

came to expect pay levels in the tens of millions. Other nonfinancial corporations followed suit. The ratio of the pay of executives to ordinary workers
went from a range of 50 to 1 to around 500 to 1.

Consumer and Labor Deregulation

Though it is not widely appreciated, other forms of deregulation beginning
in the 1970s and 1980s had devastating effects on worker incomes and job
security, as well as on consumers. The New Deal system used various forms
of regulation to protect workers, consumers, and investors, and to constrain
predatory behavior by corporations, banks, and investment bankers. A second wave of regulation ensued in the 1960s and 1970s, when activists won a
major wave of consumer and workplace protections—around food, drugs,
automobiles, airline safety, air and water, and workplace safety. These
included the Clean Air Act, the Clean Water Act, the Occupational Safety
and Health Act, the Community Reinvestment Act, Title IX of the Education Amendments Act (which prohibited sex discrimination in all aspects of
education programs that receive federal support), the Pregnancy Discrimination Act (which banned employment discrimination against pregnant
women), and many others. Many of these reforms were enacted during the
Nixon administration, which felt it had to respond, however reluctantly, to
the growing mobilization by consumer and environmental groups.

But even as the consumer, environmental, labor, and women's movements
were winning new victories, a powerful corporate backlash was brewing.
The corporate pushback was crystallized in an (in)famous memorandum
to the U.S. Chamber of Commerce in August 1971, written by Lewis Powell, a well-connected corporate lawyer (and later a Supreme Court justice),
calling on organized business to use its latent muscle to roll back consumer,
labor, and environmental protections. Richard Nixon, in his first two years,
signed several consumer and environmental laws. By the early 1970s, he
had turned against them, and so had the general climate.

The rollback of other consumer and labor regulation began not with
Republican Ronald Reagan but with Democrat Jimmy Carter. Several of the
free-market economists around Carter convinced the president (spuriously)
that regulation was one of the factors contributing to the inflationary economic conditions of the 1970s, and that deregulation would unleash com-

petition, innovation, and consumer choice and thus restrain prices. This turned out to be a fantasy. Mainly, deregulation unleashed concentration, pricing power, and a hammering down of wages.

After the New Deal, government was able to regulate several industries either as natural monopolies (too big not to regulate) or to prevent pricing abuses and predatory behavior toward rivals. These industries included electricity, telephones, broadcasting, natural gas, airlines, trucking, and hospitals. One salutary side effect of this brand of rate-and-route regulation was to carry out an old labor slogan—"Take wages out of competition." Since profits were both guaranteed and capped, companies had nothing to gain by trying to batter down wages. In these industries, corporations opted for well-trained workers, good earnings and benefits, and labor peace. These industries all became centers of effective unions. Business lobbied Congress to weaken or even eliminate many of these regulations, so there was no regulation of profits. This allowed and encouraged companies to increase profits by cutting wages and benefits, raiding pension plans, and sharpening their efforts to weaken unions. Deregulation of these industries harmed consumers and workers alike.

The New Corporate Concentration and the Death of Antitrust

In the past three decades, corporations have manipulated the laws to create new forms of concentration. Patent, trademark, and copyright laws have been rigged to give drug companies the right to patent products such as vaccines that were once treated as in the public domain. After he invented the polio vaccine, Dr. Jonas Salk was asked if he intended to patent it. An indignant Salk famously replied, "Would you patent the sun?" Today's pharmaceutical giants (or energy conglomerates) would, if they could.

Drug companies have gotten in the habit of buying old drugs and jacking up prices to whatever the market will bear. Century-old drugs such as insulin have been reformulated, patented, and turned into costly boutique products. Global drug giants have bought up generic drug makers to keep generic drugs off the market. All of these tactics not only price lifesaving drugs out of reach, but even when such drugs are covered by insurance companies, the higher costs cycle through to consumers and taxpayers in the form of higher insurance premiums, copays, and taxes to support Medicare. Economist Dean Baker has calculated that it would be more cost-effective and more conducive to scientific progress to put all pharmaceutical research and all drugs in the public domain.

In telecommunications, the breakup of the old regulated Bell monopoly has given way to unregulated concentration, as companies like Verizon and AT&T bought out independents. There is now effectively a Verizon/AT&T duopoly. In most metro areas, consumers have a "choice" of just one cable company. As a consequence of these forms of monopoly power, not only are prices higher, but American consumers have the slowest and least reliable internet service among wealthy countries. Concentrated economic power creates concentrated political power. The big telecom companies successfully fought to overturn net neutrality, which will produce even more concentration and price gouging.

In the area of health policy, merger and concentration have been the norm. Hospitals have merged with other hospitals and insurance companies with other insurance companies. There have also been mergers of drug chains, and mergers of insurance companies with hospitals and with drug retailers and "pharmacy benefit managers," yet another form of middleman that extracts profits and provides no discernible benefit. All of this is advertised as promoting efficiency. This is nonsense. These mergers are all about maximizing market power.

In the 1980s, Reagan appointed the University of Chicago's most influential conservative critic of antitrust, Robert Bork, to head the Justice Department's Antitrust Division. Bork brought with him a preposterous doctrine that he called "the antitrust paradox." Bork's doctrines played the same convenient rationalizing role for monopolists that supply-side claims did for tax cutters. They provide pseudo-academic blessing for purely opportunistic pro-corporate policies. With Bork in charge, antitrust enforcement collapsed. Mergers and acquisitions took off, supercharged by the parallel deregulation of finance. Every industry became more concentrated, with attendant price gouging.

Today, despite the profusion of ostensibly independent brands, consumer industries as varied as car rental companies, cell phones, makers of eyeglasses, cable companies, movie chains, and numerous others are dominated by two or three giants. The three largest banks, for instance, now control more than a third of all deposits. And three companies have a 92 percent market share of the cigarette- and tobacco-manufacturing industry. Two chains— Home Depot and Lowe's—control 81 percent of hardware store sales. The four largest U.S. airlines have 76 percent of the industry's revenues.

Oligopoly is the norm. This raises prices and deters innovation. Companies such as Apple rig their products so that they only work, or work better, with other Apple products. Under traditional antitrust doctrine, this was illegal. It gives rise to abuses such as the $80 power cord. Proposed mergers, no matter what their potential abuse, are hardly ever blocked. Market power is the name of the game. Not surprisingly, the big platform monopolies reap astronomical profits.

The fact that this occurred in a context of low inflation at first seemed to vindicate Bork. How could monopoly-pricing abuses coexist with low inflation? The answer to this real "antitrust paradox" is that wages are the economy's largest single cost, and due to the loss of worker power, real wages have been flat or falling. An economy where prices are rising but wages are falling can have low measured inflation on average. Indeed, the same concentrated monopoly power that enables megacorporations to gouge consumers enables them to underpay workers. With the advent of big platform companies such as Google, Amazon, and Facebook, new forms of monopoly abuse arose. The essence of the business strategy of these platform giants is to create monopolies in their space and to buy out or drive out potential rivals. Facebook and Google together control more than 90 percent of internet ads. Amazon competes with the vendors who use its search features to reach customers. The fact that these companies amass so much data on the habits of their users makes it easy for them to destroy their rivals, who either lack such data or have to pay for it. The laxity of antitrust authorities in the face of these abuses is appalling. Since 2008, Amazon, Apple, Google, Facebook, and Microsoft have bought 436 rival companies, all without a single regulatory challenge.

A new era of antitrust enforcement is on the horizon, thanks to the creative work of a new generation of antitrust scholars such as Lina Khan and Sabeel Rahman, who have devised ingenious new strategies to apply traditional antitrust concepts to new forms of abuse by platform monopolies. Much of this can be done under existing law. All it will take is the election of progressives willing to appoint aggressive, pro-consumer regulators.

Yet another abuse of corporate power is the use of compulsory arbitration, on coerced terms that favor the company over aggrieved consumers and
workers. Since the 1980s, America's leading corporations, abetted by right-
wing courts, have twisted a venerable law, the Arbitration Act of 1925, to
compel both their workers and consumers of their products to sign an agreement that requires them to submit any disputes to binding arbitration, using
arbitrators selected by the company. These agreements preclude appeals to
the courts and explicitly prohibit class-action suits. It is one more illustration
of the vicious circle of corporate power leading to more corporate power to
rig the rules leading to still more concentrated corporate wealth and power.

Tax Frauds

Ever since the Reagan administration, tax policy has been used to shift the
cost of government off of corporations and the rich and onto working families. Before the Reagan tax cuts, the American economy performed very well
with top marginal rates on individual incomes upward of 70 percent right
though the 1970s, and corporations paying about half of their net profits in
taxes in exchange for the privileges and immunities they enjoyed by being
incorporated. The slow growth and "stagflation" of the 1970s became the
pretext for cutting taxes as a form of economic and entrepreneurial stimulus,
even though the economic travails of the 1970s were actually caused by collapse of the Bretton Woods system of fixed exchange rates, the devaluation of
the dollar, and the OPEC oil price hikes, compounded by Fed chairman Paul
Volcker's cold-bath cure of putting the economy into a deliberate recession by
hiking interest rates up to over 20 percent. In truth, the economic turmoil of
that decade had nothing to do with excess taxes on corporations and the rich.

The policies that followed, however, drastically cut the tax rates on corporate profits and on high incomes, especially on income from capital, including dividends, interest, and capital gains. The right successfully rebranded
the estate tax the "death tax" and cut both the rate and the percentage of
estates covered, from about 2 percent of all estates to less than one-fifth of
1 percent. Meanwhile, in one of the less-well-appreciated tax shifts, there
was a massive increase in Social Security taxes.

In the early 1980s, following a decade of slower-than-expected wage growth, payroll tax receipts were well below projections. Social Security's actuaries began predicting that the system's trust funds would be well below what was needed to finance payouts by the mid-twenty-first century. In a grand legislative bargain between Democrats in Congress and the Reagan administration, the normal retirement age was raised and payroll taxes were dramatically increased.

While the budget was briefly brought into balance late in the Clinton presidency, with Social Security trust funds supposedly safeguarded in an imaginary "lockbox," the hard-won surplus—denying public spending that the economy needed—was soon squandered on yet another series of tax cuts, mostly for the rich, by the George W. Bush administration. The Obama administration did succeed in securing a modest increase in top marginal rates for individuals, as well as a surtax on investment income.

This was followed by the Republicans' 2017 federal tax act, a collection of provisions that will raise the deficit and thus the national debt by a projected $1.6 to $1.8 trillion over a decade. Not only was this tax cut distributionally perverse—upward of 90 percent of the cuts went to the top brackets—but it was economically perverse. It incentivized or rewarded economic behavior that will make the economy less efficient as well as less equal.

Here, the good news is that the tax act was such a travesty that Republicans, who initially planned to campaign on it in 2018 as their great achievement, soon realized how toxic it was with voters. The act turned out to be a boon to Democrats. The other piece of good news is that remedies such as restoring the top personal rate to the 70 percent that it was for most of the postwar era, restoring a serious estate tax, and even adding a general wealth tax on the very rich are not only mainstream again; they are popular.

From Public Regulation to Public Options

The cure for grotesque economic concentration and its harm to working families is first to restore necessary forms of regulation, progressive taxation, and public enterprise. This includes the following actions:

- Drastic reregulation of the financial sector.
- A modernization of antitrust laws to cover both old abuses in

new guises and especially the monopolistic practices of the platform economy. Companies like Facebook, Amazon, and Google
could be barred from buying any more competitors or from trafficking in customer data.

- New forms of corporate regulations, such as Senator Elizabeth
Warren's proposed Accountable Corporations Act. This law
would require all corporations with assets of more than $1 bil-
lion to be federally chartered. The charters would require workers to be put on boards, and place limits on executive pay ratios
and corporate political contributions.

- A new wave of consumer regulation, to limit patent, trademark,
and copyright abuses in such industries as pharmaceuticals, and
to restore basic consumer protections in industries from airlines
to telecoms. More drugs should simply be put in the public domain sooner. Under the 1980 Bayh-Dole Act, the government
has the right to require mandatory licensing of drugs urgently
needed for public health purposes. It seldom uses this authority
and should do so far more often as drug companies raise prices
to outrageous levels.

- Revise the Arbitration Act to prohibit companies from denying
workers and consumers a broad range of rights as a condition
of employment or of purchase of goods or services, as the proposed Arbitration Fairness Act—sponsored by Senator Richard Blumenthal and thirty-one Senate co-sponsors—would do.

On tax policy, we need to begin by repealing 2017's Tax Cuts and Jobs
Act. We also need to restore a basic progressive tax structure, with top marginal rates comparable to those of the postwar boom. A better alternative
to the estate tax, where the tax is paid by the estate, would be an inheritance
tax paid by their heirs at their normal tax rate after an initial exemption.
In addition, tax policy needs to discourage predatory activity of parasitic
entities such as hedge funds and private equity firms by removing the tax
deductibility of interest on loans used in leveraged buyouts. There is also
a case for a wealth tax on astronomical wealth, beginning at $50 million,

as proposed by Senator Warren and Representative Ocasio-Cortez, with majority support in the polls.

But let's face it. Regulation and taxation are not enough. When private capital wields inordinate political power, regulating corporate abuses is a game of cat and mouse that the corporate sector often wins. A close look at attempted regulation of behemoth industries such as tech, finance, and health care shows all of the maneuvers corporations and their armies of lawyers have at their disposal to frustrate regulation. Taxation, likewise, is frustrated by the ingenuity of accountants and lobbyists.

That's why we need to go beyond just regulating and taxing capitalism. The political and policy reversals that began in the 1970s and 1980s and continue to this day demonstrate that regulation and taxation are necessary but not sufficient. What our political economy needs is more public options anchored in popular politics.

If we have public banks that don't seek to maximize exorbitant profits, we don't have to worry so much about games of deception versus supervision. FDR's Home Owners Loan Corporation had no reason to come up with subprime mortgages as a profitable and opaque scam. It was there to serve, not to gouge. Universal public broadband is cheaper and more efficient than its private, for-profit equivalents. In Chattanooga, citizens enjoy America's cheapest and fastest internet, thanks to the local public power company, which happens to be a legacy of the Tennessee Valley Authority, the New Deal's program to bring electricity, water, and economic growth to Appalachia, one of the nation's poorest regions.

Genuine public infrastructure, such as public power, is more efficient and less prone to abuse than its privatized counterparts. Medicare for All is far more cost-effective than the mash-up of public-private partnerships that leaves private insurers trying to maximize profits and government holding the bag (and paying the cost.) But it also puts out of business a purely parasitic private insurance industry that is also part of the conservative corporate lobbying coalition. Social housing, forever sheltered from market pressures that raise prices and reward speculation, is far more reliable and cost-effective than throwing away money on housing vouchers that have to chase a rising private market.

One of the many virtues of a Green New Deal would be a revival of public planning and public investment, on a serious scale. Ideas such as these, with counterparts in American history, have been getting a new and respectful hearing, partly because of the sheer excesses of capitalism and its failure to deliver for regular people. There is an ongoing debate among economists about the superior efficiency of private versus public institutions, not just in theory but in practice as well. According to right-wing economists, public institutions are to be avoided because they can be corrupted by "rent seeking." Yes, they sometimes can—but recent history demonstrates that there is far greater rent seeking in the private sector, as well as a far greater potential for private corruption and for corporate power to thwart competition. That said, if public institutions are to realize their promise, they need to be anchored in, and accountable to, strong democratic politics. These two elements of a more social economy nurture each other, as a mirror image of the way that an excess of private capitalism corrupts politics.

In 1943, there was a famous argument between British economist John Maynard Keynes and one of his colleagues, the Polish-born economist Michal Kalecki. Keynes had successfully demonstrated that it was indeed possible to stabilize an essentially capitalist economy. The right mix of macroeconomic policies and regulatory policies could keep a market economy at full employment with decent wages while social investment could provide complementary services. Kalecki, who located himself somewhere between Keynes and Marx, agreed that this model was indeed possible, *as a matter of economics.* He just doubted that capitalists would permit a high-wage, full-employment economy *as a matter of politics.*[3] The debate echoed an older argument about revolutionary versus reformist socialism between Rosa Luxemburg and Eduard Bernstein.

During the postwar boom, it looked as if Keynes had won the argument. Now it looks as if Kalecki was the more prescient. In a primarily capitalist economy, it is very hard for reforms to endure, because of the relentless resistance of capitalists. If we are to reclaim a decent economy, we will need not just to revive regulation, taxation, social investments, and trade unions. We will need more public options—not just because they are both fairer and more efficient, but to weaken the political power of capital to reverse these gains. To paraphrase a famous quip by social scientist Christopher Jencks, that is what other nations call socialism.[4]

Building the People's Banks

David Dayen

AFTER DEMOCRATS SWEPT INTO CONTROL OF THE HOUSE OF REPRESENTA-
tives in the 2018 midterms, something unusual happened: almost no
incoming freshmen sought a seat on the House Financial Services Committee.[1] Not only is the panel one of the most important and wide-ranging
in Congress—with jurisdiction over banking regulations, the affordable
housing crisis, economic discrimination, retirement security, and the macro
economy—it's historically been a landing spot for swing-state Democrats
looking for a fertile source of campaign fund-raising from deep-pocketed
financiers. Yet the centrist Democrats saw more peril than promise in
accepting Wall Street donations.

This practically unprecedented situation created an opportunity for progressives who were unable to secure spots on other exclusive committees
to jump onto Financial Services, like superstar congresswoman Alexandria
Ocasio-Cortez. But overseeing the financial sector is anything but a con-
solation prize; as Occupy Wall Street taught us, the industry is right at the
heart of why the economy no longer works for most Americans.

After all, it was only a decade ago that inattention to financial maneuver-
ing led the economy to the brink of implosion, as bankers took advantage
of the opportunity to steal in the dark. The results fell most harshly on the
working poor and those struggling to improve their lot. Roughly 8.7 million jobs were lost in the Great Recession; according to a *Wall Street Journal*
article in 2015, at least 9.3 million families lost their homes, through either

foreclosure or some other transaction that forced an eviction. Most of these borrowers committed nothing more than an accident of timing, buying into a historic bubble and suffering tragic consequences.[2] The housing collapse robbed millions of families of home equity, the primary method of building wealth in the United States, particularly for families of color. Former representative Brad Miller has called the crisis "an extinction event" for the black and Latinx middle class.[3]

The Great Recession's Wall Street–directed pain at the nation's most vulnerable is no anomaly. For decades after the Depression, lenders redlined neighborhoods to keep families of color out, barred from an avenue to gathering wealth. When the Fair Housing Act of 1968 and the Community Reinvestment Act of 1977 attempted to right these wrongs and produce equitable access to the financial system for low- and moderate-income families, the industry cooked up other schemes, like subprime lending, to wipe them out. And even after the recession, banks like Wells Fargo continue to use deceptive practices to nickel-and-dime low-income customers and put them in peril. Wall Street and predatory misconduct often go hand in hand.

Timothy Geithner, then Treasury secretary, was fond of a simple dictum: "Plan beats no plan."[4] He focused with laser-sharp precision on preserving the financial system, and policymakers to his left with vague alternatives could not compete. As a result, instead of transformative financial regulation, we got the Dodd-Frank Act, and while parts of it undoubtedly have merit (such as the Consumer Financial Protection Bureau, a long-needed agency with its sole mission to protect people from financial rip-offs), for the most part it produced a complex series of technocratic tweaks, with final rules left up to banking regulators to write. After its passage, the industry predictably sent a flotilla of lobbyists to weaken Dodd-Frank and lock in the status quo. Even the Consumer Financial Protection Bureau couldn't prevent a committed opponent, Mick Mulvaney, from taking over during the Trump administration; enforcement slowed to a trickle.

Geithner, incidentally, is now running a private equity firm that owns a company called Mariner Finance, which profits off deceiving the working poor into high-interest loans. Plan beats no plan.[5]

For the emerging left, answers are available for how to rein in the financial sector; they just need to be given prominence. At a time of climate devastation, migrant abuses, and soaring inequality, it may seem boring and arcane to focus attention on loans and securities. But control of money—who has it, who can manipulate it, and who can deploy it at others' expense—must sit at the center of a left agenda.

What do we actually need a healthy financial system to do? First, it must manage payments, so we don't have to carry wads of cash around to settle major transactions. This used to mean checks and credit cards, but today we have debit cards, electronic fund transfers, online bill pay, e-commerce solutions, and even mobile payments. Second, a good financial system matches those who want to lend money with those who want to borrow—whether individuals or businesses. We mostly think about this as a bank using savings deposits to finance lending; that's not quite how it works, as we'll get to later. But peer-to-peer online services directly matching borrowers and lenders have also flourished more recently.

Banks also manage investments for families and institutions. And finally, banks provide insurance—both simple insurance against loss of savings (by putting them in a government-insured institution instead of under a mattress), and more sophisticated insurance of major assets like home or auto or family well-being, in the event of a sudden loss of the breadwinner. These functions are intended to enable investments in the real economy, so productive businesses can grow and entrepreneurship can thrive.

As John Kay, the longtime *Financial Times* writer, estimates in his book *Other People's Money*, these elements—again, all that we actually need for a functional financial system—make up only about 10 percent of total sector activity. To a far greater degree, financial institutions today trade assets, package assets for trading, and repackage those packaged assets for more trading. Trading desks have swamped more traditional banking operations in terms of growth and profit. In short, we built a financial sector and created a trading monster.

As a result, Wall Street is several orders of magnitude larger than it should be. In 2017, the financial sector took in $432 billion in profits, just under 20 percent of total net corporate income.[6] Federal Reserve banks accounted for another $79.2 billion. Put that together and nearly $1 in $4 earned by corporations in 2017 came from financial sector activity.

If anything that's an undercount, because it doesn't include parts of the nonfinancial economy where profits are conjured through financial activity.

Incredible amounts of corporate profits are derived from accounting and tax strategies that have nothing to do with the core business. Apple may make iPhones, but it also manages a $244 billion investment firm called Brae-burn Capital, like many other Fortune 500 companies that are laden with cash and deploying it in the capital markets.[7] Dozens of retail, restaurant, and consumer product brands are pawns in a financial engineering contest waged by private equity firms. A surprising chunk of activity on Amazon is effectively arbitrage trading, with upstarts securing assets they can buy low and sell high. Mergers and acquisitions, which soared to record highs in 2018, can be seen as higher-level trading of entire corporations, with banks advising and taking cuts out of the deal.[8]

Overfinancialization creates multiple problems for an economy. It increases systemic risk; if the bankers' bets go bad, there's less of a real economy to fall back on. It stifles efforts to build a more inclusive economy, as access to financial markets determines fortunes. Nearly one-third of all national income in the United States is derived from financial maneuvers like stock equity, interest, dividends, and real estate.[9] This income is generated from having money, and the financial sector facilitates this wealth built upon wealth. No less than the radical socialists at the International Monetary Fund have demonstrated that a financial sector reaches a tipping point at a certain size, where its continued development can actually damage growth.[10] The United States is currently on the wrong side of that line.

The dominance of trading lessens the importance of traditional banking, especially in what bankers would call "unprofitable" communities. Over the past decade banks have dumped branches and created financial deserts across the country. According to the Federal Deposit Insurance Corporation's most recent national survey, more than one-quarter of all American households have little or no access to financial services, deprived of an essential component of participating in the modern economy.[11]

A bloated banking sector supercharges inequality, with the earnings of those allowed inside the Wall Street casino far outpacing those of ordinary workers. That's true within the industry as well: the largest six U.S. banks control $10.37 trillion in assets, a figure that has only increased in market share after the financial crisis.[12] That may sound enormous, but it's actually less than the $12.8 trillion lent, spent, and guaranteed by the U.S. government to save the financial system after the 2008 crash.[13] Not only are lumbering banking behemoths too big to fail, granted implicit guarantees by the government that they will be rescued in the event of disaster; their sprawling operations are also too big to manage, highlighted by complexity and confusion that gives bad actors leeway—often deliberately so—to engage in misconduct. From assisting money laundering and tax evasion to rigging interest and foreign exchange rates, banks have revealed themselves as unrepentant sinners who took taxpayer cash without strings and showed no interest in reforming their behaviors.[14]

The economic power held on Wall Street routinely converts into political power. The financial sector enjoyed some of the biggest benefits from the Trump tax cuts, an unprecedented $100 billion in earnings by the biggest six banks in 2018.[15] Efforts to get banks to divest from environmental calamities like the Keystone XL pipeline, private prison companies profiting from immigration cruelties, or gun manufacturers driving America's mass shooting epidemic are in their way noble, but also faintly pathetic, as they accept as reality that banks have simply accumulated more power than democratic governance and that the only avenue to policy change lies in begging Wall Street executives to use their dominion over the country for good.

So how can we fix this? It's simple: we retain the parts of the banking system that are socially useful and necessary. We ensure equitable access to those tools, stepping in with nationalized solutions if the private sector cannot accomplish this.

And then we flay the rest and toss it into the sea.

Step 1: Breaking Trading

One provision in the Dodd-Frank reform tried to do something about excessive trading. The so-called Volcker rule intended to prevent banks that take deposits from using that money to make high-risk trades; sometimes this is known as proprietary trading. But the prohibition relies on whether regulators can differentiate proprietary trading from the carve-outs that bank lobbyists managed to force into the rule. If a bank says it's hedging risk—making a trade to offset potential losses on another trade—or engaging in market making—offering to buy and sell the same financial instrument so other investors have access to the trade—it's exempt from the Volcker rule.

And sharp bankers quickly learned how to characterize practically every trade in their portfolio as market making or hedging.

Another exception enables banks to invest up to 3 percent of their capital in hedge funds and private equity firms, effectively laundering trading through another channel. Successful lobbying for subsequent delays in implementation relieved banks from having to unwind most of their out-of-compliance trades until 2017, seven years after the Volcker rule's passage.[16]

So plenty of trading has continued, and now the Trump administration has begun the process of degrading the Volcker rule even further, by exempting more types of funds and shifting the burden of proof for compliance to regulators instead of the banks.[17] In other words, an illegal trade isn't illegal until some agency official manages to figure it out, even though regulatory budgets are a fraction of any established bank's, and regulators cannot possibly track down noncompliant trades in real time.

We already have many of the tools needed to transform the financial system. What we lack are regulators aggressive enough to use them. Under Dodd-Frank, firms that cannot credibly explain to regulators how they would be dismantled and sold off in a crisis can be forced to downsize or even break up.[18] The Financial Stability Oversight Council, a board composed of major regulators, also could declare that large firms must be busted up if they posed a systemic risk.[19] The Federal Reserve has already and can further increase capital requirements on the largest and riskiest firms in ways that could force them to pay for their own mistakes and induce them to downsize.[20] The Justice Department can jail executives who break the law or otherwise punish miscreant banks to create a deterrent against criminal behavior.

But to eliminate the risks of excessive trading, regulators would need additional tools. First, we could structurally separate trading activities from traditional banking activities like taking deposits and making loans. This is often called the Glass-Steagall reform, after the New Deal–era rule splitting investment and commercial banks.

This would reduce the interconnectedness that caused losses in housing securities to cascade throughout the financial system during the crisis. It would also break up large supermarket banks that perform both commercial and investment banking activities, like JPMorgan Chase or Citigroup, and move them down the road of being small enough to fail without disrupting the economy.

Such a rule would further establish that banks can receive government benefits like deposit insurance, discounted Federal Reserve lending, and expectations of future bailouts only if they engage in socially necessary activities. We shouldn't want ordinary Americans' deposits entangled with, and indeed funding, what amounts to high-stakes gambling. A no-transfer rule would prevent any money inside a narrow commercial bank from leaking out into the capital markets. If an investment bank wants to trade, it can do so on its own dime, with fully disclosed risks and a prescribed duty to investors.

The concept of Glass-Steagall–style structural separation has been broadly accepted throughout developed economies. The Liikanen report, produced in 2012 by a European Union task force, recommended "ring-fencing" deposits so that they could not be jeopardized by failures in trading.[21] The Vickers report in the United Kingdom reached the same conclusion.[22] The radicals in this debate are protecting the deregulatory status quo; the rest of the world has already made up its mind.

John Kay takes this even further by recommending specialized institutions for handling asset management, issuing securities, and advising corporations. His design would minimize conflicts of interest, so the same firm isn't selling securities and advising companies on what securities to buy. In Kay's view, Glass-Steagall isn't enough to fragment the system; you must broadly segment to ensure safety and break the "tight coupling" between different parts of finance. He looks at the problem as an engineer would, and redesigns the plumbing to ensure that the water keeps flowing regardless of an isolated failure.

Depriving subsidies to trading institutions limits the amount of funds available to expand trading. But there's also the option of simply banning socially unproductive trading entirely. That would return finance to its role as a facilitator of economic output, rather than the center of it.

Step 2: Deleting Derivatives and Spotlighting the Shadow Banks

Derivative trades are bets on whether a financial asset will go up or down in value, regardless of whether either side of the trade owns that asset, and they're everywhere. The most recent statistics show an outstanding value of all derivatives contracts at $544 trillion, with a *t*.[23] Derivatives originated as commodity hedges, so farmers would have some fallback in case their crops failed. Of course, there are other ways to compensate farmers for assuming risk. And noncommodity derivatives have poured money into financial markets for scant societal benefit. That's particularly true of second-order derivatives, bets on top of bets repackaged for investors to trade. During the financial crisis, collateralized debt obligations—derivatives based on the rise and fall of the housing market—exposed the entire system to the bubble collapse. Thanks to collateralized debt obligations, investors who didn't own the underlying mortgages still lost big when those mortgages failed.

Big banks and their regulators sometimes argue that derivatives are merely a risk-management tool.[24] But as we saw in the crisis, when deployed in the real world, derivatives increase financial risk by widening the amount of exposure from any single disaster across investors and firms. If they just amount to bets in a casino, close the casino.

A proposal from Morgan Ricks of Vanderbilt University addresses short-term funding markets, a $20 trillion pool of overnight lending that finances an astounding amount of trading activity.[25] The financial part of the financial crisis occurred because lenders were worried they wouldn't be paid back on their short-term debt. Overnight repurchases or money market accounts are considered as safe as money, but the crisis demonstrated that they are potentially unstable and prone to runs. Banks have reduced reliance on this type of debt, but there's still plenty of it floating around, particularly outside the traditional banking sector, as a cheap source of funding for so-called shadow banks like hedge funds and private equity firms.[26]

If only chartered banks could issue short-term debt, and if they were separated from other parts of the financial system, those banks could be monitored for excessive lending, reducing the likelihood of a debilitating crisis. It would simplify the market structure by limiting the channel through which overnight lending could flow. Plus, shadow banks would lose access to cheap capital.

This raises a bigger question: why do hedge funds exist at all, and do we need them? A loophole in the Investment Company and Investment Advisers Acts of 1940 allowed firms that cater to "sophisticated investors"—at the time wealthy families—to engage in risky profit-making activities like short sales (bets that a stock will go down instead of up), leverage (investing with borrowed funds to amplify returns and heighten risk), and corporate takeovers. Policymakers justified this by reckoning that sophisticated investors can handle the risks, while retail investors needed to be protected more stringently. The exemption expanded in the National Securities Markets Improvement Act of 1996 to include institutional investors like pension funds and university endowments; hedge fund assets subsequently increased twentyfold in twenty years.[27]

This has perverted the entire point of the 1940 acts, which was to break up giant pools of capital used for rank speculation. Now hedge fund capital, and that of its close cousin the private equity fund, has shoved itself into practically every aspect of economic life, largely outside the purview of regulatory authorities. Most retail bankruptcies in the age of e-commerce can be attributed to companies owned by private equity funds, investment firms that load up companies with debt and extract profits.[28] Hedge funds have been at the forefront of scooping up the discounted debt of struggling sovereigns like Argentina or Greece or Puerto Rico and forcing a repayment payday.[29] High-frequency trading is more and more a province of hedge funds.[30] Name a financial strategy that harms workers, businesses, and investors, and there's sure to be a hedge fund or private equity firm behind it.

We don't have to permit that. Closing the loophole and placing hedge funds under the 1940 acts would mandate disclosure, alter the industry's complex, lucrative fee structures, and eliminate the use of leverage. In effect, it would put these predatory actors out of business.

Separating bank business lines by activities, and banning harmful products, changes the system we have from a complex, interconnected agglomeration, where a failure in one area can spill over everywhere, to a more independent and stable system. Combining these ideas would reduce trading volumes and channel capital only toward necessary activity.

Step 3: Democratize Our Financial System

But eliminating or segregating the nonessential aspects of banking is not sufficient to fix the system. If separated from investment banking, the firms controlling consumer banking will need to rely even more on fees and markups and deception to hit their profit targets. We saw this with Wells Fargo, a firm mostly engaged in consumer banking, which issued millions of fake accounts to meet high sales goals.[31] That was just one of an avalanche of scandals for the bank, most of which involved ripping off its own customers. It placed unnecessary auto insurance on customer accounts, secretly changed the loan terms of mortgage borrowers in bankruptcy, and falsified records to charge mortgage applicants for its own delays in application processing, to name but a few examples.[32]

Any bank committed to that much criminality to make its profits should have its corporate charter revoked.[33] But even a scrupulous commercial bank sector would be problematic for how much of the country it leaves out. Large banks claim that poor depositors whom they cannot also sell loans to or advise on investment cost them money on average. It's worth questioning this assertion, but if commercial banks are prohibited from engaging in other profit-making activities, it's likely that rates of unbanked and under-banked Americans—concentrated in poor communities and communities of color—would increase.

Traditional banking is one area where there's been an attempt at disruption. So-called fintech firms use the internet to deliver financial services. This includes companies that let people make payments over the web or on their phones (PayPal, Stripe, Venmo); websites that offer simple bank accounts without physical bank branches (Chime, Empower); financial adviser robots that manage investments through an algorithm (Betterment); and peer-to-peer consumer lending sites that match people with excess money to those who need it (Prosper, LendingClub, SoFi). Users of these services praise their efficiency and ease of use. And it's not like traditional banking has such a sterling reputation that it couldn't do with some competition.

But there's as much peril in fintech as there is promise. Like shadow banks, LendingClub and SoFi exist somewhere outside the regulatory perimeter, unencumbered by laws that protect consumers. State regulation could provide a backstop, but federal banking regulators in the Trump administration have trotted out a fintech banking charter, which would strip state oversight and potentially allow these companies to engage in deceptive or discriminatory lending while federal authorities look the other way.[34]

It's also more and more apparent that the ultimate lenders behind these shiny internet firms are the same old bankers and financiers who dominate this industry. Morgan Stanley, Goldman Sachs, and BlackRock have plowed money into peer-to-peer lenders and issued hundreds of millions of dollars in peer-to-peer loan-backed securities.[35] This is not very different from how banks provided the capital for nonbank mortgage originators to make subprime loans during the financial crisis.

We cannot rely on Silicon Valley to get right what Wall Street has gotten wrong. New laws to give fintech consumers the same protections as bank customers are sorely needed. But even with those in place, the divide between those with and those without a bank account could simply be replaced by a digital divide, locking out lower-income people in need of financial services.[36] Plus, if an algorithm determines creditworthiness, as is the case with many fintech companies, the same biases blocking people of color from loans can slip into the process in a far more bloodless fashion.[37]

Without stable access to financial services, individuals are pushed to the fringes, where predatory actors like check-cashing stores, pawnshops, and payday lenders gouge them. According to a 2014 white paper, the average household using these alternative financial services spends $2,412 a *year* on interest and fees, roughly 10 percent of their total gross income. This is completely unacceptable, and there's a solution lurking on nearly every Main Street in America.

From 1911 to 1967, the U.S. Postal Service gave millions of customers postal savings accounts, and even today it sells money orders, a secure certified check.[38] There are more than 31,000 post office locations, one in every U.S. zip code; 58 percent of their branches are in zip codes with zero or one bank.[39] By offering basic financial services—an ATM card, an interest-bearing savings account, remittance services to friends and family abroad, even potentially small loans—the postal service can give millions a public option for simple banking, fulfilling the agency's mission of providing all citizens access to commerce, while saving them billions of dollars in unnecessary fees to sinister operators.[40] Federal benefits could be automatically loaded into postal banking accounts, and customers could seamlessly exchange payments inside the system. If banks would rather not serve low-income populations, the postal service can, more cheaply and equitably than the alternatives.

Postal banking would instantly increase convenience and give the unbanked a risk-free way to step into the modern economy. It would give everyone a way to exchange money, borrow when they need it, and have their savings protected. It could serve as the backbone of a consumer financial system, acknowledging that banking services comprise an essential piece of U.S. infrastructure, like a road or bridge.

But there are more ambitious options to democratize finance. Thomas Herndon and Mark Paul, in a 2018 report for the Roosevelt Institute, envisioned a publicly administered online marketplace for financial services, where the offerings of a postal bank and private banks could be compared side by side, with a ratings system and consumer reviews.[41] This would incentivize competition on the price and quality of loans and other financial products and give the government a mechanism to police financial services through access to the marketplace.

A more radical solution would be a public bank that does more than take deposits from individuals. The Bank of North Dakota, established in 1919, has only one depositor: the state. Those deposits, mostly tax revenues that have yet to be paid back out in salaries or services, form the base from which the bank makes in-state loans for economic development, including infrastructure projects and a student loan program.

A public bank serves as a substitute not so much for private sector banks as for the $3.8 trillion municipal bond market. When state or local governments fund large-scale projects not covered by taxes, they generally either borrow from the bond market at high interest rates, or enter into a public-private partnership with investors, who often don't have community needs at heart and slap already beleaguered municipalities with outrageous underwriting fees. A public bank can offer lower interest rates and fees, because it's not a for-profit business trying to maximize returns. Second, because the bank is publicly owned, any profit flows back to the city or state, virtually eliminating financing costs and providing governments with extra revenue at no cost to taxpayers.

The Bank of North Dakota, for example, has earned record profits for fourteen straight years, during both the Great Recession and the state's more recent downturn from the collapse in oil prices. Over the last decade, hundreds of millions of dollars in bank earnings have been transferred to North Dakota.

The objection that governments have no money to lend is spurious. Banks don't lend out their deposits, but create new money by extending credit. The deposits simply balance a bank's books. Public banks, then, expand the local money supply available for economic development.

Public banking and democratized investment vehicles could reimagine the role of finance as more than just blind profit seeking. A bank built to serve the public can channel its resources to actual public needs. It can give the American people a defined voice in the direction of their money. Instead of being at the mercy of financiers, they'd be participating in a fundamentally democratic process.

If you put these ideas together, you end up with something close to what academics Morgan Ricks, Lev Menand, and John Crawford proposed in 2018.[42] They call it the FedAccount. The FedAccount would be a personal account for all individuals and businesses at the Federal Reserve, the same as what financial institutions already have with the nation's central bank. The FedAccount would supply debit cards, direct deposit, online bill pay, and mobile banking. And post offices could serve as the retail storefront location for the enterprise.

Money that banks stash at the Federal Reserve earns the federal funds rate, not the infinitesimal rates Americans receive on their bank accounts. Banks instantly transfer funds to one another through their FedAccounts, a privilege that would be opened up to the rest of us. Because businesses would also have FedAccounts, that would curtail transaction fees for retailers and create a cheaper substitute for cash, available to all. And while personal bank accounts are only guaranteed through the FDIC up to $250,000, FedAccounts can never default, no matter how large the account balance, because the Federal Reserve prints America's money.

This would obviously increase financial access and improve the payment system. It would also eat away at the giant deposit bases of the big banks, reducing their size and potentially their risk to the financial system. But most important, it would allow the Fed to more directly influence economic policy.

Rajiv Sethi of Barnard College has explained that profits from the Fed's balance sheet—and it earned $65 billion in 2018—could be directly transmitted to Americans in times of recession, to create an immediate fiscal boost.[43] The money would go directly to debtors to pay off their bills, instead of creditors who benefit from changes to interest rates, the Fed's current policy tool. Because millions of people would have FedAccounts, the Fed's balance sheet would grow even larger, with more profits to channel during economic downturns.

In other words, the people's money would be put to work for the people. And while the authors of the FedAccount proposal restricted the Fed from direct consumer and business lending, you could envision that being added on. If you believe money is a public resource and not a privately supplied product, government allocation of credit takes on the role of sensible distribution of resources. The FedAccount could tie together all facets of a public bank, built with the public's well-being at the forefront.

Americans are currently stuck with a decrepit payment system, miscreant banks, interest-bearing bank accounts that bear no interest, and a financial sector that's thoroughly unconcerned with their lives, as they push past the public to trade their way to fortunes. Cryptocurrencies like Bitcoin inspire such frenzy because people are looking for an alternative to a broken financial system.

The architecture for that alternative already exists. It exists in regulators armed with the power to segregate functions and promote public safety. It exists in enforcement agents who can identify risk and simply eliminate it for the public good. It exists in federal agencies and central banks with missions to facilitate economic activity and prevent public suffering.

It also exists in our history, layered with numerous triumphs by ordinary people over financial greed. Progressive Era activists demanded and brought public banking to North Dakota. After the Depression, a young prosecutor named Ferdinand Pecora used a Senate committee charged with studying the causes of the crisis to lay bare the rank corruption in the banking system, leading to landmark New Deal regulation that kept the country safe from runaway finance for fifty years.[44] Activists reeling from Reverend Martin Luther King's death fought for the Fair Housing Act and an end to redlining. The Community Reinvestment Act of 1977, another grassroots initiative, strengthened fair lending laws by requiring broad investment across low- and moderate-income communities.[45] The Consumer Financial Protection Bureau began as a proposal in a magazine by a Harvard professor named Elizabeth Warren, and thanks to popular support it became the only agency in the federal government with a core mission to prevent financial scams. As Wells Fargo pursued its rapacious schemes, a group of tellers and line-level employees formed the Committee for Better Banks to expose it, which culminated in the resignation of CEO John Stumpf.[46]

In short, we know how to fix finance. We have a shelf full of ideas for this purpose, and a demonstrated capacity to leverage people power to make them reality. The only missing ingredient to accomplish this is the political will that a reinvigorated left can generate. The progressive surge onto the House Financial Services Committee provides an opportunity. Now activists and policymakers must work together not to squander it, so finance is finally, permanently, put on a leash. Nothing could be more vital to rendering a more just and prosperous America.

Democracy, Equality, and the Future of Workers

Sarita Gupta, Stephen Lerner, and Joseph A. McCartin

WHO WILL OWN THE FUTURE? THE ANSWER TO THAT QUESTION WILL depend on whether working people gain a significant voice in their workplaces and their government over the next decade, and whether they can begin to develop levers of power that allow them to reverse the trend toward inequality and diminished democracy that has marked the last half century of our history. The stakes have never been higher for those who have been struggling to create a just and sustainable economy in an America at peace with itself and the world.

Our twenty-first-century economy is driving us toward an increasingly unstable, undemocratic, unequal, and unsustainable world. The growing concentration of wealth among the superrich, the increasing influence of Wall Street that has accompanied the financialization of the economy, the upsurge of low-wage and precarious work, and the heightened power of Silicon Valley and monopolistic technology firms such as Facebook, Amazon, and Google are relentlessly undercutting worker bargaining power, triggering an explosive rise in inequality that especially impacts workers of color, and undermining what remains of democratic governance.

Even as they tighten their grip, the architects of inequality seek to control the alternatives we envision for our future. In recent years, they have promoted fevered "future of work" scenarios that imagine the potential disappearance of jobs before sweeping waves of robotization, artificial intelligence, and machine learning. Consulting companies like McKinsey and Deloitte spin off predictions of imminent job-destroying, technology-driven change, even as they offer their services to companies seeking to get ahead of the curve. Bank of America, Barclays, and other titans of finance, business publications from *Fortune* to *Forbes* to *Fast Company*, and elite thought-leader organizations from the Aspen Institute to the World Economic Forum each hype visions of the future of work that assume that capital's needs will shape the future. They never question who is driving the reorganization of work and for what purpose.

Unless we want a future in which we have no option but to conform to capital's dictates, we must challenge such thinking and make the future of *workers*, not the future of *work*, our central concern. Building a future that addresses the needs of workers in turn means confronting the forces that are increasing inequality and undermining democracy.

How We Got Here

The crux of our problem is not the potential impact of new technologies themselves, but their use in a world economy that has been transformed by financialization and globalization in ways that have allowed a tiny number of individuals and entities to gain enormous, unprecedented power—an economy in which, as Oxfam has recently shown, just eight men own the same wealth as half the world's population. That economy is epitomized by the likes of Amazon, Walmart, and lesser known entities like the Blackstone Group, the world's largest private equity firm, which controls 150 companies with a combined value of more than $400 billion and which employs approximately six hundred thousand workers. It is the largest owner of office space in the world, the world's largest private owner of real estate, the largest owner of logistics companies in Europe, and the world's largest investor in hedge funds. These entities thrive in an economy that relentlessly weakens worker bargaining power even as it works to consolidate corporate economic and political dominance.

To own the future, we must rebuild a labor movement decimated by decades of erosion and attack. Yet that rebuilding must entail not only organizing workers, but also adapting their organizations to the task of confronting twenty-first-century capitalism. And challenging white supremacy and racism is an essential part of this.

More than eighty years have passed since the National Labor Relations (Wagner) Act offered the first significant federal protections of industrial workers' rights to organize and the Social Security Act laid the basis for an attenuated American welfare state. These New Deal policies were not panaceas. Their reach was limited—African Americans, immigrants, and women never enjoyed their fruits on an equal basis with white men. Yet over time the struggles of unions and the civil rights and feminist movements widened both the protections workers were able to win from the law and their self-organization. Between World War II and the mid-1970s, as union density crested at 35 percent of the nonagricultural workforce in the 1950s and then spread through the public sector in the 1960s, the United States experienced a broadly shared prosperity.

Yet if postwar decades saw a steady if incomplete advance of the New Deal's promise of worker empowerment, the last four decades have witnessed the near total destruction of that promise. During these decades, the U.S. economy was reorganized in ways that underscored what workers *failed* to win in the postwar years: enough political leverage to ensure that private economic power remained accountable to the common good. Lacking that leverage, workers saw private interests progressively shred the limited social bargain of the postwar years.

The same workers who were often left out of the New Deal were the first workers to bear the brunt of the reshaping of the economy. Urban deindustrialization, subcontracting, outsourcing, and part-timing of work were first experienced by African American, immigrant, and women workers. Conditions first experienced by the most vulnerable workers spread more broadly in the economy by the twenty-first century.

Although globalization played an important role in this process, its impact is often overstated. Equally important was the financialization of the economy, which fostered the extraction of wealth from communities of color through subprime loans and other mechanisms, the capture of government by private interests, and the reorganization of corporate enterprises into a dizzying maze of supply chains, subcontractors, franchisees, and increasingly disposable workers. As good jobs became scarcer, corporations pitted one community against another, seeking tax incentives and subsidies that starved the public sector while routinely failing to deliver the jobs promised. In effect, such schemes accomplished a vast transfer of wealth from taxpayers to shareholders.

As tax receipts failed to keep up with the growing demand for public services, public institutions from schools to prisons were squeezed. Private interests then boldly presented themselves as solutions to problems they had fomented. They pushed such innovations as charter schools and private prisons as efficient "market-based" solutions to austerity-strapped governments, once again harming workers of color and immigrants most with these policies.

These overlapping processes undermined workers' bargaining power in both the private and public sectors over the course of the past four decades. Their impact cannot be captured adequately in figures that show the decline in the proportion of workers unionized from a high of 35 percent in 1954 to 10.5 percent overall and only 6.4 percent in the private sector by 2019. More telling is the near disappearance of strikes. In the 1970s, the United States averaged 289 work stoppages each year involving at least one thousand workers each. As bargaining power shifted decisively to employers, that average plunged over the past forty years, reaching only thirteen per year over the last decade. As their leverage declined, private sector unions increasingly bargained from a defensive posture, seeking job security and minimized benefit cuts even as corporations wallowed in cash and rising stock values. Their public sector counterparts, meanwhile, found themselves increasingly pitted against aggrieved taxpayers and forced to bargain with public employers whose governing agendas were being increasingly influenced by powerful private interests.

The decline of collective bargaining both contributed to and resulted from the erosion of political democracy in recent decades. Through the North American Free Trade Agreement and its membership in the World Trade Organization, the United States ceded the power to make some economic policy to international courts that had the authority to override congressional legislation. From *Buckley v. Valeo* (1976) to *Citizens United v. FEC* (2010) the Supreme Court undermined legislative efforts to prevent money from controlling politics, while in *Shelby County v. Holder* (2013) it invalidated key provisions of the Voting Rights Act and opened the door to increased voter suppression. Meanwhile, Republican-dominated state legislatures have preempted efforts by localities to raise wages and labor standards within their jurisdictions.

Yet there are many reasons for hope as we look to the future. Interest in unions is surging, and worker organizing is gaining ground in influential sectors, including new media and higher education. Young people have begun to question some of the central assumptions of capitalism and have revived interest in democratic socialism. The attention that activists have given to the intersectional nature of most struggles for justice has diminished the conflicts that once pitted advocates of a universalistic, majoritarian left politics against those who feared that the voices of minorities and the excluded would be marginalized in such politics. And, as the chapters in this volume attest, the left is alive with creative energy not seen in many decades.

The extent to which national politicians are beginning to address the need to rebuild worker power is also encouraging. Senators Elizabeth Warren and Bernie Sanders have each offered bills that would empower workers. Warren's Accountable Capitalism Act would require that all corporations obtain charters from the federal government and would compel those with more than $1 billion in annual revenues to designate 40 percent of the seats on their boards of directors for representatives elected by employees. Sanders's Workplace Democracy Act would ease union organizing and legalize secondary boycotts.

Although legislative initiatives like these are clearly necessary, we believe they are also insufficient. Laws will not save us. Workers' struggles and organizations must play a central role in shaping the twenty-first century if we are to win the changes we need. But workers' organizations will not be able to do that by clinging to strategies of the past. The world that gave rise to the New Deal and the Great Society in the United States and to social democracy in Europe no longer exists. The strategies that arose in response to twentieth-century capitalism, from traditional collective bargaining to co-determination, are therefore unlikely to be sufficient to the needs of the future.

In the years to come we believe that the workplace-centered economism that was characteristic of trade-union-based social democracies or New Deal America will yield to broader forms of organization, social bargaining, and democratic experimentation. The inescapable fact that work relations in twenty-first-century capitalism are intimately connected to the structure of communities, social institutions, and lived environments points in that direction. So do efforts to win justice for workers across lines of gender, race, and citizenship status. Winning bargaining power for workers and raising wages will inevitably be connected to efforts to defend public schools and mass transit, create affordable housing, repulse predatory finance, and combat climate change.

The Shape of Things to Come

The outlines of a future of empowered workers and revived democracy are visible in the recent efforts of unions and their allies to remake collective bargaining and organizing campaigns for an economy that no longer resembles the one for which the Wagner Act, industrial unionism, or traditional public sector collective bargaining were designed. These creative efforts have given rise to a conscious rethinking and broadening of the *participants*, *processes*, and *purposes* of organizing and collective bargaining. While the collective bargaining that emerged in twentieth-century America was generally binary and involved only employers and unions, recent efforts have attempted to broaden participation to give the community or other stakeholders a place at the bargaining table. While traditional collective bargaining was generally conducted behind closed doors by seasoned professionals who haggled over details, recent efforts have infused bargaining with greater militancy, opened it up to greater transparency, and employed political action as a form of bargaining. And, while traditional collective bargaining was focused on winning a serviceable contract that would signal a demobilization of the union's membership, recent efforts have undertaken contract campaigns as steps in a long-term strategy of worker empowerment. They try to build enduring alignments between unions and their allies that accumulate lasting power over time through campaign victories, a shared and increasingly fleshed-out infrastructure, and a common vision and narrative.

Labor activists' willingness to experiment can be traced to a conjuncture of developments triggered by the Great Recession and its aftermath. President Barack Obama's agenda was derailed by the 2010 midterm elections, which sidelined unions' hoped-for labor law reform, the Employee Free Choice Act; propelled anti-union Republican governors like Wisconsin's Scott Walker to power in the states; and tightened the grip of austerity politics on all levels of government. Union leaders increasingly recognized that they needed a bigger vision if they hoped to turn back the anti-union assaults that had gathered strength. After having secured Obama's reelection, they embarked on new initiatives. In 2013, President Larry Cohen of the Communications Workers of America, for instance, helped launch the Democracy Initiative, an alliance of labor, civil rights, and environmental groups to counter the corrosive influence of corporate money on politics, fight voter suppression, and address other obstacles to significant reform. Meanwhile, AFL-CIO president Richard Trumka moved to involve worker centers and other nonunion worker organizations in the planning for the 2013 AFL-CIO convention.

The most significant catalysts for change, however, were the emergence of new models of mobilization and organizing. A turning point for these came in 2011, with the launching of three such models, each of which in its own way signaled new departures. In January, the executive board of the Service Employees International Union (SEIU) approved an ambitious campaign called the Fight for a Fair Economy, which saw SEIU commit tens of millions of dollars to organizing projects among low-wage workers in multiple cities. That effort would spawn local campaigns such as Minnesotans for a Fair Economy and ultimately lead to the Fight for $15 and a Union, a national movement to gain a living wage for fast-food workers.

In July 2011, Jobs with Justice, the national network of unions and community allies, joined with the National Domestic Workers Alliance to create the Caring Across Generations campaign, a national initiative to transform the long-term-care system and empower care workers. Over time it built an alliance that united more than two hundred organizations, networking among care workers, families whose loved ones need care, and care recipients who wish to live at home with dignity and independence. Domestic workers, who are overwhelmingly women and likely to be people of color or immigrants who have been excluded from federal labor law protections, organized and built deep collaborations, shaping cutting-edge strategies and making significant gains. One victory was the creation of the Obama administration's Home Care Rule, which allowed 2 million direct care workers to receive federal minimum wage and overtime pay protections.

Finally, in September 2011, came the seemingly spontaneous eruption of the Occupy Wall Street movement. It seeded new and unexpected alliances among unions and their allies in many cities and spurred a discussion of inequality and the predatory nature of financialized capitalism that resonated well beyond the participants in its encampments.

A year later, in September 2012, a precedent-setting strike by the Chicago Teachers Union (CTU) against the austerity regime of Democratic mayor Rahm Emanuel attracted the attention of the entire labor movement and foreshadowed new approaches to bargaining. Led by Karen Lewis, whose Caucus of Rank and File Educators slate was elected to the CTU's top posts in 2010, the union prepared an innovative bargaining campaign in partnership with community groups and parents. It called for smaller class sizes, improved facilities, an end to the closing of schools in African American neighborhoods, and a host of other items that went beyond the confines of wages, hours, and other narrowly defined work issues about which the union was legally permitted to bargain. Importantly, the union also documented the schools' financial mismanagement. It showed how tax-increment funding that could have helped schools was instead lavished on private entities such as the Chicago Mercantile Exchange, and it exposed risky interest-rate swap deals, in which Chicago's school system ended up squandering more than $100 million. By making the financial industry's exploitation of the school district an issue, the CTU earned public support for its call for adequate school funding.

Although the CTU did not win all of its demands, its campaign inspired others to take on austerity politics. In 2013, the St. Paul Federation of Teachers (SPFT) mounted a contract campaign that resembled the CTU's. It patiently built an alliance with parents and community groups, and with them jointly drew up twenty-nine demands, including one insisting that the school district cease doing business with banks that foreclose on their students' families. The union refused to back down when the school district refused to negotiate over many of them. After rallying broad community support, the St. Paul teachers won most of what they sought. "I had negotiated almost a dozen previous contracts for the SPFT," explained the union's president, Mary Cathryn Ricker. "But, for the first time, I felt that signing a contract was just one step in building a larger movement." Meanwhile, SEIU Local 503, which represents home care, child care, and university and state workers, inaugurated a campaign called In It Together, that built alliances with the community by calling for a broad investigation into the ways in which banks were ripping off Oregonians and by demanding a state lawsuit against banks to recoup millions that were lost from retirement funds due to the secret manipulation of the London InterBank Offered Rate.

A new strategy of bargaining and alliance building emerged from these campaigns, and many of the activists involved in them convened in Washington in May 2014, where they gave that strategy a name: Bargaining for the Common Good (BCG). Soon that style was spreading to new settings like Los Angeles, where the city's leading public sector unions and their community-based allies launched the Fix LA Coalition in 2014. That coalition brought SEIU, the American Federation of State, County and Municipal Employees, and other public sector unions together with community groups and faith-based organizations. They exposed the fact that more taxpayer money was spent paying fees to the Wall Street firms that marketed LA's municipal bonds and other financial services than on maintaining the city's streets. Furthermore, they demanded that LA use its $106 billion worth of assets, payments, and debt issuance as leverage to "demand better deals with Wall Street, so that it can invest more in our communities." This included hiring workers from disadvantaged communities who had been hardest hit by layoffs and cuts.

At the outset, BCG campaigns were meticulously planned and the groundwork for them was carefully laid, in some cases over a period of more than a year before they were launched. Yet the basic principles of that approach have proven to be adaptable in more spontaneous struggles, as the teachers' mobilizations of 2018 illustrated. Beginning in West Virginia in January 2018, and spreading to such union-averse states as Oklahoma and Arizona, those mobilizations were, in effect, organizing, bargaining, and political campaigns all at once.

In each setting, teachers gravitated almost naturally toward a common-good framework in which they linked their struggles to the needs of their communities, and targeted the most powerful economic forces in their states. In West Virginia, teachers in all of the state's fifty-five school districts walked off the job, called attention to the fact that the state's wealthiest were paying scant taxes, and refused to return to work until all state workers had received a pay increase equal to the one the state legislature granted them. In Oklahoma, teachers protested the state's failure to fairly tax wealthy oil and gas interests. In Arizona, teachers demanded that the state enact no further tax cuts until the state's per-pupil spending on education reached the national average (and briefly succeeded in getting an initiative on the 2018 ballot that would have taxed the wealthy to fund schools before the Arizona Supreme Court had it removed on a technicality). Since the vast majority of strikers were not union members, these walkouts were massive organizing campaigns and democracy campaigns as well, since they posed such explicitly political demands as raising taxes to fund public schools more adequately. They instinctively adopted a BCG approach in that they were not just about wages or benefits but also about improving education and fighting for fairer taxation. The teacher walkouts ensured that more workers walked out on strike in 2018 than in any year since 1986.

In January 2019, United Teachers of Los Angeles extended that militancy. Not only did the union launch the eighth major teachers' strike in a U.S. city over a twelve-month span; it launched the largest one yet, and the one that most explicitly employed a BCG approach. With strong community support, teachers stayed off the job for a week. They settled for the same raise that the school district had offered at the outset, and instead used their strike to win the hiring of a nurse in every school, a reduction of class sizes, the extension of a program that exempts schools from administering random searches of their students (which disproportionately impacted students of color), and a cap on the spread of charter schools.

Innovative organizing and bargaining initiatives have not remained confined to the public sector. By 2016, the Communications Workers of America, the Committee for Better Banks, and allied organizations laid the groundwork for organizing to improve pay and benefits for the nation's more than 1 million nonunion bank workers. Employing a common-good approach similar to that pioneered by teachers unions, this coalition positioned itself as a defender of consumers and an opponent of predatory financial practices. It began demanding an end to sales goals and metrics that force bank workers to sell predatory financial products as a condition of employment, and more broadly to reform the finance system so that it serves the people instead of operating as a driver of inequality. Wells Fargo workers connected to this campaign acted as the whistle-blowers who exposed the bank's cheating scandals in 2016. Bank workers at Santander, a Spanish-based multinational bank that is the leader in the U.S. subprime auto loan market, have helped expose their employer's predatory practices. These bank worker campaigns are raising the idea that bank workers can help regulate their industry from below, exposing and stopping banks from cheating consumers and engaging in practices that threaten the broader health of the economy.

The titans of private equity have also presented a promising target for labor activists, particularly since such firms control a range of companies in multiple sectors and nations. Blackstone offers an example of how diverse campaigns targeting one such firm could be run at once, tying together a variety of different issues and organizations that could challenge the full scope of the company's activities. Organizers are planning for campaigns that would simultaneously mount organizing drives at the nonunion companies Blackstone owns, form a tenant union of Blackstone renters (since Blackstone is now the largest landlord in the country), and prevail on union pension funds to use their leverage to prevent Blackstone from foreclosing on homes in post-Maria Puerto Rico. At the same time, union allies are preparing legislation in several states that would tax private equity executives to recover the states' shares of the billions in tax revenue that are lost to the carried-interest loophole that protects the hyperwealthy executives of private equity giants.

Even mighty Amazon has not been impervious to pressure from workers and their allies. Perhaps the most difficult problem workers have faced in recent years is how to cope with the power of monopolistic corporations, which have a depressing effect on wages. Researchers have found that the rise of huge employers has led to the emergence of a monopsony in many labor markets, where those employers set wages artificially low without fear of competition for workers. No big employer has come to symbolize the problem more than Amazon, which pays its warehouse and delivery workers poverty wages even as it wrings tax incentives from the local communities where it builds its distribution centers.

Creative challenges to Amazon's power began to emerge by 2018. Somali immigrants make up a huge slice of Amazon's warehouse employees in the Twin Cities. In 2018, many of those workers began organizing through the Awood Center, an East African workers' center, to demand a voice in determining their workload, regular consultations with community representatives, and prayer time on the job, among other things. At the same time, activists in many of the cities Amazon induced into bidding for the siting of Amazon's HQ2 facility actively opposed tax giveaways and subsidies that their city leaders were offering to the nation's richest company, contending that Amazon's arrival would drive up housing costs and increase inequality. They also objected to the undemocratic and secretive process through which cities courted Amazon. Opposition was so great to Amazon's announcement that it would site one of its HQ2 centers in Long Island City, New York, that the company felt compelled to reverse its decision in February 2019.

The campaigns described in this chapter are in early stages. They are as of yet insufficient in scale, scope, and resources to challenge and win against the richest and most powerful corporate monopolies in history. Indeed, winning real power for workers at powerful giants like Amazon or Walmart is likely still years away. Nonetheless, these campaigns are first steps that offer a taste and glimpse of the role workers and their organizations could play in redistributing wealth and power and moving us toward real democratic socialism. Taken together they show that even as union density trended downward in the decade after the Great Recession, and even as unions absorbed blows like the *Janus* decision—which established a regressive Wisconsin and Michigan-style "right to work" regime throughout the country's public sector—new and promising labor initiatives have been proliferating.

Most importantly, these campaigns have begun the work of radically reimagining and redefining the goals and mission of unions. They have either implicitly or explicitly broken with the traditionally bifurcated approach pursued by the U.S. labor movement for more than a century. That approach held that workers should organize and bargain collectively to improve their wages, benefits, and working conditions, and that they should separately pursue political and legislative action to win what they could not gain through collective bargaining. It has become obvious that this approach is failing on every level.

Having been largely blocked from winning significant gains *either* through organizing and bargaining *or* through pursuing electoral and legislative strategies, workers and their organizations have increasingly strayed from the bifurcation that long separated bargaining from politics. Bargaining for the Common Good campaigns have shown that by consciously politicizing their organizing, bargaining, and strikes, workers can start to feel and demonstrate the potential power of a movement that is committed to democracy at work, in our communities, states, and country as a whole. The teachers' strikes of 2018–19 showed workers that they might win through job actions what they could not win through legislative or political action.

And the Amazon HQ2 campaign subverted the long-standing assumption that secret, taxpayer-funded corporate subsidies were effective tools to promote economic development.

Importantly, these campaigns have been waged in a context of growing public support for unions. In 2009, the depths of the Great Recession, 48 percent of respondents told Gallup pollsters that they approved of unions. By 2018, this number had leaped to 61 percent and the Pew Research Center reported that union favorables were even higher (68 percent) among people in the eighteen to twenty-nine age group. Reviewing similar findings, researchers at the Massachusetts Institute of Technology estimate that the union movement would quadruple in size if all of those who say they would like union representation were actually able to win it. This growing reservoir of goodwill is there to be leveraged in fights that expand collective bargaining beyond the limited workplace environments where our failed labor laws have helped to confine it. But unions won't be able to take advantage of this if they return to the same failed strategies of the past.

It is becoming possible to imagine a not-too-distant future where workers' organizations will begin to organize and bargain simultaneously for better housing and schools, an end to privatization, sustainable environmental practices, and more. The recent initiatives briefly reviewed in this chapter point to a future where workers will begin to bargain with the most powerful entities—the Blackstones and Amazons—whose power impacts our lives in so many different ways. They suggest that the idea of collective bargaining that had emerged in the twentieth century is being redefined and repurposed in promising ways that challenge the erosion of democracy and the rise of inequality.

In these struggles, and in the legislative proposals offered by Elizabeth Warren, Bernie Sanders, and other progressives, we believe can be discerned the aspirations of workers that an emerging left can help to realize in the years ahead. In them we can glimpse the outlines of what an American democratic socialism might look like. It will likely not imitate the European social democracies, whose political and material foundations are now crumbling, but will instead adapt some of their innovations to the challenges presented by twenty-first-century capitalism in an American context.

Such a vision has deep American roots. The recent efforts we have discussed in this chapter recall the vibrancy that characterized U.S. labor struggles in the era before the twentieth-century institutionalization of unions and traditional collective bargaining. From the Lowell Female Labor Reform Association's resistance to "wage slavery" in the New England factory towns of the early nineteenth century and the community-based assemblies of the Knights of Labor that took power in small towns like Rochester, New Hampshire, in the 1880s, to the "sewer socialism" of Milwaukee or Schenectady in the Progressive Era, unions of the past had concerned themselves not merely with the wages and hours of their members but with a defense of the common good, and the construction of what earlier American socialists like Eugene Debs called a "cooperative commonwealth." Labor's crisis is leading an increasing number of union members to rediscover that American heritage and update it for the needs of the twenty-first century. It is now for us to take up that urgent work.

Who Gets to Be Safe?
Prisons, Police, and Terror

Aviva Stahl

DOMINANT NOTIONS OF SECURITY AND INSECURITY ARE WOVEN SO DEEP within us they can feel instinctive. Every time a white woman feels a flicker of fear when she passes a black man on the street; every time a driver locks his car while driving through a neighborhood where homeless people congregate; every time a non-Muslim looks askance when a brown man with a beard boards her plane; what's bubbling up is the imprint of generations of capitalism, racism, and imperialism on our psyches. "Because white men can't / police their imagination / black people are dying," wrote poet Claudia Rankine in her 2014 book *Citizen*.[1] All of us, and not just killer cops, will need to unlearn how we think about danger and threat if we're going to build a different world.

The United States contains only about 2.3 percent of the world's population, but 25 percent of its prison population. About 2.3 million people are locked up in facilities across the country, including in state and federal prisons, local jails, ICE detention, and youth correctional facilities. In addition, about 4.4 million people are on parole or probation.[2] At the end of 2016 just under 7 million people—or one out of every fifty-five Americans—were under some form of correctional supervision, according to the Bureau of Justice Statistics.[3] If everyone who was incarcerated or on parole or probation moved to the same place, that city would be the second biggest in the country, smaller only than New York. But our criminal justice system doesn't solve the problems it purports to—instead it breaks up families, devastates communities, and fails to heal both those who commit harm and those who survive it.

This reality is incompatible with anything we might call democratic socialism. In this chapter, I draw on the work of decades of scholarship on prison abolition, including the words of organizer and educator Mariame Kaba. "For me prison abolition is two things: it's the complete and utter dismantling of prison and policing and surveillance as they currently exist within our culture," she said in a 2016 podcast. "And it's also the building up of new ways of intersecting and new ways of relating with each other."[4]

Like Kaba, I believe that decarcerating our society and building a more just future won't just require us to change things as they are—the policies implemented by the state, the economic system we live under, the way we deal with people who commit harm. It will also require us to change ourselves.

What we are taught to imagine as crime and criminals is a reflection not of the real dangers at hand but of who is in power. Prisons are filled with poor people and people of color because the criminal justice system functions to protect and uphold the interests of capital and its racialized and gendered hierarchies. For the same reason, it is both difficult and extraordinarily rare for corporations and their decision-makers—from the oil companies that drive climate change to the pharmaceutical companies that feed the opioid crisis—to be held legally responsible for the harm they cause. We won't be able to transition from the world we live in to the world we dream of unless we change how we think about what constitutes a threat, as well as the best means for staying safe.

Building a radically egalitarian future will mean rejecting the state's framing of who seeks to cause us harm—that it's not the migrant or the criminal or the terrorist who is the most likely to perpetrate violence against our bodies or our minds, but people we know and love. A democratic socialist society would imprison far fewer people, reorienting the perverse policy incentives that feed mass incarceration, and providing residents with the tenets of dignified life, from quality health care to housing; indeed, today's existing social democracies have some of the world's lowest incarceration rates. And for democratic socialism to survive and thrive, we'll need to understand that the greatest threat to our safety isn't an external one, and commit ourselves to building families and communities where everyone contributes to a culture of justice and accountability. Only by building stronger communities will we be able to address and intervene in the harm people perpetrate against one another in their day-to-day lives.

As Kaba has noted, the work of transforming ourselves and our communities must go hand in hand with the day-to-day labor of changing the world we live in now. Abolitionists seek to implement what have been called "nonreformist reforms," meaning changes that minimize the harm of the criminal justice system without ever expanding its reach—and over the last few years, activists have been securing wins to do just that. In Chicago, organizers successfully campaigned to give reparations to victims of police violence.[5] In Philadelphia, Chicago, and elsewhere, organizers have fought to kick pro-cop and pro-prison district attorneys out of office or elect DAs committed to more progressive platforms. And in California, organizers helped pass legislation to legalize marijuana and abolish cash bail. (The bail industry and its supporters have since successfully campaigned for California to hold a 2020 referendum on the elimination of cash bail.) These are just a few examples. So much more is happening elsewhere across the country. In short, abolitionist organizing has won real gains and made tangible improvements in people's lives—*and* that work is getting done in service of a more sweeping and utopian vision that's rooted in the values and mission of transformative justice.

Creating a world without prisons is undoubtedly an ambitious goal. It might even feel impossible. What's important to remember is that while a world without prisons may seem unimaginable, so, too, did a world without slavery, or one where women had the right to vote . . . until it didn't. In the time span of human civilization, prisons are actually a relatively new phenomenon. They embody a way of thinking about and addressing harm that was preceded (and will undoubtedly be superseded!) by other institutions and value systems. But it takes the dreams and ambitions of real people, and a belief in the reality of our own agency, to make the seemingly unattainable a reality.

When it comes to justice and security, reframing our locus of concern inward, toward ourselves and our communities, is both a means and an end to building the world we dream of, and a vital complement to transforming the world as it is.

The Political Economy of Fear

Marxist criminologists generally believe that the law exists to protect private property and the people who own it. So, in their view, it's not a flaw in the system that poor people who engage in property theft and crimes of survival end up behind bars, while wealthy individuals who cause much greater harm stay in the free world. As Jeffrey Reiman argued in his 1979 book, *The Rich Get Richer and the Poor Get Prison*, our system of policing and prisons isn't broken; it works exactly as intended—by locking up the poor and convincing the public they pose the greatest danger. "The system functions the way it does *because it maintains a particular image of crime: the image that it is a threat from the poor*," he writes (emphasis his).[6]

In the United States and across the world, where the categories of race and class are fundamentally intertwined, it's impossible to talk about the construction of criminality without talking about slavery and the continuing reality of anti-black racism. Scholars like Angela Davis[7] and filmmakers like Ava DuVernay[8] have traced how the end of slavery gave rise to new laws and criminal justice measures as a means of maintaining white dominance over black bodies and black labor, which ultimately led to the mass incarceration we see today. Alongside these material changes to the law came ideological ones. In *The Condemnation of Blackness*, Khalil Gibran Muhammad traces how social scientists and policymakers in the post–Civil War years used biased crime statistics to birth the myth of black criminality. "From that moment forward, notions about blacks as criminals materialized in national debates about the fundamental racial and cultural differences between African Americans and native born whites and European immigrants,"[9] he writes—notions that remain very much alive today.

Who's a Threat?

According to research released by the United Nations in November 2018, the most likely place for a woman to be killed, both in the United States and across the world, is where she lives, or at the hands of a family member or current or former partner.[10] Yet so many of us fear falling prey to a terror attack on the subway, but aren't similarly fearful of the violence that could befall us or our loved ones at the hands of people we know. According to a 2018 study by Chapman University, 49.3 percent of Americans report being afraid of "Islamic extremists" while only 19.2 percent of people fear being sexually assaulted by someone they know.[11] It's not that domestic terrorism doesn't cause any harm. The Anti-Defamation League's Center on Extremism calculated that "domestic extremists" were responsible for 387 murders between 2008 and 2017, the majority of whom (71 percent) were committed white supremacists or elsewhere on the far right.[12] But that's nothing compared to the number of people who die due to domestic violence. Each and every day in the United States, an estimated three women are murdered by a current or former partner.[13]

Spending on domestic terrorism versus domestic violence reflects the value we place on addressing these two threats. From the beginning of fiscal year 2001 to the end of fiscal year 2019, the United States was on track to expend an almost inconceivable amount of money fighting the War on Terror—$5.9 trillion, according to one estimate.[14] That amounts to about $310 billion per year, compared to the less than $1 billion in federal funds spent to combat domestic and sexual violence in fiscal years 2017 and 2018. (In addition, an estimated $2.6 billion was collected annually from people convicted of federal crimes; funds were used to assist victims of crime.)[15] As Solomon Hughes traced in his book *War on Terror, Inc.*, since the Twin Towers fell, corporations have relied on and exploited the politics of fear in the name of profit.[16] In 2016 alone, defense contractors Lockheed Martin made $5.3 billion in profit, Boeing $4.9 billion, and Raytheon $2.2 billion.[17] Our fear that we'll fall prey to a terrorist act—when we step on the subway, when we board a plane, when we walk into a bar or a house of worship—doesn't serve to protect us, but to enshrine the power of the already powerful.

Perhaps more importantly, our manufactured fear of external threats distorts our understanding of what may really cause us harm. The day after 9/11, the phrase "If you see something, say something" was coined by a Manhattan advertising agency for one of its clients, the Metropolitan Transportation Authority, which is charged with running New York City's public transit system.[18] We are trained to surveil strangers and public spaces for signs that a terrorist attack may be imminent, yet few Americans say anything when we see signs that abuse is happening to people we know. In her memoir about surviving an abusive relationship, Kelly Sundberg describes how, near the end of her marriage, she and her husband interviewed to move into and help run a dorm on campus. "It was a hot and humid day, so I wore a light sweater that ended at my elbows. I smiled, I chatted," she recalls. "I saw the resident director looking curiously at my elbow, which was still swollen large and almost black. I pulled down my sleeve."[19] Nobody asked Sundberg about the bruises and immediately after the interview the university made them a formal offer for the job. More than once, Sundberg narrates elsewhere in the book, her friend Rebecca saw bruises on her body that she did her best to explain away—that she did it in her sleep, or that she was clumsy. Rebecca never questioned what was truly happening.

"[D]espite the commonness of everyday terrorism [domestic violence] it tends to be hidden or excused: it is distanced despite its everywhereness," scholar Rachel Pain wrote in a 2014 article. "The terrorism that the state makes paradoxically banal is the one which is extremely rare."[20] Survivors become experts in hiding what's happening, but almost always there are noticeable manifestations of the harm that's occurring. We ignore them because it's easier for us to project danger onto people we don't know. It means we don't then have to consider the violence committed by those close to us, and it means we don't have to consider our role in making the violence stop.

Bringing Justice Home

Our criminal justice system is designed to capture and incarcerate the people we're told to fear—not those really doing the greatest harm. So it should come as no surprise that, by and large, the court and prison system doesn't serve the needs of people experiencing domestic violence or sexual assault, or help build a future where that violence is no longer occurring. Survivors of violence are often reluctant to come forward because they're fearful of not being believed or enduring traumatic evidence-collection exams and intensive questioning from cops. Many survivors don't want to report the violence or assault because they don't want to see their friend or loved one locked up, or because they rely on the one committing harm for money, citizenship, or other kinds of support. For people of color or undocumented folk, simply calling the police could place them in danger.

Moreover, when a person who's committed violence is arrested and prosecuted, it's not the needs, desires, or well-being of the survivor that are centered. Instead, it's the preferences of the state and the powerful that take center stage. Prosecutors are acting in the interest of their office, not the person who was harmed, which is why they sometimes pursue criminal cases against the expressed wishes of victims, and even force them to testify. Moreover, recent history has reminded us that not all perpetrators (or victims) are created equal under the law. Harvey Weinstein avoided facing criminal charges for decades; that his victims were mostly actresses who had some access to power and money underlines just how poorly the system might work for victims with no such resources. And while putting someone behind bars might prevent them from committing additional harm, it largely doesn't provide them with the opportunity to understand the pain they caused their victim or the support they need to change their conduct.

The belief that increasing policing, prosecutions, and imprisonment is the best way to address violence against women—a political stance termed "carceral feminism" by writer Victoria Law—is especially dangerous because it lands some of the most marginalized survivors behind bars instead of getting them help.[21] Ky Peterson, a black trans man, was sentenced to twenty years in prison after defending himself against a sexual assault. Marissa Alexander, a black woman, was sentenced to twenty years for firing a warning shot against her abusive ex-husband; after a worldwide campaign on her behalf, Alexander was released under a plea deal. Prisons are sites of routine physical and sexual violence, with trans and gender-nonconforming individuals and anyone perceived to be gay at a heightened risk of assault. "In aligning themselves with a deadly and racist legal system," says the group Survived and Punished, which campaigns on behalf of criminalized survivors, "anti-violence advocates have indeed sought safety from the most regular purveyors of insecurity and violence against marginalized people."[22]

Envisioning a Different Kind of Justice System

Prisons do not solve problems. They simply exacerbate or obscure them. "Incarceration serves as the default answer to many of the worst social problems plaguing this country—not because it solves them, but because it buries them," writes Maya Schenwar in her 2014 book, *Locked Down, Locked Out.* "By isolating and disappearing millions of Americans, prison conveniently disappears deeply rooted issues that society—or rather, those with power in society—would rather not attend to."[23]

A society governed by socialist norms could potentially address many of the political and economic issues that feed the prison-industrial complex. Property crime would be much less of an issue—everyone would have enough food to eat and a roof over their head. The state wouldn't endeavor to prohibit drug use or sex work, or lock people up who engaged in either. People with mental health issues would get the medical care they need, instead of being put behind bars. But things are more complicated when it comes to more immediate forms of harm. We don't know if domestic or sexual violence would exist in a socialist future—but given the resilience of misogyny throughout history (including on the left today), we can imagine that it might. So how would we address that violence if and when it did occur?

We know that our current approach doesn't work for survivors. Instead of ignoring the reality of domestic and sexual violence, or placing perpetrators behind bars, transformative justice processes seek to make this violence visible and to engage the community at large in working toward change. According to Generation Five, a group that campaigns to end the sexual abuse of children, transformative justice is a "liberatory approach [that] seeks safety and accountability without relying on alienation, punishment, or State or systemic violence, including incarceration and policing."[24] It's a survivor-centered approach premised on the notion that accountability for individual acts of violence must go hand in hand with the transformation of society as a whole.

By exploring ways that some communities endeavored to address domestic and sexual violence without resorting to incarceration, we can begin to think about what this ideal world might look like and consider how we'll have to change ourselves—and our communities—in order to make that future possible.

Healing Circles

Some indigenous communities have opted to implement healing circles to address sexual and domestic violence. In the documentary *Hollow Water* (2000), filmmaker Bonnie Dickie follows members of the Ojibway Nation living in a tiny village in Manitoba as they attempt to find a new way to address the widespread sexual abuse of Ojibway youth.[25] Although the film takes place in Canada, since the first moment of colonization through today, indigenous people across North America have had fraught relationships with police departments and other agents of the state. A 2016 investigation by *In These Times* found that Native Americans "are being killed by police at a higher rate than any other group in the country."[26]

When the film opens, community leaders say that the time to stay silent about the abuse is over—but they also say they have no interest in relying on criminal justice solutions put forward by the provincial government. Community leaders petition the Manitoba authorities for permission to work directly with the perpetrators in Hollow Water, with the hope that they could get them to admit what they'd done. People accused of violence agreed to participate in a Community Holistic Circle Healing (CHCH) to engage with each other and a counselor to come to terms with and change their behavior.

As the film illustrates, it can take a long time for someone who committed harm to recognize and name it. The two perpetrators of harm profiled in the film, Deb and Richard, spent two years in the CHCH before they acknowledged the violence they had inflicted on their children. Nor was that the end of their "sentence": by the time the film ended, Deb and Richard had spent five years in a circle, and community members were just considering whether their children could be returned to their home. But they did eventually accept responsibility for their conduct and commit themselves to change.

There was a great deal of buy-in to the CHCH approach from community members because expelling everyone who had committed harm—a substantial minority or even majority of people in Hollow Water—was simply inconceivable. People had grown up alongside one another in this rural, isolated community; everyone relied on one another to survive. "We live in a community. Offenders live in that community," said Joyce Bushie, one of the founders of the CHCH program. "There's no way those offenders can be put outside of that community. We have to live with them." The kinds of communal ties that enabled the success of the CHCH do not necessarily exist everywhere. Indeed, it is precisely because the United States treats certain people as expendable that our carceral system is possible.

Accountability Processes

In some queer, radical, and punk communities, survivors and their supporters have opted to utilize accountability processes to try to address harm when it occurs. An accountability process begins when a survivor comes forward to say she has been harmed and that she wants the person who committed the harm to take responsibility for what they've done. Processes can vary widely, but generally a team of community members is put together to support the survivor, intervene with the perpetrator, or both.

If the perpetrator agrees to be part of the process, the survivor outlines what she wants from them—for example, a public or private apology, not to have to share space with them for a given period of time, for the perpetrator to inform their close friends and current and future partners about their past conduct, and so on. In most cases, the person who committed the harm is also obligated to take steps to unlearn their behavior—for example, by completing an anti-violence curriculum designed and implemented by people on their support team.

One issue that has plagued accountability processes in many radical communities is how to evaluate whether someone is really engaging in the process in good faith or only going through the motions in order to maintain their social status. In the criminal justice system, we have a very concrete metric for measuring whether someone has atoned or been punished sufficiently for their wrongdoing—namely, when a person completes their criminal sentence. In transformative justice processes, it is inevitably more difficult to name a tangible goal, in part because the healing of the survivor, the perpetrator, and the community isn't something that can be given a definite end—for all parties involved, moving toward healing is often a lifelong process.

Moreover, in the radical communities where accountability processes are implemented, there may be an absence of the long-lasting ties that are key to fostering individual change. "Can we enforce our wishes on [a perpetrator] who isn't cooperative—and as anarchists, should we?" the CrimethInc. collective asked in a 2013 blog post on the pitfalls of accountability processes. "In a transient subculture, can we realistically commit to following up with someone for years into the future, and establishing structures of support and accountability that will last that long?"[27] The failure of so many accountability processes indicates how hard it can be to utilize transformative justice processes in communities (often privileged ones) where people aren't bound to one another in real and tangible ways. What might it look like to foster those relationships in a utopian future?

I've examined only two approaches to transformative justice in this chapter. These examples don't necessarily represent blueprints for how transformative justice will operate in the world at large. Different communities will have different needs and face different challenges in addressing harm. Abolitionist alternatives to prison will have to be developed and negotiated on a local level with the active involvement and engagement of all parties. In selecting these two examples, I hoped to illustrate one basic point: that in order for transformative justice processes to work, people need to feel tied into the communities in which they live. They need to be willing to show up when someone is accused of perpetrating harm, even and especially when it's someone they know. They need to be willing to confront and recognize the violence someone committed, but still see that individual as capable of change, and be invested in supporting them through that process. Most of all, transformative justice approaches require that people be willing to hold their friends, lovers, and comrades accountable for their behavior, and to consider how all of us—even those of us who don't perpetrate violence—help promote or sustain a culture of violence through silence and complicity. If democratic socialism envisions that workers take ownership over their workplaces, it's no great stretch from there to imagine community members taking ownership over the systems that sustain accountability and justice.

Building strong relationships and communities is essential to implementing any abolitionist solution, not just ones that address sexual or intrafamilial violence. MASK (Mothers/Men Against Senseless Killings) was founded in Chicago in 2015, when Tamar Manasseh and others decided they needed to intervene to stem the deadly shootings that were happening in their neighborhoods. During the summer, the group set up tables and chairs on a street corner in the city known for bouts of violence. They provided food for people passing by and patrolled a one-mile radius of the neighborhood on foot. Shootings and fights on the block reportedly decreased, a change Manasseh attributes to friendships fostered at the local level.

There's a symbiotic relationship between efforts to reduce the harm of the criminal justice system and efforts to build a new future. Initiatives like cop watching, where community members meet up to observe and document police misconduct, also function as a space for neighbors to meet and invest in each other's day-to-day lives. What makes these projects successful is community members seeing them through in the long term. "You have to be more committed to changing things than everybody else is to keeping things the same," Manasseh stressed in an interview with the *Chicago Reader*. "That's what I've learned. Consistency is the absolute key to everything."[28]

A society governed by socialist values would likely make the conditions for transformative justice more possible. If people were regularly engaged in democratic processes at their jobs and in their neighborhoods, and had their basic needs provided for, they would be more able and willing to sustain relationships of mutual accountability. If capital did not govern how we come to view harm or threat, we might be able to nurture a world that prioritized the safety, healing, and well-being of those around us.

Building Tomorrow's Transformative Justice Today

Here's my dream for what justice and security would look like in a radically utopian future: a world where people feel the *most* safe in their homes, intimate relationships, and families—and have a community to support them and their loved ones when violence does occur.

Creating this world will require us to first do hard work on ourselves. We'll need to dig deep when we feel afraid that we might fall prey to harm and ask ourselves to consider the political utility of that fear. We'll need to ask ourselves, each and every day, what forms of violence and harm we aren't seeing or acknowledging, even though it is undoubtedly in our midst.

Creating this world will also require us to transform how we think about those around us. We'll need to familiarize ourselves with signs of abuse and be proactive in speaking to friends and loved ones if we fear harm is ongoing. We'll commit to listening to survivors when and if they say they've been harmed by us or someone in our circles or families. We'll devote ourselves to holding people to account—even if it takes months, years, or decades before they're able to address and take responsibility for what they've done. We'll help create communities that value consent, communication, and vulnerability instead of anger, entitlement, or aggressiveness.

And as we create the world we want and need, we'll work to change the one we live in now. Today, in cities and states across the country, organizers are pushing for legislation to limit or end the use of solitary confinement; reform parole boards so that long-term and elderly prisoners can be released; prevent the construction or expansion of jails or prisons; divert people from prison through the use of restorative justice programs; and so much more. These nonreformist reforms at the city, state, and federal level must go hand in hand with the work we do on our own. Importantly, these two buckets of work are not divorced from each other. By joining community initiatives and campaigns—whether to challenge street-based violence, watch the cops, prevent the construction of new prisons or jails, or end the targeted prosecution of black and brown people—we'll foster long-term relationships of trust, respect, and accountability. Whether we live in a socialist utopia or not, it's only by building new kinds of communities that we'll be able to tear down the prison walls and rely on one another instead.

It's easy to talk about abolitionism in the abstract. The harder work is considering what we all have to change to build the world we want—one without prisons, prosecutors, or police.

On Immigration: A Socialist Case for Open Borders

Michelle Chen

BORDERS—AND THE DEBATES THAT SURROUND THEM—HAVE ALWAYS been about more than walls and papers. As political iconography and military symbol, border zones are the sieve through which whole nations project dominion and power in the public sphere—nowhere more so than in the United States. Under Trump, America's conscience has been rocked by harrowing images of the inhumanity of our immigration regime, of children ripped crying from their mothers' arms and dying of neglect in federal custody. But while his administration builds its brand on the spectacle of a nationwide barricade, the concrete political realities behind it long predate Trump's bravado; from Reagan to Obama, militarizing the border has long been a bipartisan priority, tapping into a deep seam of fear and prejudice at the core of the national psyche.

In the United States and beyond, the tensions reflected along borders speak to underlying social anxieties that have much less to do with who is at the border and why they come than with who we are and what this country fails to offer the people within its own bounds.

Even as borderlines blur, though, calls for "open borders" or even "no borders" (the distinction between which will be explored later) are dismissed as tantamount to chaos; unfettered free movement seems an unthinkable prospect. People's terror at eliminating national borders reflects a deep-seated fear of instability, economic loss, or cultural alienation—at least when it comes to the unchecked movement of people; quite the opposite for the free flow of commercial capital, of course.

Democratic socialism offers a path toward a system of government that respects human dignity above all—and there is no surer way to uphold human dignity than to elevate human rights above national sovereignty. With far-right parties ascendant at home and abroad, appeals to nationalism and nationhood are firmly the province of the right. Eradicating the kind of restrictionist, zero-sum mentality that colors migration policy around the world means rejecting those allegiances in all forms. Equity can never square with a border or with accompanying laws and institutions that criminalize the right to move. A socialist movement should demand nothing less than a vision of global liberation unbound by borders, where people's movement across territories should be as frictionless as possible.

It is impossible to plot out exactly what this would look like in every corner of the world. However, we do know that our current bordered world order is increasingly untenable—it is unconscionable on a moral, political, economic, and ecological level. Although not every wall can be demolished at once, resisting them whenever and wherever possible is integral to rebuilding society from the ground up. If the walls fall, so do many if not most of the institutional mechanisms that enforce them: the checkpoints, the papers, the barbed wire and cages, and—most of all—the fear.[1]

With these principles as a baseline, we can start to sketch out an open-borders-based policy that presumes inclusion, rather than exclusion, as its basic goal.

Who Needs Borders?

The heightened tensions around immigration control today suggest that Trump's border security obsession reflects a long-standing pillar of U.S. politics that is anchored deep in the national psyche. From a historical perspective, however, modern-day immigration controls are a recent phenomenon, emerging in the twilight of manifest destiny in the late nineteenth century with the Chinese Exclusion Act. Formal enforcement of the southern border arose only haphazardly in the early twentieth century. Mexican laborers traversed between countries more or less freely for casual jobs. It was only during the postwar period that our modern-day "border security" regime was erected as a permanent part of the federal infrastructure.[2]

The postwar revival of border ideology came amid the identity crisis besieging the United States in the wake of its defeat in Vietnam: the reign of Pax Americana seemed to have suddenly collapsed, and reactionary ideologues and liberals alike began to mull over ways to rejuvenate the cracked edifice of America's superego—to reclaim its mantle as the democratic beacon of the "free world." And because the modern free world that the American empire had christened in its image was no longer fit for colonial conquest, conservatives looked inward and sought to "take control" of its own borders instead.[3] Other aspects of the U.S. border regime are more recent still, including Immigration and Customs Enforcement (ICE), created in the aftermath of 9/11, and the network of draconian, mostly for-profit detention facilities contracted to cage apprehended immigrants, waiting indefinitely for a hearing in an absurdly backlogged court system.[4]

As the whole deportation regime has become grotesquely complex, theories about abolishing borders altogether have emerged as a rational route out of the crisis. Some envision a completely border-free global society with no territorial boundaries between nation-states, a concept often termed "no borders." A parallel vision of "open borders," meanwhile, imagines a kind of postborder national sovereignty. Under such a system, nations would likely retain considerable sovereign authority but also be more integrated into a system of mutual management of regional and global resources, labor regulation, financial and trade law, and distribution of public welfare. This new regime would not necessarily require the dismantling of sovereign nations, nor the abolition of national government as a concept. Rather, it would establish a legal framework forged on consensus among nations, as well as a shared, foundational belief that free movement is a personal right, a social entitlement, and a demographic inevitability.

A familiar analog that could serve as a model might be the multilateral treaty. This transnational framework operates today in the form of free-trade accords and economic cooperation zones, which are far more common, of course, than any kind of mutual border-sharing agreement. Going a step further, we could envision something in the shape of a contemporary global governance framework under the rubric of the United Nations, such as the International Labour Organization. There are other models designed to cope with specific regional interests, such as the European Union trading bloc and its concomitant migration arrangement, the Schengen Agreement, which in theory guarantees "free movement" within the EU. Yet all of these accords amount to half-a-loaf measures, offering some degree of stability and harm reduction yet still burdened by the moral inconsistencies endemic to national borders themselves. Ultimately, these supranational arrangements typically fail to resolve the fundamental injustice of restricting human movement.

Even the Schengen system—arguably the "purest" framework for dealing explicitly with free movement within a region—has buckled under rising bitterness among member states, primarily in reaction to an influx of refugees arriving from outside the EU seeking humanitarian protection and jobs. Previously "open" borders have been refortified, and old barriers and prejudices have resurfaced. The disintegration of the European political sphere illustrates how readily nation-states snap back into exclusion and discrimination as soon as perceived social risk from free movement begins to outweigh the prospective economic benefits of market liberalization, to which Schengen was intended as a complement. The EU Parliament, for its part, has admitted the need for comprehensive Schengen reform. Its members are concerned not only about the humanitarian situation surrounding refugees adrift in legal limbo across Europe, but also about the cost of reinstating border controls—a loss of economic activity estimated at about €100 to €230 billion over a decade.[5]

However, as long as human movement is considered valuable only for the benefits it brings to economic markets, the most essential human right of free movement will remain tethered to a system that dehumanizes and commodifies humanity. At the very least, moving toward democratic socialism demands border laws based not on commercial incentives but on priorities of public welfare. Beyond the question of managing borderlines, we need a transnational consensus on how to manage the tensions created by global inequality, while maintaining a total commitment to the principle of free movement.

Short of a completely border-free global society, we can imagine an open-borders arrangement that is both flexible and fair enough to cope much more judiciously and humanely with cross-border movements than any current system of regulation in the Global North. And even within the Global North, the examples of the EU and the relatively less securitized borders of the United States and Canada show that there are many international boundaries that exist today without militarization or heavy state regulation. As democratic socialists, we can work to build the legal foundations for transborder movement that prevents and mediates social harm at points of international or intergroup conflict. Moreover, we can work to dismantle the harm posed by the insidious symbolism of border barriers—the projections of state power in their most brutal, undemocratic forms.

The relatively fluid border system of Uganda contrasts sharply with the European bloc system that is more commonly associated with "free movement" principles. Like many other regions in the Global South, Uganda and its neighbors have been crisscrossed by multiple waves of migration, stemming from mass displacement driven by constant conflict across the region. But Uganda has a unique system of managing its refugee population, which treats them basically as authorized migrants, provides them land for resettlement in many cases, and allows them to work and move relatively freely across the country, all while accessing internationally administered humanitarian aid. Administered for years in tandem with United Nations authorities, the system has evolved to accommodate a sprawling population of some 1.5 million refugees, mostly from South Sudan and the Democratic Republic of the Congo. While the refugee population has faced deep strains in finding stability and sustenance in a nation with a per capita income of less than $700, authorities have mobilized to incorporate refugees into a longer-term institutionalized humanitarian infrastructure.

Other countries in the region have adopted varying refugee policies, ranging from Kenya's relatively repressive system of isolating refugees in vast encampments, to Ethiopia's more open program of providing hundreds of thousands of its refugees with the right to work and move freely within its borders, with plans to foster work and development opportunities that help citizens and migrants alike. Uganda's innovative approach is by no means a perfect system. The insecure, corruption-prone government is certainly challenged in providing adequate resources. Nonetheless, Uganda stands out in the region as a model for how a country with scarce resources might— by leveraging international assistance and domestic political will—achieve a kind of social equilibrium, accepting mass migration as a more or less permanent aspect of its social landscape. Despite resource gaps there that are typical of the Global South, Uganda's policies do evince a promising political reality: people are capable of coexisting in relative peace if there is a supportive social framework for cooperation. By embracing a political culture of openness, undergirded by international support, a deliberately inclusive immigration policy can bridge divides of nationality and ethnicity, while mollifying the social trauma that displacement both reflects and perpetuates. With these realities in mind, we should—and must—believe that a borderless world is one toward which human society is constantly evolving, fueled by the indomitable will of human movement that has always fueled radical movements for social progress.[6]

Migration and Markets

Today, migration places both ends of the political spectrum in the United States in unlikely alignment. The opposition to open borders on the right is, not surprisingly, fueled by xenophobia and pernicious notions of racial purity. The rhetoric that opening borders will harm U.S. workers has been molded into a racist, right-wing populist canard by archconservatives like former attorney general Jeff Sessions, who proclaimed, "It is not caring, but callous, to bring in so many workers that there are not enough jobs for them or those already living here." But even bona fide left-wingers like Vermont senator Bernie Sanders echoed this drastically oversimplified notion of scarcity of jobs and "theft" of hardworking Americans' jobs, in arguing during his first presidential campaign that "open borders" was not a progressive policy idea but rather a systemic threat to American livelihoods propped up by the Koch Brothers. An underregulated border, according to many on the left, inevitably means deregulated labor markets and a catastrophic downward spiral. Thus, whether argued from the left or the right, the anti-immigrant narrative revolves around a sense of competition—that migrants' gain would inevitably come at the expense of "our" welfare state, or "our" livelihoods.[7]

The left case for border restriction centers on protecting the "legal" workers from market competition—through a tiered workforce structure that renders "alien" workers a permanent underclass. However, transnational mobility is not inherently at odds with workers' rights. In fact, removing restrictions on labor mobility is key to combating the forces of capital that have a much greater interest in border control than ordinary workers do. After all, bosses win when they monopolize control of the definition of a worker's legitimacy, thus exploiting both "legal" and "illegal" workers simultaneously as twin planks of a tiered workforce. This dilemma cannot be fixed by dodging behind fences. It can only be combated by resisting corporate power from below. A truly fair labor law would encourage the opposite of exclusion: it would incorporate as many workers as possible under a single, just standard.

By extending labor regulations and related social protections, a government could check some of the major abuses created by immigration barriers, including the exploitation and abuse of low-wage migrant labor, as well as the scourge of human trafficking—an industry that runs on smuggling networks that capitalize on the market for "cheap" migrant labor. In addition, the many billions invested in "border security" and enforcement regimes would be largely eliminated under a system free of the draconian restrictions placed on migration, especially in the U.S. context. Trump's 2018 budget for Homeland Security, which administers border and immigration enforcement, was roughly $47 billion, $5 billion of which was spent on intensifying ICE's deportation raids and arrests—nearly double the amount spent in 2010, when the Obama administration was already deporting people at a massive rate.[8]

There are other potential material gains that would be yielded by a policy enabling people to migrate as freely as goods and services. Simply allowing workers to pursue favorable opportunities anywhere they see fit, according to one cost-benefit projection, would boost global GDP by 20 to 60 percent. More generous estimates project gains ranging from 67 to 250 percent of world GDP due to increased, unrestricted trade and international investment. (These are, however, projections for overall economic growth, so by current standards, these statistics alone tell us little about how wealth would be redistributed under such a system, which is obviously of primary concern when mapping out a socialist transformation.)

From a socialist perspective, of course, any case for open borders must go beyond optimistic projections of resulting economic growth. The value of free movement lies in the freedom itself, not in the profit yielded from migration as a vehicle for growth.

Defining Freedom Across Borders

Today's border controls have less to do with "securing" borders, than with a desire to punish, humiliate, and abuse the people crossing them. They typically reflect and amplify forms of unfreedom that operate within borders;

in the absence of the constitutional protections reserved for citizens, border control becomes social control. One major benefit of eliminating border controls, with both economic and social ramifications, is the eradication of the social harms associated with illicit migration.

Both efforts to "manage" migration and ban entry by certain groups stem from the same impulses of defensiveness against outside threats and fears of "alien" invaders. Those granted access under limited immigration systems are generally sorted based on an elaborate set of social sieves, from racial cues to political ideology to literacy tests. Many asylum protections, moreover, are awarded based on whether the applicant meets some threshold of desperation seen as meriting humanitarian relief: pleading for protection based on specific criteria like religious or political persecution, or other immediate threats such as war, genocide, or torture. Discriminatory filters at the border are sometimes also biased toward accepting "women and children" refugees—a category based on the most limited Western cultural norms of gender and family structure—as opposed to single boys or men.[9]

Similarly, state "anti-crime" agendas have also facilitated the mass detention and deportation of undocumented migrants. In the United States, the entanglement of the civil immigration laws with the criminal justice system has solidified stereotypes of migrant criminality while intensifying the prison-industrial complex's oppressive presence in communities of migrants, people of color, and other marginalized groups.

Another channel for legal migration in the postwar United States, family reunification between resident migrants and relatives who arrive later, aims ostensibly to keep households together by allowing close relatives to rejoin immigrant relatives. Generally the rules restrict admission to one's close relatives or spouse, and additional restrictions on permanent residency and work authorization might further relegate women in particular to economic dependency on male partners—a situation that easily shades into abuse when women's legal status is premised on the relationship to a male spouse.[10]

Removing territorial and legal distinctions based on immigration status would be critical for eliminating all forms of discrimination in the legal system, not only because foreign or undocumented status itself becomes a barrier to equity and opportunity, but also because the immigration regime itself serves to legitimize other forms of discrimination based on race, gender, religion, or ideology.

For situations of humanitarian crisis, such as an influx of refugees that strains the capacity of the host country's existing welfare system, the humanitarian and legal tools that have long been in place under the Geneva Convention Relating to the Status of Refugees could be a tangible starting point for developing a system for triaging migrant welfare provision. The process would obviously not be easy or conflict-free, but there are models of solidarity-based aid programs that break out of hierarchical models of official international aid and provide a scaffold for adjusting a society's care resources to support people's needs in the long and short term, without regard to nationality or migration status. To create a system of global justice, these principles must be enshrined in a legal framework that is not just reserved for "emergencies," but implemented in full cognizance of enduring crises that have become a fact of twenty-first-century life. While governmental jurisdiction across regions, groups, and communities might vary, the first principle of border dismantlement must be that basic rights to food, housing, and personal dignity be respected by any host and afforded to any arrival, no matter who they are or from whence they came.

Changing Climates

The need for a more equitable and rational multilateralism will only grow in the coming years as societies struggle with environmental stressors and climate crisis. The vast scope of our impending existential ecological challenges includes mass migration itself, as climate refugees are displaced to other regions. Social infrastructure must be resilient and flexible enough to deal with continual interregional or intraregional movement of populations. Whether they are farmers displaced by drought or desertification, or survivors of environmental calamity in coastal cities, migrants will be constantly on the move, and any comprehensive social welfare system must be resilient enough to absorb the social impact of constant environmentally induced demographic shifts.

Migration must be a guiding determinant of a global, cooperative approach to protecting human rights and welfare in the era of climate crisis.

People will need to relocate to escape disasters like drought, flooding, or desertification. But these processes must be negotiated and managed via a legal process that is public facing, democratic, and rooted in mutual consent. Environmentally conscious socialism embodies the collective need for a truer, freer human condition, balancing in coexistence with the ecology enveloping us; socialism across borders necessarily entails socialism against borders, and—ultimately—socialism without borders.

The reality of the climate crisis underlines what would be true even if planetary destruction weren't looming. There must be a universal right to free movement as well as universal rights to health, welfare, personal dignity, education, and equality before the law. We must acknowledge that the movement of people from one society to another is as old as any social structure, and arguably much more intuitive and necessary for human survival than money, property rights, or even work.

Pathways Toward a Postborder World

Moving toward a socialist mode of production in a relatively wealthy country would not necessarily break the system of migrant trafficking that revolves around the market for low-wage surplus labor. But redistributing wealth, establishing public ownership of workplaces, and eliminating the corporate predation that ties the government's interests to those of capital would certainly mitigate the deep inequality, within and across borders, that drives many to foreign lands. A more equitable economic system would in turn help stabilize communities and make it possible for people to work, live, pursue an education, and care for their families without having to leave home.[11] A socialist society would not only safeguard people against the social trauma that leads to displacement—it would actually serve human aspiration, by offering a level of social decency, peace, and liberty that fosters social cohesion, resulting in people simply opting to remain where they are.

But people everywhere have always moved and will always be moving—a process that must be understood as part of any global compact. In terms of how a single state might begin to fashion a more humane immigration policy, the U.S. Bill of Rights might be one clear, if imperfect, starting point. There are some foundational principles of democracy and even democratic socialism that we can build upon in that document, with the aim of expanding them universally regardless of nationality or citizenship: a universally accessible social welfare system; a system for resolving legal disputes with guaranteed due process of law; a system of democratic representation in government or direct democracy with free expression; and protections against discrimination. Current constitutional jurisprudence is in many respects designed explicitly to exclude such protections, denying many noncitizens the right to legal representation, welfare entitlements, health care, and higher education. But no society could claim to honor equal rights, justice, and welfare for all unless those social benefits are truly afforded to all, and provided to the maximum extent possible.

Even absent a full open-borders-type policy, a just immigration policy for any nation-state (including the United States) would be founded on equality of citizenship and the recognition of a form of global citizenship, even if not shared worldwide. If national laws are applied selectively, there should be minimal, if any, status differentiation between the rights of immigrants and those of nonimmigrants, to ensure that migrants are not placed on a lower tier of rights or excluded from benefits. We already have some living examples of how this might work. Undocumented immigrants are at least technically eligible for minimum-wage standards, union rights, and other basic labor protections.[12] And despite the many legal barriers they face, noncitizens can petition on the basis of habeas corpus and other due process rights in the court system. None of these legal structures could be considered fully "equal justice," but they do show that lawmakers have historically accepted the principle that, generally, justice is better served by handling all cases with the same legal standards.[13]

The need to uphold universal rights and foster political empowerment in a postborder world order challenges us to reimagine participatory democracy. Yet the social enfranchisement of migrants may be more intuitive than we think. Consider refugee communities, uprooted from their homelands but also reconstituting a social infrastructure as a resettled community. In these fluid, essentially stateless social spaces, the emergent concept of self-organized government illustrates what a postborder system of enfranchisement might look like. UN refugee camps have established governing councils to deal with internal administrative and governance issues, for example. And indigenous nations that exist within and across formal nation-states too have developed their own codes that allow free migration and exchange outside the realm of territorial national law. International trade unions have offered full membership regardless of immigration status.[14]

In many cities around the world, immigrants have been increasingly incorporated into local politics, even if they are denied a formal vote. College Park, Maryland; San Francisco; and Chicago all allow undocumented immigrants to vote in at least some local elections.[15]

Throughout the United States and around the world, so-called sanctuary cities have become self-declared protected zones for migrants' rights, enabling many to access government services without regard to status. While by no means a substitute for real rights and recognition under the law, the sanctuary city framework concretizes a commitment (at least in theory) that the municipal government will do all it can to shield the undocumented from federal immigration enforcement. This allows them to enjoy, to some extent, equal rights as political subjects of the city where they have resettled—an act of both community solidarity and civic self-determination. Other innovative systems of local enfranchisement can mirror forms of citizenship to enhance social inclusivity; a citywide ID card can grant access to local public institutions and services, for example. Or municipalities can issue driver's licenses or licenses for businesses and professionals. Political engagement outside of traditional electoral politics can also take the form of participation in civic, religious, or educational communities, neighborhood cooperatives, or, of course, political movements.

These subnational moves toward inclusion cannot just encourage defiance of border restrictions, but also foster aspirations toward new forms of citizenship. As geographer Harald Bauder writes, "Sanctuary discourses disrupt the nation state's monopoly on defining who deserves to belong and who does not, and shift the scale of belonging from the national to the local. . . . Refugees and illegalized migrants are constituting themselves as political subjects in the space of sanctuary cities and thus deny the nation state the authority to decide who is a legitimate member of the polity."[16]

A final consideration for sculpting a fair migration policy is the need for recognition of a "right to return." This might mean allowing travel back to one's homeland, or, alternately, guaranteeing and facilitating a migrant's right to continue taking responsibility for the unfolding conditions in the homeland, by participating in diaspora-based political movements and institutions, or by investing remittances in the migrant's home community as part of a broader effort to develop and rehabilitate the country, particularly as part of recovery from disaster or conflict. This capacity to share allegiance across borders is one principle that is codified in the UN Global Compact for Migration as a basic way to ensure maximum democratic participation for an individual who acts as a stakeholder in two societies—in the place where one was born, and wherever one later landed, by choice or happenstance or some combination, one should have a say in how both societies are governed. Transnational cultures rooted in histories of hybridity cannot be divided; transnational people cannot be forced to trade one citizenship for another.[17]

The case for opening or eliminating borders is both radical and pragmatic. It's a radical idea in that emancipating society from borders is perhaps the most extreme version of an inclusive society—that is, an infinitely welcoming one. It chafes against all the social conventions we are trained to obey: possession of property, prioritizing individual interests over the collective, competition as the ideal mechanism for distributing resources. But reframing social policy from a perspective of openness and coexistence, rather than a stance of mistrust and restraint, offers an alternative path to what we truly seek when we desire ownership, security, self-determination, and autonomy in our lives. What we are actually seeking is simply a stable peace for ourselves and our communities. In a rapidly shrinking world, the only practical approach to making peace is to remove as many artificial divisions as possible. The most pragmatic choice, in the end, is to abolish the arbitrary barriers inherited from a time when erecting walls was the standard way to safeguard communities. In order to restructure society as a realm of limitless potential, rather than one of pervasive lack and instability, we must find security through taking apart, not building, walls separating "us" and "them." To reject their migration is to reject the right—and the social imperative—of free movement. To exclude migrants is to deny our own humanity. To live in freedom and peace, in a world that ensures the dignity of all, is to live in a world of universal fellowship, with no strangers among us.

On Foreign Policy: War from Above, Solidarity from Below

Tejasvi Nagaraja

DURING THE 1940s, THE "AMERICAN CENTURY" OF GEOPOLITICS WAS born. The period after World War II saw U.S. leaders create a new national security state amid the Cold War, and America embraced both militarization and anti-leftist interventionism at home and abroad. Within a few decades—and owing partly to America's failed war in Vietnam—the centrality and coherence of American power in shaping world affairs began to decline. Many analysts now predict that the sun will have fully set on the American primacy in geopolitics by the 2040s, giving way to a more complex geopolitical order. The CIA-affiliated National Intelligence Council has predicted that "by 2030, no country . . . will be a hegemonic power," with centers of gravity shifting toward power "networks and coalitions in a multipolar world." Even so, America's capacity to dole out destruction the world over shows few signs of slowing down.

How might democratic socialists face the path to and through this multipolar world? The most obvious work will be responding to short-term and outrageous harms of U.S. foreign policy, from ongoing wars in the Middle East to flirtations with interventions elsewhere. Yet if movements want to transform the conditions that create militarism, impoverishment, and climate change—those which make the next war more likely—they will have to do much deeper bottom-up, long-term organizing and policy making to shift the domestic and global balance of forces and build new horizons of possibility. While paying close attention to powerful interests, the priority in this work should always be the needs and concerns of ordinary people, from Baltimore to Basra to Bahia. "Anti-war" must not only be a negative rhetorical response to each new war. It must also come with a positive and tangible anti-war agenda—domestically and abroad—to make peace possible.

From where we stand now, at the end of the second decade of the twenty-first century, there's plenty to be against. In at least eight countries there are well-documented U.S. Armed Forces, or CIA-sustained air or ground operations, where American personnel themselves drop bombs or shoot guns: Afghanistan, Iraq, Pakistan, Yemen, Somalia, Libya, Syria, Niger. Soon after his inauguration, President Trump sharply escalated every front of U.S. war-making, compared to what he inherited from his predecessor. Aggressive U.S. sanctions were imposed on Iran, North Korea, and Venezuela, tied to the threat of overt or covert U.S. war. The consequences of U.S. troop wars, air wars, drone strikes, and special ops include brutality and suffering faced by local people. They also involve the empowerment of reactionary forces in those regions as well as the destabilization of civil and democratic spaces for progressive activists and policymakers. The Pentagon or CIA oversees covert or support missions in many dozens more countries, especially—increasingly—across the African continent. U.S. military aid and arms sales flow to dozens of countries, including those involved in direct human rights violations with those weapons, such as Saudi Arabia, Israel, and Egypt. U.S. diplomacy has long been implicated in anti-democratic meddling from Iran to Chile to Honduras to Venezuela. U.S. foreign and domestic military and policing policies blur together in the wars on terror, crime, and drugs as well as migration and border affairs. Beyond issues of so-called hard power, American foreign policy also involves the U.S. role in the global economic order: trade, poverty, and inequality, as well as the regulation of wealth and finance. And it includes realms such as nuclear weapons reduction, the regulation of the arms trade, disaster relief, HIV/AIDS, refugee affairs, humanitarian aid, and, of course, climate change.

Being against destructive, U.S.-led state violence around the world should be a given for democratic socialists. Yet undoing the militarism that spawns such violence also means working to reorganize the economic structures and political culture that sustain it in our own backyard.

Building Peace, Taking Power

Given how entrenched the machinery of warfare is in American and world affairs, we will not achieve a utopian U.S. foreign policy or a nonviolent geopolitics in the near term, but we can take meaningful strides in that direction—in dynamic relationship with counterparts in dozens of other countries. None of this will be simple or straightforward. In the 2010s, we saw some openings for challenges to a long-standing foreign policy status quo—from President Obama's diplomacy with Iran and Cuba to progressive and liberal Congresspeople starting to criticize Saudi Arabia and Israel as never before. Yet the tenor of our foreign policy remains far to the right of where democratic socialists should be pushing it.

Indeed, in each period of leftward breakthroughs in federal policy—in the 1860s, 1930s, and 1960s—progressives had to negotiate compromises, if not complicities, with a warfare state and imperial expansion. The peak period of left and labor influence on U.S. politics, FDR's New Deal, culminating in World War II, reached its climax under a patriotic total-war machine. Over the 1930s and 1940s, activists and policymakers challenged economic inequality, while some made real efforts to fight racism at home and imperial meddling abroad. In a cruel turn, the momentum from the left pushing for egalitarian expansions of state power also facilitated decidedly repressive expansions of state power and empowered reactionary forces. In order to gain support for certain pro-union and redistributive policies in the New Deal and home-front war mobilization, left-leaning advocates compromised with and empowered southern Democrats and some northerners, too, who perpetuated race and gender inequalities in implementing these programs. The war machine built to fight the global far right also targeted and interned Japanese Americans. And shortly after the end of World War II, the Cold War ushered in a permanent militarization that targeted the global and domestic left. The era that inaugurated a Social Security paradigm built a national security one, too, birthing a pervasive welfare state along with an osmotic warfare state.

Today as well, domestic and foreign policy and welfare and warfare legislation and coalitions will continue to blur together, in ways that are beyond progressives' total control. If policymakers want to pass bold health care, climate, or jobs bills that benefit the majority of the population in the coming years, they will of course have to forge broad coalitions and make some compromises. They will have to try to do that in a way that doesn't betray or stigmatize minority populations, or fall into complicity with discriminatory or militarist agendas and expenditures. How, for instance, will Green New Deal advocates balance their need to work with large-scale, defense-adjacent public agencies and private companies like the Department of Energy and Boeing?

These trade-offs are even more relevant as democratic socialists start contesting for power at higher and higher levels. Through the Cold War and the War on Terror, progressives who have tried to advance social democratic and anti-racist policies have been undermined with accusations that they are weak in the face of violent, racialized threats to security; that they are naively neglecting grave dangers to the American public in favor of more apparently parochial concerns like poverty. Politicians, including democratic socialists Bernie Sanders and Alexandria Ocasio-Cortez, have navigated this hostile terrain by taking a strong alternative stance against some foreign policies—coming out strongly against U.S. support for the Saudi war in Yemen, for example—while compromising or conceding on others. Progressive politicians will continue to make some mixed bag of calls on key foreign policies in the coming decades.

Should dozens of progressive and even socialist politicians fill the Capitol—or if one even lands in the White House—they would be responsible for leading not only the redistributive agencies of the government, but the carceral and militarist ones too. However endeared and committed they are to the left, those politicians would face this responsibility every single day, mostly lacking the power to set the agenda themselves, but rather having to respond to unfavorable events and controversies far beyond their control. Given all this, social movements and activists will have to maintain a degree of independence from progressive and even socialist politicians, not offering uncritical support, but holding them accountable when they disappoint or betray on one or another front—particularly when it comes to foreign policy.

Toward a New Internationalism

As progressives mount a principled opposition to the range of U.S. war making, part of doing so must also involve building solidarity with those who have been on the other end of U.S. military interventions. We can begin by looking to models from the 2000s and 2010s, to see what this work of bottom-up solidarity could look like in the future. For example, the organization About Face: Veterans Against the War built ties with the Organization for Women's Freedom in Iraq, as they envisioned a shared Right to Heal. Seeing their struggles as not identical but linked, they demand U.S. accountability for American veterans' trauma and injuries as well as the violence and environmental justice damage of the U.S. war for Iraqis. While the goals of this campaign are ultimately for material outcomes, this is also about changing the culture and the symbols of international affairs to promote solidarity from below and to recognize common humanity. Even many of the most sincere leftists who are horrified by U.S. wars can instinctively imagine Iraqis and Afghans only as dead people or as helpless victims fated for wave upon wave of violence. Latin America is imagined as a place of economic justice struggles, but "war-torn countries" often aren't. Solidarity work highlighting Afghan and Iraqi labor, feminist, economic, and environmental justice is an anti-racist intervention in itself. The less we allow the United States and the world to see certain places as "shithole countries," in Donald Trump's words, the less they will seem available and vulnerable for further war and plunder.

The principal task of a left worth its name is to see glimpses of bottom-up democratic struggle, especially in the contexts where they seem most unlikely—and to imagine an accountable solidarity, even if those relationships are hard and slow to build. In an effort to do just that, a host of progressive diasporic groups have emerged in the United States and elsewhere, such as the Iraqi Transnational Collective and Afghans United for Justice, which are building bridges across countries and generations. In the 2010s, Yemeni, Kurdish, and Syrian civil society initiatives asked powerful geopolitical stakeholders, including the United States, to be part of negotiating a de-escalation of multipolar regional wars, and attending to humanitarian, refugee, rebuilding, and reparative needs. While maintaining a vigilant criticism of the harm the United States causes on the world stage, those on the left will also have to evaluate and debate proposals for potentially positive, diplomatic uses of America's global power.

Today, progressive legislators who have a voice in the federal government could try to help scale up these types of solidarity efforts—of, say, building relationships with Iraqi counterparts to strategize reparations.

They could find ways to hold CIA officials accountable, in conversation with the Center for Constitutional Rights and outspoken survivors such as Maher Arar, whom the United States rendered to the Assad regime for torture in Syria. Building on the 2010s congressional testimonies of drone attack survivors and others harmed by U.S. militarism, progressive legislators will have to use their power to raise such voices for accountability and justice. With a more progressive Congress, there are a number of initiatives that could gain steam—like Senator Chris Murphy's successful resolution to end U.S. support for the Saudi-led war in Yemen. Similar efforts could take off as well, like Representative Hank Johnson's bill to restrict U.S. military aid to Honduras and Representative Betty McCollum's bill to restrict U.S. military aid to Israel.

While attending to U.S. foreign policies in the Middle East and Africa, progressive policymakers and activists must also pay heed to diverse Americans' disproportionate diasporic connections to Latin America and the Caribbean. The Grassroots Global Justice Alliance, a coalition of community organizations, for example, has been a dynamic force in linking front-line working-class organizing across the United States with economic and climate justice movements from Haiti to Honduras to the U.S.-Mexico border. Human rights and aid groups like Doctors Without Borders have built bridges of solidarity with victims of militarism, war, and global injustice. United Students Against Sweatshops and the Workers Rights Consortium not only have been watchdogs against labor exploitation by multinational apparel corporations in Latin America and Asia, but also helped set up a model garment factory in the Dominican Republic (Alta Gracia), where workers have safe working conditions, good pay, and a union producing clothing sold by U.S. universities. As the Trump years have shown, from Hurricane Maria in Puerto Rico to barbaric immigration policies, the United States' treatment of colonially acquired territories and of migrants on either side of the border must be front and center for facing our interlinked domestic and foreign policy nightmares and dreams.

Any twenty-first-century internationalism should reach out further still, beyond an inherited framework of America's natural allies and kindred spirits globally. This is especially urgent as top U.S. Republican operatives are increasing their stake in far-right internationalism—in affinity with chauvinistic authoritarian parties in Brazil, Hungary, Saudi Arabia,

Israel, Russia, France, and elsewhere. Within the realm of left-leaning parties, the European leftist Yanis Varoufakis has appealed to Bernie Sanders to help build a Progressive International and an International Green New Deal. Such conversations can transcend static notions of "the West" and "the rest," or even a simplistic read of the Global North and Global South. Going further, they can help redefine and debate among themselves what kind of right-wing forces we face, and what a left worth its name should actually look like today from the standpoint of poor and working-class people around the world. While working to bridge divides between Europeans and Latin American leftists—often seen as counterparts for fair-trade and climate-justice conversations—progressives in the coming years can also build ties with allies in Palestine, Iraq, and other Middle Eastern countries around economic and environmental justice, and around moving from extractive, fossil-fueled neoliberalism toward sustainable fair trade.

As Martin Luther King Jr. asserted, true peace cannot be achieved with "merely the absence of tension" but also requires "the presence of justice." The number of billionaires has been increasing, and the taxes they pay have been decreasing, while about 3.4 billion people—almost half the world's population—live on less than $5.50 a day.

A progressive, internationalist approach to foreign policy—which looks to de-escalate conflicts and stem the rising authoritarian right—will thus have to tackle corporate and plutocratic power as well. One of the most urgent foreign policy tasks for progressive policymakers in the near- and midterm future will be aggressively taxing and regulating the wealth and transactions of rich firms and individuals—in part to curb their ability to meddle in and capture politics, in their own country or any other. The successful campaign of Google employees, who refused to consult on U.S. drone war, is one glimpse of the shape of shared struggles to come. On another front, JPMorgan Chase is invested in the high-tech firms that are driving China's anti-Muslim mass incarceration, with McKinsey & Company profiting as China's management consultants and Academi (formerly known as Blackwater) ready to play an armed mercenary role patrolling reeducation camps in Xinjiang. How might the next generation of U.S. policymakers—working with allies around the world—regulate and block these American corporations' role in global human-rights abuses, whether against those who are caged in China, sieged in Yemen, bombed in Gaza, or exploited in Zambian mines?

Transitioning Livelihoods:
Toward a Peace Economy

If progressive politicians gain more power in government in the not-too-distant future, their ambitiously egalitarian fiscal agenda—for Medicare for All, for a Green New Deal—will run up against a federal discretionary budget, half of which reliably goes toward defense and a military-industrial complex of weaponized economics. In the twenty-first century, America has had about eight hundred military bases at any given time, six hundred of those overseas across seventy countries. Among the almost 170 governments that have a military, the United States accounts for more than one-third of all global military spending. The United States spends more on defense than China, Russia, Saudi Arabia, India, France, the United Kingdom, and Japan combined. This sustains a 2 million–strong armed forces and its robust military welfare state. Under the auspices of the GI Bill, the Military Health System, and Veterans Affairs, career service members, veterans, and their loved ones have access to a social safety net including health care, education, child care, housing, affirmative action, legal resources, and other welfare supports. Progressives, of course, want the federal government to provide these kinds of services to everyone—but in a much better and demilitarized form. These programs should be universal and put us all in the same boat, rather than segmenting the perceived interests of so-called military communities off from their civilian neighbors.

Indeed, when Medicare for All or a Green New Deal is proposed, a "guns versus butter" logic will be used to argue that the desired funds are scarce because the military needs them. Such progressive policies will be challenged by entrenched interests invested in a divide between the military and civilian welfare state and by Pentagon contractors who would be stigmatized for their own environmental harms and massive carbon footprints by comprehensive climate legislation. American defense firms dominate the world's $398 billion arms sales industry, according to the Stockholm International Peace Research Institute. In 2017, Lockheed Martin had $44.9 billion in defense contracts, followed by Boeing ($26.9 billion), Raytheon ($23.9 billion), Northrop Grumman ($22.4 billion), and General Dynamics ($19.5 billion). The combined compensation for the CEOs of these five companies was $96 million. Any effort to advance a democratic socialist or social democratic agenda has to face head-on the military budget and a military-industrial economy. At least for now, war is work, and war is welfare. As a consequence, domestic economics and policies are inextricable from foreign policy.

It's for this reason that the mid-twenty-first century demands not only a Green New Deal toward a sustainable, zero-carbon economy, but also a transition from military jobs and welfare toward an economy based on civilian jobs that address human needs. To lead a shift toward a peace economy, American progressives can't just moralize about militarism. They have to strategize a *just transition* of economic livelihoods. Between armed forces service members, their loved ones, and veterans, millions of Americans depend on the military welfare state. Many more live and work in military-base towns and counties or in other civilian employment for the warfare state. Others live and work in company towns and counties, with employment dominated by Pentagon-contracting firms. This military-industrial complex implicates not only corporations branded as weapons contractors supplying the U.S. Armed Forces, its allies, and other regimes around the world, like Lockheed Martin and Raytheon. It also includes Amazon, Microsoft, Verizon, Motorola, Caterpillar, Hewlett-Packard, Johns Hopkins University, General Electric, and a host of "civilian"-branded industries that rely on Pentagon contracts to subsidize their research and nonmilitary business too. Across military service and the military-industrial complex, many millions of Americans' employment and welfare are bound up in the war machine. And because of the outsize role of military service, military bases, or Pentagon-procurement industries in hundreds of counties—as well as official and unofficial cultural propaganda—the *perception* among many millions of Americans of having a military-linked livelihood is even greater.

Previous social movements have hoped for a reconversion from a militarized economy to a more peacefully productive one. At the end of World War II, Walter Reuther of the United Auto Workers emerged as the most visible labor leader in the New Deal coalition; Congress of Industrial Organizations unions had skyrocketed in membership and influence amid the World War II war machine's demand for weapons, war supplies, and fossil fuels. In the postwar moment, Reuther argued that since American citizens had massively subsidized the military-industrial war production machine, the reconversion process should take the shape of robust nationalization. Inspired by the

New Deal's Tennessee Valley Authority, industries, he suggested, could be reoriented to producing nonmilitary consumer goods and social goods like housing and transportation. In Reuther's formulation, this would require an "unswerving will to plan and work together for peace and abundance, just as we joined forces for death and violence." Writing one month after the U.S. bombings of Hiroshima and Nagasaki, Reuther concluded, "If we fail, our epitaph will be simply stated: we had the ingenuity to unlock the secrets of the universe for the purposes of destruction, but we lacked the courage and imagination to work together in the creative pursuits of peace."

Reuther's vision did not prevail. Within two years, Cold War "national security" ideas took hold. Social and economic and global power struggles were deeply interlinked. It was disproportionately the anti–civil rights and anti-union southern right wing who were empowered by the wave of permanent bases and Pentagon contracts to come. Reuther, too, would accommodate to the postwar boom in military-industrial economics justified by Cold War ideology.

The United Auto Workers' Emil Mazey was the central leader of soldier protest in the Philippines in 1946, when soldiers themselves were the vanguard of protesting postwar U.S. foreign policy. He reflected on the American labor movement's complicity in the Cold War as a top union leader two decades later. As the U.S. war in Vietnam escalated in 1966, he noted that it was not only aircraft corporations but also sectors of defense workers who had a "vested interest" in the continuation of U.S. militarism. This was "because our government has no plans, on how to use the defense plants for peacetime production." Even as the Vietnam War intensified, it was not enough to only criticize U.S. foreign policy. It was also necessary for policymakers and activists to transform economic planning, to "guarantee full employment to the workers now engaged in military production," Mazey argued. At the end of the Vietnam War, when testifying to Congress in support of a full-employment program, civil rights leader Coretta Scott King lamented, "This nation has never honestly dealt with the question of a peacetime economy."

How can progressives today imagine a just transition to make the Green New Deal away from fossil fuels also a Peace New Deal? Policymakers involved in advancing a Green New Deal, Medicare for All, basic-income, or job-guarantee agendas will have to evaluate and articulate how these proposals interface with military-service and military-industrial realms, and how they can pose an attractive alternative to war work and war welfare. From the era of a significant armed forces draft (1940–73) to the era of the "all-volunteer army" coinciding with the rise of neoliberalism (1973–present), military service is unfortunately the closest thing we have to a federal employment program. A new agenda of green and guaranteed jobs or income for all on the "producer" end, as well as a single-payer guarantee of health care, education, child care, housing, transportation, and other welfares on the "consumer" end, could prove to be a lifesaving anti-war infrastructure. If progressives can drastically reduce the military defense budget, this would further free up money, resources, labor, energies and political capital—for climate justice, health care, education, child care, housing, and transportation at home, and for global support for climate justice, fair trade, public health, disaster relief, and refugee assistance, as well as for reparations to those unjustly harmed by U.S. wars overseas.

Most military spending is highly capital intensive—weighted more toward machinery than workers. Most other forms of public spending, including education, child care, health care, clean energy, and infrastructure, do or would create more jobs per dollar than spending on war, according to studies by the National Priorities Project and other groups. The dilemma is how to guarantee both job retraining and income support for those workers in the military and defense-related industries during the transition from a war to a peace economy.

Progressive policymakers and their activist supporters will have to navigate and debate a fraught agenda for dismantling and reconverting a massive, messy beast. Over the 2010s, for example, Senator Bernie Sanders was criticized for supporting the F-35 Lightning II stealth fighter. The largest and most expensive military program ever, the $1 trillion Lockheed Martin aircraft program is considered flawed and unnecessary, harmful to humans and the environment. But it promises hundreds of direct and indirect jobs, across military service and defense industries, in Sanders's home state. In advocating for a Green New Deal, Representative Rashida Tlaib has invoked the World War II war machine's heart in Michigan industry: "We were the Arsenal of Democracy and helped save the planet from real darkness decades ago, and there's no reason why we couldn't be one of the regions to build America's green energy infrastructure and help save the planet again in the process." Like-minded policymakers can lead a conversation about a peace transition—by visiting and building relationships with constituents who are reliant on welfare and employment linked to military service and military industries, such as workers in Pentagon-procurement factories in their districts. Through building relationships and trust over a period of time, they might put forward pilot programs for converting a factory or a military base in their district toward a peaceful, public sector alternative industry. This work could create models to be scaled up in service of saving the planet, not destroying it.

Vision and Coalition, Intersectional to International

In the 2010s, the most compelling articulation of a progressive U.S. foreign policy agenda was the Movement for Black Lives (M4BL) platform. The platform advocates an "invest-divest" agenda, redistributing and reimagining priorities away from military wars abroad and carceral wars at home in the form of mass incarceration. The M4BL demands transformative reforms that would instead support quality education and universal health care, as well as full employment and just climate transition, now further articulated in the Green New Deal. The M4BL notes that "the U.S. military is the largest contributor to emissions," as the "war economy drives fossil fuel economy." The platform demands a shift in "national resources away from war making institutions to peace-making," criticizing U.S. aid to rights-violating regimes such as Israel, and U.S. drone and dirty wars from Somalia to Niger. The M4BL advocates drastic cuts in the military budget and the closure of hundreds of bases, expressly to "severely limit" America's "war-making ability." Cutting the Pentagon budget, activists note, would free up money for universal social programs, for reparations for past and continuing harms from slavery to mass incarceration, and for U.S. reparations to "countries and communities devastated by American war-making, such as Somalia, Iraq, Libya and Honduras." The M4BL's invest-divest and reparations call—bridging Americans' and Iraqis' needs and demands—is a lodestar for a progressive foreign policy agenda.

In the face of imperial surges and military base building, the left will have to embrace intersectional insurgencies and grassroots base building. While the peace movement is often stereotyped as old and white, a few peace and anti-war organizations such as War Resisters League and About Face: Veterans Against the War have put strategic energies toward supporting working-class-centered, diverse movements against domestic expressions of militarism, from Ferguson to Standing Rock. This work is not at the expense of opposing U.S. wars in the Middle East and Africa—but rather designed to endear and embed that work within the most dynamic U.S. movement visions and strategies that are already in motion.

Moreover, Americans have become increasingly skeptical of U.S. military interventions overseas, including, according to a 2018 poll, both the physical involvement of the U.S. military and extending to military aid in the form of funds or equipment as well. The poll found that 86.4 percent of Americans believe that the military should be used only as a last resort, while 57 percent think that U.S. military aid to foreign countries is counterproductive. The poll found overwhelming support for Congress to reassert itself in the oversight of U.S. military interventions, with 70.8 percent agreeing that Congress should pass legislation to restrain military action overseas.

From a Green New Deal to Medicare for All, winning any of the progressive movement's bold goals will be a heavy lift and require massive popular mobilization, even if a new progressive U.S. president had campaigned in support of those goals, and even if Congress has several dozen more progressives. The leadership and organizing skills of base-building movements for racial justice will be critical—to guide ethics and strategy, build popular buy-in, and push for an intersectional array of just transitions.

Progressives have to map the ties between local, national, and global struggles for justice. In doing so, they will have to not only speak of a statically imperial "America" and a statically tragic "Iraq"—but also draw further parallels between the black-led struggle for accountability for the Chicago police torture at Homan Square warehouse, which activists rightly compared to a CIA "black site"; the Iraqi feminist environmental-justice organizing in Hawija; native Hawaiian self-determination campaigns against U.S. military activities; and Yemeni civil society's fight for food sovereignty as the Saudi war machine choked the port of Hodeidah.

The human struggles of the likes of Homan, Hawija, Hawaii, and Hodeidah invite specific measures of U.S. accountability, reparation, and transition from U.S. activists and policymakers. If they hope to have wins for economic, social, ecological, and global justice—and if these wins are to be proud and durable ones—an American left will have to *wage anti-war* with as much resolve and commitment as the American right wages war.

Part III

The Right to a Good Life

Livable Cities

Thomas J. Sugrue

IT'S NOW AXIOMATIC AMONG URBAN PLANNERS, JOURNALISTS, AND MANY scholars that "cities are back." After decades of disinvestment, capital flight, population loss, racial and ethnic strife, and escalating crime, most of the nation's top fifty cities have seen at least a modest uptick in population, crime rates at their lowest in more than half a century, and a massive infusion of capital, particularly in real estate and downtown redevelopment projects. Once bleak cityscapes—rubble-strewn vacant lots, abandoned factories, and boarded-up stores—now sprout coffeehouses, art galleries and performance spaces, loft apartments, craft distilleries and gastropubs. In many cities, long-neglected parks have been rebuilt, often with substantial contributions from philanthropies and local businesses. One of the most striking urban phenomena, after decades of urban racial conflict and white flight, is the reappearance of white faces in formerly segregated, mostly African American or Mexican American neighborhoods.

The narrative of "comeback cities" is seductive, but it obscures the larger reality. America's metropolitan areas are highly segregated by income and race. Suburban sprawl is accelerating. The fastest job growth takes place in outer suburbs, far from where most people live and poorly served by public transit. Americans remain more dependent on cars than residents of any other affluent society, contributing to traffic congestion, accidents, high insurance rates, pollution, and global warming. The "revitalization" of some older city neighborhoods and downtowns forces middle-class and low-income households to compete for scarce housing, triggering rising rents, gentrification, and displacement. Housing costs in cities and suburbs alike are skyrocketing much faster than income increases.

America is now a suburban nation, but suburbia is no longer dominated by white, heteronormative middle- and upper-class families. Today a majority of African Americans live in suburban communities. Most new immigrants, regardless of class or place of origin, settle outside of central cities. A majority of Mexican immigrants live in suburban places. America's quintessential suburbs are now remarkably diverse. Central New Jersey, once dominated by working- and middle-class whites, is one of the most ethnically heterogeneous places in America, with sizable enclaves of immigrants and their children from India, China, Honduras, and Mexico. Orange County, California, the ground zero of the 1960s right-wing insurgency, is now majority nonwhite, its landscape defined by Vietnamese shopping malls, storefront Spanish-language churches, and postwar single-family homes turned into multigenerational residences and, sometimes, boardinghouses. Suburbs are far more racially mixed than they have ever been, and also home to a growing population of economically insecure poor and working-class residents. More than half of the nation's poor now live in suburbs, but not in the same areas as middle-income suburbanites. Most nonwhite and working-class suburbanites live in secondhand suburbs, namely, communities with older, smaller houses, decaying shopping districts, relatively underfunded public schools, and shrinking tax bases. Demographers Sean Reardon and Kendra Bischoff have found that in the 117 largest metropolitan areas in the United States, the percentage of residents living in affluent and poor communities has increased sharply, while the number living in middle-class communities has dropped sharply. Racial segregation, still a fundamental characteristic of our urban regions, has been steadily (but slowly) declining, but income and wealth segregation has been rising.

The nation's widening economic divide—greater than at any time since the Gilded Age—is reflected in metropolitan labor markets. At the top is a small class of highly educated managers and professionals, most of them white, thriving in finance, insurance, real estate, tech, and creative jobs, living in affluent enclaves in cities and suburbs. They are supported by a mass of unskilled service sector workers, disproportionately immigrant, female, and poor, who cook their meals, deliver their groceries, watch their children and care for their elderly parents, and clean their houses and offices. The metropolitan middle class, by contrast, has been shrinking, under siege from four decades of austerity policies, private sector restructuring, cuts to government jobs, and corporate assaults on labor unions. Between 2000 and 2014, rents across the United States rose by nearly 13 percent, while household income fell by 7 percent. The wage gap contributes greatly to many Americans' housing and employment insecurity.

Where you live determines your health and life expectancy, your job prospects, the quality of your public services and schools, your personal safety, and your experience as a consumer, including access to grocery stores, banks, and medical services. The unequal geography of metropolitan America is the result of both long-term public policies, dating back to the first half of the twentieth century, and profound changes in local, regional, national, and even international economies over the last few decades.

Housing

At the core of the crisis of metropolitan America is the lack of high-quality affordable housing. The United States has always been a stingy provider of affordable housing—standing in sharp contrast to most Western democracies, which have constructed and maintained mixed-income social housing rather than relying primarily on the private sector.

America's failure dates back to the two-tiered housing policy of the Progressive Era and especially the New Deal, which offered massive subsidies (through federally guaranteed home loans and mortgage interest tax deductions) to homeowners but not to renters. The federal government introduced public housing during the Depression, but lobbying pressure from the real estate industry led Congress to limit it to the poor, underfund it, allow local governments to build it on marginal land and racially segregate it, and allocate insufficient funds for maintenance. Public housing and its residents soon became stigmatized.

Beginning in the late 1960s, the federal government began the long process of replacing public housing programs with various market subsidies. The Department of Housing and Urban Development provided incentives to home builders and nonprofits to construct or rehabilitate housing for the poor. In practice, speculators took advantage of the subsidies, bought

housing cheaply, invested little in it, and sold or rented it at substantial profits. In 1974, the federal government introduced Section 8, a housing voucher
program that channeled funds to the private sector and brought new public
housing construction to a near halt. Vouchers help families pay the rent *if*
they can find a landlord willing to accept them. Beginning in the 1990s, the
federal government launched HOPE VI, a program to demolish existing,
mostly high-rise housing projects and replace them with mixed-income,
suburban-style low-rise developments. As a result, the affordable housing
inventory shrank steadily over the next several decades. Congress currently allocates enough funds for only 2 million vouchers and 1 million public
housing apartments. As a result, only one-quarter of America's low-income
families receive any government subsidy to help them afford housing, leaving most of them to the mercy of the private rental market. Not surprisingly,
waiting lists for public housing are enormous nearly everywhere.

　　Meanwhile, federal policy beginning during the New Deal and after
World War II encouraged banks to redline—denying government-insured
mortgage loans to families, particularly African American families, who
wanted to buy homes in cities or suburbs. The federal government underwrote the migration of middle-class white families to the suburbs while
trapping black (and in some places Latinx and Asian) families—even
middle-class families of color—in a predatory housing market, where home
seekers faced two equally bad choices. They could buy homes in segregated
neighborhoods with financing from the unregulated fringe banking system,
which issued costly and risky loans. Or they could live in absentee-owned
apartments, where they faced the constant threat of eviction. In the 1950s
and 1960s, the federal government's urban renewal program bulldozed
many working-class neighborhoods (misleadingly called "slum clearance")
to make way for highways, convention centers, hotels, office towers, and
luxury housing, further displacing families and small neighborhood businesses and worsening housing insecurity.

　　Starting in the 1990s, predatory lenders engaged in a process of "reverse
redlining." Banks and lenders marketed subprime, high-interest loans, frequently underwritten by dubious appraisals, to residents of neighborhoods
that had long lacked access to conventional mortgages. The impact was
disastrous, resulting in the mortgage meltdown and recession in 2007. Over
the following decade, nearly 9 million American households had suffered

foreclosures. In many large cities and overbuilt suburbs, neighborhoods were pockmarked with abandoned houses.

The biggest legacy of these policies and practices is a massive, persistent gap in household wealth between whites and everyone else. For most Americans, the home was and is their single most significant holding, dwarfing stocks, bonds, savings accounts, and other assets. Americans use home equity to subsidize their children's education and as collateral for loans. Eventually, many pass down the value of their homes as inheritances. Insecure homeowners, subject to predatory loans and frequent foreclosures, and renters, who hold no equity in their housing, have virtually no assets. By 2011, the household wealth of blacks and Latinxs reached a record low of only one-twentieth that of white Americans. African American and Latinx households that year had a median net worth of a little more than $5,000.

The nation's overall homeownership rate declined from 69 percent in 2006 to 64 percent in 2018, but it fell most significantly among black and Latinx households. This exacerbated the racial gap in homeownership: in 2018, 78 percent of whites but only 42 percent of African Americans and 47 percent of Latinxs owned their own homes, the lowest rates since the 1960s.

More families now compete for scarce rental housing, which has pushed up rents. In the postcrash years, predatory investors have become landlords, gobbling up foreclosed homes and aging apartment complexes and profiting from the unmet demand for rental properties. Blackstone Group, one of the world's largest private equity firms, is now America's largest landlord. Rental prices nationwide have risen nearly 50 percent since 2000. A 2017 study showed that 17 percent of renters paid more than half their income in rent and 21 percent paid more than one third. The result is rental insecurity and what sociologist Matthew Desmond has called an "eviction epidemic." Frequent evictions and turnover often lead to a cascade of fees and penalties, litigation, poor credit ratings, and even greater financial and housing vulnerability, including a growing number of homeless Americans, many of whom work but still cannot afford a roof over their heads.

Transportation

Exacerbating these problems is America's failed transit system. In the mid-twentieth century, the nation's automobile, gas, tire, steel, and construction industries successfully lobbied Congress to fund an interstate highway system, one of the most expensive infrastructure ventures in modern history. Public transit, on the other hand, mostly remained the responsibility of local and state governments or regional transit authorities, with stingy federal support. No other affluent country has such a dramatic government bias toward cars over public transit. As a consequence, working Americans spend a substantial share of their income on transportation, especially privately owned cars. The poor are least likely to own cars, because of the high purchase costs and expensive insurance, gas, and repairs, and other expenses like tolls and parking.

With the federal government paving the way to sprawl with subsidized homes and highways, it is hardly surprising that underfunded local mass transit systems have failed to connect people to the places where they work. Those cities with subways and regional rail systems face the consequences of aging infrastructure and deferred maintenance. Washington's Metro system has struggled with frequent maintenance-related shutdowns and station closures. New York's subway system is plagued by delayed trains and breakdowns. Regional rail systems, like New Jersey Transit, Chicago's Metra, and the Southeast Pennsylvania Transit Authority, have cut service for decades, even as transit ridership has begun rising. Securing funding for buses, in particular, has been challenging because affluent voters are reluctant to support what they see as a service for the poor. Most cities that have improved their transit systems in recent years have built high-profile but usually low-ridership, short-distance light rail systems, primarily to attract investors and tourists to downtowns and adjoining neighborhoods.

The United States stands alone among major nations for its inadequate public transportation. The negative consequences of transit poverty are profound. Medical researchers have documented the negative health outcomes of lengthy automobile commutes, including higher rates of obesity and chronic pain. Car exhaust contributes heavily to atmospheric pollution and global warming. And excessive petroleum consumption—like highways, heavily subsidized in the United States—has devastating economic and environmental implications.

Schools

Metropolitan areas are the ground zero of educational inequality. Public schooling remains profoundly separate and unequal, the consequence of patterns of racial segregation that have steadily worsened since the 1980s. The quality and funding of public schools is closely associated with the wealth of residents and businesses within school districts, meaning that the poor and working class are more likely to attend schools with the greatest needs and the fewest resources to address them. Separate and unequal school systems, struggling for funding, reinforce long-standing economic and racial inequalities.

System Failure, Policy Crisis

The inequities in housing, jobs, transit, and schooling stem from the growing problem of an almost unregulated capitalist system that puts the profits of employers, banks, developers, automakers, and education technology companies over human needs. Lenders and investors profit from predatory lending and rentals. Developers have catered to high-end buyers, rather than expanding the pool of affordable housing. Public goods like schools and transit are seldom profitable. The drive for profit has been exacerbated by the failure of government officials to challenge corporate priorities.

Since the 1970s, cities have fallen victim to massive public disinvestment. That disinvestment happened in Washington and in state capitals, largely as the result of the declining political clout of cities, in part the consequence of a shift in the balance of legislative power away from cities and to suburban and outlying constituencies. As middle-class Americans moved to suburbia, they largely rejected federal and state programs to improve urban infrastructure, provide affordable housing, desegregate schools by race and class, and expand assistance to the most insecure. Between 1979 and 2017 alone, the share of federal contributions to municipal budgets fell from nearly 14 percent to just 4 percent. Most states did not step in to fill the gap. Cities had to close libraries, parks, and playgrounds and cut other essential services, while deferring maintenance on roads and bridges.

As middle-class families and major employers fled cities for suburbs, cities faced serious fiscal crises, even bankruptcy. This gave corporations—banks, developers, high-tech companies, and professional sports teams—greater leverage to pit cities against one another, desperate to attract private investment. Companies like Amazon, Boeing, Tesla, and many others triggered bidding wars to see which cities would offer the biggest combination of tax breaks and other subsidies, on the flimsy pretext that their benefits would trickle down to poor and working-class residents in the form of jobs and, over the long run, enhanced tax revenues.

Money that could have gone to restore parks and expand affordable housing went to big corporations and their rich shareholders. Many cities used property tax abatements to attract private developers to build housing for well-to-do residents. Cities made deals with private corporations to pay for enhanced sanitation and security services, as well as parks, in downtowns and in wealthy enclaves. Private corporations and wealthy residents encouraged the privatization of education, primarily through charter schools that competed with public schools, depleting them of much-needed funding. Poor and working-class districts paid the price for austerity, with little ongoing park maintenance and inadequate trash pickup. Conservative politicians lambasted spending on metropolitan infrastructure, affordable housing, education, and social welfare as wasteful, even though they had few objections to corporate subsidies or massive federal spending on highways and agriculture that disproportionately benefited nonurban areas.

Thinking Small: Austerity and Its Alternatives

For the last fifty years, cities have been one of the most important bases of progressive activism. In the 1960s, activists and organizers turned their energies toward organizing in impoverished urban neighborhoods, striking against exploitative landlords, building community centers, and providing social services, including after-school and recreation programs. Many of these activists were skeptical, with good reason, that mayors, city councils, and school boards could be effective agents of change. They viewed themselves as outsiders, pressuring elected officials through protests or working through legal advocacy organizations to fight and sometimes win victories in the courts to protect social services from cutbacks, to stem cuts in school spending, and particularly to reform the rapidly expanding carceral state.

These activists called for community control in policy making. That meant favoring small-scale, neighborhood-based efforts to rebuild neighborhoods, led by community development corporations. The emphasis on community control reflected democratic aspirations for giving voice to urban residents rather than mayors, city councils, or professional planners. But such efforts had unintended consequences. Small-scale development programs meshed well with the center-right agenda that cut funding for social programs, drastically reduced state and federal spending on cities, and called for the devolution or downsizing of government generally.

The most successful efforts by community-based developers involved the construction of affordable housing. But they were limited in scope and scale. It was simply not possible for grassroots groups to meet the huge demand for affordable housing without access to substantial subsidies. Private foundations often provided funding for community housing, but even the most generous philanthropic support could not make up for the loss of federal dollars. The strength of the nonprofit community developers was to offer an alternative vision and a model of well-designed and well-managed social housing—many of which included social services, community centers, health clinics, job training programs, and even innovative schools. Under the right political conditions, those programs could be expanded.

In recent decades, conservative state legislators and governors worked diligently to destroy public sector unions, which they viewed not only as bastions of labor power and well-paid jobs but also as threats to big business's efforts to weaken government rules and regulations. They scored some major victories, including huge losses of public jobs (including teachers) in states that were once union strongholds, like Michigan, Ohio, and Wisconsin.

In most states and cities, however, public sector unions not only survived the conservative onslaught but have found new strength. Many older unionists were veterans of the battle against workplace discrimination in the postwar years. Their efforts bore fruit, opening up unprecedented opportunities for people of color, especially women, in local, state, and federal government jobs. Public sector workers resisted efforts to outsource public services and replace municipal workers with workfare recipients. In many cities, teachers unions and student allies joined to protest inequitable school funding and classroom overcrowding.

Since the 1990s, a large wave of progressive activists and elected officials have gained a political foothold in the nation's major cities. Like their
predecessors, they confronted the dilemmas of running cities with inadequate tax bases, crumbling infrastructure (like aging pipes and poisoned
water), and substandard housing. To compensate for this "hollow prize"—
a shortage of public funds—progressives introduced policies that required
business to act more responsibly—minimum-wage laws, rent control,
inclusionary housing, community benefit agreements, community- and
worker-owned enterprises, and new environmental rules to clean up ports
and toxic facilities—while cracking down on racial profiling by police and
racist redlining by banks.

The resurgence of urban progressivism was made possible by new coalitions of community organizations, environmental justice groups, and newly
militant and progressive unions, especially those representing government
employees and low-wage workers (including many immigrants in the service sector). These coalitions fought attempts by state and local politicians and their business allies to downsize government and privatize public
services. Janitors, hotel workers, and other service employees pushed for
worker-friendly transit policies and living-wage ordinances and marched in
favor of immigration reform.

Intrepid community and union organizers, many of them people of color,
had to depend on grassroots organizing and dramatic tactics to gain media
attention and win legislative victories, because they lacked the deep pockets
that developers, real estate interests, and big corporations had available to
lobby city officials. They had to overcome the challenges of getting poor
and working-class residents to attend community meetings and meet with
politicians. Civic participation requires time and energy, both scarce in
communities whose residents struggled to make ends meet in a labor market characterized by job insecurity, low pay, and unpredictable hours. The
fruits of their labor can be found in pocket parks, community education
centers, and neighborhood after-school and arts programs, many with dedi-
cated staff. But they could scarcely fill the gap left by decades of disinvestment in community and social services.

A related current of community politics—led largely by young residents,
many of them new to cities—is characterized by do-it-yourself (DIY)
urbanism. DIY urbanites have stepped in where local governments have

opted out. They have greened cities with new bike lanes and pocket parks
on empty lots. Well-meaning urbanites supplemented struggling public
libraries with "little free libraries," pretty lawn boxes with donated books
to barter or borrow. DIY urbanists have made artisanal lemonade from
the lemons of urban disinvestment, reimagining urban change on a small
scale, celebrating the virtues of neighborhood self-help in lieu of capturing
city councils, of local empowerment in place of social welfare and public
spending.

Along with the DIY ethos have come two other trends: an emphasis on
community and self-sufficiency, concepts that have a long tradition on the
left. A new urban economy, based on local production and local consumption, stands athwart a consumer economy dominated by multinational chain
stores, replacing mass consumption with a new localism, one that ostensibly
empowers communities. The most utopian urban visionaries imagine creating cities as alternative sustainable economies, undoing decades of urban
ecological devastation and environmentally disastrous agribusiness. Many
big cities now have hundreds of urban farms, former industrial brown-
fields and rubble-strewn vacant lots reclaimed for the cultivation of fruits
and vegetables, even hydroponically grown herbs and flowers. But while
urban agriculture has provided some green oases in urban food deserts,
it is too small in scale to meet the needs of the millions of food-insecure
Americans. Notions of self-sustainability and do-it-yourself urban reform
have a certain romantic, even utopian appeal. But they are too local and
too fragmentary—by design—to make a dent in the deep inequality that
plagues metropolitan America.

The most influential current in community-based activism today focuses on gentrification, the takeover—some would say settler colonization—
of once poor and working-class neighborhoods by affluent, mostly white,
professionals. The narrative of gentrification combines a critique of economic and cultural injustice, namely, the devastation of long-standing
communities by imperious newcomers seeking authenticity and afford-
ability on what they see as the urban "frontier," enabled by avaricious
developers displacing established residents in service of rising property
values and new development. Once solid working-class neighborhoods—
such as Williamsburg, Bushwick, and Bedford-Stuyvesant in Brooklyn,
and Boyle Heights and Highland Park in Los Angeles—are now full of

overpriced lofts, trendy restaurants, and bespoke clothing retailers. There, developers who convert old industrial buildings into apartments and fill vacant lots with new houses often benefit from tax abatements and other incentives, drawing money that would be better spent improving public services in poor and working-class neighborhoods. But those developments are more a symptom than a cause of the massive nationwide crisis of low-wage employment, unaffordable housing, and predatory lending and renting.

Almost every city has experienced some degree of gentrification, but it is a major problem in only a handful of cities (especially New York, Boston, Seattle, San Francisco, Los Angeles, and Washington), where high-tech and finance have utterly reshaped real estate markets. Most of Detroit's gentrification is confined to 7.2 of the city's 139 square miles. Vast sections of Chicago, only minutes from the wealthy lakefront and the latte belt of the near West Side, are windswept and neglected by investors and city officials other than the police. The core neighborhoods of Baltimore and Philadelphia are full of renovated row houses and fashionable restaurants and bars, but vast sections of both cities continue to experience massive disinvestment and deep housing insecurity. Places as diverse as Bakersfield, California; Milwaukee, Wisconsin; Trenton, New Jersey; and Orlando, Florida, have experienced little gentrification but still struggle with an acute shortage of decent, affordable housing.

A focus on urban gentrification also draws attention away from older, unfashionable urban neighborhoods—untouched by gentrification—and especially the increasingly diverse suburbs, where speculators and exploitative landlords are marketing houses and apartments at inflated prices to urban refugees, most of them people of color, in search of better jobs, schools, and public services. Housing insecurity is not primarily the result of gentrification-related displacement, but rather the fact that working-class and poor Americans are largely trapped in low-value, declining housing stock, including older single-family homes in neighborhoods losing population, cheaply built, aging tract housing that is costly to maintain, sprawling suburban town house and apartment complexes that are milked for profit by neglectful owners, and peripheral trailer parks.

In response to the housing crisis, a right-to-housing movement has emerged around the world, particularly in cities hard hit by the 2008 fore-closure and the eviction crises. From Barcelona and Madrid to Cleveland; Chicago; and Jackson, Mississippi, neighborhood activists have reinvigo-rated a tradition of tenant and homeowner organizing that flourished dur-ing the Depression and during the late 1960s and early 1970s. The human tragedy of evictions—police officers serving eviction notices, movers pil-ing up families' belongings on sidewalks and curbs, and the process hap-pening over and over again—has served as a powerful organizing tool to galvanize communities. In some cities, right-to-housing activists have gone from blockading evictions to pooling resources to buy foreclosed properties, bank land for new affordable housing, and support community-run housing cooperatives. These efforts build on the democratic social-ist tradition of providing affordable housing for lower-income people. In Philadelphia and New York, to name two prominent examples, trade unions and religious organizations have been building and maintaining housing cooperatives since the 1920s and 1930s. But there have been some victories, too, because in the midst of a severe shortage, families cannot wait for government or for-profit developers to build more housing. Since roughly 2012, housing activists—often with the support of unions and faith-based groups—have escalated battles for tenants rights and rent con-trol, winning victories in Oregon, Washington, California, Illinois, Min-nesota, and other states.

As part of the resurgent urban progressivism, democratic socialists have built bases of power from the bottom up in many big cities, taking over hidebound electoral wards, challenging candidates who are closely tied to big developers, and gaining footholds on some city councils and school boards. But left-leaning activists have conceded most suburbs and exurbs to conservatives and, increasingly, moderates (that is, voters who identify as economically conservative and socially liberal, at once opposed to the con-struction of affordable housing and the creation of equitable school funding and, at the same time, alienated by the rise of the Christian right and white nationalism). Progressives and leftists need to expand their efforts beyond city borders. A healthy sign is the founding of Local Progress, a network of progressive and radical local officials, founded in 2012, that seven years later had members in more than five hundred cities and forty-six states.

Thinking Bigger:
Toward a New Metropolitan Policy

Are we on the brink of a revolution in metropolitan policy? In the three-quarters of a century since Franklin Delano Roosevelt promised Americans "the right to a decent home," the housing market has remained both a cause of America's racial and economic inequality and a woefully inadequate solution to it. Today, a decade after the financial crash of 2008, even in a period of rapid economic growth, the home-finance and rental markets are still failing most Americans. But, as in the Depression, a new generation of politicians are putting urban issues at the center of the national agenda. Congressional candidates ranging from Minnesota's Ilhan Omar to Hawaii's Kaniela Ing have called for Housing for All, including rent-stabilization programs and a new infusion of federal subsidies for construction of affordable housing. In New York City, where half of renters are paying more than a third of their income on housing, Alexandria Ocasio-Cortez is calling for an end to subsidies for luxury developments and to redirect funds to expand housing for low-income and middle-class residents. Activists in Queens successfully protested against a $3 billion city and state subsidy for Amazon's expansion into Long Island City, making an argument that the dollars would be better spent on infrastructure and public education. In February 2019, Oregon governor Kate Brown signed a first-in-the-nation statewide rent-control law, putting a limit on how much landlords could raise rents.

Democratic socialist alternatives must begin by rejecting the last generation of policies—austerity, corporate subsidies, the collapse of civil rights, and the deregulation of the housing, rental, and financial markets. A left metropolitan policy must also start big—building on the lessons of the last few decades of urban activism. Grassroots change starts from below but cannot stop there: the scale of metropolitan problems is too large for small-scale, neighborhood-based efforts to make a real change. That requires acknowledging that locally oriented, community-control activism and do-it-yourself urbanism are microlevel solutions to macrolevel problems. It must recognize that gentrification is one symptom, and not usually the cause, of urban inequality. A new metropolitan policy must begin with the recognition that the yawning gap between white and nonwhite and between the 1 percent and the 99 percent is metropolitan-wide in scale. That also means thinking regionally, remembering that the fate of cities and suburbs are fundamentally linked, not antithetical.

A new, just metropolitan policy must address the policies that incentivize both high-profile downtown development and, simultaneously, the ongoing sprawl of population and jobs. It must address, especially, the maldistribution of resources spatially, between wealthy communities and poor and working-class neighborhoods, whether in the city or suburbs. A just metropolitan policy requires, above all, moving the battle for policy to build on the energies of protest but turn attention to political institutions, both urban and suburban. Voluntary organizations, whether DIY park builders or community development corporations, offer a compelling vision of what a just city might look like, but gaining power in city councils, in mayors' offices, in state governments, and in Congress is essential to bring the just city to fruition.

Political power is necessary to challenge the developer-centered city halls, anti-urban state legislatures, and a federal government that has shunted cities to the margins for decades. For decades, mainstream urban policy has relied on an implicit trickle-down theory: namely, rebuilding downtowns and providing tax incentives for corporations and well-to-do homebuyers have exacerbated inequality. Second, democratic socialist activists need to stand up to politicians who put corporate profits over human needs. Several decades of experiments in market-based urbanism and deregulation have left the problems of transit, infrastructure, and housing unsolved or worse.

Overcoming the current crises will require a deeper transformation that puts the right to the city—the right to decent housing, decent public transportation and services, and secure employment—at the forefront. The left needs to learn from what has worked—and what has not—over the last several decades, and use that knowledge to launch a comprehensive metropolitan policy.

To address the housing crisis, a democratic socialist program should include mixed-income social housing, with federal and state funding. That housing needs to be built across metropolitan areas, not just in the impoverished communities that have been the focus of nonprofit initiatives over the last fifty years. There is an especially acute need to build affordable housing in suburban areas with strong labor markets, but little good-quality, affordable housing stock. Modest federal support for successful nonprofit housing programs, such as limited-equity cooperatives, outside the speculative market will also expand affordable housing options. Especially pressing is the need to reduce rental burdens. More cities and suburbs must introduce rent control.

The transit crisis needs urgent action. It is time for a renewal of federal funding for public transportation—buses, light-rail systems, subways, and regional rail systems—that connect cities and suburbs, as well as suburbs and suburbs, with a national goal of reducing auto ridership. Currently, the federal government provides massive subsidies for highways and tax breaks for commuter parking. Those resources could be easily diverted to incentives for employers to help employees take public transit or bike or walk to work.

Addressing economic insecurity requires creating jobs, particularly around the long-deferred reconstruction of metropolitan infrastructure. America's crumbling schools, bridges, parks and playgrounds, sewers, and water systems are in need of a massive overhaul. A public green jobs and infrastructure program will lead to full employment at a living wage, with job training and job creation initiatives that target distressed urban and suburban areas.

We need federal incentives for states and cities to adopt land-use regulations that limit unplanned suburban sprawl, instead of subsidizing more highways and off-ramps. Outdated zoning laws, such as large lot size requirements and single-family zoning that encourage sprawl and keep housing unaffordable, must be replaced by state-mandated inclusionary zoning laws so that existing suburbs—especially wealthy ones—will allow affordable housing. Federal and state funds should be directed to create and maintain green spaces and parks in underserved areas as well as more public spaces that serve as meeting grounds for diverse populations.

The vast majority of Americans live in metropolitan areas, a trend that is likely to continue for the foreseeable future. Cities and suburbs are places of extraordinary vitality and opportunity, but also of wrenching inequalities. If the United States is to become a more just and equitable society in the future, the process will begin in our metropolitan areas.

What Does Health Equity Require? Racism and the Limits of Medicare for All

Dorothy Roberts

PERHAPS THE MOST OBVIOUS HUMAN NEED THE GOVERNMENT SHOULD meet in a democratic socialist society is health care. Because health care is a human right, its distribution can't be left to the market, which privileges the wealthy and leaves cash-poor and working-class people with inadequate services. A capitalist health care system is antithetical to a radically egalitarian society because corporate executives will provide only as much care as is profitable.[1] Health care, therefore, is one of the basic services government should guarantee by providing it to the public for free. Democratic socialists may not insist on immediate or total state control of all parts of the economy, but replacing private, for-profit corporate insurance with universal, government-provided health care is fundamental to their platform.

Health care is what makes the United States stand out the most from other industrialized nations. The European Union, Great Britain, Canada, and Japan all have a single system that guarantees medical services for every resident, regardless of age or income. By contrast, the United States maintains a hodgepodge of models for different classes of people centered on corporate rather than government providers. While Medicare is a national insurance plan for people over sixty-five, most Americans are insured privately through their employers, and 45 million uninsured Americans get only the health care they can afford to pay out of pocket.[2] As James Petras summarizes, "The US is the only developed country relying on a private, for-profit insurance system to fund and deliver medical care for its working age population."[3] Thus, the United States alone is out of step with a model of health care motivated by egalitarian principles.

Democratic socialists advocate for Medicare for All as the main strategy for protecting the human right to health care, achieving greater health equity, and bringing the United States in line with other industrialized nations. But America's long legacy of white supremacy makes universal guaranteed medical insurance inadequate to dismantle the racist barriers to equal health. Institutionalized racism creates the unequal living conditions that are the main cause of health disparities and racial bias among health care professionals, is structured into the distribution of health care, and generates inferior treatment of patients of color even when they have the same health insurance as white patients. Only an anti-racist approach to democratic socialist health policy can create the social conditions needed for health equity and the political conditions needed for radical change.

The Case for Universal Health Care

The Democratic Socialists of America (DSA) makes the struggle for universal health care a prominent part of its platform, and voted to make it one of the organization's three priority campaigns at its 2017 national convention.[4] Medicare for All is the group's chief strategy for making health care available to everyone regardless of their employment or economic status, pushed at the state and national levels alongside progressive groups, labor unions such as National Nurses United, and left-leaning politicians. It would establish a single, public, universal health insurance system, managed by the federal government, providing free comprehensive care on demand. As Bernie Sanders writes, "Health care is a right. The United States must join the rest of the industrialized world and guarantee health care to every man, woman, and child through a national Medicare for All single-payer system."[5] The party endorses H.R. 676, the Expanded and Improved Medicare for All Act, introduced by John Conyers, and Sanders's S. 703, the American Health Security Act of 2009.

The democratic socialist approach to health care stands out from the congressional debate focused on the Affordable Care Act because it relies on government insurance only and completely eliminates for-profit insurance companies. While the mainstream controversy over Obamacare hinges on how to regulate free-market forces to deliver health care to more people, democratic socialists push for a radical departure from the capitalist approach to health care as a business by making it a guaranteed public service. Some experts have pointed out that "Medicare for All" is a misleading label for DSA's platform because Medicare as currently structured allows private insurance companies, and not only the government, to manage care. Democratic socialists like Sanders are calling for a publicly funded program that covers everyone in which the federal government alone manages and pays for care. Though eliminating private insurance, Medicare for All would cover privately operated, as well as government-provided, services, in contrast to almost fully nationalized health services in some European countries, such as Norway and Sweden. In sum, U.S. democratic socialist health insurance would go beyond the Affordable Care Act to create a single-payer system that excludes private insurance companies, but not go as far as the Nordic model that provides all citizens equal access to government-operated services. At a minimum, any national health care reform legislation must include the option to choose a government-run public plan that has the ability to negotiate drug prices and reimbursement rates. Furthermore, individual states should be able to opt out of the national system to establish their own single-payer plans using Medicare, Medicaid, and similar federal health care funding sources.

Publicly funded and delivered health plans provide greater access to essential medical services than the market based system in the United States. In this country, more than 20 percent of working-age people report that they avoid visiting a doctor because they can't afford the cost.[6] A substantial percentage of people with health insurance report having trouble paying health care bills, as is true for most people without insurance.[7] The capitalist marketing of health care for profit spikes up health care costs and generates wasteful spending on advertising, bureaucracy, lobbying, and CEO compensation.[8]

Not having access to health care is a serious violation of human rights and social equality. The inability to pay health care bills bankrupts hundreds of thousands of Americans each year, while the ability to afford needed health care unjustly privileges wealthy people. The discrepancy is deadly: as T.R. Reid reports, "More than twenty thousand Americans die in the prime of life each year from medical problems that could be treated, because they can't afford to see a doctor."[9] Despite spending twice as much per capita on health care than in the EU, the United States falls far behind in life expectancy, infant and maternal mortality, chronic diseases, and other key health outcomes.[10] A study published in the *Journal of the American Medical Association* found that, in 2016, the United States spent 17.8 percent of its gross domestic product on health care, compared to spending in other high-income countries, which ranged from 9.6 percent (Australia) to 12.4 percent (Switzerland).[11] Why does the United States spend so much on health care yet yield such poor population health outcomes? The study found that the main drivers of U.S. spending are higher administrative costs and prices of labor and goods, including pharmaceuticals and devices. These costs would be lower in a single-payer system that was governed by patient care rather than by profit. The study also found that the United States had the highest proportion of private health insurance and the lowest percentage of the population with health insurance. Societies that guarantee access to health care and that generally distribute resources more equally are healthier for everyone.[12]

Indeed, by many measures, health in the United States is getting worse. The for-profit system also leads to the dangerous overuse of technologies and pharmaceuticals to address health problems in order to increase corporate profits while putting patients at risk of injury, side effects, and addiction.[13] As a result, the United States has the highest rates of cesarean sections and lethal drug overdoses among industrialized nations. In other words, the capitalist health care system not only fails to provide needed medical services to millions of Americans; it also affirmatively harms Americans' health. Among eleven industrialized nations whose health care systems were evaluated in 2014, the United States had the highest costs and the worst performance.[14]

Medicare for All Is Not Enough

The democratic socialist platform on health policy basically boils down to guaranteeing universal, government-provided health insurance. In pushing for Medicare for All, democratic socialists seek to protect health by eliminating economic barriers to accessing health care services. Although DSA recognizes that "health is social" because it depends on the social conditions of life for American workers, its policy prescriptions concentrate on providing medical services for all as the goal, on inability to pay for them as the barrier, and on the profit-driven model of health care as the problem.[15] On its website, for instance, DSA explains that Medicare for All is one of its three key campaigns because "health care is a huge segment of our economy and health care access is a deeply and widely felt need."[16] It goes on to contrast access to health care under capitalism versus socialism: "In the capitalist system, you have to pay to get care or go without, and under a democratic socialist system, we would collectively provide care as a society." Although Medicare for All would greatly increase access to health care and bring the United States in line with the rest of the industrialized world, it is an inadequate remedy for this nation's atrocious health disparities.

An exclusive focus on guaranteed medical care fails to account for the impact of America's particular history of institutionalized racism and white supremacy on health. First, institutionalized racism produces unequal health outcomes that cannot be corrected by access to health care alone. Second, racial bias negatively affects the health care people of color receive even when they have equal access to medical insurance, including government-provided insurance. Finally, the investment white workers have in their racial identity, which has outweighed their concerns about economic justice and even about their own health, poses a formidable barrier to the social change needed to achieve health equity in America.

Racism's Impact on Health and Access to Health Care

In 1967, Dr. Martin Luther King Jr. launched the Poor People's Campaign, which connected the ongoing movement for black people's civil rights to a new call for the radical redistribution of political and economic power—a move some see as marking King as a socialist.[17] He identified racism, poverty, and militarism as related evils that systematically fueled an unjust social order and that had to be fought together to build a better world. A year earlier, Dr. King singled out one form of inequality as especially egregious: "Of all the forms of inequality, injustice in health is the most shocking and inhuman."[18] By highlighting injustice in health, Dr. King recognized the relationship between racial health disparities and the institutionalized racism and economic inequality that were at the heart of the widening civil rights struggle.[19]

Health disparities are not just a biological reality; they are a form of social inequality because they are structured according to unjust power arrangements. Social stratification drives group disparities in health, so health status reflects social status.[20] Public health advocates use the term "health inequities" to describe these differences in health because they result from the systemic, unjust, and avoidable distribution of social, economic, political, and environmental resources needed for health and well-being. Numerous studies have established that the best predictor of health is an individual's position in the social order.[21] Poor health is a function of occupying a disadvantaged position in our society, while having better health is a benefit of being socially privileged.[22] The classic Whitehall study of British civil servants, with data spanning more than two decades, compared heart disease and mortality in employees at four civil service levels: administrators, professional and executive employees, clerical staff, and menial workers.[23] The study found that health got worse and mortality increased with each step down the occupational hierarchy.

People of color in the United States experience greater rates of morbidity and mortality than white people.[24] In one generation, between 1940 and 1999, more than 4 million black Americans died prematurely relative to whites.[25] Race matters at the beginning of life, too. Black infants are more than two times as likely as white infants to die before their first birthday and more than three times as likely as white infants to die from complications related to low birth weight.[26] Recent research shows that the maternal mortality rate is actually *increasing* in the United States, unlike in any other developed nation, and departing even from most of the developing world.[27] Black women in the United States are almost four times more likely than white women to die from pregnancy-related causes.[28] For black women, Chickasaw County, Mississippi, is a deadlier place to be pregnant than Kenya or Rwanda.[29]

A growing field of empirical research demonstrates that racism negatively affects the health of black Americans through a variety of pathways.[30] Scientists are now uncovering the biological mechanisms that translate inequities in wealth, employment, health care, housing, incarceration, and education, along with experiences of stigma and discrimination, into disparate health outcomes.[31] Institutionalized racism in these systems restricts access to resources required for health and well-being. For example, a 2014 study using novel measures of structural racism—political participation, employment status, educational attainment, and judicial treatment—found that blacks living in states with high levels of structural racism were more likely to report past-year myocardial infarction (heart attack) than those living in low-structural-racism states.[32]

In addition, experiencing racial discrimination causes chronic stress and other negative psychological responses that are related to disease.[33] Recent studies indicate that red blood cell oxidative stress,[34] sleep deprivation,[35] allostatic load,[36] and cortisol dysregulation[37] are pathways by which racial discrimination increases cardiovascular disease, diabetes, and premature aging. A 2007 study showed that experiencing daily racial microaggressions, which often has been dismissed as benign, actually has biological consequences that gravely damage black and Latinx adolescents' health.[38] A 2018 study found that police killings of unarmed black Americans had an adverse effect on the self-reported mental health of other black Americans in the U.S. general population.[39]

Residential segregation—resulting from the forcible exclusion of black people from white neighborhoods by private terror, government housing policies, and state-sponsored legal mechanisms, such as restrictive covenants—is one of the most potent mechanisms of persistent health inequality.[40] Numerous studies have identified racially segregated housing as a key contributor to health disparities because it concentrates poverty and minimizes resources needed for good health in predominantly black areas.[41] As a group of health researchers recently summarized, racial residential segregation harms health in multiple ways, including "the high concentration of dilapidated housing in neighborhoods that people of color reside in, the substandard quality of the social and built environment, exposure to pollutants and toxins, limited opportunities for high-quality education and decent employment, and restricted access to health care."[42] Thus, by geographically concentrating racism and poverty, residential segregation creates neighborhood environments for black residents that are extraordinarily destructive to their health.

Unequal Treatment

Universal health insurance would mitigate the unequal health burdens caused by institutionalized racism and help to shrink the racial gaps in well-being. But Medicare for All cannot transform the unequal living conditions that produce disparities in health in the first place. Nor will government-provided medical care ensure equal treatment of patients. Health inequities in America today are deeply rooted in a long-standing relationship between white supremacy and the very concept of race as a natural division of human beings. Scientific claims of biological distinctions between races were essential to justifying the enslavement of Africans in a nation founded on a radical commitment to liberty, equality, and natural rights.[43] During the slavery era, doctors developed the racial concept of disease—that people of different races suffer from different diseases and experience common diseases differently—as proof not only that race was biological but also that black pathology caused racial inequality.[44] They argued that the biological peculiarities of black people made enslavement the only condition that allowed them to be productive, disciplined, and healthy. After slavery ended, locating blacks' subordinated status in biological susceptibility provided an excuse to retain white supremacy instead of dismantling the social order inherited from slavery. The biological concept of race and the racial concept of disease continue to govern medical practice today and to generate inequities in health care.[45]

Numerous studies show that black patients receive inferior care even when they have the same private or state health insurance as white patients. In 2002, the health arm of the National Academy of Sciences, the Institute of Medicine (now the National Academy of Medicine), documented widespread racial disparities in health care and found that they stemmed, at least in part, from physician bias. Its 562-page report, *Unequal Treatment: Confronting Racial and Ethnic Disparities in Health Care*, stated that, although these disparities are associated with socioeconomic status, the majority of studies it surveyed "find that racial and ethnic disparities remain even after adjustment for socioeconomic differences and other healthcare access-related factors," including medical insurance. Other researchers have documented the disparaging and inhumane treatment that cash-poor and low-income black mothers in particular receive when they seek prenatal, obstetric, and family-planning services from Medicaid providers and public hospitals.[46]

Black patients' vulnerability to harmful biases and stereotypes is manifested as well in the undertreatment of pain based on commonly held myths that black people as a race feel less pain, exaggerate their pain, or are predisposed to drug addiction.[47] A 2016 study conducted at University of Virginia School of Medicine found "a substantial number of white medical students and residents hold false beliefs about biological differences between blacks and whites"—beliefs such as black people have thicker skin and less sensitive nerve endings than white people—"and these beliefs predict racial bias in pain perception and treatment."[48]

Another striking example of unequal treatment is the delay in lifesaving therapies that black heart attack victims receive from hospital staff, leading to lower rates of survival.[49] A 2018 multicenter study of more than twelve thousand outpatients with atrial fibrillation found that black patients were significantly less likely to receive stroke-preventing treatment than white patients, even after controlling for clinical and socioeconomic features.[50] In a 2004 study, Yale researchers discovered that black patients tended to be admitted to hospitals with the worst procedures for treating heart attacks.[51] But they also found that, even holding the hospital constant, there remained racial disparities in timeliness of treatment. Thus, ending the inequitable treatment of black patients requires both tackling individual physician bias and making systemic changes in access to high-quality hospitals. Providing black patients with an insurance card won't solve either problem.

Medicare for All can guarantee access to medical services, but it can't guarantee those services will be made available or delivered with the same quality of care to patients of color. A democratic socialist health policy must attend to the long-standing racial bias in medicine that will not be eliminated by universal insurance alone.

Racism as a Barrier to Universal Health Care

Democratic socialists must also address white Americans' racism, which has been a tenacious barrier to implementing national health insurance as well as to transforming the social structures and modes of production that produce ill health. Medicare for All would secure desperately needed medical care for millions of Americans. It would help to dissolve the stigma associated with need-based public assistance. But reliance on universalism underestimates the degree of white Americans' unwillingness to accept people of color as full citizens deserving of equal human rights, including the right to health care. Privileged racial identity gives whites a powerful incentive to leave the existing social order intact. A majority of white Americans have been unwilling to create social programs that will facilitate blacks' full citizenship, even when those benefits would benefit whites.

Even white workers' and feminist movements have compromised their most radical dreams in order to strike political bargains that sacrifice black people's rights.[52] Northern Democrats gained the support of southern Democrats for New Deal legislation by systematically denying black workers' eligibility for social insurance benefits. Core programs allowed states to define eligibility standards and excluded agricultural workers and domestic servants in a deliberate effort to maintain a black menial labor caste in the South.[53] Although by the 1970s African Americans had the highest unionization rates of any group, in prior decades they were overtly discriminated against and excluded from membership by labor unions, especially those affiliated with the American Federation of Labor.[54] Let's remember, socialists have embraced eugenicist strategies for improving population health.[55] The renowned British socialist Havelock Ellis, for example, argued in his 1912 book, *The Task of Social Hygiene*, that socialist societies needed to eliminate their nonproductive members in order to advance. Swedish social democracy embraced eugenic ideas to create a productive "national stock" and passed sterilization policies in 1934 and 1941 to integrate these ideas in its welfare program aimed at egalitarian redistribution.[56]

W.E.B. DuBois explained white resistance to labor and education reform during Reconstruction by the fact that poor and laboring whites preferred to be compensated by the "public and psychological wage" of racial superiority.[57] Historian Jill Quadagno argues convincingly that the War on Poverty failed because whites opposed it as an infringement on their economic right to discriminate against black people.[58] Decades later, a chief threat to the Affordable Care Act is the white backlash against any government-backed reforms that will benefit black citizens and Mexican immigrants—even at the risk of harming their own health. In his 2019 book *Dying of Whiteness: How the Politics of Racial Resentment Is Killing America's Heartland*,

Jonathan Metzl quotes a forty-one-year-old uninsured Tennessean suffering from an inflamed liver who nevertheless supported the state legislature's refusal to expand Medicaid coverage. "Ain't no way I would ever support Obamacare or sign up for it," he told Metzl. "I would rather die." Why? Because "no way I want my tax dollars paying for Mexicans or welfare queens," he explained.[59] Because of white supremacy, the United States has failed to adopt the Nordic model of universal, government-provided medical services that ensures that every citizen has equal access to health care. Indeed, growing anti-immigrant sentiment in European nations like Sweden is threatening to cut back their generous social welfare policies.[60]

Toward Anti-Racist Democratic Socialist Health Policy

Medicare for All focuses on implementing a restructured health insurance program without paying sufficient attention to the racism that structured the current system. It leaves racist social structures and biases in place, relying on the universal distribution of benefits to relieve the problems these structures and biases create. To achieve their radically egalitarian vision, democratic socialists must instead propose a health agenda that is anti-racist as well as universal. Recognizing health care as a human right by guaranteeing universal, state-supported, high-quality health care for everyone is essential. But health equity also requires eliminating the living conditions that unjustly damage the health of socially disadvantaged communities. This means enacting policies aimed at changing the structures, systems, and institutions grounded in white supremacist ideologies and practices, that unequally distribute resources that affect people's health. A critical aspect of this transformation is ending mass incarceration and police violence that wreak havoc on the health of entire neighborhoods, as well as carceral approaches that lock up and punish people for having health problems, such as drug addiction, mental illness, and trauma from experiencing violence.[61]

Democratic socialists should also join with feminists of color in the reproductive justice movement to promote a vision of freedom based on social justice rather than individual choice.[62] In contrast to the dominant goal of protecting individuals' choices—especially the decision to have an

abortion—from government interference, the reproductive justice framework calls for social change needed for everyone to have equal access to
the resources and living conditions needed for reproductive health and
freedom as a human right. In 2004, the national reproductive rights rally
on the Washington Mall departed dramatically from prior events, which
had been led by mainstream pro-choice organizations, because women of
color organizations were included among its sponsors. The women of color
leaders changed its name from March for Freedom of Choice to March for
Women's Lives and shifted its focus from choice to social justice. Bringing a
reproductive justice approach to the leadership helped to mobilize new supporters, making the 2004 march the largest and most diverse of its kind in
U.S. history.[63] Since then, reproductive justice organizations such as Sister-
Song Women of Color Reproductive Justice Collective have led campaigns
to abolish the Hyde Amendment, which denies federal funding for abortion
services; repeal state laws that limit public assistance benefits for women
who have children while receiving welfare; and oppose state and federal
bills that criminalize "race and sex selective" abortions on grounds they
stigmatize black and Asian women.[64]

In addition, health inequities should be addressed by pushing for medical
schools to train health professionals to be more structurally competent.[65]
Medical education in the United States typically perpetuates biological concepts of race, the racial concept of disease, and stereotypes about racial differences that contribute to inferior treatment of black patients.[66] Rather than
grapple with racist ideas embedded in the curriculum, medical schools have
sought to address physician bias by requiring students to be trained in "cultural competency" to better understand patient lifestyles and attitudes.[67] A
growing movement called "structural competency" radically departs from
these biological and cultural approaches by contending that "many health-
related factors previously attributed to culture or ethnicity also represent
the downstream consequences of decisions about larger structural contexts,
including health care and food delivery systems, zoning laws, local politics,
urban and rural infrastructures, structural racisms, or even the very definitions of illness and health."[68] Structurally competent health care professionals must recognize the legal, social, and economic structures that affect
their patients' health and shape clinical interactions. Although these structures include financial and other barriers to access to services, they also

include a much wider range of living conditions supportive of or harmful to patient well-being. Becoming structurally competent, then, requires health care professionals to learn from other disciplines and from the communities they serve about incorporating knowledge about structural racism, sexism, classism, and other inequalities into their practice. It also requires imagining innovative structural interventions that depart from traditional clinical treatment of patients' illnesses. Democratic socialists, in turn, can learn from health care scholars and practitioners who are advancing structural competency how to move beyond Medicare for All to address the unequal structures that affect health. At the same time, democratic socialists can facilitate the expansion of structural competency in medical care by supporting campaigns in medical schools to adopt this approach in their curriculums and by advocating for the structural changes needed to increase health equity.[69] Health care providers need to be more competent at recognizing and addressing their own racist beliefs as well as the upstream structural factors that determine patients' health and create health disparities.

Democratic socialists' call for Medicare for All is critical to a radically egalitarian society that recognizes everyone's human right to health care. It would put the United States on par with every other industrialized country, which guarantee residents universal access to medical services regardless of their ability to pay for them. It would help to eliminate the despicable gaps in health that link life and death to social status. But universal health insurance is woefully inadequate to correct the devastating impact of institutionalized racism on the nation's health and on efforts to transform health policy. By crafting a deliberately anti-racist health agenda, democratic socialists will have a better chance of succeeding at their mission to build a more humane America.

The Family of the Future

Sarah Leonard

A fundamental goal of the 1971 Welfare Reform Act was to strengthen the role of the family as the basic unit in society.

—*California's Blueprint for National Welfare Reform*, 1974

One person cannot raise a child. Neither can two.

—Toni Morrison, interview on *Charlie Rose*, 1993

Family Enforcement

Capitalism wants everything and nothing from the family. Trying to create any kind of household in twenty-first-century America feels like a battle with bad odds: housing is expensive, high-quality child care almost nonexistent, and debt the new norm, along with three jobs, no union, and unpredictable hours. Millennials have, logically enough, responded by having kids later and later. This is probably smart since America also has the highest maternal mortality rate among wealthy countries[1]—and merciful since we have the highest infant mortality rate as well.

It's not hard to see why anyone who wants to make a family is hard-pressed to do so. Since the 1970s, real wages have been falling, making the idealized household with one breadwinner a thing of the past, or a thing for the rich. Two wages are needed now—an impossibility for many and a severe stretch for others. Women, who continue to do the majority of the child care and cleaning, also work for wages, disproportionately in poorly paid, unpredictable service sector jobs. Notoriously, America has almost no high-quality affordable child care: the annual cost of child care in most states is approaching the cost of in-state college tuition.[2] At the same time, the bottom dropped out of the welfare state, with the slow, cruel march of welfare cutbacks beginning in the seventies and including the defeat of major child care bills in Congress. The gaps in care get filled in at home. Women are being stretched impossibly thin. In families with enough money, domestic labor picks up the slack left by the state, typically through the hiring of immigrant women of color, often undocumented, far from their own children and confronting ugly labor violations in an underscrutinized sector. In Nancy Fraser's words, there is a full-blown crisis of care.[3]

At the same time, capitalism's greatest defenders seem to see the family as a sort of magical cure-all. Mitt Romney has suggested that two-parent homes would reduce gun violence. Bill Clinton thought the family would reduce poverty. Hillary pointed to crime. Reaching back further, Vice President Dan Quayle thought the sitcom *Murphy Brown* was "mocking the importance of fathers, by [having the title character] bearing a child alone." More recently, when Obama gave a speech on MLK Day at Morehouse College in 2013, he cited family responsibility as a source of communal uplift among black Americans. Politicians from Reagan to Bush and Obama have pushed marriage incentives. Why does having a family feel so hard to sustain and yet so . . . mandatory?

A big part of the answer lies in America's history of using the family to absorb burdens that the ruling class doesn't want to pay for. Policy has long positioned the family as the first measure of defense against poverty rather than the state. At the same time, a confluence of religious morality, conservative values, and the like has served to paint this practice with a veneer of naturalness. Here and there in this dire history, we can glimpse moments in our recent past when things might've developed in a more liberatory direction.

Social scientist Melinda Cooper has written in her book *Family Values* that capitalists need the family to care for and reproduce workers at no cost, while social conservatives need the family as a symbol and keeper of so-called traditional moral values. She places the origin of our obsession with family responsibility in seventeenth-century industrializing England, when the state instituted the first poor laws in order to manage the country's new permanent class of poor people, uprooted by land enclosures and shuffled into industry. The laws mandated that money be distributed through church parishes and demanded that family members do everything possible to care for any dependents, young or old, before receiving funds, so as not to unduly burden the community. This basic framework has been with us ever since.

The thirteen American colonies carried poor laws over from England. According to Cooper, poor laws were first aggressively used to coerce marriage after the Civil War. The Freedmen's Bureau, designed to help formerly enslaved Americans transition to freedom, compelled formerly enslaved people who were coupled but unmarried, were cohabitating, or were in multiple relationships to wed. The government feared the burden of so many newly free, destitute people and quickly pushed men into becoming legal heads of households, responsible for the welfare of those therein. "As soon as they became applicable to African Americans," Cooper writes, "marriage laws were enforced ruthlessly."

This relationship between state provision and marriage enforcement ebbs and flows throughout the subsequent history of the welfare state. During the Gilded Age, responsibility shifted to private charities, which pioneered the use of surveillance to ensure that women receiving charity did not have men in their lives. Charities and poor laws reinforced the idea that a woman's well-being should be tied to an individual man and, only failing that, the state. Other reformers believed that a more universal form of social insurance would better protect families, since it could fill any gaps in the man's family wage, an argument that undergirded some support for universal New Deal provisions like Social Security.

A brief period of family law liberalization in the sixties—primarily the result of the Welfare Rights Movement—meant that women could receive welfare support without acute moral surveillance.[4] Even the Aid to Families with Dependent Children program, long representative of family responsibility-oriented poor laws, allowed single women with children to receive aid without "moral" conditions. In other words, welfare had become a "social wage for unmarried women."[5] If policy had continued in this direction, we might have moved closer to a feminist welfare state, or at least the basic provisions of modern Europe, where social benefits to support children are widespread, often without means testing. But the very freedom that these policies made possible terrified America's leading proponents of family values. They hastened to slam shut this narrow window of opportunity for families not dependent on men.

Ronald Reagan played a pivotal role in this turning tide, pioneering welfare reform as governor of California that cut benefits, reinstituted relentless surveillance of anyone receiving them, and, as a result, saw far fewer people applying for welfare. He introduced the virulently racist and enduring idea of "welfare queens" to a wide audience. His strategy was fully realized at a national level under Bill Clinton, when New Democrats and conservatives saw eye to eye on the importance of family, if on little else. New work requirements and marriage incentives created a regime much like the old poor laws, but on a national level. These new laws mandated that states identify and locate fathers and spend significant resources enforcing child support, often amounting to small sums from impoverished or working-class men. The message over and over again has been that moral families should absorb individuals' needs. Don't look to the state. In this light, the market is terribly family-friendly.

What's more, it should be obvious from the quite brutal enforcement required to shape people into so-called traditional family structures that there has never been anything particularly natural about a nation of identical nuclear families. If there were, it wouldn't have taken a crusade of hundreds of years and the charisma of Ronald Reagan and Bill Clinton combined.

Unfortunately for social conservatives and neoliberals alike, the one eternal thing about the family is that it has always been in flux. In her study *The Way We Never Were*, scholar Stephanie Coontz notes that in no era has the ideal family been a reality—the idealized Victorian family, for example, was materially supported by enslaved families and industrial workers who sent their children to labor in factories.[6] There is no one "traditional" family, but rather a variety of kinship networks that have evolved in response to systems of work and efforts by the ruling class to control labor, money, and mobility. In the midst of this push and pull, it is difficult to imagine what *we* want from the family. As socialists, are we for or against it? Is the family a bastion against capitalism or another realm of exploitation? What the hell are families for?

Families and Freedom

Toni Morrison's *Beloved* is a story about a mother's love and the murder of a child. Sethe has escaped slavery. While she and her children are fleeing, they are nearly caught and brought back to the plantation. When she believes that capture is imminent, she cuts the throat of her youngest child. Under slavery, Morrison said in conversation with Junot Díaz, your children "weren't yours. They could be sold, *were* sold. To be a mother, was an unbelievable freedom. And so when Margaret Garner [the real-life model for Sethe] cut that girl's neck, she was saying 'this child is mine.' And to claim her. Even if it had to go and become bloody, nevertheless that was the freedom, that was the ability, that was the mothering."[7]

Dorothy Roberts's classic study of race and reproduction, *Killing the Black Body*, begins with slavery and tells a story about how efforts to control black women's reproduction have shaped both anti-feminism and racism in America. The book is an intellectual cornerstone of the reproductive justice movement founded by black women in 1994. As Roberts documents, family structures beyond the two-parent home have long been a strategy to deal with the pressures of racism and poverty. Because families were constantly torn apart during slavery, she writes, "slave communities created networks of mutual obligation that reached beyond the nuclear family related by blood and marriage. . . . During and following the Civil War, ex-slaves throughout the South took in Black children orphaned by wartime dislocation and death ('motherless children') who were excluded from formal adoption services." She goes on to describe the ugly alliance between eugenics and the movement for birth control, and the ensuing legacy—extending up until the 1970s—of doctors sterilizing black, brown, and poor women without their consent because they were deemed unfit to have children; roughly sixty thousand Americans are estimated to have been sterilized without their consent.

The fixation on poor and black mothers as the drivers of America's problems, especially poverty, is absurd on its face, if an impressively brazen exercise in blaming the victims of capitalism for its outcomes. The Clinton administration's brutal welfare reform meant not only cuts to state support but also the reinforcement of the family as a zone of personal responsibility. The thrust of such restrictions hasn't been to support families in whatever form they might take, but to enforce judgments about who is worthy of procreation. That ever-flexible notion of worthiness seldom includes poor people and people of color because it isn't meant to; unworthiness is a club that's useful to wield to control resources. The very notion of blackness, suggests Roberts, has been written out of national tropes of good motherhood. "American culture," she writes, "reveres no Black madonna."

Roberts theorizes that in our social policies, we need both liberty and equality. A liberal view of negative liberty in the sphere of reproductive rights—demanding an end to abortion bans, for example—fails to take into account how affluent people benefit from a rights-based approach while neglecting poor women, who are more likely to be coerced by the government or private insurance companies. "Mainstream reproductive rights organizations practically ignored the explosion of government policies in the 1990s, such as welfare 'family caps' and prosecution for using drugs while pregnant, principally aimed at punishing childbearing by black women who received public assistance," she later wrote in *Dissent*, adding that such groups' "promotion of birth control as a way to save taxpayer money spent on unintended, welfare-dependent children . . . masks its potential for racial and class bias and coercion, as well as the systemic and structural reasons for social inequities."[8] Thus, the framework of reproductive justice doesn't take the rights to birth control and abortion as simple social goods, but rather situates them within a more comprehensive program for justice that acknowledges that these tools have been for good and for ill.

Accordingly, reproductive rights campaigners have pushed more mainstream organizations to acknowledge the full scope of what it means to protect reproductive freedom. In 2014, for instance, SisterSong executive director Monica Simpson chided Planned Parenthood in Mississippi for only working to block one of two conservative ballot initiatives. They fought one that would have established fetal personhood at the moment of conception, but not another to implement voter ID laws. As Simpson wrote in an open letter to the organization, the latter left "Mississippi more vulnerable to new 'personhood,' anti-abortion, and other discriminatory and counterproductive laws in the future."

The contours of coercion identified by reproductive justice movement activists and scholars give us unparalleled insight into how freedom will actually be achieved: not by ticking off a list of formal rights, but by making major structural changes to what is valued. Morrison addressed this shift in an interview with *Time* magazine in 1989. The interviewer cites the "depressingly large number of single-parent households and the crisis in unwed teenage pregnancies." Morrison responds by dismissing the limited definition of a good family, noting that "I don't think a female running a house is a problem, a broken family. It's perceived as one because of the notion that a head is a man. Two parents can't raise a child any more than one. . . . And the little nuclear family is a paradigm that just doesn't work. It doesn't work for white people or for black people. Why we are hanging onto it, I don't know. It isolates people into little units—people need a larger unit."

The interviewer presses her: isn't she worried about teen pregnancies? Couldn't these girls have realized their dreams, become teachers perhaps? "They can be teachers," Morrison responds. "They can be brain surgeons. We have to help them become brain surgeons. That's my job. I want to take them all in my arms and say, 'Your baby is beautiful and so are you and, honey, you can do it. And when you get to be a brain surgeon, call me—I will take care of your baby.' That's the attitude you have to have about human life. But we don't want to pay for it. I don't think anybody cares about unwed mothers unless they're black—or poor. The question is not morality, the question is money."

The Luxury of Communism

In the excellent and titillating documentary *Do Communists Have Better Sex?*, the filmmaker talks with a group of social scientists who studied sex in divided Germany before 1989.[9] Now, to be clear, this "better sex" was not happening in any kind of utopia—the stagnant economy and the Berlin Wall ensured that. But at the same time, due to ideology, practical politics, and competition with the West, East Germany had some useful innovations when it came to sex. The German Communists believed strongly in sex education, occasionally of the soft-porn variety. And they sought to replace guilt and coercion in marriage with something more liberated and rational. Kurt Starke, sex researcher, noted that "marriage lost the function of legitimizing sexuality very early in East Germany. Over 90%, 99%,

almost 100% of people had premarital sex." In a black-and-white sex education video, two beautiful young Germans have sex, a baby is conceived, and
the young man says with downcast eyes, "I guess we'll have to get married,
then." The young woman looks at him evenly: "I don't know if I want to."

In East Germany, the voice-over continues, "The cost of living is low.
Young people are only entitled to their own housing once they've produced
children. So half the women in East Germany become mothers at the age
of twenty-two." Far from destroying their society, subsuming it in a wave
of tragic youthful pregnancies—a guarantee, Americans would have you
believe, of poverty and criminality—Dietrich Mühlberg, a cultural studies
researcher, explained that "back then . . . for students and young workers,
having children wasn't a problem. It didn't throw them off course." An interviewer asks a young woman if "when you're twenty-one or twenty-two you'll
have a baby or two and you'll be studying and working, don't you think it's a
bit much?" She responds, "Not if you work together. If you share the housework it ought to be fine." And it wasn't just about shared housework: East
Germany had a robust child care system, and, far from being stigmatized,
families were expected to use it. In this, it benefited from the Communists'
rejection of gendered fictions of natural womanhood, so freighted in the
West with the labor of mothering and the guilt of not mothering.

"Financially and otherwise," the voice-over intones, "children are not
a hindrance under totally subsidized socialism." Under the socialism we
seek, the overwhelming mass of obligations that under capitalism have been
thrust onto the nuclear family in the name of responsibility must be returned
to the community. And the policies created must be designed to support a
multiplicity of family forms and structures; just as today's policies coerce
people into a narrow set of structures, socialist policy should set them free.

Of course, we don't have to go back to East Germany to see some good
examples of sex ed and gender equal social policy. The Nordic countries
famously provide good models. Sweden has had comprehensive sex education since 1956.[10] In the Netherlands, comprehensive sex education can
start as young as four, and Dutch teens are much more likely than their
American counterparts to describe their first sexual experiences as fun and
positive.[11] All of the Nordic states boast liberal abortion laws (though they
have recently come under threat) and universal health care, and they have

some of the lowest maternal mortality rates in the world.[12] These countries boast social policies that actively aim toward gender equality. Denmark, for instance, specifically incentivizes men to take parental leave, recognizing that just providing social benefits may not change the gendered division of labor. As a result, the maternal employment rate in Denmark is over 80 percent. Such generous social safety nets also ensures that women are not compelled to marry to tolerate men for mere survival. And finally, while people in Nordic countries enjoy a higher quality of life than the average American, they work fewer hours. Everyone simply spends more time at home.

There is no one policy that will solve the crisis of care, because when we talk about care, we are really talking about life: everything that sustains us day to day that is not wage exploitation. Transforming our world into a socialist one is by definition a question of care. In no particular order, here are a few basic policy suggestions for socialist reproductive justice and care.

Universal Twenty-Four-Hour High-Quality Communal Child Care

Every attempt at getting universal child care in this country has been met with a backlash that uses moralizing about motherhood to thrust sole responsibility and expense for children back on the small family unit. Back in 1997, Mike Pence said that "for years, we have gotten the message from the mouthpieces of the popular culture that you can have it all, career, kids and a two-car garage. The numbers in this federally funded study argue that the converse is true. Sure, you can have it all, but your day care kids get the short end of the emotional stick." Your day care kids! Pence was right that trying to "have it all" is a trap that disguises the contradictions inherent in capitalist labor (surely what he meant). But study after study has shown that kids do great in day care and parents are more able to participate in public life. One would think that someone who calls his wife "Mother" might be more open to nontraditional family forms.

Socialist Johanna Brenner has pointed out that there's an additional reason for socialists to fight for child care: while women still do the bulk of child care, it will always be hard for them to participate in political organizing. Organizing where women are not represented is likely to be organizing that fails to address concerns that disproportionately affect women. Indeed, worker action in general can be subsidized by policies that allow them to organize by loosening individual responsibility for care work.

In Denmark, every child is guaranteed preschool.[13] Providers can't charge more than a quarter of what it costs, and it's free if the family can't afford it. This basic level of care is a good starting point, and Mike Pence will be glad to know that Danes seem not to have grown sociopathic as a result of early childhood services. Brenner has warned that for-profit child care providers are likely to try to shape any future programs in the United States. She wisely proposes that child care be built into the public school system, a model that allows for both democratic access and some local control. She suggests, too, that child care be structured as worker cooperatives, a form that could better include parents and other community stakeholders in decision-making. The care sector must, of course, be organized: what is today one of the greatest sites of the exploitation of immigrant labor should instead be a site of feminist labor power for the women of color who disproportionately currently work in the sector.

Housing as a Human Right

Communities of care do, typically, begin at home, and there's no reason that home should be either a crowded, run-down apartment building or an isolated, inefficient suburban house. Right now, housing in America is being done all wrong from the perspective of care.

Consider our cities: throughout America, urban areas are being sold off to developers to create luxury properties, many of which appear to be money-laundering schemes for the international oligarchy.[14] Meanwhile, about half a million people are homeless on any given night of the year.[15] We need hundreds of thousands of units of housing. The only solution is to build massive amounts of *public* housing. A mixed-income building here and there won't do it.

While public housing is often run-down and denigrated in America, it needn't be this way. Famously, prewar Red Vienna saw the construction of beautiful public housing that stands to this day, with everything from modern kitchens to swimming pools to lovely courtyards, maintained with pride by the taxpayer.[16] As Harvard professor Eve Blau notes, the housing was part of a comprehensive urban development scheme intended to improve the quality of life for the whole city, and provided "a vast new infrastructure of health and welfare services, clinics, childcare facilities, kindergartens, schools, sports facilities, public libraries, theatres, cinemas, and other institutions."[17] Sometimes child care and elder care were combined with housing. It stands as a strong example of how to create a built environment for socialist care.

In 1930s New York, a number of housing developments experimented with collective governance and were built to facilitate democratic collective control over all kinds of care work, ranging from child care to elder care to gardening and entertainment. Built on the so-called Rochdale Principles for collectives, some of these experiments were sponsored directly by labor unions to provide their members with good affordable housing. Rochdale Village in Queens was a city project that emphasized racial integration. When estate pressures and incentives, as well as the end of government subsidies, drove the boards to abolish the Rochdale structure in the 1980s, many community members mourned what they saw as an ideal living situation. "This is probably one of the best integrated housing communities—racially, culturally, socioeconomically," one member told the *New York Times*.[18] "There are probably some very successful professionals who are beyond middle income and some who are borderline working poor or lower." The possibility was there for not just good housing, but housing that had begun to democratize daily life and the world of the family.

Free Abortion on Demand

The freedom to have an abortion is great, and abortion should be free. Without it, women live constantly under the threat of being forced to give birth. With it, women are free to have sex without worrying that if a condom breaks they've made a lifelong commitment to parenthood. And they're free to plan their families, not fall backward into them.

We are perilously close to an abortion-free dystopia in many parts of the country: as of this writing, Missouri looks likely to become the first state without an abortion clinic while five other states have only one left. Forty-five states allow health care providers to refuse to participate in abortions, and twenty-seven states have waiting periods.[19] Pregnant people jump through endless humiliating hoops to get access to their health care.

These regulations give the distinct impression that pregnant people are not quite human, not able to make their own choices, moral minors. These barriers often can only be overcome with resources to travel and pay doctors. Every week in America, women give birth against their will because they are poor.

We know that women will have abortions whether or not abortion is legal. In 1955, when abortion was illegal, experts estimated that there were between two hundred thousand and 1.2 million occurring every year in the United States. Today, experts favor something near the higher figure. Complications including sepsis were frequent. At least one hundred women died annually from abortion complications until it was legalized, an annual massacre that we could see again soon in America.[20]

What would it take to give women access to this basic tool of autonomy and family planning? First, stop treating it like exceptional health care. It should be available at public hospitals for free and not shunted onto private clinics. Universal health care would benefit all women enormously, and must include abortion without exception. Learning to perform abortions is not currently required in medical school, and many offer it as an elective and with little training. Treating women's health care as a lesser subject is unacceptable, and doctors should become well versed in performing abortions and related care. Finally, abortion must be absolutely on demand; unless we're going to start adding waiting periods before men's colonoscopies, waiting periods are simply a mark of contempt for women. Of course, birth control should also be free and widely accessible, part of a person's fundamental right to control her own body. It will not replace abortion: accidental pregnancies are unlikely to disappear entirely; about 13 percent of women say that the health of the fetus contributed to their decision to have an abortion, 12 percent cite their own health, and, well, pregnant people change their minds.[21]

Ending Policing

There are about sixty thousand kids incarcerated in America today. Schools in New York have more cops than counselors.[22] Ordinary acting out at school is increasingly criminalized, especially for black and brown children. Children who are incarcerated are more likely to be incarcerated as adults, and this lifelong cycle of suffering can begin in elementary school. Former death penalty mitigation specialist Ethan Brown wrote that "nearly all of my adult clients had been incarcerated as kids, a profoundly adverse, life-altering experience that was as much a part of their trauma history as having a sibling murdered, being physically or sexually abused by a family member or teacher, or suffering from lead poisoning."[23] He added that when kids were sent to adult prisons instead of (also appalling) juvenile jails, they were five times more likely to be sexually assaulted and thirty-six times more likely to commit suicide.

This is a reproductive justice issue that affects an entire community. Not only does this sort of policing produce traumatized children who often grow into traumatized adults; it traumatizes parents and turns schools into war zones. A criminal record often makes it near impossible to get a job and reinforces cycles of poverty and stigma. America is exceptional in the length of its prison sentences: about two hundred thousand people are serving life sentences or virtual life sentences (defined as likely to die in prison) today. Meanwhile in Norway, mass murderer Anders Behring Breivik was sentenced to twenty-one years—a longer sentence doesn't exist. With 2.3 million Americans behind bars, communal life in many areas has become punctuated by the absence and reappearance of loved ones.

As Aviva Stahl notes elsewhere in this volume ("Who Gets to Be Safe? Prisons, Police, and Terror"), the route to ending mass criminalization and incarceration runs through more health care, including mental health care, less poverty, and more housing security—all core socialist goals—and restorative and transformative justice offer more human alternatives.

Now, I know what some of you are thinking: how can all these things be part of a reproductive justice movement—won't you dilute the struggle? I'd say just the opposite. By understanding the intersections of reproductive justice with other struggles against capitalism, we can build a far stronger movement.

Consider the 2019 teacher strikes that rocked Los Angeles. The teachers didn't demand just wages, but full-time school nurses, smaller classes, counselors, less standardized testing. They described an entire realm of human development that was suffering: they couldn't do their jobs and the students couldn't learn. Schools are enmeshed in the reproduction of communities. One teacher decried the factory mentality of higher-ups in the education system, telling journalist Sarah Jaffe, "Our widget is a human who has trauma and who has been through things. I have a student in my classroom right now whose mother was incarcerated when she was 2. Her father was shot the next year. She is living with her great-grandparents."[24] When the teachers went on strike, one poll showed that two-thirds of LA residents supported them, with just 15 percent against the strike.[25] Far from the family-first attitude of "getting the best for my kids," the strike turned education into a reproductive justice issue and built solidarity among parents, teachers, and kids.

Extended Family

There are plenty of other ways to expand our definition of what constitutes a family. Nontraditional family forms have often come about from a mix of preference and survival. In *Zami: A New Spelling of My Name*, the poet, theorist, and activist Audre Lorde writes about the circles of gay-girls (her term) who came together out of love, friendship, and mutual aid. "However imperfectly," she writes of one period in the 1950s, "we tried to build a community of sorts where we could, at the very least, survive within a world we correctly perceived to be hostile to us; we talked endlessly about how best to create that mutual support which twenty years later was being discussed in the women's movement as a brand-new concept."[26] This isn't a utopia—Lorde is clear that mutual aid was necessary in the face of poverty and homophobia, and that her circle at the time consistently failed to recognize racism—but it was a loving family and entirely female. As Stephanie Coontz writes in *The Way We Never Were*, the 1950s, often represented as the quintessential era of family values, were an era of severe Cold War repression, where "a 'normal' family and vigilant mother became the 'front line' of defense against treason; anti-communists linked deviant family or sexual behavior to sedition," so that gay-baiting and red-baiting went hand in hand. Coontz notes that, in such a context, marriage was often a defensive act. For Lorde, her found family was an affirmative act, but one fraught with risk.[27]

In Armistead Maupin's classic series, Tales of the City, about the tenants of a building in 1970s and '80s San Francisco, much of the dire risk is removed—his characters are mostly white and more often employed than not—but each character has fled a "normal" biological family in order to become fully themselves. More than one tenant is in hiding from such a normal family due to their queerness. In these stories, the house itself forms the family; it's cheap, big, pleasant, and overseen by a benevolent woman with a loose conception of timely rent. There's no better example of the role of real estate in creating a community of like-minded friends and lovers. (Though it should also be noted that San Francisco exemplifies how America's wildly deficient housing protections have resulted in marginalized communities both acting as the perpetrators of gentrification as people of color are pushed out, and then becoming its victims as wealthy people move in.[28])

In Canada recently, I met with a friend who is an artist and writer who has grappled in print and life with her own ideas about family. She told me she had a good arrangement: a couple she knew had a child and shared caretaking with her and another friend who lived in their building. They were all semibroke artists, but they had free health insurance, low rent, and a pretty happy community of care. She thought often about moving to New York. "I add everything up and I think I can do it," she told me. "And then I remember health care."

The big question for socialists is whether we can build a world that recognizes the diversity of family forms and supports them with resources instead of trying to discipline them. Even a socialist society will be full of unsolvable human differences, even traumas, including within biological families. People will probably always desire a wide range of living arrangements that may or may not be biological. Further, the family will continue to evolve, and should.

In a world radically transformed by revolution, technology, and the simple fact of time, we cannot make some perfect blueprint and thank god for that. The theorist Donna Haraway made the case in her 1985 "Cyborg Manifesto" that boundaries between people and machines and animals should and would become increasingly porous. Feminist theorist Shulamith Firestone declared pregnancy and birth unnaturally gruesome and proposed that all babies be grown outside the body. Both have actually turned out to be prophetic: rates of in vitro fertilization have risen steadily, and there is a booming surrogacy industry for those who can afford it, staffed by working-class women who do the work of gestating the baby. We are in a wild era of reproductive technologies.

Now, it goes without saying that today those methods are for people who can afford them, and regularly exploit the underpaid labor of women of the Global South. Americans are outsourcing reproductive labor to many of the same countries to which American corporations outsource telemarketing and clothing manufacturing. But it also means that in a society that was no longer obsessed with enforcing the nuclear family, these new reproductive technologies could allow for all kinds of family arrangements, kinship networks, and relationships of care. In her book *Full Surrogacy Now*, writer and geographer Sophie Lewis expands the idea of surrogacy, saying "labor (such as gestational labor) and nature (including genome, epigenome, microbiome, and so on) can only alchemize the world together by transforming one another. We are all, at root, responsible, and especially for the stew that is epigenetics. We are the makers of one another. And we could learn collectively to act like it."[29] In other words, what if we were able to incorporate these new technologies into a utopian vision of diverse and expansive families?

In this sense, a socialist vision of family expands the very definition of the term. It forces us to recognize that a healthy society demands many forms of care that exist outside the household. On the other hand, it offers us a new way to *create* households that are free to take many forms and free from the burdens forced on them by an austerity state. Perhaps the key feature of our neoliberal world is that work has expanded to fill every bit of time, putting unsustainable pressure on all nonmonetized work, and on the humane pleasures of building community with others. A socialist vision flips this formula, putting economics in service to human well-being and relationships. Those relationships are then free to take shape from human comfort and desire instead of survival and coercion. This vision of multiplicitous families deviates radically from mainstream discussions of family. But it doesn't challenge so much as support the families that actually exist.

Defending and Improving Public Education

Pedro Noguera

PUBLIC EDUCATION IS THE ONLY SOCIAL ENTITLEMENT IN AMERICAN SOCI-
ety that is available to all children. Education is also one of the few sectors
here that is mandated by law to pursue some degree of equity and equal
opportunity for children.[1] There are myriad reasons for progressives and
democratic socialists to fight for public education, but this may be the most
important: the United States' education system is among the closest things
we have to socialism.

In a society where none of our basic rights, including precious needs such
as food, housing, health care, safety, or even clean air or water, are guaranteed or protected, the inclusive nature of public education makes it the most
important and enduring component of the American social welfare system
and safety net for children. Public schools are the only institution where
children are provided a meal (sometimes two), adult supervision, heat in the
winter, and some measure of safety.

Despite its incredible promise, America's public education remains deeply flawed and profoundly unequal. The services that public schools provide
are, more often than not, inadequate to address the needs of our most vulnerable children, and too often our schools fail to achieve the basic purpose
of education—namely, imparting academic skills in literacy and numeracy.
Moreover, in most of the country, education is characterized by extreme
inequities in learning conditions. In every major city, and in many suburban
and rural communities as well, public schools almost exclusively serve the
poor. Presently, more than 20 million children in the public school system

qualify for free lunch and one out of five come from families at or below the poverty line.[2] Moreover, despite the historic *Brown v. Board of Education* decision to integrate schools, many remain deeply segregated on the basis of race and class.[3] None of this negates the importance of the institution, nor its potential. It does, however, make it vulnerable to criticism and attack.

Many politicians, Republicans as well as many Democrats, have done little more than blame schools and the people who work there for the problems that beset many public schools. In so doing, they avoid addressing the structural issues—poverty and institutionalized racism—that make it more likely that many public schools will continue to fail. Many politicians would prefer to espouse lofty platitudes such as describing education as the "civil rights issues of the twenty-first century" rather than taking on the underlying issues that make it difficult to ensure that *all* children receive an adequate education.

Under both Republican and Democratic administrations, policies that were intended to reduce race and class disparities in academic outcomes—the so-called achievement gap—have proven to be largely inadequate and even harmful to public education. For some time, individual schools and districts have been left to themselves to devise strategies to address rising poverty rates and to counter the effects of social and economic inequality on education. The results of these efforts have been fairly unimpressive, both because the problems they are attempting to address are formidable, and because the policy strategies that have been pursued have largely been weak (e.g., expanding the number of charter schools, closing failing schools, etc.) and even harmful.

To support and revitalize public education, progressives who are in charge of school systems must approach efforts to reform and improve education by directly challenging inequality and injustice. This does not mean that we should simply defend public education as is, accepting its flaws or tolerating the glaring inequities that too often relegate poor children to an inferior education. The public expects more, and, to be relevant, progressives must offer a pragmatic vision for change. As a policymaker, educator, and researcher, I will use this chapter to propose ways to change the education system, both because I think it is irresponsible to merely offer a critique of current policies, and because I believe there are possibilities for enacting changes that can improve the lives and opportunities available to children and families. In the remainder of this chapter I spell out some of the policy changes that are needed.

Bringing about sustainable, meaningful change—and defending public education because of its importance to democracy—requires us to contend with what presently constitutes "education reform." For the last several years, neoliberal reform has dominated both Republican and Democratic education policies. Its well-known recipe consists of the following: raising academic standards through the adoption of the Common Core curriculum; increasing accountability on students, schools, and, in several states, teachers and principals, through high-stakes testing; shutting down "failing" schools and replacing them with publicly financed but privately run charter schools. In several cities, the reforms have gone further and included rating teachers (and schools) based on their effectiveness in raising student test scores, and sometimes publishing the results in newspapers; expanding school choice either through the creation of voucher programs or by expanding the number of charter schools; mayoral control of schools in big cities; and state takeovers of failing districts, most of which happen to serve poor black and Latinx children. For example, not long ago every urban school district in New Jersey was under state control, and despite the state's failure to bring lasting improvement to schools in Newark, Paterson, Trenton, and Camden after several years of receivership, none of the state's high-ranking public officials were held accountable. At the same time, charter schools have proliferated in these cities, supported by donations from Facebook CEO Mark Zuckerberg and backed by politicians like former governor Chris Christie and current U.S. senator Cory Booker.[4]

For democratic socialists, there is no reason why pushing back on this agenda should mean accepting the indifference that too often characterizes the way in which policymakers typically tolerate the abysmal conditions in schools serving poor children or the disregard that poor parents are often subjected to by school systems.

Teachers unions have been at the leading edge of opposition to voucher initiatives, the proliferation of charter schools, the use of tests to rate teachers, and other parts of the agenda. Sometimes, as in the case of the teachers strike in Chicago in 2012 or more recently the Los Angeles teachers strike, not only have teachers unions been successful in defeating the neoliberal reform agenda; they have also managed to advocate for broader changes such as reducing the size of classes and hiring more counselors and social workers. The 2018 wave of teacher strikes in Oklahoma, West Virginia, Arizona, and Kentucky—and in LA a year later—brought the fight for public education to the Trump administration and its allies. The strikes and the wellspring of public support they generated showed that when teachers organize to address the systematic disinvestment in public education that has occurred in many Republican-led states (and some blue states like California), they can generate considerable public support.

As striking teachers have made clear, schools generally reflect and embody the inequities present in our society. The so-called achievement gap—the problem the last twenty years of federal education policy has attempted to take on—is actually an educational manifestation of social and economic inequality. We have known for some time that factors such as family income and parental education are the strongest predictors of student academic performance.[5] We have also known that under the guise of "local control," the United States has become one of few Western nations that intentionally allocates and spends more money to educate the children of the affluent than it does to educate the children of the poor.[6]

Given that our society remains deeply stratified by race and class, it is hardly surprising that most schools reflect these patterns. Yet, with progressives in charge of many school systems and school boards across the country, and the growing popularity of politicians like Bernie Sanders and Alexandria Ocasio-Cortez—each calling to expand our system of free public education to the college level—progressive leaders will need more than slogans. To be credible, they must have policies and strategies to address the larger structural inequalities that hamper public education. Democratic socialists and progressives alike must be prepared to put forward a vision for education rooted in social justice that compliments and echoes the demands of teachers striking to defend quality education from West Virginia to California.

A Bold Agenda for Reform

In the spring of 2008, a large group of progressive academics, policymakers, educators, and advocates released an editorial in the *New York Times* calling for a "Broader and Bolder Approach to School Reform." Sensing the strong possibility of an Obama victory in the November elections, the group referred to as BBA (Broader and Bolder Approach) hoped that it could influence the new administration to pursue a different policy direction upon assuming office. While the specific policy reforms called for by BBA were relatively modest and uncontroversial—expanded access for children to health care, after-school and summer school enrichment, and universal access to preschool—there was a larger point to the advocacy that reformers saw as threatening. The crafters of BBA were hoping to shift the direction of education policy away from standards-based accountability toward an agenda that emphasized expanding opportunity and equity. In a sign of what was to come from the Obama administration, BBA's op-ed prompted a swift repudiation by former New York City chancellor Joel Klein (who was rumored to be under consideration for appointment by Obama to secretary of education), the Reverend Al Sharpton, and former U.S. House of Representatives Speaker Newt Gingrich, who formed the Education Equity Project, in part to counter BBA.[7]

Though the Broader and Bolder Approach has never been embraced as federal policy, there are now openings in some states (e.g., California, New Mexico, Washington, and Oregon) as well as school districts to begin embracing such an agenda. In the final section, I outline what a progressive education agenda should consist of. This is by no means an exhaustive or comprehensive list. Rather, it should be seen as the beginnings of a framework for policy and a means to ensure that education is central to any progressive agenda for change.

Capacity Building, but Not in a Vacuum

Several Democratic and Republican leaders have responded to failing schools—most of them serving poor black and Latinx students—by either shutting them down or taking them over, effectively removing them from democratic governance. In nearly every case, there has been no evidence of improvement.[8] Another favorite tactic is firing hordes of "bad teachers" (e.g., those who cannot raise test scores) and principals. Under New York mayor Mike Bloomberg, 161 schools, almost all of which served poor black and Latinx students, were shut down during his twelve years in office. Many of the schools that were labeled "failing" were replaced by charter schools, based on the assumption that they would be more effective.

The alternative to mass firings, threats, or shutting down struggling schools is capacity building. In essence, capacity building involves state or district officials assessing the factors that have contributed to a school's troubles and then devising a plan *with* school staff to make sure that needs are addressed. This may involve training or even replacing personnel or providing critical resources (e.g., social workers, counselors, after-school programs, etc.) to meet student needs.

This is the strategy that Michael Fullan argues has been the key to success in Toronto, arguably the highest-performing urban school district in North America.[9] When a school in Toronto is identified as struggling by the Ontario Ministry of Education, a strategy is devised to address the causes of the problems and to build capacity in areas of weakness.

We now have a clearer sense of the areas where capacity building is needed, particularly in struggling schools. In a 2010 study of school reform,[10] researchers with the University of Chicago's Consortium on School Research identified five essential ingredients that must be present for schools to experience sustained improvement, as follows:

- A coherent instructional guidance system
- Ongoing development of the professional capacity of staff
- Strong parent-community-school ties
- A student-centered learning climate / culture
- Shared leadership to drive change

By focusing on these five essentials, schools are more likely to improve over time. However, it is important to note that capacity building is a long-term process and not a quick fix. Under Mayor Bill de Blasio, New York City's Department of Education adopted a capacity building approach to support its struggling schools. However, existing evidence shows that the impact has thus far been negligible.[11] The limited success can be attributed to New York City's approach to capacity building, which focused on bringing social services into schools but did not adequately address their academic challenges.

Additionally, in the United States, we still rely too heavily on schools to address a broad range of social needs that are common among poor children (e.g., lack of housing, health care, etc.). It makes little sense to expect schools to address needs that they have neither the resources nor the expertise to meet, but this is how things have been done for many years in the United States. Unlike in the U.S., universal access to health care and preschool has been part of the Canadian welfare system for many years. Without broader societal efforts to address poverty and structural inequality, it is highly unlikely that we will see large-scale improvements in public schools that serve poor children.

Focusing on the Whole Child

Acknowledgment that children's physical health, emotional well-being, and social stability have an impact on their academic performance is not a new idea. In fact, it was a central focus of Lyndon B. Johnson's War on Poverty. The Elementary and Secondary Education Act passed in 1965 as part of that combination of programs aimed at alleviating and compensating for the effects of poverty. That Johnson had once been a teacher in a poor Texas town near the Mexican border undoubtedly reinforced his recognition that, in order for education to play a role in reducing or breaking the cycle of poverty across generations, schools serving poor children would need help in countering the effects of poverty.

Despite the bold rhetoric that accompanied its passage, the idea that schools should focus on the needs of the whole child was lost in No Child Left Behind. Even at the height of the Great Recession—with unemployment soaring and many families unable to make ends meet—neoliberal reform advocates cast efforts to focus on the whole child as making excuses for the effects of poverty. In a 2010 editorial for the *Washington Post*, Joel Klein, Janet Murguía of the National Council of la Raza, and Michael Lomax of the United Negro College Fund wrote:

> In the debate over how to fix American public education, many believe that schools alone cannot overcome the impact that economic disadvantage has on a child, that life outcomes are fixed by poverty and family circumstances, and that education doesn't work until other problems are solved. This theory is, in some ways, comforting for educators. . . . Problem is, the theory is wrong. It's hard to know how wrong—because we haven't yet tried to make the changes that would tell us—but plenty of evidence demonstrates that schools can make an enormous difference despite the challenges presented by poverty and family background.

Despite their opposition, and the ongoing tendency to blame teachers for their inability to solve problems that are not academic in nature (e.g., homelessness), recognition of the need to adopt a more holistic approach to educating children is growing—and not just in blue cities like New York City. Several states are now embracing what are known as community schools to enhance the ability of schools to address the nonacademic needs of children. For example, despite the fact that Oklahoma has persistently underfunded its schools (in many districts in the state, students attend school only four days a week), the state has long been a leader in early childhood education. Many of the schools in Tulsa, Oklahoma City, and Union now offer a comprehensive range of services, including preschool and after-school programs. Some community schools are equipped with clinics, while others offer food pantries, coats for children in the winter, or housing and job placement services for parents.[12] While the costs associated with creating community schools are high, advocates point out that the costs of ignoring the needs of children are much higher. In a nation where more than half of the nation's children in public schools qualify for free or reduced-price lunch, the need for such an approach is increasingly clear.

From Using Assessment as a Weapon to Using It as a Tool

One of the most controversial aspects of the No Child Left Behind Act enacted under President George W. Bush was its requirement that children be tested on a regular basis—in third, fifth, and eighth grade, on math and literacy—to monitor their achievement. The idea was widely embraced, and most states now require students to be assessed at the end of each year.

As a result of No Child Left Behind's use of testing to hold schools accountable for student learning, subjects that were not on the tests often received considerably less attention and funding in many schools, particularly those serving poor children. Art, music, and physical education programs—and in some cases science and social studies—have been cut as a result.[13] Tests have been used to make "high-stakes" decisions that in many cases have harmful effects on students and educators. For example, in states such as Massachusetts, students who don't pass state exams are held back or denied a high school diploma.

The real issue here isn't testing itself but *how* the tests are used. While standardized testing has become controversial, it is important to note that few educators argue against the need for assessment. After all, how can one know if children are learning, or have acquired the skills and knowledge deemed to be most important if they aren't assessed? However, it has become increasingly clear that in many schools, preparing students for standardized tests has replaced the need to focus on teaching and learning. Many scholars have argued that instead of using tests to rank students, teachers, or schools, they should be used to diagnose learning needs and provide teachers with useful information on how to meet them.[14] If tests are used in this way, testing can instead serve as a useful tool to guide interventions and educational supports.

From Parents as Consumers to Parents as Partners

School choice is based on the principle that parents should be able to choose which school their child attends. In practice under most choice systems, particularly those that include charter schools, parents are treated as consumers. They are expected to be informed about the quality of schools they can choose from and to know when and how to apply or enter the lottery for admission. If they don't like what a school has to offer—or if they are unhappy with how they or their child is treated—then like a shopper at a department store or restaurant they can choose to go elsewhere and patronize another school. The market logic behind this system is that there will be high demand for "good" schools, and underperforming schools will be underenrolled and eventually close due to a lack of students.[15]

In reality, choice often exacerbates inequality. The most informed and motivated parents are most likely to get their children into the better schools, while those who are less informed, or who have children regarded as less desirable (e.g., students with special needs, English learners, children with behavior problems, etc.), are more likely to be stuck in less desirable schools. While the idea of treating parents as consumers in an open education marketplace has been appealing to many—especially to parents dissatisfied with the neighborhood schools that their children have typically been required to attend—in reality school choice is always limited by parents' unequal access to transportation and reliable information about the quality of schools. Moreover, research shows that in many cases the most highly regarded schools are unlikely to choose the most disadvantaged children. Similar patterns can be observed in many magnet schools and schools that require an entrance exam to gain admission. Typically, such schools screen out the most disadvantaged students, further exacerbating inequities among schools.

It is important to point out that middle- and upper-class parents almost always have some form of choice. They can, and often do, choose to move if they don't like the school in their neighborhood, or pay to send their child to private school. This is one of the reasons why schools in most cities in the United States today remain segregated by race and class despite the *Brown* decision.[16]

Given the pervasive inequality in society, school choice is a poor way of ensuring access to a quality education. However, even if one is opposed to choice, the question of how parents should be involved in the education of their children is still relevant and important. Several studies have shown that when parents reinforce the value of learning at home, students are more likely to perform at higher levels. While many schools claim to value parent involvement, too often they fail to recognize that the most important form of parental involvement occurs at home, and not at the school itself. Many working parents, meanwhile, lack the time to volunteer or attend meetings at their children's school. Low-income and immigrant parents often encounter barriers to their involvement, such as a lack of translation and transportation, and some feel intimidated when interacting with school officials.

Given the importance of parental involvement to student success, a truly progressive education agenda must include a deliberate, well-devised effort to engage parents as partners in the educational endeavor. To do this, schools must view parent involvement as an organizing strategy and have the resources to carry it out: reaching out to parents where they live, cultivating trust by demonstrating respect and empathy, and training teachers in how to work with and communicate with parents from different race, class, linguistic, and educational backgrounds.

From Punitive to Preventative School Discipline

In the aftermath of the mass shootings at Columbine High School in 1994, several states adopted zero-tolerance school discipline policies that were intended to increase school safety.[17] In addition to increasing the presence of armed security guards, law enforcement personnel, surveillance cameras, and metal detectors, zero-tolerance policies also led to an increase in the number of young people who were suspended, expelled, and arrested at school throughout the country.[18] The impact of zero-tolerance policies was particularly harsh in schools serving black, Latinx, and low-income children generally, even though most school shootings have been carried out by middle-class white males in middle-class white communities. Several studies have shown that racial disparities in school discipline are pervasive throughout the United States, and a 2014 study by the U.S. Department of Education Office of Civil Rights found that one out of four black male preschool children had been suspended at least once.

While almost everyone agrees on the absolute need for safety and order in schools, there is growing recognition that punitive approaches to school discipline are actually an obstacle to the goal of reducing racial disparities in student achievement and carrying out the central mission of education. Several states and school districts have begun to actively pursue strategies to reduce suspensions and racial disparities in school discipline. However, a progressive vision for educational reform must go further. Schools must adopt preventative strategies to maintain order and safety, and they must develop healthy cultures that support children and address the underlying issues that affect behavior (e.g., poverty, trauma, and academic difficulties).

Equitable Funding

There are more than thirteen thousand local school districts in the United States. They vary considerably in terms of wealth, income, and tax base, and thus the ability to pay for decent schools. A recent report by EdBuild found that there is a gap of $23 billion in funding between predominantly white school districts and districts that serve mostly students of color. According to the report, "For every student enrolled, the average nonwhite school district receives $2,226 less than a white school district."[19]

Ironically, even as the federal government has been focused on finding ways to reduce the disparities in how well students do in school (that is, the so-called achievement gap), it has largely ignored the wide and significant disparities in the amount of resources devoted to students in wealthy and less wealthy school districts. Americans spend roughly $650 billion a year on K–12 education. Traditionally, the bulk of funds used to support public schools has been generated revenue from local property taxes. Given the high degree of race and class segregation throughout the country, this has ensured that inequality in per-pupil spending is the norm, with few exceptions. Since the 1970s, there have been several lawsuits over inequity in funding for education. As a result, several states have improved their funding for local school districts and reduced some of the disparity in spending.

Overall, about 40 percent of all school funding comes from states and 40 percent comes from local school districts. But states vary dramatically in how much they spend on education—from $20,744 per student in New York to $6,751 in Utah. Furthermore, there is often considerable variation in how funds are allocated within states and school districts. Some states are more generous and progressive than others in funding school districts with the largest proportion of low-income students. However, in many districts and states, schools serving the poorest children receive less money.

Money matters. It impacts teacher salaries, the quality of facilities and resources available to students, and their ability to provide supplemental support services such as social workers and after-school and preschool programs. In a social democratic America, the federal government—which now provides only 10 percent of K–12 funding—would make equity in funding for schools a priority. This can be done by increasing the federal government's contribution to schools in high-poverty areas and by requiring states to adopt more equitable funding policies. In a fair system committed to educational equity, funds would be allocated based on need (i.e., the proportion of students from low-income families). States and local school boards would have autonomy to design the curriculum and set school standards so long as they meet a basic national threshold. This is how most social democratic nations today in Europe organize their school systems, and their students generally outperform American students in global comparisons of math, science, and other subjects. There's no good reason why the United States can't learn from their success and follow their example.

Mutual Accountability

Under the "standards and accountability" approach of neoliberal education reform, the general pattern has been that those with the most power have the least accountability. Governors, state legislatures, mayors (when they have authority), and superintendents are generally much less likely to be held accountable for school performance than students, teachers, and principals. Though the latter group typically has no control over the resources they have access to, it's the former who tend to avoid any responsibility for their role in managing and governing schools.

The alternative to top-down reform is the concept of mutual accountability. Under such an approach, the responsibilities of all stakeholders—students, parents, teachers, administrators, legislators, and governors—must be clearly laid out by state and district officials. While there is little that public officials can do to compel parents and students to do their part, several schools have shown that they are more likely to if asked respectfully. Since each stakeholder plays an important role in the educational process, spelling out what each must do to achieve desired results is important.

Choice, Charters, and Competition

Although several states have no provision to allow for the creation of charter schools—publicly financed, privately operated for-profit and nonprofit schools—in nearly every major American city, charter schools have become a significant option that parents can exercise when choosing a school. School choice and the creation of charter schools have become two of the few features of the reform movement that show no signs of fading away. While in several states the pace at which charter schools are being authorized has slowed considerably, there is no sign that the ones that are presently in existence will disappear anytime soon. Moreover, in some cities—Washington, DC, New Orleans, and Detroit—charter schools now make up the majority of schools available.

Most charter schools are nonunion, and many find ways to screen out the most disadvantaged children, which is why progressives and their allies (e.g., teachers unions and some civil rights groups such as the NAACP) almost uniformly oppose them, as well as school choice more generally. Their concerns that charter schools exacerbate existing inequities among schools by siphoning off the better-prepared students and undermining public schools by depriving them of needed funding are well-founded and supported by evidence. Public schools continue to serve 90 percent of America's children, and any policy that threatens their future viability should be challenged.

However, I believe a democratic socialist agenda for education should adopt a more nuanced approach toward charter schools. Most serve low-income students of color whose parents have chosen to enroll their children because they are not satisfied with the existing public schools—and most are content with the choice they made. Furthermore, middle-class and affluent parents always have some degree of choice, and they exercise it. It makes no sense for progressives to make the parents who support charter schools or the teachers who work in them their opponents.

Any effort to create and promote a democratic socialist educational agenda cannot be based on a prescribed list of policy positions, but on a careful reading of the politics and sentiments of the local community where it is to be executed. Schools always reflect the character—particularly with respect to race, class, and language—of the communities where they are located. As a consequence, organizers, activists, and aspiring politicians who hope to improve schools must be in dialogue with the parents, educators, and students they hope to lead, and the agenda they adopt must reflect their aspirations in the broadest sense. In other words, it has to be as democratic as it is socialist.

As with any other policy field, none of these changes will be effective if they are executed from the top down. If there is to be any possibility of advancing a progressive agenda during or after the Trump era, we must acknowledge that it will only emerge and gain traction through organizing and educating, particularly with people too often left out of the political decisions that govern their schools and communities.

The future of America will be determined not only by what happens in Washington but also by what happens to children in schools all over the country. As we have seen with striking teachers in Los Angeles and Denver, and with the Parkland students who have taken on the NRA to push for gun control, we can organize to create schools that are safe and responsive to the needs of the communities they serve. Democratic socialists must go further and take on the structural inequality that today sets up too many schools and students for failure. We can do this by developing and advocating for a democratic socialist agenda in America that is rooted in a bold vision for change in education.

Reclaiming Competition: Sports and Socialism

David Zirin

I LOVE SPORTS. I GREW UP IN THE NEW YORK CITY OF THE 1980s OBSESSED with the Mets, Jets, and Knicks, losing streaks and all. In other words, being a sports fan has never been easy. I played every sport that I could, almost always—to my great luck—with coaches who gave a damn about their players as people and not just instruments of their own egos. I never gave much thought to the politics of sports. That changed dramatically for me when Mahmoud Abdul-Rauf—a guard for the NBA's Denver Nuggets—made the decision in 1996 not to stand for the national anthem before a game. Rauf said that he made this daring decision because he believed while the American flag was "a symbol of freedom for some, it's a symbol of oppression and tyranny to others." In the aftermath, I heard announcers speak about Rauf being in "the tradition of activist athletes like Muhammad Ali, Billie Jean King, Tommie Smith, and John Carlos." At age twenty-two, I had no idea that such a tradition existed—despite what I thought was an extensive knowledge of sports history—so I set about attempting to learn this past. This too-often invisible history of struggle and resistance in the hyperexalted, celebrity-obsessed, brought-to-you-by-Nike world of sports should compel us in the present to both critique sports and attempt to envision the kind of sports world we want to see in the future.

This is why it resonated with me so strongly in 2018, when Kaniela Ing, a member of the Hawaii House of Representatives and the Democratic Socialists of America, asked a simple question: "What dreams would you pursue if your basic needs were met?" It's a query that I believe is also worth asking of our culture. What would film look like? What would music sound like? What would life be like, if people—all people—had the time, energy, and mental space to devote to shaping our world?

Writing about games that adults play has been my livelihood for the last fifteen years, and I've often thought about what the sports world could look like in a country not scarred by war, poverty, and the mercenary priorities of profit. I've wondered what sports would or could look like if the athletic industrial complex wasn't such a cutthroat big business and sports weren't so divided between those who play and those who only watch.

I'm a big believer that sports are like fire and fire can be used to burn down your house or cook a meal. We are in a moment when the house is burning—and that goes for the sports world as well as the real world it inhabits. But imagine if we could harness that fire for the greater good. I believe strongly that sports can be different, better, democratized, and less harmful in a world with true political and economic democracy—a tool to build community instead of tearing it down.

Sports are such a bloated leviathan of greed that it has long suspended any pretense of moral or community accountability. None of the billionaires that oversee the sports world or the sportswriters who act more like stenographers, advertising the billionaires' products without criticism, ever ask themselves: Are we doing harm? Are we doing harm by making games so expensive to watch and play? By selling products—especially sneakers that are made under sweatshop conditions and are unaffordable for the bulk of our young fan base, are we doing families a disservice? Are our sports being used to sell more than games, but war through joint commercial sponsorships with the military? Are we promoting an endeavor where "everyone can play" and "get in the game," or are those just marketing phrases to ease the guilt of consumers who love the action but recoil at the stench of what lies beneath? There are so many people who love sports but hate what they have become. They want to enjoy the games but don't desire to check their morality at the door, and are trapped in a relationship with sports that borders on the abusive.

We are all affected by sports whether we play or not and whether we watch or not. We are affected economically, culturally, and socially, and we all have an interest in being critics of how it operates, how it gets in our lives, whether by choice or through more insidious means. In a world where newscasters regularly describe what happens on Capitol Hill in terms of end zones and home runs, and where today's athletes could be tomorrow's politicians, we should all be questioning every aspect of this system. The minders of the sports world certainly aren't, and they have created a product where nothing is pure.

Keep It Fun

It would be easy to begin critiquing sports as they are at the top, in the big sports leagues. But it makes more sense—and is perhaps more urgent—to start at the base: youth sports.

At their best, youth sports can be a place of friendship, exercise, and healthy competition. But they're far from their best for the overwhelming majority of young people in this country. Leave aside for a moment the millions who don't get to play organized sports because of shuttered community centers, slashed physical education, and lack of access, due to either community circumstance, disability, or some combination of the two. (I taught at a public elementary school without physical education. It was deemed a luxury.) Let's talk about those who do in fact have access to play.

Despite massive early participation—the American Youth Soccer Organization claims membership of more than fifty thousand teams, with more than 630,000 participants—recent polling by the National Alliance for Youth Sports finds that roughly 70 percent of children in this country stop playing organized sports by the age of thirteen. Burdened by the expectations of frustrated adults, they simply say, "It's just not fun anymore." The first act of rebellion for many children is taking a stand and choosing not to play. The research shows that this is because there is too much pressure, too many coaches who think that they are Vince Lombardi, and an avalanche of messages that unless they are "good," then they are wasting everyone's time. Far from the myth that sports today are some soft reality where "everyone gets a trophy," the reality is far different. Instead it becomes a brutal reflection of our survival-of-the-fittest culture instead of a place to grow. This teenage act of rebellion means that these young people—and this is maddening—*choose* to pull themselves out of a situation that potentially could be a site of growth, friendship, and community, and understandably so. They are voting with their feet, proclaiming in communities across the country that youth sports are little more than a cauldron of angst. The rise of health problems for young people, like early onset diabetes, is directly related to this reality. The number of girls who are pushed away from sports is even higher, as the pressure to not play becomes tied up with gender expectations and homophobia. With public programs and facilities dwindling and the costs of private lessons, luxury equipment, and league fees growing by the year, youth sports overall have become privatized and cost above and beyond what can be a reasonable part of a family's budget.

That is a travesty. As Mark Hyman's terrific book, *The Most Expensive Game in Town*, details, sports for the young are engulfed in what he compellingly describes as a "destructive trend of commercialization." Hyman details how this prices out some working class families, but others scrimp and save so their kids can get into the game, paying for travel, equipment, and league entry fees. Now the act of play has become an issue of family sacrifice. Our children are playing for profit until they burn out, but it doesn't have to be this way. There should be universal physical education and there should be access for all, regardless of ability, status, or economic class. Sports should not exist only for the few.

It also should be noted that as privatized sports become the avenue of play for a majority of young people, these leagues allow themselves to be exempt from Title IX legislation, which means that there is no legally mandated equal opportunity for girls to play, further limiting their access.

This is not every youth sports experience. Mine—only because I had coaches who gave a damn—was transformational. But, to use the language of former Baltimore Colts lineman Joe Ehrmann, far too many of these coaches are "not transformational but transactional": in it for themselves and taking no prisoners.

Power to the Players

After this social Darwinist winnowing experience of youth sports, ever fewer choose to keep playing as adults. An even smaller number of high school athletes—less than 1 percent—earn scholarships to play at the

Division I collegiate level. Here they come face-to-face with an organization that makes their youth sports experience look like an innocent, Disneyfied walk in the park. Here they have to face one of the most unjust institutions on the sports landscape: the cartel of so-called amateur sports, the National Collegiate Athletic Association. There is so much wrong with the NCAA, one hardly knows where to begin. It's best to start with its revenue-producing sports, men's basketball and football. These sports pull in billions of dollars in profit from cable television deals, virtually all of which goes to NCAA executives. The top football and basketball coaches make millions of dollars per year. In thirty-nine of the fifty states in this country, according to the most recent survey, the highest-paid public employee is the football or basketball coach at the big state school. Yet the players, disproportionately African American, don't receive a dime. Or rather, they receive a mangled education where they don't have free choices in classes or schedule. As all-American basketball player Laron Profit once said to me, "They call us student athletes but really we are 'athlete students' because the minute we get to campus, it is made very clear just what our priorities should be and who we are to serve." When looking at the NCAA through this lens, it becomes strikingly clear that it isn't the educational "nonprofit" that it purports to be. It is a multibillion-dollar operation designed for the theft of black wealth.

This is a civil rights issue, a fact that was made manifestly clear to me by one of the great chroniclers of the civil rights movement, Taylor Branch, the Pulitzer Prize–winning author of a magisterial three-volume series on Martin Luther King Jr.'s life and times. In an article for *The Atlantic* in October 2011 called "The Shame of College Sports," Branch sparked a discussion that has been amplified by the inevitable scandals that plague college sports on an annual basis. "For all the outrage," he wrote, "the real scandal is not that students are getting illegally paid or recruited, it's that two of the noble principles on which the NCAA justifies its existence—'amateurism' and the 'student-athlete'—are cynical hoaxes, legalistic confections propagated by the universities so they can exploit the skills and fame of young athletes. . . . The NCAA makes money, and enables universities and corporations to make money, from the unpaid labor of young athletes."

Branch added that "slavery analogies should be used carefully. College athletes are not slaves. Yet to survey the scene—corporations and universities enriching themselves on the backs of uncompensated young men, whose status as 'student-athletes' deprives them of the right to due process guaranteed by the Constitution—is to catch an unmistakable whiff of the plantation."

In addition, Dr. Harry Edwards, the great sports sociologist who has been part of sporting movements for social justice since the 1968 Olympics, has called the reformation of the NCAA "the civil rights sports issue of our time." Comparisons to the Old South have come not just from those branded as "outsiders," like Branch. Walter Byers, the association's executive director from 1951 to 1987 and the man most responsible for the modern NCAA, saw the light toward the end of his life. After his retirement, he told sportswriter Steve Wulf: "The coaches own the athletes' feet, the colleges own the athletes' bodies, and the supervisors retain the large rewards. That reflects a neo-plantation mentality on the campuses."

This "neo-plantation mentality" can be seen at a place like Clemson University in South Carolina, an institution of higher learning built on an actual plantation. They won college football's national championship in 2019 and their coach, Dabo Swinney, received several million dollars in bonuses on top of his $6.5 million base salary. When Clemson won the national championship in 1981, their coach, Danny Ford, made just $50,000 ($139,000 in today's dollars). The profession has become lucrative, well beyond any pretense of amateurism, yet that cudgel is still used to keep players in line. They are powerless, especially in football, where there is no minor league path to get to the NFL, and players come from disproportionately poor backgrounds from the former Jim Crow South. These players are at risk of injury not only to their bodies but also to their brains. Institutions of higher learning are setting players up for devastating degenerative brain damage and ailments like ALS (Lou Gehrig's disease), and they have no recourse, no workers' compensation, not even health care.

In addition to the above maladies, seventeen college football players have died in off-season drills since 2000, most from dehydration or heat exhaustion. This should be a national scandal. If such a number existed at the NFL level, there would be congressional hearings. And yet because it persists among a workforce that is supposed to be "grateful" for their scholarships, their voice and their plight remain muted.

The best—and most realistic—solution in the here and now is for players to unionize so they can have a collective voice about not only pay, but also workouts and their health care. This is not some stray fantasy. The football players at Northwestern attempted to unionize and challenge college football to its foundation. In addition, lawsuits, and speak-outs by rebellious current players and former players in the NFL, all show that if the "student-athletes" were truly free to organize, then they would do so. If I could have a magic wand, I'd delink revenue-producing sports from institutions of higher learning altogether and make the pro sports leagues pay for their own minor leagues. But absent that possibility, let's treat the players like the employees they are and allow them to enjoy the fruits of their labor instead of having them live and die at the whims of a cartel like the NCAA.

Out with the Old

Challenging this NCAA setup is part of a broader and necessary fight to make sure that sports are a racism-free zone. If sports and play are truly going to be for all, they can't also be a place where people are marginalized on the basis of race. That's why any movement for better sports should also, as a point of pride, stand against all Native American mascotry. The American Psychiatric Association has written that mascotry harms Native American kids. It also serves to make the very real problems that indigenous communities face invisible. It's archaic and needs to go.

There is one particular case where this kind of mascotry extends beyond all reasonable comprehension and descends to the level of an open racial slur. That's the moniker of the NFL team in the nation's capital.

For decades, Native American activists and allies have fought to get the Redskins of Washington, DC, to change its name. For decades, they have pointed out that the name is a demeaning insult. For decades, they have argued that it is the dishonorable product of the team's original owner, George Preston Marshall, an archsegregationist with a love of minstrelsy whose team was the last in the NFL to sign African American players. For decades, these arguments have fallen on deaf ears. Every league commissioner and subsequent owner has refused to listen. But no one's hearing has been quite as impaired as current owner Dan Snyder's, who bought the team in 1999. Snyder has told reporters, "We'll never change the name. It's that simple. NEVER—you can use caps." He disparages and punishes members of the media who take him to task, restricting access to the team. He is a plutocratic brute. A mass people's movement should see eradicating his bigotry as a central task. It means just following the advice of every indigenous civil rights group in North America, all of whom have called for this team that represents the nation's capital to change their damn name. But as mentioned, the Redskins is only the ugliest manifestation of mascotry. It all deserves to be thrown in the dust heap of history.

Challenging racism in sports is a necessity for creating the kind of sports world—and the kind of real world—that we want and need. Any social democratic movement worth its salt would also need to speak out for an end to Native American mascotry, and a broad-based anti-racist movement could even have the players in the NFL feeling empowered to speak out against the racial slur that brands the team in our nation's capital.

Sports should be a refuge for all who want to play, a place where oppression is challenged, not where it festers and spreads. It should also be a space where sexism, toxic masculinity, and homophobia have no place. The exclusion of black and brown people and women was baked into the cake of organized sports at their very beginning in the nineteenth century. The panic over LGBTQ people being part of who takes the field has also been a constant, as the men's locker room has been the most stubborn of closeted environments, while women have faced homophobia from the earliest days of their fight to even play.

When Jason Collins, in 2013, came out of the closet and played for the NBA's Brooklyn Nets, tennis star Martina Navratilova wrote that this would be a "game changer." She wrote, "Now that Collins has led this watershed moment, I think—and hope—there will be an avalanche. Come out, come out wherever and whoever you are. It is beautiful out here and I guarantee you this: You will never, ever want to go back. You will only wonder why it took so long." Yet an avalanche has not taken place. Instead we have seen just more of the same: more homophobia, more toxic masculinity, more athletes in the closet. No one should have to live this way. It has been slightly better in women's sports than men's sports, but the idea that women's sports are some kind of Shangri-la against homophobia is a myth as well. It is true that the WNBA has seen more players be open and out with their sexuality. But men's sports have been a very different story, especially in the most popular sports of baseball, basketball, and football. There the door of the closet remains strong. The goal is for sports to be a voice against homophobia, against sexism, and against sexual assault. As rape survivor Brenda Tracy says when she speaks to teams on the intersection between sports culture and rape culture, we should "set the expectation" that teams are forces to change how their communities interact, not battering rams of the worst that society has to offer.

Ending the Stadium Racket

Just as we should "set the expectation" that teams are forces for the greater good, we should ask no less of the places where they play. Sports have a profound impact not only on the individual athlete, whether amateur or professional, but also in the communities where they roost. In too many cities, professional sports have become neoliberal bulldozers of gentrification. Adam Silver, commissioner of the NBA, has said that arenas are the "town halls" and "public squares" of the twenty-first century. It's a bizarre "town hall" indeed that costs a fortune to enter and lines the pockets of the 1 percent.

Over the last generation, University of Maryland sports economist Dennis Coates and University of Alberta's Brad R. Humphreys have estimated that we've seen $30 billion in public funds spent on stadiums for professional teams. These monuments to plutocratic greed and the ways that the rich can rob the public till have been presented as photogenic solutions to deindustrialization, declining tax bases, and suburban flight. The building of stadiums is basically the closest thing there is to a comprehensive urban policy in this country.

The results are now in, and they don't look good for the home teams. Coates and Humphreys studied stadium funding going back more than thirty years and failed to find a single, solitary example of a sports franchise lifting or even stabilizing a local economy. They concluded the opposite, writing that there has been "a reduction in real per capita income over the entire metropolitan area. . . . Our conclusion, and that of nearly all academic economists studying this issue, is that professional sports generally have little, if any, positive effect on a city's economy."

These projects achieve so little because the jobs that are created tend to be low-wage, service-sector, seasonal employment. They also pull needed funds away from other necessities. Instead of being solutions for urban decay, they exacerbate gentrification and displacement. Stadiums, which were once symbols of community cohesion, have been tools of organized theft: sporting shock doctrines—to borrow a phrase from Naomi Klein's seminal book about disaster capitalism—for our ailing cities.

As Neil deMause, co-author of the book *Field of Schemes*, said to me, "The history of the stadium game is the story of how, by slowly refining their blackmail skills, sports owners learned how to turn their industry from one based on selling tickets to one based on extracting public subsidies. It's been a bit like watching a four-year-old learn how to manipulate his parents into buying him the new toy that he saw on TV; the question now is how long it takes our elected officials to learn to say no."

Even in liberal Los Angeles, new stadium complexes for the National Football League are rising from the ground at the same time that homelessness reaches epidemic proportions. Cities like Las Vegas are welcoming the Raiders from Oakland at the expense of their school system. Meanwhile, the city of Oakland will be making payments in the millions on the Oakland Coliseum for years after the Raiders finally move. At the risk of stating the obvious, a sane society would have billionaires pay for their own damn stadiums. Failing that, sports teams should become the equivalent of public utilities. For every public dollar that goes into a team, the public should get a share. That way, anytime one sees a jersey or team jacket being worn by a fan, they'll know that this money spent is actually aiding their community instead of robbing it blind.

Speaking of Los Angeles, the city is also planning—and bracing—for hosting the 2028 Olympics. When it comes to sporting shock doctrines, the Olympic Games make the building of football stadiums seem tame. In addition to being orgies of nationalism, the games bring debt, displacement, and the militarization of public space. Example after historic example demonstrates this. From the hosting of the games in 1936 in Hitler's Germany to the recent disaster in Brazil, where corruption and broken promises surrounding the 2016 Rio games led to the rise of protofascist president Jair Bolsonaro, the Olympics are simply not good for the health of a country. If we are going to have the Olympic Games—and Olympic sports are truly beautiful and should be celebrated—then let them be in one country. That way, at least, the construction and upkeep of Olympic facilities will actually have some use value after the cheers have stopped and the confetti has been swept away.

The Olympics are the sharpest expression of the way sports—particularly in the United States—is used to promote not only patriotism but militarism as well, especially since the attacks of September 11, 2001. An entire generation since then has grown up only knowing sports as a place where the military blasted ads and support for war was just a part of the game. Fighting to delink the constant calls for war—and the financial partnerships between the Pentagon and major sports leagues—would have to be a part of this project.

Nothing Without a Fight

These injustices—the ways that sports can be used to pump the most reactionary politics through their play—are outrageous, and it's time for a change. Sports are a mirror and sports will change, no matter how stubbornly, as our society changes. Yet while the arc of history might bend toward justice, someone, and more often than not many thousands of people, has to bend it. We need a movement of fans who are willing to separate what they love about sports from what they cannot stand so they can demand that it change. We shouldn't have to choose between having our kids play youth sports and seeing them on the sidelines because of a megalomaniacal coach. We shouldn't have to choose between going to a game and not supporting a taxpayer-funded arena. We shouldn't have to choose between playing for a team that uses Native American mascots and not playing. We shouldn't have to choose between staying in the closet and taking the field. The trans community shouldn't be forced to play for a team that does not comply with their gender. It will take more than sports radio complaints—although bringing these politics into the confederate confines of most sports radio is very welcome.

Taking on the NCAA would require explicit political movements against racism, because this cartel primarily exploits, uses up, and throws away the black and brown athletes who make up the heart of college basketball and football. Fighting the NCAA could become a part of this new civil rights movement. LGBTQ people in the sports world, however few, have always been a part of the movement for LGBTQ rights. That can only continue. Any movement for social democracy also must be a movement for women's rights and LGBTQ liberation.

Sports for the Many, Not the Few

Seeing all of our youth having access to sports and our tax money not mis-used in the subsidizing of arenas would hopefully whet a collective appetite for more change. If we expand access as well as the attitudes toward sports at the youth level—having young people healthier, happier, and better adjusted through exercise—that alone could trigger a tremendous change in our society. Imagine seeing an end—at long last!—to corporate welfare in sports. But our imagination needs to be bolder than even that.

For sports to become all they can be, we need a world where people aren't so exhausted by the end of the workday that all they can do is watch. U.S. workers labor longer than they did a generation ago and for less pay. As the gap between rich and poor has relentlessly grown, we are also see-ing an absence of leisure time. It should be unacceptable that this coun-try can be both obsessed with sports and so physically unhealthy. Leisure time was a demand during the movement for the eight-hour workday in the nineteenth century, and it tragically needs to become an animating demand again.

It's not hard to envision the better way to play that could flow from that world. Imagine a youth sports community that has equal access for boys and girls, and a youth sports complex that doesn't immediately segregate boys and girls, that allows them to play together, if that's the choice that any girl wants to make.

Imagine instead a situation where you don't have to be some kind of star athlete to continue to play, where you can take the field because you want to build community, make friends, and exercise, where sports for kids don't exist to satisfy the egos of parents but are, heaven forbid, fun. Imagine Title IX being strengthened and enforced to make sure that girls have the same access as boys to play. Imagine instead taking the profit motive out of youth sports, a very recent historical development, and going back to a model where if a kid wants to play, the resources are there to make it a reality.

Imagine a system where our institutions of higher learning aren't factories of indentured servitude, producing billions in profit and creating a millionaire class of head coaches. Imagine NCAA athletes not being branded with the fictitious label of "student-athlete" but being treated with the dignity that comes from being organized workers, with full labor rights. Hell, imagine if the NFL and NBA didn't use our schools as their de facto minor leagues and instead subsidized their own farm system to groom the next generation of players.

Imagine a sports world where sexism and homophobia are challenged instead of winked at or abided. It's remarkable how, particularly in men's sports, there remains, in the twenty-first century, a glass door on the locker room. It's a hell of a vision.

Sports and Social Movements: A Winning Team

The potential for a better model of sports is profound. And we don't have to create or re-create the wheel to make it a reality. Sports have always been an area of political struggle and, occasionally, a path breaker for social justice. It is impossible to consider the civil rights movement without mentioning Jackie Robinson, who broke baseball's color barrier in 1947, as part of a broad progressive movement to challenge the sport's segregationist practices. Dr. King called Robinson "a sit inner before sit ins and a freedom rider before freedom rides."

It is impossible to talk about the 1960s without speaking of the struggle of Muhammad Ali, the most famous athlete on earth and the most famous draft resister who ever lived, who gave up his heavyweight titles to speak out against the war in Vietnam. In doing so, he inspired millions to question the war in Vietnam at great personal sacrifice. He's the man who said, "Why should they ask me to put on a uniform and go ten thousand miles from home and drop bombs and bullets on brown people in Vietnam," he said, "while so-called Negro people in Louisville are treated like dogs and denied simple human rights?"

Champion tennis player Billie Jean King fought for Title IX legislation as an extension of the women's movement, later reflecting that "in the seventies we had to make it acceptable for people to accept girls and women as athletes. We had to make it okay for them to be active," and "I wanted to use sports for social change." Her activism helped lead to the passage of Title IX legislation in 1972, which has dramatically increased women's participation in sports. Signed into law by Richard Nixon, it had a revolutionary effect on the access women and girls would have to sports. In 1971, the year before Congress passed Title IX, only three hundred thousand girls—less than 4 percent—participated in high school sports. Today, participation is up to 40 percent, or 3.4 million.

Colin Kaepernick taking a knee during the national anthem to protest police violence and racial inequity became one of the most striking images of the Black Lives Matter movement. As Kaepernick said, "I am not going to stand up to show pride in a flag for a country that oppresses black people and people of color."

Athletes can be leaders in the struggle to reform sports, and can join alongside a people's movement for fairer play. They can also be reflections of our own aspirations for what we want this world to be. But the starting point has to be that we can only truly pursue our athletic dreams if our basic needs are in fact met. This is a world worth fighting for.

What About a Well-Fed Artist? Imagining Cultural Work in a Democratic Socialist Society

Francesca Fiorentini

I PERFORM STAND-UP COMEDY IN FRONT OF LIVE AUDIENCES MULTIPLE nights a week. There is no money in 99 percent of stand-up. Sometimes we are paid less than the gas or transit money it took to get to the venue. Other times we're paid in drink tickets—always extra cruel for the sober comics. Shows are often free for audience members and a hat is passed around, which once led me to being tipped with a Safeway coupon for $0.50 off Yoplait yogurt. Probiotics are indeed useful when stomaching a life in the performing arts under capitalism.

If you've watched fictional representations of comics hitting it big overnight, you might be under a different impression about the craft. For the majority of stand-ups, things are much less glamorous; most will eventually quit and become the funniest person in the office. Many stand-ups, like many artists, are not very good. But let's not allow capitalism's survival-of-the-fittest mentality to trick us into thinking only the most talented comics are entitled to put food on the table. We can't be Lenin when it comes to factory workers and Milton Friedman when it comes to cultural ones.

There's nothing romantic about starving artists. Allowing our culture to fetishize and celebrate the starving artist who goes from rags to riches signifies that we're okay with the majority of artists living in rags.

It's past time to think about cultural work as a commodity, and successful artists as Cinderella stories. The way we produce and enjoy art is part and parcel of revolutionary social change. Instead, let's interrogate how hyper-consumerist capitalism creates cultural rot, and how different our lives and communities and Saturday nights would be if arts were publicly funded. This all might be an elaborate thesis for free Beyoncé concerts, so follow closely.

The Right's War on Fun

Before we can imagine what democratic socialism might mean for culture, we first have to assess how capitalism has bludgeoned it. The "free market" has a unique way of loving artistic production for its monetary value and criminalizing the rest. Both neoliberal plutocracies and authoritarian regimes know that from culture come things like historical memory, new ideas, and therefore potentially subversive things like pluralism and democracy.

Which is why every time a right-wing government comes into power around the world, there's almost always a concerted shutdown of culture that lives outside the bounds of capitalism's reach—whether via the harassing of street performers in Mexico City when Enrique Peña Nieto came to power in Mexico or the shutting down of cultural centers in Buenos Aires when Mauricio Macri assumed the Argentine presidency.

In the United States, right-wing think tanks and politicians have consistently lobbied to cut public funding for culture and the arts. They're not even sure they believe in one of those things. The Heritage Foundation has argued for decades to cut government spending on the arts, claiming that the National Endowment for the Arts supports the "radical virus of multiculturalism,"[1] an objectively great name for a punk rock band. From Reagan to Newt Gingrich to the American Family Association, which successfully got Congress to cut the NEA's budget in 1996, all the way through to Andrew Breitbart, the right somehow thinks that spending *less than* *$0.50 per American* on arts funding and access is more of a waste than a now near $1 trillion military budget.

The right will call the arts, as they do higher education, elitist and out of touch, even though the entire point of the NEA is to make art more accessible to underserved communities in both rural and urban areas. Half of NEA-funded events occur in areas where the median household income is less than $50,000 a year.

But of course this isn't about fiscal conservatism or perceived elitism. It's about conformity as a key pillar of autocracy, whether to military power or to robot pop. What we're left with is what I call "Coors Light Sharia," a cultural handmaid's tale that looks a lot like the 2017 presidential inauguration, in which country singer Toby Keith sang his hit "Beer for My Horses." Cringe.

Accordingly, it makes sense that the Trump administration has introduced budgets that would put the NEA, the National Endowment for the Humanities, and the Corporation for Public Broadcasting on life support.

The danger that public arts poses for autocrats, aspiring and otherwise, is that it isn't driven by money or even popularity necessarily, but by a broader project of inclusion, community, memory, and history. The vital role that culture plays in democratic and free thought is precisely what motivated the act that established the National Endowment for the Arts and the Humanities in 1965:

> An advanced civilization must not limit its efforts to science and technology alone, but must give full value and support to the other great branches of scholarly and cultural activity in order to achieve a better understanding of the past, a better analysis of the present, and a better view of the future.

> The world leadership which has come to the United States cannot rest solely upon superior power, wealth, and technology, but must be solidly founded upon worldwide respect and admiration for the Nation's high qualities as a leader in the realm of ideas and of the spirit. . . .

> It is necessary and appropriate for the Federal Government to help create and sustain not only a climate encouraging freedom of thought, imagination, and inquiry but also the material conditions facilitating the release of this creative talent.

> It is vital to democracy to honor and preserve its multicultural artistic heritage as well as support new ideas. . . .

Concretely that's meant support for things like an indigenous art show in Alaska, the designs for the Vietnam Veterans Memorial, or Vermont's Poetry Out Loud high school competition. You know, commie shit, or—as the Heritage Foundation calls it—"evaluating artistic efforts based on race, ethnicity and sexual orientation instead of artistic merit." For proof positive of their theory, look no further than the mediocre career of obscure author Alice Walker, who received an NEA grant ten years before writing *The Color Purple.*

Of course, capitalism and neoliberalism are adept at co-opting the aesthetics of cultural resistance without the politics. But that co-optation is becoming harder to pull off under such crippling inequality so obviously induced by capitalism's failures. Nike can make Colin Kaepernick the face of its new ad campaign, but it would never do the same for a Korean sweatshop organizer. Everything has its limits.

Anywhere Else Model

I didn't start performing stand-up in the United States, but in Argentina. In the Buenos Aires neighborhood of San Telmo, a mixed crowd of expats, Argentines, and tables of unamused Danish tourists watched me, a new comic, work out material as the host of a weekly show called GrinGo. Even though I had only months of stand-up under my belt, I received the equivalent of about $75 per show from the venue. My future American stand-up self would've been astounded, her mouth gaping wide with Yoplait.

I lived in Buenos Aires for five years, working as a freelance journalist, English teacher, comedian, and YouTuber, and came to understand a few things about countries that are even a few degrees less all-consumingly neoliberal than the United States. For example, a noncitizen friend of mine got a free appendectomy in a public hospital. And as an aspiring stand-up, I looked around and realized there were other aspiring comics, actors, dancers, musicians—hell, even magicians and clowns—who were making a living as artists. They sometimes had other jobs, but it wasn't a rule like it is in the United States. And when they weren't getting paid to perform, they were using their skills to help teach other comics, actors, dancers, musicians, magicians, and clowns, because nonartist working professionals had both the interest and the *time* to seek out artistic endeavors. They weren't completely overtired at the end of the day to the point where streaming services became their only way to unwind.

Before the recent right-wing crackdown, there were hundreds of cultural centers strewn across the city that offered low-cost classes and space for artists to both perform and teach. And when I say cultural centers we're not talking the place your grandma does Zumba, but gritty, bohemian, late-night, wine-soaked venues where for a small fee you could watch tango quartets bang out Astor Piazzolla and split a $5 liter of beer with friends.

There are hugely successful artists in Argentina, but there was a palpable feeling that artists—however talented or well-known—don't starve. There wasn't a "famous or nothing" cultural inequity, despite being in the Global South in a more economically unequal country. Rather, artists there were compensated and given space for their work in ways that made art a seamless and vital part of Argentine culture.

In comparison to what comparably wealthy countries spend on arts, the United States is culturally destitute. Germany, the fastest-growing economy in Europe, spends about $20 per person on arts and culture, and France's Ministry of Culture has a budget of $10 billion. That's the equivalent of two of Trump's border walls and about a week and half of the occupation of Iraq. In fiscal year 2009–10, Australia spent *$311 per person* on the arts.

The Norwegian Arts Council directed $21 million to its music industry in 2010, and neighboring Sweden's support of bands like the Knife have helped it gain international recognition. The Scottish government regularly helps local musicians get to international festivals like SXSW. As Marc Hogan writes for *Pitchfork*, the UK's "generous art-school environments and government assistance programs enabled the nation that gave us the Beatles, the Rolling Stones, and the Who to become the nation that gave us the Smiths, the Jesus and Mary Chain, Blur, Pulp, Saint Etienne, and so many more."

Just like some of the mixed economies of these countries, mixed arts funding allows cultural workers to play a role in society beyond their monetary contributions. Rather, they contribute to the free thought, cultural traditions, and cultural innovations of a healthy democratic society.

We Did It That One Time

Public arts funding during times of political and economic change, however, is not a foreign concept to the United States. We need only look to a time when capitalism could no longer be the reliable cultural role model because it—as it tends to do—failed.

After the Great Depression, the Works Progress Administration didn't just provide building and infrastructure jobs to millions of workers. It employed and trained artists, musicians, writers, and actors under Federal Project Number One. That meant $27 million ($500 million by today's standards) was infused into the newly created Federal Theatre Project, Federal Art Project, Federal Music Project, and the Federal Writers' Project. Those projects supported artists like Duke Ellington, Langston Hughes, Jackson Pollock, Charlie Chaplin, and Orson Welles, among others.

The Federal Theatre Project had five regional centers and reached more than 30 million people in two hundred theaters, churches, parks, and streets nationwide. It also established the Negro Theatre Unit offshoot, which operated in four cities. The Federal Art Project established one hundred community art centers around the country and employed more than ten thousand artists.

While the initial goal was to help out-of-work artists, the impact of this relief was the creation of class-conscious cultural content with a vast reach that continues to enrich American culture to this day. The works created were a product of their precarious times. Working people who bore the brunt of inequality and unemployment were politicized by their disillusionment with capitalism's promises and began to join unions and warm to socialist ideas. American studies professor Michael Denning writes in *The Cultural Front* that the relief projects "meant that many plebian artists found work writing, painting and performing for the federal government, and they brought the aesthetic and politics of the proletarian avant-garde and the labor movement culture."

Themes tackled in relief productions included unionization and corporate corruption in the hugely successful 1937 play *The Cradle Will Rock*; a skewering of dictatorship in the satire *It Can't Happen Here*, adapted from the Sinclair Lewis book; and unemployment through the eyes of college students in the play *Class of '29*. The Federal Writers' Project underwrote anthologies like the Slave Narrative Collection, which collected for the first time 2,300 first-person accounts and images of American slavery. The local Chicago writers' project helped launch the careers of Richard Wright, author of the 1940 book *Native Son*, and author Zora Neale Hurston was employed by the writers' project in Florida.

As Denning notes, "The federal arts projects became a crucial site where alliances were formed by established artists and intellectuals who dominated non-relief personnel." Artist unions that had existed prior to the relief projects were bolstered and new guilds formed, filled with rank-and-file cultural workers. Nowadays just the idea of "rank-and-file cultural workers" is an awesome thought.

By 1939, Red Scare tactics deployed by the House Un-American Activities Committee helped to gut and eventually shutter Federal Project Number One just four years after it was established. Once again, artists eating is a very, very dangerous concept. But the lasting mark of these cultural workers on everything from theater and music to eventually the film and television industries continues to this day.

What's remarkable is that during the worst depression in American history, federal funds were directed toward the arts. Maybe during times of economic crisis attitudes toward arts and culture mark the difference between authoritarianism and democratic societies. Whereas authoritarianism sees such spending as superfluous and a threat to social control, a democracy recognizes the arts' role in rebuilding and envisioning a new future. And no doubt these federal works, including the posters commissioned to advertise everything from the Rural Electrification Administration to the Civilian Conservation Corps, were key in culturally buoying the bold political project of the New Deal itself.

A Revolution of Artistic Values

Part of a political revolution toward socialism will necessitate a revolution of values. Those values won't come from the top down but from culture up. We can use Denning's notion of a "cultural front"—in this case, to save us from our cultural ass. Right now the United States is working at a deficit. Our identities and aesthetics are deeply tied into capitalism—no disrespect to rapper Cardi B and her love of money. But unlearning money worship and our worth being determined by what we can accumulate is going to be vital to any socialist change. And as during the 1930s and '40s, and in so many times in American history, there will be a symbiotic relationship between the creation of cultural space and the creation of political change. I am but a mere comedian / web journalist / podcast host. I don't think I can offer a blueprint of how the arts industry will work in a democratic socialist society. But I'm an artist, so I can imagine one.

Firstly, it has to be noted that if and when other democratic socialist goals are met, the life of cultural workers will inevitably improve. If we don't have to worry about health care, affordable housing, or going into hundreds of thousands of dollars in debt for college training in our chosen craft, we're already in a far better place. But there should absolutely be a plan for arts and culture under democratic socialism, just as there should be for health care, housing, and more.

Culture, like wealth, does not trickle down. Any top-down imposition of music or theater won't last and will probably suck. Still, government can create the space in which art can flourish. Fighting for that space will be the beginning of a cultural front in and of itself. Just as Federal Project Number One put artists to work, we need a bold New Deal–style plan for cultural workers that can do the same. Think of what a half-billion-dollar infusion into the arts would mean today. We might expand the NEA's and NEH's reach, offer tax incentives for small venues, and give assistance when they are under threat of closure. We could bolster local film production, offer localized and accessible studio space, increase grants for artists, and—just as during the New Deal—employ cultural workers on large-scale murals and projects. We could make Burning Man free.

If the arts are to thrive under democratic socialism, they should be independent and free of censorship, from both the right and the left. We need none of the McCarthyist onslaughts nor the imposed "socialist realism" of the Soviet Union, no disrespect to the artists who made some incredible agitprop. Of course, propaganda and art are crucial to selling a broad national project to the people—they raise consciousness and stir political activity. But marrying the state with artistic direction is not the goal.

The Danes, while a tough crowd at my shows in Buenos Aires, have established the so-called arm's-length principle under their Music Act of 1971, where the government can decide a framework for funding music but doesn't meddle in which projects get approved. Ted Cruz shouldn't decide who goes to SXSW (or really anything).

Given that so much of artistic production is disseminated and consumed via the internet, television, film, and radio, I don't see how any bold proposal for the arts in the twenty-first century can survive without dramatically democratizing telecommunications. That means not only protecting net neutrality but breaking up telecommunications monopolies that have a grip on our cultural consumption. It might also look like major private-public partnerships between places like Netflix and the National Endowment for the Humanities.

Beyond the critical interplay of media, rebuilding artistic industries will need robust and inclusive unions. That means expanding all entertainment unions—SAG-AFTRA (Screen Actors Guild–American Federation of Television and Radio Artists), the Writers Guild of America, and the International Alliance of Theatrical Stage Employees—and making membership more accessible. It also means organizing the unorganized cultural workers, including web creators, bloggers, stand-up comics, musicians, and other smaller-stage performers. Yes, a spoken-word guild.

The socialist democratization of the arts would increase the sites of cultural creation. In the stand-up world, being called a "local comic" is always a knock, usually implying that you're in a B comedy town that's fighting tooth and nail to keep open its handful of performance spaces. You're a big fish drowning in a tiny pond. Oftentimes performers simply end up moving to Los Angeles or New York to be wholly swallowed by a whale.

But in a radically democratized art world that would decentralize production, we could stop the cultural drain toward the coasts, and smaller cities and towns would become competitive, medium-size lagoons. Same goes for the film and television industry. If suddenly there were funds for people to tell their own stories rather than have them warped through Hollywood's gaze, how would that kind of representation shape local communities?

If some of the monetary incentives behind arts were gone, our winner-take-all, race-to-the-bottom entertainment culture would shift dramatically. Robot pop would have to compete with diverse and original music that would actually stand a chance at a record deal. The alternative and subculture scenes would flourish and find new audiences, with messages that don't merely glorify money.

I know what some of you are thinking when I talk about supporting different kinds of underground culture: "I'm just not that into burlesque." Well, imagine if dancers made more money than the dollars they picked up in their thongs, and had the funding to train to nail that triple-axel aerial bra removal and leave you breathless.

If the world in which artists are allowed to operate expands—from the streets to opera houses—art itself will get better and culture will thrive. Cultural work under democratic socialism will mean more work. (Not to mention far fewer creeps in entertainment.) And with $10 Hamilton tickets, The Color Purple playing in public parks, and Toby Keith charged with animal cruelty, my guess is fascism in America doesn't stand a chance.

Art is more than entertainment; it is an experience, an education, and a collective mirror to gaze at our multicultural, multiethnic, multifaith pluralist democracy—one with some pretty sweet talent. Our democracy also has deep wounds and a deep history of struggle that we can honor through our cultural work. We can remember the play *The Cradle Will Rock* and think, "Let's stage a revival, but with Beyoncé!"

Told you.

How Socialism Surged, and How It Can Go Further

Harold Meyerson

In 1960, the young socialist Michael Harrington traveled to Ann Arbor to provide what help he could to the fledgling radical movement at the University of Michigan, and to see if he could recruit some students to the Young People's Socialist League. He had particularly long talks with Tom Hayden, the twenty-year-old editor of the *Michigan Daily* (the student newspaper). Though the two hit it off, Harrington couldn't make the sale. "He accepted much of my analysis," Harrington later wrote, "yet he balked at the socialist idea itself."

Harrington was no slouch at converting progressives to socialism; an unusually high percentage of the members of the Democratic Socialist Organizing Committee (which he founded in 1973) and its successor organization, the Democratic Socialists of America (which he co-founded in 1982), signed up after having been intellectually and emotionally persuaded by one or more of Harrington's speeches. Nonetheless, DSA's membership never grew to more than eight thousand during Harrington's lifetime (he died in 1989). Hayden was just one of many American leftists who either balked at the socialist idea or saw no future for it in real American politics.

It's taken some time for an America more receptive to democratic socialism to emerge, but, in an epochal and largely unforeseen shift in the political and cultural landscape, emerge it has. In 2018, a Gallup poll found that the share of Democrats with a favorable view of socialism stood at 57 percent, while those with a favorable view of capitalism had dwindled to 47 percent.

The year before, a YouGov poll of millennials (not just millennial Democrats) showed that 44 percent would prefer to live in a socialist nation, exceeding the 42 percent who wanted to live in a capitalist nation, with the remaining 14 percent (alas!) evenly split between nations that are either communist or fascist.

According to that 2018 Gallup survey, the share of *all* Americans with a positive view of socialism was 37 percent. As there were 252 million voting-age Americans in 2018, that means that a mind-boggling 93 million of our compatriots over the age of seventeen have a favorable view of socialism—a number well in excess of the population of any European social democracy. Polling also shows clear majority support for such social democratic policies as universal taxpayer-supported child care and Medicare for All—the primary reason why many Democratic presidential candidates scurry to champion social democratic reforms.

So: Tom Hayden, who perhaps more than anyone personified the new left radicalism of the 1960s, consistently refused to identify as a socialist, while today, many millions of Americans, few of whom adhere to anything resembling Hayden's deep and lifelong radicalism, say that socialism is their preferred economic and social system. More than sixty thousand of them—most of them not much older than Hayden was when he turned Harrington down—have now joined DSA.

Between 1960 and today, what had changed?

In a word, capitalism.

"The enemy of the conventional wisdom," wrote economist John Kenneth Galbraith (who coined the term "conventional wisdom"), "is not ideas but the march of events."

For almost all of our history, the conventional wisdom about the United States has been that it is uniquely inhospitable to socialism. Hayden's thinking was anything but conventional, yet he clearly believed that socialism—or at least policies that most Americans believed were socialist—was not going to take root on American soil.

The most famous formulations of this conventional wisdom have come from two sociologists—Werner Sombart and Daniel Bell. In 1906, Sombart, a German colleague of Max Weber's, wrote a small book, *Why Is There No Socialism in the United States?* In it, he argued that American workers' living standards and prospects for upward mobility were higher than their European counterparts'—too high to drive them into the socialist column. Even immigrants who came to America and were compelled to take the worst, lowest-paying jobs knew they were doing better than they'd be had they stayed in Europe. They'd been down so long, one might say, that America looked like up to them. Sombart was writing at a time of rising worker incomes. "On the reefs of roast beef and apple pie," he wrote, "socialistic Utopias of every sort are sent to their doom."

In 1952, Bell—a New Yorker who in the 1930s and '40s had been an active member of the Socialist Party—authored an essay, "The Failure of American Socialism," in the *Antioch Review*. In it, he argued that the party, whose membership had by then dwindled to perhaps a thousand, was in many ways the author of its own demise. It continually had failed, he contended, to make the hard decisions that political life required, since such decisions often involved compromising its moral ideals. The party, he famously pronounced, "was trapped by the unhappy problem of living in but not of the world."

At the time, Bell was the labor beat writer for *Fortune* magazine. It was he who'd called the United Auto Workers' historic 1950 contract with General Motors "the Treaty of Detroit," since it signaled an end to the ferocious labor-versus-capital battles that had wracked the auto industry for the preceding fifteen years. By offering workers not just raises, but annual productivity and cost-of-living increases, on top of pension benefits and job security, Bell presciently foresaw that the UAW's social democratic and socialist leaders had reached a modus vivendi with capitalism, one that created a more secure and prosperous working class and concomitantly heralded what he termed "the end of ideology," to the extent that ideology—that is, socialism—had ever factored into American politics.

In the simplest terms, what underpinned both Sombart's and Bell's obituaries for American socialism (actually, for even the *prospect* of American socialism) was the rising prosperity of American workers. Even more than Sombart, Bell was writing during a period of unprecedented job security and steady increases in workers' income and standard of living. Bell may have blamed the extinction of the socialists on their lack of political hard-headedness, but the economy in the years preceding his essay sounded a louder death knell than socialists' stubbornness. From 1941 through 1950, the real after-tax income of the poorest quintile of Americans rose by

41 percent, for the next quintile by 37 percent, for the next by 24 percent, for the next by 16 percent, and for the highest, wealthiest quintile, by just 8 percent. The wealthiest 5 percent actually saw their after-tax income decline by 2 percent. This was the cumulative effect of World War II's economic expansion, of a host of New Deal programs, of the power wielded by newly created militant industrial unions, and of steeply progressive taxes.

Michael Harrington was trying to recruit Tom Hayden right at the midpoint of the great postwar boom, the one period in American history of relatively broadly shared prosperity. Both Harrington and Hayden knew there were millions left out of that boom—Harrington was to memorably expose the extent of the nation's poverty two years later with his 1962 book *The Other America*, while Hayden was regularly traveling to Mississippi to document the ferocious discrimination and poverty to which blacks were subjected—but Hayden saw little reason to think that any significant share of Americans was going to embrace socialism. If only on that question, he subscribed to the conventional wisdom.

Then—at first imperceptibly, then in a rush—that conventional wisdom was overturned, not by ideas but by the march of events.

In the half century between Harrington and Hayden's discussions and Gallup's recent discovery of American socialists, most of the political constraints placed on American capitalism in the 1930s and '40s were lifted—at capital's insistence. The broadly shared prosperity of the New Deal and post–World War II order—in which unions were strong, taxes progressive, wages rising in tandem with productivity, domestic investment (both public and private) high, and the power of finance and major investors limited—all but vanished. As economist Simcha Barkai has documented, between 1984 and 2014, the share of the nation's gross domestic product going to profits rose by 13.5 percent, while the share going to worker pay and benefits and corporate investment declined by a corresponding 13.9 percent.[1] In the parlance of economist Thomas Piketty, author of *Capital in the Twenty-First Century*, r (the rate of return on investment) was a hell of a lot greater than g (the rate of economic growth).

Economic and political power had grown so unbalanced that as the nation climbed out of the ditch dug by the Wall Street–generated collapse of 2008, almost all the recovery's gains went to the wealthiest Americans, particularly the owners of the bulk of corporate stock. More than nine million families lost their homes; millennials entered a fissured and not very remunerative job market, and their rate of family formation and home buying lagged those of their older siblings, their parents, and their grandparents. In 2002, 46 percent of millennials had described themselves as middle-class; by 2014, that figure had fallen to 35 percent—a record low—while 57 percent called themselves working-class, and 8 percent lower-class. America could no longer brandish its economic calling card to the rest of the planet—its historically high rates of economic mobility—because its rates fell well behind those of Europe and China.

Amid the tortuously slow recovery, polls began to pick up the shattering of the conventional wisdom on socialism, particularly among the young. It wasn't that Americans were impressed by socialist arguments, organizations, or legislation—none of which loomed large, if at all, on the nation's political landscape. It was the march of events—not ideas—that was driving the nation to the left.

In 2010, DSA was down to roughly five thousand largely inactive members, myself included. Alexandria Ocasio-Cortez and Julia Salazar (now a congressional representative and New York state senator, respectively) were still in college. Most Americans couldn't pick Bernie Sanders out of a police lineup. Wall Street and Zuccotti Park had yet to be occupied. And hardly anyone had heard of, much less read, Thomas Piketty.

Yet because of the severity of the financial crash and ensuing recession, in 2010 Gallup decided to conduct a poll on the popularity of economic systems, and found that 53 percent of Democrats had a favorable view of socialism. The following year, the Pew Research Center poll found that 49 percent of Americans under thirty looked favorably on socialism, which exceeded by 2 percentage points the share of Americans under thirty who felt that way about capitalism.

Despite this fairly stunning shift in sentiment, socialist groups were not yet growing and discussions of socialist policies were still hard to find in the media. Then, in 2015, Vermont senator Bernie Sanders announced he was running for president as a democratic socialist—and within the Democratic Party. And with that, the dam broke.

"Political change happens slowly, until it doesn't," says Dan Cantor, the longtime leader of the Working Families Party, a progressive electoral organization that operates chiefly within the Democratic Party. "Bernie has changed what it's possible to say."

Sanders brought three distinctive features to his candidacy: first, the rock-solid authenticity of a life spent outside, and devoted to destroying, the nexus of money and politics; second, a detailed (if largely unchanging) stump speech that assailed American capitalism directly; and third, a range of social democratic proposals that had not previously been "possible to say" within mainstream political discourse, much less in the glaring light of a major presidential campaign.

The evidence of his success is all around us. As Barry Goldwater's 1964 presidential campaign set the lamentable template for Republican politics for decades to come, so Sanders's campaign brought such social democratic policies as Medicare for All, free college educations, and more progressive taxation into the Democratic mainstream—so much so that they not only poll well with all Americans but were embraced by most of the 2020 Democratic presidential field.

That's a tribute to Sanders, but it also reflects the readiness of millions of his compatriots to join him in embracing democratic socialism—a readiness charted in polling for half a decade before he ran, but a readiness unvoiced until he began campaigning. The Sanders campaign didn't create a new left; it revealed it—both to the nation and to that new left itself.

That new left was not simply an outgrowth of economic conditions, however, nor did it define itself in narrowly economistic terms. It was also inextricably intertwined with the contemporaneous explosion of left activism on issues of race, gender, sexual orientation and identity, and climate change and the very future of the planet. Socialism's reemergence on the American scene has coincided with the growth of such movements as Black Lives Matter; the DreamActivists seeking legalization for undocumented immigrants; the Women's Marches, with their millions of participants; the #MeToo uprising; and the opposition to the nation's dependence on fossil fuels, epitomized by the Sunrise Movement.

There is, after all, an intersectionality of subordination. Women, minorities, and workers face systemic discrimination that's at once social, economic, and existential. Targeting a particular form of that discrimination often offers the most fruitful path to improved conditions—as, say, the Civil Rights Act of 1964 did—and such reforms are vitally important. But many of today's socialists understand their socialism either as comprising one of a set of left agendas that must all be realized in order to make life more rewarding and fair, or as itself encompassing all these agendas.

Many of today's progressive movements, and particularly their most devoted and militant activists, are drawn disproportionately from the young—the cohort most attuned to social subordination and environmental concerns, not to mention having been saddled with record levels of debt and thrown into a largely unrewarding job market. To look at public opinion polling, election results, or the composition of progressive groups is to conclude that millennials and members of Generation Z (the group younger than millennials) constitute the leftmost generation at least since the generation that came of age in the 1930s—if not in all of American history. And not only American: exit polling in both the 2016 Democratic presidential primaries and the 2017 parliamentary election in the United Kingdom shows that support for Sanders in the United States and for Jeremy Corbyn's Labour Party in the United Kingdom grew stronger with each successively younger age cohort.

The growth of socialism's support in America is also due to Bernie Sanders's decision to run within the Democratic Party rather than as a third-party also-ran. By so doing, Sanders was able to appear in numerous televised debates and compete in one high-profile primary election after another, winning incomparably more media coverage than he would have as a minor-party candidate. By so doing, he gave his volunteers around the nation a steady stream of state campaigns in which they could involve themselves, thrilling them by winning a number of those contests, which only ratified the power of his and their ideas. By so doing, he busted socialism out of the irrelevance and spoiler status of third-party candidacies in a plurality-winner-take-all electoral system, enabling him to pull down fifteen times the vote of his hero, Eugene Debs, who ran for president five times on the Socialist Party ticket. That Sanders won 43 percent of the Democratic primary votes is a major reason why so many 2020 Democratic presidential candidates and other

Democratic elected officials announced their support for many of the causes he advanced, most especially Medicare for All. Neither Debs nor six-time Socialist Party presidential candidate Norman Thomas, nor, for that matter, Ralph Nader or any Green presidential nominee, had any comparable success in compelling the Democrats to fundamentally alter their policy agendas.

The story of Sanders's ability to redefine much of the Democratic agenda by working from within the party (notwithstanding his incongruous insistence that he's an independent, which doesn't meet the walk-like-a-duck test) has been repeated by Alexandria Ocasio-Cortez, another socialist working within the Democratic Party. After upsetting a powerful incumbent in the Democratic primary in her Bronx-Queens district in June 2018, she was elected to Congress in November of that year. Once in office, she placed both the Green New Deal and radically more progressive taxation onto the party's and the public's agendas. Ocasio-Cortez is a certifiable genius at messaging, but if she didn't represent a rising tendency within the Democratic Party, her messaging would be for naught.

The idea that socialists should do their electoral work largely within the Democratic Party isn't new. Since he founded DSOC in 1973, Harrington had argued that working openly as socialists within the Democratic Party created a far clearer path to socialist visibility and viability than remaining within the ghetto of third-party challenges, which even socialists might hesitate to support if that meant splitting the progressive vote and enabling a right-winger to win election. The surge of new members to DSA that accompanied both Sanders's and Ocasio-Cortez's campaigns is just one reflection of the strategic soundness of Harrington's perspective. Less than four years after Sanders declared his candidacy, DSA membership had increased ninefold—from roughly six thousand to roughly sixty thousand by late 2019, with its three major surges in membership coinciding with Sanders's campaign, Donald Trump's election, and Ocasio-Cortez's victory in her 2018 Democratic primary. A more significant index of the success of that strategy is the degree to which Democrats, most especially Democratic presidential candidates, are now advancing social democratic policies—not just Medicare for All, but also universal taxpayer-funded child care, planned full employment, and a much more progressive taxation of income and wealth to fund such policies.

One reason for socialism's growing popularity is a long-term shift in the public's understanding of the term. When Sanders delivered a speech at Georgetown University in the fall of 2015, which he'd billed as providing his definition of socialism, he cited as his precedents Franklin Roosevelt's creation of Social Security, Lyndon Johnson's creation of Medicare, and Martin Luther King's commitment to an egalitarian society. His vision of socialism, he emphasized, was light-years distant from a society in which all private enterprise, particularly small- and medium-size businesses, were taken over by the state.

Crucially, that seems to be the public's definition of socialism as well. In September of 2018, Gallup asked Americans for their "understanding of the term 'socialism.'" One-third—33 percent—answered that it meant a society with equal standing for everybody, in which benefits and services were free for all. When Gallup had asked Americans the same question in September of 1949, at the height of the Cold War, just 14 percent gave that answer, while 34 percent answered that it meant government ownership of all business and control of society. Just half that total—17 percent—gave that answer in 2018. (Other answers drew far less support.) That is, the public's idea of socialism has shifted over the past seventy years from one verging on totalitarianism to one far closer to social democracy. The disappearance of Soviet communism has clearly contributed to that shift, but the transition over those same seventy years to a radically more vicious form of capitalism has likely also prompted many to define socialism as the more egalitarian system they seek—"the name of our desire," as Irving Howe and Lewis Coser defined it in a 1954 issue of *Dissent* magazine.

Where We Need to Go, What We Need to Surmount

The Constitution of the United States is not our friend, and in this, socialists are not alone. The nation's governing document presents a host of obstacles to all progressive reform, beginning with the anti-majoritarian bias that's encoded in both the Senate and the electoral college, both of which violate the principle of one-person, one-vote. Socialists need to work with liberals and all fellow Americans who simply support majority rule to eliminate the electoral college and do what they can to abolish or mitigate the power of the Senate (which, constitutionally, is very difficult). Socialists also need to work with liberals to take money out of politics—putting justices on the Supreme Court who will reverse *Buckley v. Valeo* (the ruling that first protected all campaign spending as free speech), and passing legislation at the federal, state, and local levels that limits the size of campaign contributions and creates public matching funds for low-dollar donations, for ballot measures no less than for candidates.

Socialists and progressives will find—and are finding—fewer obstacles to reform in blue Democratic states and even bluer Democratic cities. As cities have become increasingly home to a share of millennials and people of color that's far higher than the national average, they've almost uniformly moved left over the past couple of decades. Today, an overwhelming majority of the nation's fifty largest cities have Democratic mayors and councils, many of them progressive, even in the reddest of states. In the 2018 midterm elections, Democrats won Republican-held congressional seats in Oklahoma City, Salt Lake City, and Charleston, South Carolina.

It was left-wing groups in liberal cities that began the campaigns for progressive reforms that since have become commonplace in Democratic thinking and law in Democratic-controlled states. The Fight for $15 was begun by a New York community organization; the Living Wage campaign and the policy of requiring developers to hire local residents were begun by union-backed Los Angeles policy groups; San Francisco enacted its own semi-universal health insurance plan; Seattle was the first city to mandate a $15 wage.

It's in cities such as these where DSA also has its greatest strength, and, of course, it was in New York and Detroit where DSA members Alexandria Ocasio-Cortez and Rashida Tlaib, respectively, won congressional seats in November 2018. Neither of their campaigns was incubated by DSA, and, famously, Ocasio-Cortez joined the organization only after she saw DSA members involve themselves in her campaign.

All of which is to argue that cities are where socialists can have the greatest impact in the near future, if they make common cause with the progressive communities and progressive groups that shape the cities' political climate. Cities afford socialists the best opportunities to run for and win elective office, but also, the best opportunities to build powerful alliances with unions, community and ethnic organizations, and other progressive groups. In 2019 city elections, for instance, Chicago voters sent five DSA members to the city council. We haven't seen an upsurge like this since the wave of municipal socialism in the early 1900s.

As in the first decades of the twentieth century, cities are also the places where some specifically socialist or social democratic policies stand the best chance of enactment. Public banks, public utilities, social housing, worker- and community-owned cooperative enterprises (like the Evergreen Coops in Cleveland)—these are all institutions whose creation or expansion has been made more likely by the glaring failure of private markets and institutions. Just to focus for a moment on California, the track records of Wells Fargo, PG&E, and the real estate developers suggest that campaigns for public banks, public utilities, and mixed-income social housing might do very well in the Bay Area and Los Angeles, and perhaps even statewide.

Obviously, the creation of such institutions is not dependent on having avowedly socialist majorities on city councils or in statehouses—no more so than it required an avowedly socialist Congress to create Social Security in 1935 or Medicare in 1965. Nor, if the Democrats control Congress and the White House in 2021, will it require a socialist caucus that constitutes a congressional majority to enact social democratic policies.

But a bigger socialist caucus, and a bigger House Progressive Caucus, would surely help. The 2018 election brought a number of avowed progressives to Congress (not all of them representing urban districts, either). Today, 102 House Democrats (out of a total of 235) belong to the Progressive Caucus—an all-time high. The delegation also included a socialist caucus of two—Ocasio-Cortez and Tlaib. The more social democrats (whether they term themselves socialists or progressives) in Congress, the more likely it will be that health coverage will be a truly universal, taxpayer-funded entitlement, rather than a crazy quilt of public and private plans, some of which scale patient benefits to patient payments.

But, as is ever the case, legislative outcomes will depend on the outside game as well as the inside one. Overcoming the opposition of major economic interests will require a mix of militant action, door-to-door canvassing, and the continual construction and nurturing of coalitions.

For members of a group like DSA, that raises the question of whether their organization should support candidates who back policies like Medicare for All or co-determination on corporate boards, but who are not themselves socialists. In 2018, New York Democratic gubernatorial candidate Cynthia Nixon won the primary endorsement of DSA after she declared herself a socialist, while in Florida and Georgia, Democratic gubernatorial candidates Andrew Gillum and Stacey Abrams, whose politics were generally as left as Nixon's, made no such declaration and received no such formal backing. Nixon lost by a landslide, but Gillum and Abrams came within razor-thin margins of winning. Socialists need to be strategic about where they put their resources. A few hundred DSA members walking precincts for Gillum and Abrams might have made a big difference, perhaps adding enough votes to put them in the winners' columns. Then again, New York (particularly New York City) is a place where a DSA endorsement actually can help a candidate, given the city's political climate and the group's ability to consistently mobilize many hundreds of volunteers. In Florida and Georgia, by contrast, a prominent endorsement from a socialist group isn't going to help a statewide candidate—it could possibly even damage them—barring a sea change in those states' politics. A non-endorsement, however, doesn't preclude substantial volunteer involvement in a campaign.

The one way socialists would be almost certain to subvert—actually, undo—the gains they've made in recent years would be to repudiate work within the Democratic Party for the chimera of focusing on building an independent third party. Most third-party campaigns do more harm than good for activists and organizations that espouse them, not to mention for the nation as a whole, as the candidacies of Green Party presidential nominees Ralph Nader and Jill Stein lamentably demonstrated.

Contemporary American socialists—including most DSA members— are unlikely to make that mistake in today's political climate. After all, most DSA members joined the organization because it was involved in a variety of candidate campaigns that won unprecedented (for socialists) levels of publicity and approval precisely because they were conducted within the Democratic Party (that is, the campaigns of Sanders and Ocasio-Cortez). To shift to a third party now, when social democratic policies have won considerable traction within the Democratic Party and its field of presidential candidates, and when the electoral alternative to the Democrats is

Trumpian fascism, would surely—and rightly—destroy not only DSA, the only socialist organization to have made an impact on American politics since the 1930s, but also the broader progressive movement that includes many people who consider themselves socialists but are not affiliated with a socialist organization.

That said, what are the policies that can supplant capitalist institutions and markets with socialist or social democratic institutions—or at least weaken those capitalist institutions and markets while strengthening their socialist alternatives—that progressives and socialists can credibly advance in the coming years?

One such policy is already atop the left's agenda: Medicare for All. While there are strategic questions as to the best way to get to Medicare for All, the end goal of removing health care from the tyranny of markets is essential. Other popular policies that can advance social rights and dispel the rule of money are free public higher education and free universal child care. Still another—perhaps the most fundamental—is to take money out of politics through a system of public financing of campaigns.

But socialists must be cognizant of the fact that capitalist institutions have been able to erode many of the gains that parties of the left and center left achieved in the decades following World War II. That makes it particularly important for socialists to focus on policies that build social power and weaken capitalist power. For this reason, socialists need to push a range of changes that shift the balance of social and economic power in our nation. They need to champion changes in labor law that enable workers to form effective unions again (an effort that should encompass the repeal of the Taft-Hartley Act). They should back changes to the structure of corporations by requiring that their boards be split between worker and shareholder representatives (with the possibility of a three-way split encompassing workers, shareholders, and public representatives). They need to advocate establishing public banks on a scale so large that they diminish the power of Wall Street, and to further diminish Wall Street's sway by breaking up its megabanks. They must call for transferring ownership of the corporate sector to its employees and the public through such means as directing a share of the profits to employees (as Labour Party Shadow Chancellor John McDonnell has proposed in the United Kingdom), or requiring corporations to pay their taxes in the form of stock (as economist Dean Baker has long suggested), or establishing a social wealth fund along the lines of Norway's. In particular, as an increasing number of corporations will be seeking to replace human labor with technology, it's crucial that workers and the public become part of the corporate decision-making process, not just to save old jobs or structure new ones, but also to ensure that the gains in productivity are not confined, as they currently are, to wealthy shareholders.

Is today's socialist movement large enough to credibly advance these goals and turn them into law? Clearly not.

This isn't to make light of DSA's ninefold gain in members over the past few years. Coupled with the electoral successes of Sanders and Ocasio-Cortez, with which its growth is inextricably linked, DSA has played a nontrivial role in shifting public discourse and enabling many social democratic policies to be seriously debated and considered on the floors of Congress and legislatures and on to the presidential campaign trail.

But the roughly 60,000 members of DSA amount to 0.4 percent of the 13.2 million Americans who voted for Bernie Sanders in 2016. They amount to 0.17 percent of the 93 million Americans whom Gallup says hold a favorable view of socialism.

Barring a retreat into third-party futility or some equally self-marginalizing posture, DSA will likely continue to grow, which is one—but only one—factor in assessing the prospects for socialist or social democratic policies. But the size of avowedly socialist organizations has never been *the* critical determinant of whether a nation adopts such policies. To be sure, the actions of socialist and communist militants (for instance, organizing the unemployed and instigating general strikes) helped prod New Deal—era politicians to enact more rights and benefits for workers. But such breakthroughs have always required the support of far greater numbers of citizens, most of whom are not members of any socialist organization but who have decided to vote for candidates who support socialist, social democratic, or simply progressive reforms. It's through just such a combination of socialist organizational activity and the socialists' cultivation of support for specific reforms from a far broader public that enabled the nations of Western Europe to adopt social democratic policies.

"An unorganized socialist is a contradiction in terms," Michael Harrington frequently said, and if socialism is to become a genuine force in American politics and life, it needs both to organize many thousands of unorganized socialists into a more powerful socialist organization, and to help in the process of building far broader support for social democratic reforms. For perhaps the first time ever in American history, these goals are now possible—provided socialists choose to be both in and of the world.

Afterword: A Day in the Life of a Socialist Citizen

Michael Walzer

This essay has been very lightly adapted from a piece of the same name, first published in Dissent *in 1968. We think it holds up.*

IMAGINE A DAY IN THE LIFE OF A SOCIALIST CITIZEN. HE HUNTS IN THE morning, fishes in the afternoon, rears cattle in the evening, and plays the critic after dinner. Yet he is neither hunter, nor fisherman, nor shepherd, nor critic; tomorrow he may select another set of activities, just as he pleases. This is the delightful portrait that Marx sketches in *The German Ideology* as part of a polemic against the division of labor.[1] Socialists since have worried that it is not economically feasible; perhaps it is not. But there is another difficulty that I want to consider: that is, the curiously apolitical character of the citizen Marx describes. Certain crucial features of socialist life have been omitted altogether.

In light of the contemporary interest in participatory democracy, Marx's sketch needs to be elaborated. Before hunting in the morning, this unalienated man of the future is likely to attend a meeting of the Council on Animal Life, where he will be required to vote on important matters relating to the stocking of the forests. The meeting will probably not end much before noon, for among the many-sided citizens there will always be a lively interest even in highly technical problems. Immediately after lunch, a special session of the Fishermen's Council will be called to protest the maximum catch recently voted by the Regional Planning Commission, and the Marxist man will participate eagerly in these debates, even postponing a scheduled discussion of some contradictory theses on cattle rearing. Indeed, he will probably love argument far better than hunting, fishing, *or* rearing cattle. The debates will go on so long that the citizens will have to rush through dinner in order to assume their role as critics. Then off they will go to meetings of study groups, clubs, editorial boards, and political parties, where criticism will be carried on long into the night.

Oscar Wilde is supposed to have said that socialism would take too many evenings. This is, it seems to me, one of the most significant criticisms of socialist theory that has ever been made. The fanciful sketch above is only intended to suggest its possible truth. Socialism's great appeal is the prospect it holds out for the development of human capacities. An enormous growth of creative talent, a new and unprecedented variety of expression, a wild proliferation of sects, associations, schools, parties: this will be the flowering of the future society. But underlying this new individualism and exciting group life must be a broad, self-governing community of equals.

A powerful figure looms behind Marx's hunter, fisherman, shepherd, and critic: the busy citizen attending the endless meetings. "Society regulates the general production," Marx writes, "and thus makes it possible for me to do one thing today and another tomorrow."[2] If society is not to become an alien and dangerous force, however, the citizens cannot accept its regulation and gratefully do what they please. They must participate in social regulation; they must be social men and women, organizing and planning their own fulfillment in spontaneous activity. The purpose of Wilde's objection is to suggest that just this self-regulation is incompatible with spontaneity, that the requirements of citizenship are incompatible with the freedom of hunter, fisherman, and so on.

Politics itself, of course, can be a spontaneous activity, freely chosen by those men and women who enjoy it and to whose talents a meeting is so much exercise. But this is very unlikely to be true of all men and women all the time—even if one were to admit what seems plausible enough: that political life is more intrinsic to human nature than is hunting and cattle rearing or even (to drop Marx's rural imagery) art or music. "Too many evenings" is a shorthand phrase that describes something more than the sometimes tedious, sometimes exciting business of resolutions and debates.

It suggests also that socialism and participatory democracy will depend upon, and hence require, an extraordinary willingness to attend meetings, and a public spirit and sense of responsibility that will make attendance dependable and activity consistent and sustained. None of this can rest for any long period of time or among any substantial group of people upon spontaneous interest. Nor does it seem possible that spontaneity will flourish above and beyond the routines of social regulation.

Self-government is a very demanding and time-consuming business, and when it is extended from political to economic and cultural life, and when the organs of government are decentralized so as to maximize participation, it will inevitably become more demanding still. Ultimately, it may well require almost continuous activity, and life will become a succession of meetings. When will there be time for the cultivation of personal creativity or the free association of like-minded friends? In the world of the meeting, when will there be time for the tête-à-tête?

I suppose there will always be time for the tête-à-tête. Men and women will secretly plan love affairs even while public business is being transacted. But Wilde's objection is not silly. The idea of citizenship on the left has always been overwhelming, suggesting a positive frenzy of activity and often involving the repression of all feelings except political ones. Its character can best be examined in the work of Rousseau, from whom socialists and, more recently, new leftists directly or indirectly inherited it. In order to guarantee public spiritedness and political participation, and as a part of his critique of bourgeois egotism, Rousseau systematically denigrated the value of private life: "The better the constitution of a state is, the more do public affairs encroach on private in the minds of the citizens. Private affairs are even of much less importance, because the aggregate of the common happiness furnishes a greater proportion of that of each individual, so that there is less for him to seek in particular cares."[3]

Rousseau might well have written these lines out of a deep awareness that private life will not, in fact, bear the great weight that bourgeois society places upon it. We need, beyond our families and jobs, a public world where purposes are shared and cooperative activity is possible. More likely, however, he wrote them because he believed that cooperative activity could not be sustained unless private life were radically repressed, if not altogether eradicated. His citizen does not participate in social regulation as one part of a round of activities. Social regulation is his entire life. Rousseau develops his own critique of the division of labor by absorbing all human activities into the idea of citizenship: "Citizens," he wrote, "are neither lawyers, nor soldiers, nor priests by profession; they perform all these functions as a matter of duty."[4] *As a matter of duty*: here is the key to the character of that patriotic, responsible, energetic person who has figured also in socialist thought, but always in the guise of a new man, a new woman, freely exercising their human powers.

It is probably more realistic to see these citizens as the product of collective repression and self-discipline. They are, above all, *dutiful*, and this is only possible if they have triumphed over egotism and impulse in their own personalities. They embody what political theorists have called "republican virtue"—that means, they put the common good, the success of the movement, the safety of the community, above their own delight or well-being, *always*. To symbolize their virtue, perhaps, they adopt an ascetic style and give up every sort of self-decoration: the men wear *sans-culottes* or unpressed khakis; the women go without makeup. More important, they forgo conventional careers for the profession of politics; they commit themselves entirely. It is an act of the most extreme devotion. Now, how is such a person produced? What kind of conversion is necessary? Or what kind of rigorous training?

Rousseau set out to create virtuous citizens, and the means he chose are very old in the history of republicanism: an authoritarian family, a rigid sexual code, censorship of the arts, sumptuary laws, mutual surveillance, the systematic indoctrination of children. All these have been associated historically (at least until recent times) not with tyrannical but with republican regimes: Greece and Rome, the Swiss Protestant city-states, the first French republic. Tyrannies and oligarchies, Rousseau argued, might tolerate or even encourage license, for the effect of sexual indulgence, artistic freedom, extravagant self-decoration, and privacy itself was to corrupt men and women and turn them away from public life, leaving government to the few. Self-government requires self-control: it is one of the oldest arguments in the history of political thought.[5]

If that argument is true, it may mean that self-government also leaves

government to the few. At least, this may be so if we reject the disciplin-
ary or coercive features of Rousseau's republicanism and insist that citizens
always have the right to choose between participation and passivity. Their
obligations follow from their choices and do not precede them, so the state
cannot impose one or the other choice; it cannot force the citizens to be self-
governing men and women. Then only those citizens will be activists who
volunteer for action. How many will that be? How many of the people you
and I know? How many ought they to be? Certainly no radical movement
or socialist society is possible without those ever-ready participants, who
"fly," as Rousseau said, "to the public assemblies."[6] Radicalism and socialism make political activity for the first time an option for all those who relish
it and a duty—sometimes—even for those who do not. But what a suffo-
cating sense of responsibility, what a plethora of virtue would be necessary
to sustain the participation of everybody all the time! How exhausting it
would be! Surely there is something to be said for the irresponsible nonpar-
ticipant and something also for the part-time activist, the half-virtuous man
or woman (and the most scorned among the militants), who appears and
disappears, thinking of Marx and then of his dinner? The very least that can
be said is that these people, unlike the poor, will always be with us.

We can assume that a great many citizens, in the best of societies, will do
all they can to avoid what Melvin Tumin has called "the merciless masochism of community-minded and self-regulating men and women."[7] While
the necessary meetings go on and on, they will take long walks, play with
their children, paint pictures, make love, and watch television. They will
attend sometimes, when their interests are directly at stake or when they
feel like it. But they will not make the full-scale commitment necessary for
socialism or participatory democracy. How are these people to be represented at the meetings? What are their rights? These are not only problems
of the future, when popular participation has finally been established as the
core of political and economic life. They come up in every radical movement; they are the stuff of contemporary controversy.

Many people feel that they ought to join this or that political movement;
they do join; they contribute time and energy—but unequally. Some make
a full-time commitment; they work every minute; the movement becomes
their whole life, and they often come to disbelieve in the moral validity of life

outside. Others are established outside, solidly or precariously; they snatch hours and sometimes days; they harry their families and skimp on their jobs, but yet cannot make it to every meeting. Still others attend scarcely any meetings at all; they work hard but occasionally; they show up, perhaps, at critical moments; then they are gone. These last two groups make up the majority of the people available to the movement (any movement), just as they will make up the majority of the citizens of any socialist society. Radical politics radically increases the amount and intensity of political participation, but it does not (and probably ought not) break through the limits imposed on republican virtue by the inevitable pluralism of commitments, the terrible shortage of time, and the day-to-day hedonism of ordinary men and women.

Under these circumstances, words like "citizenship" and "participation" may actually describe the enfranchisement of only a part, and not necessarily a large part, of the movement or the community. Participatory democracy means the sharing of power among the activists. Socialism means the rule of the people with the most evenings to spare. Both imply, of course, an injunction to the others: join us, come to the meetings, participate! Sometimes young radicals sound very much like old Christians, demanding the severance of every tie for the sake of politics. "How many Christian women are there," John Calvin once wrote, "who are held captive by their children!"[8] How many "community people" miss meetings because of their families! But there is nothing to be done. Ardent democrats have sometimes urged that citizens be legally required to vote; that is possible, though the device is not attractive. Requiring people to attend meetings, to join in discussions, to govern themselves: that is not possible, at least not in a free society. And if they do not govern themselves, they will, willy-nilly, be governed by their activist fellows. The apathetic, the occasional enthusiasts, the part-time workers: all of them will be ruled by full-timers, militants, and professionals.

But if only some citizens participate in political life, it is essential that they always remember and be regularly reminded that they are . . . only some. This is not easy to arrange. The militants in the movement, for example, do not represent anybody; it is their great virtue that they are self-chosen, volunteers. But since they sacrifice so much for their fellows, they readily persuade themselves that they are acting in their name. They take the failure of the others to put in an appearance only as a token of their oppression. They are certain that they are the agents of the people's liberation. I suppose they are not simply wrong. The small numbers of participating citizens in the United States today, the widespread fearfulness, the sense of impotence and irrelevance: all these are signs of social sickness. Self-government is an important human function, an exercise of significant talents and energies, and the sense of power and responsibility it brings is enormously healthy. A certain amount of commitment and discipline, of not-quite-merciless masochism, is socially desirable, and efforts to evoke it are socially justifiable.

But many of the people who stay away from meetings do so for reasons that the militants do not understand or will not acknowledge. They stay away not because they are beaten, afraid, uneducated, lacking confidence and skills (though these are often important reasons), but because they have made other commitments; they have found ways to cope short of politics; they have created viable subcultures even in an oppressive world. They may lend passive support to the movement and help out occasionally, but they will not work, nor are their needs and aspirations in any sense embodied by the militants who will.

The militants represent themselves. If the movement is to be democratic, the others must *be represented*. The same thing will be true in any future socialist society: participatory democracy has to be paralleled by representative democracy. I am not sure precisely how to adjust the two; I am sure that they have to be adjusted. Somehow power must be distributed, as it is not today, *to* groups of active and interested citizens, but these citizens must themselves be made responsible *to* a larger electorate (the membership, that is, of the state, movement, union, or party). Nothing is more important than that responsibility; without it we will only get one or another sort of activist or apparatchik tyranny. And that we have already.

Nonparticipants have rights; it is one of the dangers of participatory democracy that it would fail to provide any effective protection for these rights. But nonparticipants also have functions; it is another danger that these would not be sufficiently valued. For many people in America today, politics is something to watch, an exciting spectacle, and there exists between the activists and the others something of the relation of actor and audience. Now, for any democrat this is an unsatisfactory relation. We rightly resent the way actors play upon and manipulate the feelings of their audiences. We dislike the aura of magic and mystification contrived at onstage. We would prefer politics to be like the new drama with its alienation effects and its audience participation. That is fair enough.

But even the new drama requires its audience, and we ought not to forget that audiences can be critical as well as admiring, enlightened as well as mystified. More important, political actors, like actors in the theater, need the control and tension imposed by audiences, the knowledge that tomorrow the reviews will appear, tomorrow people will come or not come to watch their performance. Too often, of course, the reviews are favorable and the audiences come. That is because of the various sorts of collusion that commonly develop between small and co-opted cliques of actors and critics. But in an entirely free society, there would be many more political actors and critics than ever before, and they would, presumably, be self-chosen. Not only the participants, but also the nonparticipants, would come into their own. Alongside the democratic politics of shared work and perpetual activism, there would arise the open and leisurely culture of part-time work, criticism, second-guessing, and burlesque. And into this culture might well be drawn many of the alienated citizens of today. The modes of criticism will become the forms of their participation and their involvement in the drama the measure of their responsibility.

It would be a great mistake to underestimate the importance of criticism as a kind of politics, even if the critics are not always marked, as they won't be, by "republican virtue." It is far more important in the political arena than in the theater. For activists and professionals in the movement or the state do not simply contrive effects; their work has more palpable results. Their policies touch us all in material ways, whether we go or do not go to the meetings. Indeed, those who do not go may well turn out to be more effective critics than those who do: no one who was one of its "first-guessers" can usefully second-guess a decision. That is why the best critics in a liberal society are citizens-out-of-office. In a radically democratic society they would be people who stay away from meetings, perhaps for months at a time, and only then discover that something outrageous has been perpetrated that must be mocked or protested. The proper response to such protests is not to tell the laggard citizens that they should have been active these past many months, not to nag them to do work that they do not enjoy and in any case will not do well, but to listen to what they have to say. After all, what would democratic politics be like without its kibitzers?

Acknowledgments

WE'D LIKE TO THANK JULES BERNSTEIN FOR HIS FRIENDSHIP AND SUPPORT for this book. This project wouldn't have been possible without the ample support of the *Dissent* staff, past and present—Colin Kinniburgh, Natasha Lewis, Nick Serpe, Kaavya Asoka, and more—who helped shepherd this book into existence. We'd also like to thank Marc Favreau, The New Press's executive editor, along with Emily Albarillo and the rest of the team there, for helping us bring this book project from an idea to a finished product in record time.

Notes

Introduction

1. Mohamed Younis, "Four in 10 Americans Embrace Some Form of Socialism," Gallup, May 20, 2019, https://news.gallup.com/poll/257639/four-americans-embrace -form-socialism.aspx.

2. Zack Beauchamp, "A Clinton-Era Centrist Democrat Explains Why It's Time to Give Democratic Socialists a Chance," *Vox*, March 4, 2019, www.vox.com/policy-and -politics/2019/3/4/18246381/democrats-clinton-sanders-left-brad-delong.

3. Intergovernmental Panel on Climate Change, "Summary for Policymakers of IPCC Special Report on Global Warming of 1.5°C Approved by Governments," IPCC, October 8, 2018, www.ipcc.ch/2018/10/08/summary-for-policymakers-of-ipcc-special -report-on-global-warming-of-1-5c-approved-by-governments.

4. Ellen Barry and Martin Selsoe Sorensen, "In Denmark, Harsh New Laws for Immigrant 'Ghettos,'" *New York Times*, July 1, 2018, www.nytimes.com/2018/07/01 /world/europe/denmark-immigrant-ghettos.html.

5. Ian Haney Lopez and Heather McGhee, "How Populists Like Bernie Sanders Should Talk About Racism," *The Nation*, January 28, 2016, www.thenation.com/article /how-populists-like-bernie-sanders-should-talk-about-racism.

Toward a Third Reconstruction

1. Lani Guinier and Gerald Torres, *The Miner's Canary: Enlisting Race, Resisting Power, Transforming Democracy* (Cambridge, MA: Harvard University Press, 2003).

2. Alan Flippen, "Black Turnout in 1964, and Beyond," *New York Times*, October 16, 2014.

3. Algernon Austin, "The Unfinished March: An Overview," Economic Policy Institute, June 18, 2013, https://www.epi.org/files/2013/EPI-The-Unfinished-March -An-Overview.pdf.

4. Sharon Dolovich, "Exclusion and Control in the Carceral State," *Berkeley Journal of Criminal Law* 16:2 (Fall 2011), 259–339.

5. See Melany De La Cruz-Viesca et al., "The Color of Wealth in Los Angeles," Federal Reserve Bank of San Francisco, 2016, http://www.aasc.ucla.edu/besol /color_of_wealth_report.pdf.

6. See Henry S. Farber et al., "NBER Working Paper No. 24587: Unions and Inequality over the Twentieth Century: New Evidence from Survey Data," National Bureau of Economic Research, May 2018, https://www.nber.org/papers/w24587.

A Three-Legged Stool for Racial and Economic Justice

1. Mark Paul, William Darity Jr., and Darrick Hamilton, "The Federal Job Guarantee—A Policy to Achieve Permanent Full Employment," Center on Budget and Policy Priorities, March 9, 2018, www.cbpp.org/research/full-employment/the-federal -job-guarantee-a-policy-to-achieve-permanent-full-employment.

2. Mark Paul, William Darity Jr., and Darrick Hamilton, "An Economic Bill of Rights for the 21st Century," *American Prospect,* March 5, 2018, prospect.org/article /economic-bill-rights-21st-century.

3. James Smith and Finis Welch, "Black Economic Progress After Myrdal," *Journal of Economic Literature* 27:2 (June 1989), 519–64.

4. Peter Gottschalk, "Inequality, Income Growth, and Mobility: The Basic Facts," *Journal of Economic Perspectives* 11:2 (Spring 1997), 21–40; William A. Darity and Patrick L. Mason, "Evidence on Discrimination in Employment: Codes of Color, Codes of Gender," *Journal of Economic Perspectives* 12:2 (Spring 1998), 63–90.

5. Darrick Hamilton, "The Federal Job Guarantee: A Step Toward Racial Justice," *Dissent,* November 9, 2015, www.dissentmagazine.org/online_articles/federal-job -guarantee-racial-justice-darrick-hamilton.

6. Janelle Jones and John Schmitt, "A College Degree Is No Guarantee," Center for Economic and Policy Research, May 2014, http://cepr.net/documents/black-coll-grads -2014-05.pdf.

7. Ibid.

8. Darrick Hamilton, William Darity Jr., et al., "Umbrellas Don't Make It Rain," National Asset Scorecard and Communities of Color, April 2015, http://www.insightcced .org/wp-content/uploads/2015/08/Umbrellas_Dont_Make_It_Rain_Final.pdf.

9. Darrick Hamilton, "Racial Equality Is Economic Equality," Biden Forum, February 14, 2018, https://bidenforum.org/racial-equality-is-economic-equality -64fca8e8bfc0.

10. Darrick Hamilton and Trevon Logan, "Here's Why Black Families Have Struggled for Decades to Gain Wealth," Marketwatch, March 4, 2019, www.marketwatch.com /story/heres-why-black-families-have-struggled-for-decades-to-gain-wealth-2019-02 -28.

11. Darrick Hamilton, "How 'Baby Bonds' Could Close the Wealth Gap," TED, September 2018, https://www.ted.com/talks/darrick_hamilton_how_baby _bonds_could_help_close_the_wealth_gap?language=en.

12. This measure is known as "U-3" in the monthly employment report from the Bureau of Labor Statistics.

13. Paul, Darity, and Hamilton, "The Federal Job Guarantee—A Policy to Achieve Permanent Full Employment."

14. Bureau of Labor Statistics, "Job Openings and Labor Turnover Summary," U.S. Department of Labor, January 2018, www.bls.gov/news.release/pdf/jolts.pdf.

15. Tomaz Cajner, Tyler Radler, David Ratner, and Ivan Vidangos, "Racial Gaps in Labor Market Outcomes in the Last Four Decades and over the Business Cycle" (Finance and Economics Discussion Series 2017-071, Washington, DC, Board of Governors of the Federal Reserve System, June 2017), www.federalreserve.gov/econres/feds/files/2017071pap.pdf.

16. Helen Lachs Ginsburg, "Historical Amnesia: The Humphrey-Hawkins Act, Full Employment and Employment as a Right," *Review of Black Political Economy* 39, no. 1 (2012): 121–36.

17. The act was an amendment to the 1946 Employment Act drafted by Leon Keyserling.

18. Karthik Muralidharan, Paul Niehaus, and Sandip Sukhtankar, "General Equilibrium Effects of (Improving) Public Employment Programs: Experimental Evidence from India" (NBER Working Paper No. 23838, National Bureau of Economic Research, 2017), www.nber.org/papers/w23838.

19. For an in-depth discussion of Argentina's Jefes y Jefas program, see Pavlina Tcherneva and L. Randall Wray, "Employer of Last Resort Program: A Case Study of Argentina's Jefes de Hogar Program," *SSRN* (2005), papers.ssrn.com/sol3/papers.cfm?abstract_id=1010145.

20. See Paul, Darity, and Hamilton, "The Federal Job Guarantee—A Policy to Achieve Permanent Full Employment."

21. Pavlina Tcherneva, "Working Paper No. 902: The Job Guarantee: Design, Jobs and Implementation," Levy Economics Institute of Bard College, April 2018, www.levyinstitute.org/pubs/wp_902.pdf.

22. See Matthew Boesler, "'Baby Bonds' Could Help the U.S. Wealthy Gap," *Bloomberg*, April 5, 2019, https://www.bloomberg.com/news/articles/2019-04-05/-baby-bonds-could-help-the-u-s-wealth-gap.

23. See Sarah Kliff, "An Exclusive Look at Cory Booker's Plan to Fight Wealth Inequality: Give Poor Kids Money," *Vox*, October 22, 2018, https://www.vox.com/policy-and-politics/2018/10/22/17999558/cory-booker-baby-bonds.

24. Naomi Zewde, "Universal Baby Bonds Reduce Black-White Wealth Inequality, Progressively Raise Net Worth of all Young Adults," November 2018, https://static1.squarespace.com/static/5743308460h5e922a25a6dc7/t/5c4339f67ha7fc4a9addb819/1547909624486/Zewde-Baby-Bonds-WP-10-30-18.pdf.

25. Hamilton, "How 'Baby Bonds' Could Close the Wealth Gap."

26. See Darrick Hamilton and Trevon Logan, "Why Wealth Equality Remains Out of Reach for Black Americans," *The Conversation*, February 28, 2019, https://theconversation.com/why-wealth-equality-remains-out-of-reach-for-black-americans-111483.

27. Hamilton and Logan, "Here's Why Black Families Have Struggled for Decades to Gain Wealth."

28. See Cheryl I. Harris, "Whiteness as Property," *Harvard Law Review* 106:8 (June 1993), 1707–1791; David Roediger, *The Wages of Whiteness: The Making of the American Working Class. Rev. ed.* (London and New York: Verso, 1999).

29. Kenneth C. Schoendorf et al., "Mortality Among Infants of Black as Compared with White College-Educated Parents," *New England Journal of Medicine* 326 (June 4, 1992), 1522–1526, https://www.nejm.org/doi/full/10.1056/NEJM199206043262303# t=article; Darrick Hamilton and Jennifer Cohen, "Race Still Trumps Class for Black Americans," *The Guardian*, March 27, 2018, https://www.theguardian.com /commentisfree/2018/mar/27/race-trump-class-black-americans.

30. Darrick Hamilton, "The Moral Burden of Economists," Institute for New Economic Thinking, April 13, 2017, https://www.ineteconomics.org/perspectives/blog /the-moral-burden-on-economists.

We the People: Voting Rights, Campaign Finance, and Election Reform

1. See Raj Chetty, David Grusky, Maximilian Hell, Nathaniel Hendren, Robert Manduca, and Jimmy Narang, "The Fading American Dream: Trends in Absolute Income Mobility Since 1940," *Science* 356:6336 (2017), 398–406.

2. Howard R. Gold, "Never Mind the 1 Percent: Let's Talk About the 0.01 Percent," *Chicago Booth Review*, Winter 2017/18, review.chicagobooth.edu/economics/2017 /article/never-mind-1-percent-lets-talk-about-001-percent.

3. Anthony Cilluffo and Rakesh Kochhar, "How Wealth Inequality Has Changed the U.S. Since the Great Recession, by Race, Ethnicity and Income," *Pew Research Center*, November 1, 2017, www.pewresearch.org/fact-tank/2017/11/01/how-wealth-inequality -has-changed-in-the-u-s-since-the-great-recession-by-race-ethnicity-and-income.

4. See, for example, Martin Gilens, *Affluence and Influence: Economic Inequality and Political Power in America* (Princeton, NJ: Princeton University Press, 2012); Larry Bartels, *Unequal Democracy: The Political Economy of the New Gilded Age* (Princeton, NJ: Princeton University Press, 2008); Kay Lehman Schlozman, Sidney Verba, and Henry E. Brady, *The Unheavenly Chorus: Unequal Political Voice and the Broken Promise of American Democracy* (Princeton, NJ: Princeton University Press, 2012); Larry M. Bartels, Benjamin I. Page, and Jason Seawright, "Democracy and the Policy Preferences of Wealthy Americans," *Perspectives on American Politics* 11:1 (March 2013), 51–73, faculty.wcas .northwestern.edu/~jnd260/cab/CAB2012%20-%20Page1.pdf.

5. "Voter Turnout by Income, 2008 US Presidential Election," Demos, www.demos .org/data-byte/voter-turnout-income-2008-us-presidential-election.

6. "What Is the Minimum Wage?," U.S. Department of Labor, https://webapps.dol .gov/elaws/faq/esa/flsa/001.htm; "Living Wage," Federal Safety Net, federalsafetynet .com/living-wage.html.

7. Jennifer Marlon, Peter Howe, Matto Mildenberger, Anthony Leiserowitz and Xinran Wang, "Yale Climate Opinion Maps 2018," Yale Program on Climate Change Communication, August 7, 2018, climatecommunication.yale.edu/visualizations-data /ycom-us-2018/?est=prienv&type=value&geo=national; Michael Greshko, Laura Parker, et. al, "A Running List of How President Trump Is Changing Environmental Policy," *National Geographic*, May 3, 2019, news.nationalgeographic.com/2017/03/how -trump-is-changing-science-environment.

8. Ibid.

9. David E. Broockman and Christopher Skovron, "Bias in Perceptions of Public Opinion Among Political Elites," *American Political Science Review* 112:3 (2018), 553, stanford.edu/~dbroock/published%20paper%20PDFs/broockman_skovron_bias _in_perception_of_public_opinion_among_political_elites.pdf.

10. Ibid., 551.

11. See "Legislative Staff and Representation in Congress," *American Political Science Review* (2018), staticl.squarespace.com/static/5b6f913085edela17e4c2bf7 /t 5bd7934af4e1fc0b2cbfd564/1540856026626/Hertel-Fernandez_Mildenberger _Stokes_2018_APSR_forthcoming_Legislative_Staff_and_Representation _in_C.pdf.

12. See Broockman and Skovron, "Bias in Perceptions of Public Opinion"; "Legislative Staff and Representation in Congress," *American Political Science Review* (2018), staticl.squarespace.com/static/5b6f913085edela17e4c2bf7/t/5bd7934af4e1fc0b2cbfd564 /1540856026626/Hertel-Fernandez_Mildenberger_Stokes_2018_APSR _forthcoming_Legislative_Staff_and_Representation_in_C.pdf, generally.

13. See "ALEC Exposed," The Center for Media and Democracy, www.alecexposed .org/wiki/ALEC_Exposed.

14. Lisa Graves, "A CMD Special Report on ALEC's Funding and Spending," prwatch .org, July 13, 2011, www.prwatch.org/news/2011/07/10887/cmd-special-report-alecs -funding-and-spending.

15. Ibid.

16. Ibid.

17. See "Revolving Door," opensecrets.org, www.opensecrets.org/revolving.

18. "Revolving Door: Former Members of the 114th Congress," opensecrets.org, www.opensecrets.org/revolving/departing.php?cong=114.

19. See *Buckley v. Valeo*, 424 U.S. 1 (1976) and *Citizens United v. Federal Election Commission*, 558 U.S. 310 (2010).

20. *Buckley.*

21. "Cost of 2018 Election to Surpass $5 Billion, CRP Projects," opensecrets.org, October 17, 2018, www.opensecrets.org/news/2018/10/cost-of-2018-election.

22. "Cost of Election," opensecrets.org, www.opensecrets.org/overview/cost.php

23. Benjamin I. Page, "How Money Corrupts American Politics," *Scholars Strategy Network*, June 19, 2013, scholars.org/how-money-corrupts-american-politics.

24. Norah O'Donnell, "Are Members of Congress Becoming Telemarketers?," *60 Minutes*, April 24, 2016, www.cbsnews.com/news/60-minutes-are-members-of -congress-becoming-telemarketers.

25. Uri Friedman, "American Elections: How Long Is Too Long?," *The Atlantic*, October 5, 2016, www.theatlantic.com/international/archive/2016/10/us-election -longest-world/501680.

26. Thomas K. Grose, "Elections: Is There a Better Way Than America's?," *U.S. News & World Report*, November 9, 2016, www.usnews.com/news/best-countries /articles/2016-11-09/the-us-elections-is-there-a-better-way.

27. Ibid.

28. Sruthi Gottipati and Rajesh Kumar Singh, "India Set to Challenge U.S. for Election-Spending Record," *Reuters*, www.reuters.com/article/us-india-election-spen ding/india-set-to-challenge-u-s-for-election-spending-record-idUSBREA280 AR20140309.

29. J. Mijin Cha and Liz Kennedy, "Millions to the Polls: Practical Policies to Fulfill the Freedom to Vote for All Americans," Demos, 2014, 19, www.demos.org/sites/default /files/publications/m2p-Main.pdf.

30. "The Effects of Shelby County v. Holder," Brennan Center for Justice, August 6, 2018, www.brennancenter.org/analysis/effects-shelby-county-v-holder.

31. Ibid; see also *Shelby County v. Holder*, 570 U.S. 529 (2013).

32. See "The Effects of Shelby County v. Holder."

33. Ibid.

34. "Voter ID History," National Conference of State Legislatures, May 31, 2017, www.ncsl.org/research/elections-and-campaigns/voter-id-history.aspx.

35. "Resources on Voter Fraud Claims," Brennan Center for Justice, June 26, 2017, www.brennancenter.org/analysis/resources-voter-fraud-claims.

36. "Debunking the Voter Fraud Myth," Brennan Center for Justice, January 31, 2017, www.brennancenter.org/analysis/debunking-voter-fraud-myth.

37. Andrew Prokop, "What Is Gerrymandering?," *Vox*, November 14, 2018, www.vox.com/2014/8/5/17991938/what-is-gerrymandering.

38. Ibid.

39. "Election 2012: Pennsylvania Election Results," *New York Times*, www.nytimes .com/elections/2012/results/states/pennsylvania.html.

40. Lena Groeger, Olga Pierce, et al., "House Seats vs. Popular Vote," December 21, 2012, projects.propublica.org/graphics/seats-vs-votes.

41. "League of Women Voters of Pennsylvania v. Commonwealth of Pennsylvania," Brennan Center for Justice, October 29, 2018, www.brennancenter.org/legal-work /league-women-voters-v-pennslyvania.

42. Christopher Ingraham, "Pennsylvania Supreme Court Draws 'Much More Competitive' District Map to Overturn Republican Gerrymander," *Washington Post*, February 20, 2018, www.washingtonpost.com/news/wonk/wp/2018/02/19/pennsylvania -supreme-court-draws-a-much-more-competitive-district-map-to-overturn-republican -gerrymander.

43. "Pennsylvania Election Results," *New York Times*, May 15, 2019, www.nytimes .com/interactive/2018/11/06/us/elections/results-pennsylvania-elections.html.

44. Juhem Navarro-Rivera and Emmanuel Caicedo, "Public Funding for Electoral Campaigns," Demos, June 28, 2017, www.demos.org/publication/public-funding -electoral-campaigns-how-27-states-counties-and-municipalities-empower-sma.

45. See "CEP Overview," State of Connecticut State Elections Enforcement Commission, seec.ct.gov/Portal/CEP/CEPLanding; Neil Vigdor, "The Ins And Outs Of Public

Campaign Financing in Connecticut," *Hartford Courant*, www.courant.com/politics/hc
-pol-public-campaign-financing-20180601-story.html.

46. J. Mijin Cha and Miles Rapoport, "Fresh Start: The Impact of Public Campaign
Financing in Connecticut," Demos, April 29, 2013, www.demos.org/publication/fresh
-start-impact-public-campaign-financing-connecticut.

47. Ibid.

48. "Revised Grant Amounts for 2018 Primaries and General Election and 2018
and 2019 Special Elections (Public Acts 17-2, 17-4, & 18-81)," State of Connecticut State Elections Enforcement Commission, seec.ct.gov/Portal/data/CEP/news
/2018GrantAmounts.pdf.

49. See Cha and Rapoport, "Fresh Start: The Impact of Public Campaign Financing
in Connecticut."

50. Ibid.

51. Karl Evers-Hillstrom, "Beto O'Rourke Smashes Quarterly Fundraising Record
with $38 Million Haul," opensecrets.org, October 12, 2018, www.opensecrets.org/news
/2018/10/beto-orourke-smashes-quarterly-fundraising-record.

52. Karl Evers-Hillstrom, "Ocasio-Cortez Enters the House with Highest Portion of
Small Contributions," opensecrets.org, December 17, 2018, www.opensecrets.org/news
/2018/12/ocasio-cortez-enters-the-house-as-most-popular-member-with-small-donors.

53. Karl Evers-Hillstrom, "The Most (and Least) Popular Candidates Among Small
Donors," opensecrets.org, November 1, 2018, www.opensecrets.org/news/2018/11
/popular-candidates-4-small-donors.

54. "Restore Democracy Amendment," Citizens Take Action, citizenstakeaction.org
/restore-democracy-amendment.

55. For The People Act of 2019, H.R.1, 116th Cong. (2019).

56. Drew Desilver, "U.S. Trails Most Developed Countries in Voter Turnout,"
Pew Research Center, May 21, 2018, www.pewresearch.org/fact-tank/2018/05/21/u
o voter-turnout-trails-most-developed-countries.

57. Ibid.

58. "Voter Turnout in U.S. Presidential Elections Since 1908," Statista, 2019, www
.statista.com/statistics/262915/voter-turnout-in-the-us-presidential-elections.

59. "Voter Turnout Demographics," United States Elections Project, www
.electproject.org/home/voter-turnout/demographics.

60. See Cha and Rapoport, "Fresh Start: The Impact of Public Campaign Financing
in Connecticut."

61. Ibid.

62. Ibid; "Same Day Voter Registration," National Conference of State Legislators,
April 17, 2019, www.ncsl.org/research/elections-and-campaigns/same-day-registration
.aspx; Charlotte Hill and Jake Grumbach, "Data for Politics #27: Same Day Registration
Can Increase Voter Turnout," October 8, 2018, www.dataforprogress.org/blog/2018/10
/8/data-for-politics-27-same-day-registration-can-increase-voter-turnout.

63. "Automatic Voter Registration," National Conference of State Legislators, April 22, 2019, www.ncsl.org/research/elections-and-campaigns/automatic-voter-regist-ration.aspx#states%20auto%20reg.

64. Ibid; J. Mijin Cha, "Registering Millions: The Success and Potential of the National Voter Registration Act at 20," Demos, May 20, 2013, www.demos.org/registering-millions-success-and-potential-national-voter-registration-act-20.

65. "The National Voter Registration Act of 1993 (NVRA)," U.S. Department of Justice, www.justice.gov/crt/national-voter-registration-act-1993-nvra.

66. Ibid.

67. Alex Vandermaas-Peeler, Daniel Cox, et al., "American Democracy in Crisis: The Challenges of Voter Knowledge, Participation, and Polarization," PRRI, July 17, 2018, www.prri.org/research/American-democracy-in-crisis-voters-midterms-trump-election-2018.

68. "What Is Compulsory Voting?," Institute for Democracy and Electoral Assistance, www.idea.int/data-tools/data/voter-turnout/compulsory-voting.

69. Ibid.

70. "Voter Turnout—2016 House of Representatives and Senate Elections," Australian Election Commission, www.aec.gov.au/About_AEC/research/files/voter-turnout-2016.pdf.

71. "Voter Turnout in U.S. Presidential Elections Since 1908."

72. "Voting Within Australia—Frequently Asked Questions," Australian Election Commission, www.aec.gov.au/FAQs/Voting_Australia.htm; "Electoral Background-er: Compulsory Voting," https://Australian Election Commission, www.aec.gov.au/about_aec/publications/backgrounders/compulsory-voting.htm.

73. Anthony Fowler, "Electoral and Policy Consequences of Voter Turnout: Evidence from Compulsory Voting in Australia," *Quarterly Journal of Political Science* 8 (2013), 159–182, projects.iq.harvard.edu/files/westminster_model_democracy/files/fowler_compulsoryvoting.pdf.

74. "Australia Votes to Repeal Carbon Tax," BBC News, July 17, 2014, www.bbc.com/news/world-asia-28339663.

75. "Electoral Backgrounder: Compulsory Voting."

Confronting Corporate Power

1. "Historical Highest Marginal Income Tax Rates," Tax Policy Center, February 19, 2015, www.taxpolicycenter.org/sites/default/files/legacy/taxfacts/content/PDF/toprate_historical.pdf.

2. "The Productivity-Pay Gap," Economic Policy Institute, August 2018, https://www.epi.org/productivity-pay-gap.

3. Michal Kalecki, "Political Aspects of Full Employment," *Political Quarterly* 14 (1943): 322–31, mronline.org/2010/05/22/political-aspects-of-full-employment.

4. Christopher Jencks, *Equality* (New York: Basic Books, 1972), 265.

Building the People's Banks

1. Tory Newmeyer, "The Finance 202: Incoming Democratic Frosh Don't Want to Serve on House Financial Services Panel," *Washington Post*, December 14, 2018.

2. Center on Budget and Policy Priorities, "Chart Book: The Legacy of the Great Recession," *Center on Budget and Policy Priorities*, July 9, 2019, www.cbpp.org/research/economy /chart-book-the-legacy-of-the-great-recession; Laura Kusisto, "Many Who Lost Homes to Foreclosure in Last Decade Won't Return—NAR," *Wall Street Journal*, April 20, 2015.

3. Zoë Carpenter, "Five Years After Dodd-Frank, 'It's Still a Financial System That Needs Reform,'" *The Nation*, July 23, 2015.

4. Timothy Geithner, "Remarks by Secretary Tim Geithner at the Commencement Ceremony for the Johns Hopkins University Paul H. Nitze School of Advanced International Studies," U.S. Department of Treasury, May 24, 2012, https://www.treasury.gov /press-center/press-releases/Pages/tg1593.aspx.

5. Peter Whoriskey, "'A Way of Monetizing Poor People': How Private Equity Firms Make Money Offering Loans to Cash-Strapped Americans," *Washington Post*, July 1, 2018.

6. Erin Duffin, "Corporate Profits in the United States in 2018, by Industry (in Billion U.S. Dollars)," *Statista*, June 26, 2019, www.statista.com/statistics/222122/us -corporate-profits-by-industry.

7. Thomas Gilbert and Christopher Hrdlicka, "Apple Is a Hedge Fund That Makes Phones," *Wall Street Journal*, August 23, 2018.

8. Dana Mattioli and Dana Cimilluca, "M&A Market Headed for a Record, Powered by Tech Disruption, AT&T Ruling," *Wall Street Journal*, July 1, 2018.

9. Matt Bruenig, "The Problem Is Capital," *Jacobin*, August 7, 2017.

10. Ratna Sahay, Martin Čihák, Papa N'Diaye, Adolfo Barajas, Ran Bi, Diana Ayala, Yuan Gao, Annette Kyobe, Lam Nguyen, Christian Saborowski, Katsiaryna Svirydzenka, and Seyed Reza Yousefi, "Rethinking Financial Deepening: Stability and Growth in Emerging Markets" (IMF Staff Discussion Note, SDN/15/08, May 2015), www.imf.org/external/pubs/ft/sdn/2015/sdn1508.pdf.

11. Federal Deposit Insurance Corporation, "2017 FDIC National Survey of Unbanked and Underbanked Households," *FDIC*, October 22, 2018, www.fdic.gov /householdsurvey.

12. Amanda Dixon, "America's 15 Largest Banks," *Bankrate*, May 30, 2019, www.bankrate.com/banking/americas-top-10-biggest-banks/#slide=1.

13. "The True Cost of the Bank Bailout," *PBS*, September 3, 2010, www.pbs.org /wnet/need-to-know/economy/the-true-cost-of-the-bank-bailout/3309.

14. Aruna Viswanatha and Brett Wolf, "HSBC to Pay $1.9 Billion U.S. Fine in Money-Laundering Case," *Reuters*, December 11, 2012; Samuel Rubenfeld, "Corruption Currents: BNP Paribas Settles U.S. Tax-Evasion Case," *Wall Street Journal*, November 20, 2015; James McBride, "Understanding the Libor Scandal," *Council on Foreign Relations*, October 12, 2016, www.cfr.org/backgrounder/understanding-libor-scandal; Philip Augar, "How the Forex Scandal Happened," *BBC*, May 20, 2015.

15. Jim Tankersley, "Banks Are Big Winners from Tax Cut," *New York Times*, January 16, 2018; Hannah Levitt and Max Abelson, "It's Official: Wall Street Topped $100 Billion in Profit," *Bloomberg*, January 16, 2019.

16. Zach Carter, "Fed Delays Volcker Rule, Giving Wall Street Another Holiday Gift," *HuffPost*, December 19, 2014.

17. Pete Schroeder, "Exclusive: U.S. Regulators Examine Wall Street's Volcker Rule Wish List—Sources," *Reuters*, February 28, 2018.

18. David Dayen, "Big Bank 'Living Wills' Are a Failure—and Point to a Bigger Problem," *Fiscal Times*, April 15, 2016, www.thefiscaltimes.com/Columns/2016/04/15/Big-Bank-Living-Wills-Are-Failure-and-Point-Bigger-Problem.

19. George Zornick, "Enforce Dodd-Frank: Break Up Bank of America," *The Nation*, January 26, 2012.

20. Rortybomb, "JPMorgan Slimming Down Because Dodd-Frank's Capital Requirements Are Working," *Reuters*, October 16, 2015.

21. Erkki Liikanen, "Final Report" (High-Level Expert Group on Reforming the Structure of the EU Banking Sector, Brussels, October 12, 2012), ec.europa.eu/info/system/files/liikanen-report-02102012_en.pdf.

22. Tim Edmonds, "The Independent Commission on Banking: The Vickers Report and the Parliamentary Commission on Banking Standards," *U.K. Parliament*, December 30, 2013, researchbriefings.parliament.uk/ResearchBriefing/Summary/SN06171.

23. Bank for International Settlements, "Global OTC Derivatives Market," *BIS*, n.d., www.bis.org/statistics/d5_1.pdf.

24. National Association of Pension Funds Limited, " Derivatives and Risk Management Made Simple," *J.P.Morgan*, December 2013, www.jpmorgan.com/jpmpdf/1320663533358.pdf; Comptroller of the Currency Administrator of National Banks, "Risk Management of Financial Derivatives: Comptroller's Handbook," *Office of the Comptroller of the Currency, U.S. Department of the Treasury*, January 12, 2012, www.occ.treas.gov/publications/publications-by-type/comptrollers-handbook/risk-mgmt-financial-derivatives/pub-ch-risk-mgmt-financial-derivatives.pdf.

25. Morgan Ricks, "Reforming the Short-Term Funding Markets: Harvard University John M. Olin Center for Law, Economics and Business Discussion Paper No. 713," Scholars Strategy Research Network, May 18, 2012, https://ssrn.com/abstract=2062334.

26. Peter Eavis and Keith Collins, "The Banks Changed. Except for All the Ways They're the Same," *New York Times*, September 12, 2018.

27. David Dayen, "What Good Are Hedge Funds?" *American Prospect*, April 25, 2016, prospect.org/article/what-good-are-hedge-funds.

28. Ben Unglesbee, "Retail's Largest Private Equity Buyouts and How They've Panned Out," *Retail Dive*, November 9, 2018, www.retaildive.com/news/the-biggest-buyouts/541078.

29. David Dayen, "How Hedge Funds Deepen Puerto Rico's Debt Crisis," *American Prospect*, December 11, 2015, prospect.org/article/how-hedge-funds-are-pillaging-puerto-rico.

30. Miles Weiss and Zachary Mider, "Legendary Hedge Fund Wants to Use Atomic Clocks to Beat High-Speed Traders," *Bloomberg*, July 7, 2016.

31. Paul Elias, "Lawyers: Wells Fargo Created About 3.5 Million Fake Accounts," *U.S. News & World Report*, May 12, 2017.

32. Gretchen Morgenson, "Wells Fargo Forced Unwanted Auto Insurance on Borrowers," *New York Times*, July 27, 2017; Gretchen Morgenson, "Wells Fargo Is Accused of Making Improper Changes to Mortgages," *New York Times*, June 14, 2017; James Rufus Koren, "Wells Fargo Stuck Mortgage Borrowers with Extra Fees, Whistle-Blower's Lawsuit Says," *Los Angeles Times*, July 14, 2017.

33. David Dayen, "Give Wells Fargo the Corporate Death Penalty," *New Republic*, August 1, 2017.

34. Stacy Cowley, "Online Lenders and Payment Companies Get a Way to Act More Like Banks," *New York Times*, July 31, 2018.

35. Shelly Banjo, "Wall Street Is Hogging the Peer-to-Peer Lending Market," *Quartz*, March 4, 2015, qz.com/355848/wall-street-is-hogging-the-peer-to-peer-lending-market; Edward Robinson, "As Money Pours into Peer-to-Peer Lending, Some See Bubble Brewing," *Bloomberg*, May 14, 2015.

36. Sidney Fussell, "Who Wins When Cash Is No Longer King?" *CityLab*, December 26, 2018, www.citylab.com/equity/2018/12/who-wins-when-cash-no-longer-king/578983.

37. Peter Rudegeair, "A $150,000 Small Business Loan—From an App," *Wall Street Journal*, December 28, 2018; Robert Bartlett, Adair Morse, Richard Stanton, and Nancy Wallace, "Consumer-Lending Discrimination in the FinTech Era," *UC Berkeley*, May 2019, faculty.haas.berkeley.edu/morse/research/papers/discrim.pdf.

38. United States Postal Service, "Postal Savings System," *USPS*, July 2008, about .usps.com/who-we-are/postal-history/postal-savings-system.pdf; United States Postal Service, "Domestic Money Orders," USPS, n.d., www.usps.com/shop/money-orders .htm.

39. United States Postal Service, "FY2017 Annual Report to Congress" (USPS, 2017), about.usps.com/who-we-are/financials/annual-reports/fy2017/fy2017.pdf.

40. Pew Research Center, "Remittance Flows Worldwide in 2017," *Pew Research Center*, April 3, 2019, www.pewglobal.org/interactives/remittance-map

41. Mark Paul and Thomas Herndon, "A Public Banking Option as a Mode of Regulation for Household Financial Services in the United States," *Roosevelt Institute*, August 14, 2018, rooseveltinstitute.org/public-banking-option.

42. Morgan Ricks, John Crawford, and Lev Menand, "Central Banking for All: A Public Option for Bank Accounts," *Great Democracy Initiative*, June 2018, greatdemocracy initiative.org/wp-content/uploads/2018/06/FedAccountsGDI.pdf.

43. Rajiv Sethi, "The Payments System and Monetary Transmission," *Rajiv Sethi* [personal blog], November 20, 2013, rajivsethi.blogspot.com/2013/11/the-payments -system-and-monetary.html; Board of Governors of the Federal Reserve System, "Credit and Liquidity Programs and the Balance Sheet," Federal Reserve, December 26, 2018, www.federalreserve.gov/monetarypolicy/bst_fedsbalancesheet.htm.

44. Gilbert King, "The Man Who Busted the 'Banksters,'" *Smithsonian Magazine*, November 29, 2011.

45. Peter Dreier, "The Future of Community Reinvestment: Challenges and Opportunities in a Changing Environment," *Journal of the American Planning Association* 69:4 (2004), 341–353.

46. King, "The Man Who Busted the 'Banksters.'"

Who Gets to Be Safe? Prisons, Police, and Terror

1. Claudia Rankine, *Citizen: An American Lyric* (Minneapolis, MN: Graywolf Press, 2014).

2. The Prison Policy Initiative, "Mass Incarceration: The Whole Pie 2019," March 19, 2019, www.prisonpolicy.org/reports/pie2019.html.

3. Bureau of Justice Statistics, U.S. Department of Justice, "Probation and Parole in the United States, 2016," April 2018, www.bjs.gov/content/pub/pdf/ppus16.pdf.

4. Damon Williams and Daniel Kisslinger, "Episode 29: Mariame Kaba," *AirGo* podcast, February 2, 2016, soundcloud.com/airgoradio/ep-29-mariame-kaba.

5. Yana Kunichoff and Sarah Macaraeg, "How Chicago Became the First City to Make Reparations to Victims of Police Violence," *Yes! Magazine*, March 21, 2017, www.yesmagazine.org/issues/science/how-chicago-became-the-first-city-to-make -reparations-to-victims-of-police-violence-20170321.

6. Jeffrey Reiman and Paul Leighton, *The Rich Get Richer and the Poor Get Prison* (London: Pearson Education, 1979).

7. Angela Davis, *Are Prisons Obsolete?* (New York: Seven Stories Press, 2011).

8. Ava DuVernay, *13th*, Netflix, 2016.

9. Khalil Gibran Muhammad, *The Condemnation of Blackness* (Cambridge: Harvard University Press, 2010), 4.

10. United Nations Office on Drugs and Crime, "Global Study on Homicide: Gender-Related Killings of Women and Girls," November 2018, www.unodc.org/documents/data -and-analysis/GSH2018/GSH18_Gender-related_killing_of_women_and_girls.pdf.

11. Chapman University Survey of American Fears, "America's Top Fears 2018," October 16, 2018, blogs.chapman.edu/wilkinson/2017/10/11/americas-top-fears-2017.

12. Anti-Defamation League, "Murder and Extremism in the United States in 2017," January 17, 2018, www.adl.org/resources/reports/murder-and-extremism-in-the -united-states-in-2017#the-perpetrators.

13. Chris Nichols, "Fact-Checking Sad Statistic on Women Murdered by Intimate Partners in U.S.," *Politifact California*, February 19, 2018, www.politifact.com/california /statements/2018/feb/19/jackie-speier/fact-checking-sad-statistic-number-women -murdered-.

14. Watson Institute for International and Public Affairs at Brown University, "Summary of War Spending, in Billions of Current Dollars, FY2001–FY2019," November 2018, watson.brown.edu/costsofwar.

15. National Network to End Domestic Violence, "VAWA and Related Programs Appropriations for Fiscal Years 16, 17, 18, 19, and 2000," March 2019, https://nnedv.org /?mdocs-file=8444.

16. Solomon Hughes, *War on Terror, Inc.: Corporate Profiteering from the Politics of Fear* (New York: Verso, 2007).

17. Samuel Stebbins, "20 Companies Profiting the Most from War," *24/7 Wall St.*, February 20, 108, 5, 247wallst.com/special-report/2018/02/20/20-companies-profiting -the-most-from-war/5.

18. Manny Fernandez, "A Phrase for Safety After 9/11 Goes Global," *New York Times*, May 10, 2010.

19. Kelly Sundberg, *Goodbye Sweet Girl* (New York: HarperCollins Publishers, 2018), 193.

20. Rachel Pain, "Everyday Terrorism: Connecting Domestic Violence and Global Terrorism," *Progress in Human Geography* 38, no. 4 (2014), 531–50.

21. Victoria Law, "Against Carceral Feminism," *Jacobin*, October 17, 2014, www .jacobinmag.com/2014/10/against-carceral-feminism.

22. Survived and Punished. "#SurvivedAndPunished: Survivor Defense as Abolitionist Praxis," https://view.publitas.com/survived-and-punished/toolkit/page/1.

23. Maya Schenwar, *Locked Down, Locked Out* (Oakland, CA: Berrett-Koehler Publishers, 2014).

24. Generation Five, "Toward Transformative Justice: A Liberatory Approach to Child Sexual Abuse and Other Forms of Intimate and Community Violence," June 2007, www.usprisonculture.com/blog/wp-content/uploads/2012/03/G5_Toward_Trans formative_Justice.pdf.

25. Bonnie Dickie, "Hollow Water," National Film Board of Canada, 2000.

26. Stephanie Woodard, "The Police Killings No One Is Talking About," *In These Times*, October 17, 2016, inthesetimes.com/features/native_american_police _killings_native_lives_matter.html.

27. CrimethInc, "Accounting for Ourselves Breaking the Impasse Around Assault and Abuse in Anarchist Scenes," April 13, 2017, crimethinc.com/2013/04/17/accounting -for-ourselves-breaking-the-impasse-around-assault-and-abuse-in-anarchist-scenes.

28. Maya Dukmasova, "Abolish the Police? Organizers Say It's Less Crazy Than It Sounds," *Chicago Reader*, August 25, 2016, www.chicagoreader.com/chicago/police -abolitionist-movement-alternatives-cops-chicago/Content?oid=23289710.

On Immigration: A Socialist Case for Open Borders

1. Hurst Hannum, "Rethinking Self-Determination," *Virginia Journal of International Law* 34, no. 1 (1993). Also published in *Self-Determination in International Law*, ed. Robert McCorquodale (Farnham, UK: Ashgate Publishing, 2000), ssrn.com /abstract=1940662; Hurst, "Self-Determination," Oxford Index, March 2013, dx.doi.org /10.1093/obo/9780199743292-0125.

2. Domenic Powell, "How to Abolish ICE," *Jacobin*, June 29, 2018, www.jacobinmag .com/2018/06/abolish-ice-immigration-cbp-deportation; Gilberto Cárdenas, "United States Immigration Policy Toward Mexico: An Historical Perspective," *Chicana/o Latina/o Law Review* 2 (1975), escholarship.org/uc/item/0fh8773n; Elaine Godfrey, "What 'Abolish ICE' Actually Means," *The Atlantic*, July 11, 2018, www.theatlantic.com /politics/archive/2018/07/what-abolish-ice-actually-means/564752.

3. Greg Grandin, "The Vast, Stupid, Useless Wall," *Jacobin*, January 11, 2018, jaco-binmag.com/2019/01/immigration-wall-trump-borge.

4. Lucy Steigerwald, "The Case for Abolishing ICE," *The Week*, July 6, 2018, theweek.com/articles/782486/case-abolishing-ice.

5. European Parliament, "The Schengen Area Is at a Crossroads," May 30, 2018, www.europarl.europa.eu/news/en/press-room/20180524IPR04217/the-schengen -area-is-at-a-crossroads.

6. Harald Bauder, "Perspectives of Open Borders and No Border," *Geography Compass* 9 (2015), 395–405, www.researchgate.net/publication/280156538_Perspectives _of_Open_Borders_and_No_Border; Alexander Betts, "What Europe Could Learn from the Way Africa Treats Refugees," *The Guardian*, June 26, 2018, www.theguardian .com/commentisfree/2018/jun/26/europe-learn-africa-refugees-solutions; Tessa Coggio, "Can Uganda's Breakthrough Refugee-Hosting Model Be Sustained?," Migration Policy Institute, October 31, 2018, www.migrationpolicy.org/article/can-ugandas -breakthrough-refugee-hosting-model-be-sustained; Austin Bodetti, "What Arab Countries Can Learn from Uganda's Humane Approach to Neighbouring Refugees," *New Arab*, February 12, 2019, www.alaraby.co.uk/english/indepth/2019/2/12/what -arab-countries-can-learn-from-ugandas-immigration-policies; Asad Hussein, "I Grew Up in the World's Biggest Refugee Camp—What Happens When It Closes?," September 23, 2016, www.theguardian.com/world/2016/sep/23/kenya-dadaab-refugee-camp -what-happens-when-it-closes-asad-hussein.

7. Susan Ferriss, "How Trump and Sessions Cherry-Picked Data to Blame Immigrants for Lower Wages," The Center for Public Integrity, April 30, 2018, publicintegrity .org/immigration/how-trump-and-sessions-cherry-picked-data-to-blame-immigrants -for-lower-wages; Richard Eskow, "'Open Borders': A Gimmick, Not a Solution," *Democracy Daily*, republished in *Huffington Post*, August 5, 2015, www.huffpost.com /entry/open-borders-a-gimmick-no_b_7945140. See also Manjoo, Farhad, "There's Nothing Wrong with Open Borders," *New York Times*, January 16, 2019, www.nytimes .com/2019/01/16/opinion/open-borders-immigration.html; Angela Nagle, "The Left Case Against Open Borders," *American Affairs*, Winter 2018, Volume II, 4, americanaf-fairsjournal.org/2018/11/the-left-case-against-open-borders; Atossa Araxia Abra-hamian, "There Is No Left Case for Nationalism," *The Nation*, November 28, 2018, www.thenation.com/article/open-borders-nationalism-angela-nagle.

8. "Department of Homeland Security Statement on the President's Fiscal Year 2019 Budget," US Department of Homeland Security, February 12, 2018, www.dhs.gov/news /2018/02/12/department-homeland-security-statement-president-s-fiscal-year-2019 -budget.

9. Alice Edwards, "Age and Gender Dimensions in International Refugee Law," January 12, 2010, *Refugee Protection in International Law: UNHCR'S Global Consultations On International Protection*, E. Feller, V. Türk, and F. Nicholson, eds., 46–80, Cambridge University Press, 2003, www.unhcr.org/419c74784.pdf; Patrick Kingsley, "Canada's Exclusion of Single Male Refugees May Exacerbate Syrian Conflict," *The Guardian*, November 24, 2015, www.theguardian.com/world/2015/nov/24/canada-exclusion-refugees-single-syrian-men-assad-isis.

10. Kate Morrissey, "Immigration Status Can Make Matters Worse for Domestic Violence Victims," *San Diego Union-Tribune*, January 7, 2017, www.sandiegouniontribune.com/news/immigration/sd-me-domestic-violence-20170107-story.html; Bridget Anderson, Nandita Sharma, and Cynthia Wright, "Editorial: Why No Borders?" *Refuge* 26, no. 2 (2009), refugeeresearch.net//wp-content/uploads/2016/11/Anderson-et-al-2009-Why-no-borders_.pdf.

11. David Bacon, "Building a Culture of Cross-Border Solidarity," UCLA: Institute for Research on Labor and Employment, 2011, escholarship.org/uc/item/05f6g6s7.

12. "Undocumented Workers' Employment Rights," Legal Aid at Work, legalaidatwork.org/factsheet/undocumented-workers-employment-rights.

13. Gretchen Frazee, "What Constitutional Rights Do Undocumented Immigrants Have?," *PBS News Hour*, June 25, 2018, www.pbs.org/newshour/politics/what-constitutional-rights-do-undocumented-immigrants-have. Immigration Policy Center and the Legal Action Center, "Two Systems of Justice: How the Immigration System Falls Short of American Ideals of Justice Due Process and the Courts," American Immigration Council, March 19, 2013, www.americanimmigrationcouncil.org/sites/default/files/research/aic_twosystemsofjustice.pdf.

14. Julie St. Louis, "Tribal Border Alliance Calls for Better Access to Native Lands," January 28, 2019, www.courthousenews.com/tribal-border-alliance-calls-for-better-access-to-native-lands; Harald Bauder, "Sanctuary Cities: Policies and Practices in International Perspective," *International Migration (2016)*, www.researchgate.net/publication/311529902.

15. John Haltiwanger, "Immigrants Are Getting the Right to Vote in Cities Across America," September 13, 2017, *Newsweek*, www.newsweek.com/immigrants-are-getting-right-vote-cities-across-america 664467.

16. Bauder, "Sanctuary Cities," 9.

17. "Global Compact for Migration," United Nations, adopted July 13, 2018, refugeesmigrants.un.org/migration-compact.

What Does Health Equity Require? Racism and the Limits of Medicare for All

1. Alan Maass, *The Case for Socialism* (Chicago: Haymarket Books, 2010), 24.

2. T.R. Reid, *The Healing of America: A Global Quest for Better, Cheaper, and Fairer Health Care* (New York: Penguin, 2009), 20–21.

3. James Petras, "Socialism, Capitalism and Health Care," *Global Research*, November 28, 2017, https://www.globalresearch.ca/socialism-capitalism-and-health-care/56 20412.

4. Democratic Socialists of America, "DSA Priorities Resolution 2017," September 13, 2017, https://www.dsausa.org/democratic-left/dsa_priorities_resolution_2017.

5. Bernie Sanders, *Guide to Political Revolution* (New York: Henry Holt, 2017).

6. Petras, "Socialism, Capitalism and Health Care"; Reid, *Healing of America*, 207–208.

7. Sanders, *Guide to Political Revolution*, 84.

8. Sanders, *Guide to Political Revolution*, 85; Reid, *Healing of America*, 34–44.

9. Reid, *Healing of America*, 2, 210–11.

10. Reid, *Healing of America*, 31–34.

11. Papanicolas, L.R. Woskie, and A.K. Jha, "Health Care Spending in the United States and Other High-Income Countries," *Journal of the American Medical Association* 319, no. 10 (2018): 1024–39, doi:10.1001/jama.2018.1150.

12. Richard Wilkinson and Kate Pickett, *The Spirit Level: Why More Equal Societies Almost Always Do Better* (London: Allen Lane, 2009); Karen Feldscher, "What's Behind High U.S. Health Care Costs," *Harvard Gazette*, March 13, 2018, news.harvard.edu /gazette/story/2018/03/u-s-pays-more-for-health-care-with-worse-population-health -outcomes.

13. Petras, "Socialism, Capitalism and Health Care."

14. Sanders, *Guide to Political Revolution*, 98.

15. Democratic Socialists of America, *Medicare for All Organizing Guide*, January 2018, medicareforall.dsausa.org/organizing-guide/launching-a-medicare-for-all -campaign.

16. Democratic Socialists of America, www.dsausa.org.

17. "Why a Poor People's Campaign? Dr. King's Vision: The Poor People's Campaign of 1967–68," Poor People's Campaign, www.poorpeoplescampaign.org/history.

18. "Dr. Martin Luther King on Health Care Injustice," Physicians for a National Health Program, October 14, 2014, www.pnhp.org/news/2014/october/dr-martin -luther-king-on-health-care-injustice.

19. Ibid.

20. See Commission on Social Determinants of Health, World Health Organization, *Closing the Gap in a Generation: Health Equity Through Action on the Social Determinants of Health* (Geneva: World Health Organization, 2008).

21. Donald A. Barr, *Health Disparities in the United States: Social Class, Race, Ethnicity, and Health* (Johns Hopkins University Press 2014), 45–47; Nancy E. Adler and David H. Rehkopf, "U.S. Disparities in Health: Descriptions, Causes, and Mechanisms," *Annual Review of Public Health* 29, no. 235 (2008): 242–43.

22. Barr, *Health Disparities in the United States*, 42.

23.   Michael G. Marmot, Martin Shipley, and Peter J. Hamilton, "Employment Grade and Coronary Heart Disease in British Civil Servants," *Journal of Epidemiology and Community Health* 32 (1978): 244; Michael G. Marmot, Martin J. Shipley, and Geoffrey Rose, "Inequalities in Death: Specific Explanations of a General Pattern?," *Lancet* 323 (1984): 1003.

24.   National Center for Health Statistics, Centers for Disease Control and Prevention, *Health, United States, 2015: With Special Feature on Racial and Ethnic Health Disparities* (Hyattsville, MD: National Center for Health Statistics, 2016), 37–38, 100–101, www.cdc.gov/nchs/data/hus/hus15.pdf; Robert S. Levine, James E. Foster, and Robert E. Fullilove, "Black-White Inequalities in Mortality and Life Expectancy, 1933–1999: Implications for Healthy People 2010," *Public Health Reports* 116 (2001): 474, 480; David R. Williams, "Miles to Go Before We Sleep: Racial Inequities in Health," *Journal of Health and Social Behavior* 53 (2012): 279, 280.

25.   Levine, Foster, and Fullilove, "Black-White Inequalities in Mortality and Life Expectancy," 474–75.

26.   Office of Minority Health, U.S. Department of Health and Human Services, "Infant Mortality and African Americans," November 9, 2017, minorityhealth.hhs.gov /omh/browse.aspx?lvl=4&lvlid=23.

27.   Marian F. MacDorman, Eugene Declercq, Howard Cabral, and Christine Morton, "Is the United States Maternal Mortality Rate Increasing? Disentangling Trends from Measurement Issues," *Obstetrics and Gynecology* 128 (2016): 447, 450.

28.   Centers for Disease Control and Prevention, Department of Health and Human Services, "Pregnancy Mortality Surveillance System," www.cdc.gov/reproductivehealth /maternalinfanthealth/pregnancy-mortality-surveillance-system.htm.

29.   Miriam Zoila Pérez, "New Report Says U.S. Health Care Violates U.N. Convention on Racism," *Colorlines*, August 28, 2014, www.colorlines.com/articles/new-report -says-us-health-care-violates-un-convention-racism.

30.   Elizabeth Brondolo, Linda C. Gallo, and Hector F. Myers, "Race, Racism and Health: Disparities, Mechanisms, and Interventions," *Journal of Behavioral Medicine* 32 (2009): 1; David R. Williams and Selina A. Mohammed, "Racism and Health I: Pathways and Scientific Evidence," *American Behavioral Scientist* 57 (2013): 1152.

31.   Zinzi D. Bailey, N. Krieger, M. Agénor, J. Graves, N. Linos, and M.T. Bassett, "Structural Racism and Health Inequities in the USA: Evidence and Interventions," *Lancet* 389 (2017): 1453, 1456–58.

32.   Alicia Lukachko, Mark L. Hatzenbuehler, and Katherine M. Keyes, "Structural Racism and Myocardial Infarction in the United States," *Social Science and Medicine* 103 (2014): 42, 46–47.

33.   Williams and Mohammed, "Racism and Health I," 1163; Jules C. Harrell et al., "Multiple Pathways Linking Racism to Health Outcomes," *Du Bois Review* 8 (2011): 143, 143–44; Nancy Krieger, "Discrimination and Health Inequities," *International Journal of Health Services* 44 (2014): 643, 644.

34.   Sarah L. Szanton et al., "Racial Discrimination Is Associated with a Measure of Red Blood Cell Oxidative Stress: A Potential Pathway for Racial Health Disparities," *International Journal of Behavioral Medicine* 19 (2012): 489, 490.

35. Bridget J. Goosby, Elizabeth Straley, and Jacob E. Cheadle, "Discrimination, Sleep, and Stress Reactivity: Pathways to African American–White Cardiometabolic Risk Inequities," *Population Research and Policy Review* 36 (2017): 699, 700.

36. Nancy E. Adler and David H. Rehkopf, "U.S. Disparities in Health: Descriptions, Causes, and Mechanisms," *Annual Review of Public Health* 29 (2008): 235, 245–46.

37. Amy S. DeSantis et al., "Racial/Ethnic Differences in Cortisol Diurnal Rhythms in a Community Sample of Adolescents," *Journal of Adolescent Health* 41 (2007): 3, 4.

38. Desantis et al., "Racial/Ethnic Differences in Cortisol Diurnal Rhythms," 11–12; Derald Wing Sue et al., "Racial Microaggressions in Everyday Life: Implications for Clinical Practice," *American Psychologist* 62 (2007): 271, 273.

39. Jacob Bor et al., "Police Killings and Their Spillover Effects on the Mental Health of Black Americans: A Population-Based, Quasi-Experimental Study," *Lancet* 392 (2018): 302, 307–8.

40. See Douglas S. Massey and Nancy A. Denton, *American Apartheid: Segregation and the Making of the Underclass* (Cambridge, MA: Harvard University Press, 1993), 35–37; Richard Rothstein, *The Color of Law: A Forgotten History of How Our Government Segregated America* (New York: Liveright, 2017), vii–xv.

41. See Joy Rayanne Piontak and Michael D. Schulman, "School Context Matters: The Impacts of Concentrated Poverty and Racial Segregation on Childhood Obesity," *Journal of School Health* 86 (2016): 864, 865; David R. Williams and Chiquita Collins, "Racial Residential Segregation: A Fundamental Cause of Racial Disparities in Health," *Public Health Reports* 116 (2001): 404, 410–11; Williams and Mohammed, "Racism and Health I," 1158–59.

42. Bailey et al., "Structural Racism and Health Inequities in the USA," 1456. See also Williams and Mohammed, "Racism and Health I," 1159; Sue C. Grady, "Racial Disparities in Low Birthweight and the Contribution of Residential Segregation: A Multilevel Analysis," *Social Science and Medicine* 63 (2006): 3013, 3014; James W. Collins Jr. et al., "Very Low Birthweight in African American Infants: The Role of Maternal Exposure to Interpersonal Racial Discrimination," *American Journal of Public Health* 94 (2004): 2132; Abigail A. Sewell, "The Racism-Race Reification Process: A Mesolevel Political Economic Framework for Understanding Racial Health Disparities," *Sociology of Race and Ethnicity* 2 (2016): 402, 414; Robert J. Sampson and Alix S. Winter, "The Racial Ecology of Lead Poisoning: Toxic Inequality in Chicago Neighborhoods, 1995–2013," *Du Bois Review* 13 (2016): 4–5, 8.

43. Barbara J. Fields, "Ideology and Race in American History," in *Region, Race, and Reconstruction: Essays in Honor of C. Vann Woodward*, ed. J. Morgan Kousser and James M. McPherson, 148–49 (New York: Oxford University Press, 1982); Ibram X. Kendi, *Stamped from the Beginning: The Definitive History of Racist Ideas in America* (New York: Nation Books, 2016); Dorothy Roberts, *Fatal Invention: How Science, Politics, and Big Business Re-create Race in the Twenty-first Century* (New York: The New Press, 2011).

44. Lundy Braun, *Breathing Race into the Machine: The Surprising Career of the Spirometer from Plantation to Genetics* (Minneapolis: University of Minnesota Press, 2014); W. Michael Byrd and Linda A. Clayton, *An American Health Dilemma: A Medical History*

of African Americans and the Problem of Race, Beginnings to 1900 (New York: Routledge, 2000); Rana Hogarth, *Medicalizing Blackness: Making Racial Difference in the Atlantic World, 1780–1840* (Chapel Hill: University of North Carolina Press, 2017); Harriet Washington, *Medical Apartheid: The Dark History of Medical Experimentation on Black Americans from Colonial Times to the Present* (New York: Doubleday, 2006).

45.   John Hoberman, *Black and Blue: The Origins and Consequences of Medical Racism* (Berkeley: University of California Press, 2012), 32–37; Roberts, *Fatal Invention.*

46.   Dorothy Roberts, *Killing the Black Body: Race, Reproduction, and the Meaning of Liberty,* 2nd ed. (New York: Vintage, 2017); Khiara Bridges, *Reproducing Race: An Ethnography of Pregnancy as a Site of Racialization* (Berkeley: University of California Press, 2011).

47.   Monika K. Goyal, "Racial Disparities in Pain Management of Children with Appendicitis in Emergency Departments," *JAMA Pediatrics* 169 (2015): 996; Kelly M. Hoffman et al., "Racial Bias in Pain Assessment and Treatment Recommendations, and False Beliefs About Biological Differences Between Blacks and Whites," *Proceedings of the National Academy of Sciences of the United States of America* 113 (2016): 4296; Knox H. Todd et al., "Ethnicity and Analgesic Practice," *Annals of Emergency Medicine* 35 (2000): 11.

48.   Hoffman et al., "Racial Bias in Pain Assessment and Treatment Recommendations," 4300.

49.   Paul S. Chan et al., "Delayed Time to Defibrillation After In-Hospital Cardiac Arrest," *New England Journal of Medicine* 358 (2008): 9.

50.   Utibe R. Essien et al., "Association of Race/Ethnicity with Oral Anticoagulant Use in Patients with Atrial Fibrillation," *JAMA Cardiology* 3 (2018): 1174–82.

51.   Elizabeth H. Bradley et al., "Racial and Ethnic Differences in Time to Acute Reperfusion Therapy for Patients Hospitalized with Myocardial Infarction," *Journal of the American Medical Association* 292 (2004): 1563.

52.   Angela Y. Davis, *Women, Race, and Class* (New York: Vintage Books, 1981); Herbert Hill, *Black Labor and the American Legal System* (Madison: University of Wisconsin Press, 1977).

53.   Linda Gordon, *Pitied but Not Entitled: Single Mothers and the History of Welfare* (New York: Free Press, 1994), 276–77.

54.   Jake Rosenfeld and Meredith Kleykamp, "Organized Labor and Racial Wage Inequality in the United States," *American Journal of Sociology* 117, no. 5 (2012): 1460–1502.

55.   Alberto Spektorowski, "The Eugenic Temptation in Socialism: Sweden, Germany, and the Soviet Union," *Comparative Studies in Society and History* 46 (2004): 84–106.

56.   Spektorowski, "The Eugenic Temptation in Socialism," 90–98.

57.   W.E.B. DuBois, *Black Reconstruction in America 1860–1880* (1935; repr., New York: Atheneum, 1985), 700.

58.   Jill Quadagno, *The Color of Welfare: How Racism Undermined the War on Poverty* (New York: Oxford University Press, 1994).

59. Jonathan Metzl, *Dying of Whiteness: How the Politics of Racial Resentment Is Killing America's Heartland* (New York: Basic Books, 2019), xi.

60. Maureen A. Eger, "Even in Sweden: The Effect of Immigration on Support for Welfare State Spending," *European Sociological Review* 26, no. 2 (2010): 203–17.

61. Beth E. Richie, *Arrested Justice: Black Women, Violence, and America's Prison Nation* (New York: New York University Press, 2012), 127; Dora M. Dumont et al., "Public Health and the Epidemic of Incarceration," *Annual Review of Public Health* 33 (2012): 325, 328–29; Michael Massoglia, "Incarceration, Health, and Racial Disparities in Health," *Law and Society Review* 42 (2008): 275, 280–81. See generally David Cloud, "On Life Support: Public Health in the Age of Mass Incarceration," Vera Institute of Justice, 2014, www.vera.org/publications/on-life-support-public-health-in-the-age-of-mass-incarceration.

62. Roberts, *Killing the Black Body*; Loretta J. Ross and Rickie Solinger, *Reproductive Justice: An Introduction* (Berkeley: University of California Press, 2017); Jael Silliman et al., *Undivided Rights: Women of Color Organize for Reproductive Justice* (Cambridge, MA: South End Press, 2004).

63. Dorothy Roberts, "Reproductive Justice, Not Just Rights," *Dissent*, Fall 2015.

64. SisterSong, "Mobilizing the RJ Movement," trustblackwomen.org, 2018, trustblackwomen.org/mobilizing-the-rj-movement; Alveda King, "What Is PreNDA?," *Alveda King's Blog*, April 1, 2009, civilrightsfortheunborn.com/blog/index.php/about/what-is-prenda; Sara Jayden, "Choice and the 2004 March for Women's Lives," National Communication Association, June 1, 2009, www.natcom.org/communication-currents/choice-and-2004-march-womens-lives.

65. Jonathan M. Metzl and Helena Hansen, "Structural Competency: Theorizing a New Medical Engagement with Stigma and Inequality," *Social Science Medicine* 103 (2014): 126–133; Jonathan M. Metzl and Dorothy E. Roberts, "Structural Competency Meets Structural Racism: Race, Politics, and the Structure of Medical Knowledge," *AMA Journal of Ethics* 9 (2014): 674, 683–84, journalofethics.ama-assn.org/article/structural-competency-meets-structural-racism-race-politics-and-structure-medical-knowledge; Margaret Mary Downey and Anu Manchikanti Gómez, "Structural Competency and Reproductive Health," *AMA Journal of Ethics* (2018).

66. Roberts, *Fatal Invention*, 92–101; Hoberman, *Black and Blue*, 198–233.

67. Sunil Kripalani et al., "A Prescription for Cultural Competence in Medical Education," *Journal of General Internal Medicine* 21 (2006): 1116.

68. Metzl and Roberts, "Structural Competency Meets Structural Racism," 674.

69. Ibid.

The Family of the Future

1. Nina Martin, "U.S. Has the Worst Rate of Maternal Deaths in the Developed World," NPR, May 12, 2017, www.npr.org/2017/05/12/528098789/u-s-has-the-worst-rate-of-maternal-deaths-in-the-developed-world.

2. Darla Mercado, "Forget College Tuition. Annual Child-Care Costs Exceed

$20,000 in These States," August 28, 2018, www.cnbc.com/2018/08/28/forget-college
-tuition-annual-childcare-costs-exceed-20000-here.html.

3.   Sarah Leonard and Nancy Fraser, "Capitalism's Crisis of Care," *Dissent*, Fall 2016,
www.dissentmagazine.org/article/nancy-fraser-interview-capitalism-crisis-of-care.

4.   Melinda Cooper, *Family Values: Between Neoliberalism and the New Social Conservatism* (Cambridge, MA: MIT Press, 2017), 95.

5.   Cooper, *Family Values*, 97.

6.   Stephanie Coontz, *The Way We Never Were: American Families and the Nostalgia
Trap* (New York: Basic Books, 2000), 5.

7.   Toni Morrison and Junot Díaz Live at New York Public Library, published Dec
13, 2013, www.youtube.com/watch?v=J5kytPjYjSQ.

8.   Dorothy Roberts, "Reproductive Justice, Not Just Rights," *Dissent*, Fall 2015,
www.dissentmagazine.org/article/reproductive-justice-not-just-rights.

9.   *Do Communists Have Better Sex?* Dir. by André Meier, 2006. Retrieved from www
.youtube.com/watch?v=9cMccZG-dGc.

10.   Sally Weale, "Swedish Sex Education Has Time for Games and Mature Debate,"
The Guardian, June 5, 2015, www.theguardian.com/education/2015/jun/05/swedish
-sex-education-games-mature-debate.

11.   Saskia de Melker, "The Case for Starting Sex Education in Kindergarten," May 27,
2015, www.pbs.org/newshour/health/spring-fever.

12.   Central Intelligence Agency, "Country Comparison: Maternal Mortality
Rate," World Factbook, 2015 www.cia.gov/library/publications/the-world-factbook
/rankorder/2223rank.html.

13.   "People in Denmark Are Much Happier Than People in the United States. Here's
Why," *The Nation*, July 17, 2017, Retrieved: www.youtube.com/watch?v=YKuRiigagkU.

14.   Joseph Lawler, "Money Laundering Is Shaping US Cities," March 27, 2017, www
.washingtonexaminer.com/money-laundering-is-shaping-us-cities.

15.   National Alliance to End Homelessness, "State of Homelessness," 2018,
endhomelessness.org/homelessness-in-america/homelessness-statistics/state-of
-homelessness-report.

16.   Meagan Day, "We Can Have Beautiful Public Housing," *Jacobin*, November 13,
2018, jacobinmag.com/2018/11/beautiful-public-housing-red-vienna-social-housing.

17.   Eve Blau, "Re-visiting Red Vienna," Austria Embassy Washington, www.austria
.org/revisiting-red-vienna.

18.   Nadine Brozan, "For Low-Cost Co-op, a Pricing Quandry: A Co-op Ago-
nizes Over Price Ceilings," *New York Times*, February 3, 2002, web.archive.org/web
/20061101143944/http://www.kossarsbialys.com/times%2525252520coop.htm.

19.   "An Overview of Abortion Laws," Guttmacher Institute, accessed March 2019,
www.guttmacher.org/state-policy/explore/overview-abortion-laws.

20.   L. B. Tyrer, "Health Benefits of Legal Abortion: An Analysis," *Plan Parent Rev.*,
Summer 1985, www.ncbi.nlm.nih.gov/pubmed/12340404.

21. Lawrence B. Finer, Lori F. Frohwirth, Lindsay A. Dauphinee, Susheela Singh, and Ann M. Moore, "Reasons U.S. Women Have Abortions: Quantitative and Qualitative Perspectives," Guttmacher Insitute, 110 Perspectives on Sexual and Reproductive Health, September 2005, www.guttmacher.org/sites/default/files/pdfs/journals /3711005.pdf.

22. Mariame Kaba, "How the School-to-Prison Pipeline Works," *Teen Vogue*, October 10, 2017, www.teenvogue.com/story/how-the-school-to-prison-pipeline-works.

23. Ethan Brown, "Caging Kids Is an American Tradition," *The Appeal*, January 3, 2019, theappeal.org/caging-kids-is-an-american-tradition.

24. Sarah Jaffe, "This Model of Education Is Not Sustainable," *The Nation*, January 15, 2019, www.thenation.com/article/la-teachers-strike-interviews-class-size.

25. ABC7.com staff, "Exclusive Poll: LA Public Supports Striking Teachers," ABC7 .com, January 14, 2019 abc7.com/education/exclusive-poll-la-public-supports-striking -teachers/5077986.

26. Audre Lorde, *Zami: A New Spelling of My Name* (Berkeley, CA: Crossing Press, 1982), 179.

27. Coontz, *The Way We Never Were*, 36.

28. Peter Moscowitz, "When It Comes to Gentrification, LGBTQ People Are Both Victim and Perpetrator," *Vice*, March 16, 2017, www.vice.com/en_us/article/nz5qwb /when-it-comes-to-gentrification-lgbtq-people-are-both-victim-and-perpetrator.

29. Sophie Lewis, *Full Surrogacy Now* (London: Verso, 2019), 19.

Defending and Improving Public Education

1. I. Katznelson and M. Weir, *Schooling for All* (Berkeley: University of California Press, 1985).

2. Kids Count Data Center, report, Annie E. Casey Foundation, Washington, DC, 2018.

3. Gary Orfield and Erica Frankenberg, with Jongyeon Ee and John Kuscera, "Brown at 60: Great Progress, a Long Retreat and an Uncertain Future," UCLA Civil Rights Project/Proyecto Derechos Civiles (CRP), May 15, 2014.

4. D. Rusakoff, *The Prize: Who's in Charge of America's Schools?* (New York: Houghton Mifflen, 2015).

5. James S. Coleman, "Equality of Educational Opportunity," National Center for Education Statistics, 1966.

6. U.S. Commission on Civil Rights, "Public Education Funding Inequity in an Era of Increasing Concentration of Poverty and Resegregation," January 11, 2018.

7. R. Sisk, "Gingrich and Sharpton Team Up to Rally for Education," *Daily News*, May 16, 2009.

8. A. Greenblatt, "The Problem with State Takeovers," *Governance*, June 2018.

9. Michael Fullan and Joanne Quinn, *Coherence: The Right Drivers in Action for Schools, Districts and Systems* (New York: Corwin, 2015).

10.   Anthony S. Bryke et al., *Organizing Schools for Improvement: Lessons from Chicago* (Chicago: University of Chicago Press, 2010).

11.   M. Akter, "De Blasio's School Renewal Plan Spirals to Failure," *Science Survey*, May 1, 2018.

12.   D. Kirp, *Kids First: Five Big Ideas for Transforming Children's Lives* (New York: Public Affairs, 2011).

13.   P. Noguera and R. Rothstein, "The Reauthorization of ESEA," *New York Times Blog*, October 16, 2010.

14.   A.W. Boykin and P. Noguera, *Creating the Opportunity to Learn: Moving from Research to Practice to Close the Achievement Gap* (Washington, DC: ASCD, 2011).

15.   Anna J. Egalite and Patrick J. Wolf, "A Review of the Empirical Research on Private School Choice," *Peabody Journal of Education* 91, no. 4 (2016): 441–54, https://doi.org/10.1080/0161956X.2016.1207436.

16.   E. Frankenberg, S. Diem, and C. Cleary, "School Desegregation After Parents Involved: The Complications of Pursuing Diversity in a High-Stakes Accountability Era," *Journal of Urban Affairs* 39, no. 2 (2017), 160–184.

17.   Brian Knowlton and International Herald Tribune, "Zero-Tolerance Injustices Multiplying, Critics Say : A Backlash in the U.S.," *New York Times*, February 14, 2000.

18.   Office for Civil Rights, U.S. Department of Education, "Civil Rights Data Collection (CRDC) for the 2013-14 School Year," June 7, 2016.

19.   "$2.3 Billion," EdBuild, February 2019, https://edbuild.org/content/23 -billion.

What About a Well-Fed Artist? Imagining Cultural Work in a Democratic Socialist Society

1.   "Ten Good Reasons to Eliminate Funding for the National Endowment for the Arts," The Heritage Foundation, April 23, 1997, www.heritage.org/report/ten-good -reasons-eliminate-funding-the-national-endowment-orthe arts.

How Socialism Surged, and How It Can Go Further

1.   Simcha Barkai, "Declining Labor and Capital Shares," 2016, home.uchicago.edu /barkai/doc/BarkaiDecliningLaborCapital.pdf.

Afterword: A Day in the Life of a Socialist Citizen

1.   Karl Marx and Friedrich Engels, *The German Ideology*, ed. R. Pascal (New York: International Publishers, 1947), 22.

2.   Marx and Engels, *German Ideology*, 22.

3.   Jean-Jacques Rousseau, *The Social Contract*, trans. G.D.H. Cole (New York: E.P. Dutton and Company, Inc., 1950), bk. 111, chap. 15, 93.

4.   Jean-Jacques Rousseau, "Considerations on the Government of Poland," in *Political Writings*, trans. Frederick Watkins (Edinburgh: Thomas Nelson & Sons, 1953), 220.

5.   It is sympathetically restated by Alan Bloom in his introduction to Rousseau's "Letter to M. D'Alembert on the Theatre," in *Politics and the Arts* (Glencoe, IL: Free Press, 1960), xv–xxxviii.

6.   Rousseau, *Social Contract*, bk. III, chap. 15, 93.

7.   Melvin Tumin, "Comment on Papers by Riesman, Sills, and Tax," *Human Organization* 18 (Spring 1959): 28.

8.   John Calvin, *Letters of John Calvin*, ed. Jules Bonnet, trans. David Constable (Edinburgh, 1855), vol. l, 371. Of all alternate communities, the family is clearly the greatest danger to the movement and the state. That is not only because of the force of familial loyalty, but also because the family is a place of retreat from political battles: we go home to rest, to sleep.

Contributor Biographies

J. Mijin Cha is assistant professor of urban and environmental policy at Occidental College. Her current research agenda focuses on "just transition"—how to transition communities and workers economically dependent upon fossil fuel extraction and use into a low-carbon future in a way that is equitable and just.

Michelle Chen is a contributing writer at *In These Times* and *The Nation*, a contributing editor at *Dissent*, and a co-producer of the magazine's *Belabored* podcast. She teaches about history and labor at the City University of New York.

David Dayen is the executive editor of the *American Prospect*. His work has appeared in *The Intercept*, the *New Republic*, *HuffPost*, the *Washington Post*, *Los Angeles Times*, and more. His first book, *Chain of Title: How Three Ordinary Americans Uncovered Wall Street's Great Foreclosure Fraud*, winner of the Studs and Ida Terkel Prize, was released by The New Press in 2016.

Francesca Fiorentini is a correspondent and stand-up comedian. She is the host and head writer for *Newsbroke* on AJ+. She is also a regular guest on *The Young Turks* and a correspondent with *Explorer* on the National Geographic Channel. Follow her @franifio.

Bill Fletcher Jr. is a longtime labor writer and activist, having worked for several unions as well as having served as a senior staff person in the national AFL-CIO. He is also the former president of TransAfrica Forum. Fletcher is the author of three nonfiction books focusing on the labor movement and is most recently the author of the mystery novel *The Man Who Fell from the Sky*, dealing with race, justice, revenge, and Cape Verdean Americans.

Andrea Flynn is a fellow at the Roosevelt Institute, where she research-es and writes about race, gender, and economic inequality. She is a co-author of *The Hidden Rules of Race: Barriers to an Inclusive Economy* and her writing has appeared in the *Washington Post*, *Time*, *The Atlan-tic*, the *New Republic*, *Cosmopolitan*, and *Salon*.

Sarita Gupta is a nationally recognized expert on economic, labor, and political issues affecting working people, particularly women and those employed in low-wage sectors. She is the director of the Ford Foun-dation's Future of Work(ers) program and the former co-executive director of Jobs With Justice and Caring Across Generations.

Darrick Hamilton is a stratification economist, the executive director of the Kirwan Institute for the Study of Race and Ethnicity at The Ohio State University, and a fellow at the Roosevelt Institute. His academic work is widely published in peer-reviewed journals, book chapters, and popular media press, such as the *New York Times* and the *Washington Post*. In addition, his media appearances include Al Jazeera America, NPR, MSNBC, and the BBC.

Susan Holmberg is a political economist and a fellow at the Roosevelt Institute, where she researches and writes on inequality, corporate governance, and climate change issues. She is the author and co-author of numerous books, reports, and articles, including *The Hidden Rules of Race: Barriers to an Inclusive Economy*.

Naomi Klein is an award-winning journalist and *New York Times* bestselling author of books including of *This Changes Everything: Capitalism vs. the Climate* and *The Shock Doctrine: The Rise of Disas-ter Capitalism*. She is a senior correspondent for *The Intercept*, a Puffin Writing Fellow at Type Media Center, and the inaugural Gloria Steinem Chair in Media, Culture and Feminist Studies at Rutgers University. Her latest book is *On Fire: The (Burning) Case for a Green New Deal*.

Robert Kuttner is co-founder and co-editor of the *American Prospect*, and professor at Brandeis University's Heller School. His latest book is

The Stakes: 2020 and the Survival of American Democracy. In addition to writing for the *Prospect*, he writes for *HuffPost*, the *Boston Globe*, and the *New York Review of Books.*

Sarah Leonard is a writer and editor in New York. She is on the masthead of *The Nation*, *Dissent*, and *The Appeal.* She has co-edited two books: *Occupy! An OWS-Inspired Gazette*, with literary magazine *n+1*, and *The Future We Want: Radical Solutions for the 21st Century.*

Stephen Lerner is a fellow at Georgetown University's Kalmanovitz Initiative for Labor and the Working Poor and architect of the Justice for Janitors campaign. He is an American labor and community organizer. He has organized janitors, farm workers, garment workers, and other low-wage workers into unions.

Joseph A. McCartin teaches history and directs the Kalmanovitz Initiative for Labor and the Working Poor at Georgetown University. His research focuses on the intersection of labor, politics, and public policy. Among his books are *Collision Course: Ronald Reagan, the Air Traffic Controllers, and the Strike That Changed America* and *Labor in America: A History* (co-authored with Melvyn Dubofsky).

Harold Meyerson is the editor-at-large at the *American Prospect.* He was a longtime op-ed columnist at the *Washington Post* and is an op-ed contributor to the *Los Angeles Times.* His articles on politics, labor, the economy, foreign policy, and American culture have also appeared in the *New Yorker*, *The Atlantic*, the *New Republic*, *The Nation*, the *New Statesman*, the *New York Times*, numerous other publications.

Tejasvi Nagaraja is assistant professor of history at the New York State School of Industrial and Labor Relations at Cornell University. He previously worked at New York University, Harvard, and the New School. His research considers how social movements grapple with war, militarization, empire, and solidarity—from New Deal labor unions and World War II to black freedom and Vietnam, and beyond.

He is completing a book on intersecting movements among the anti-fascist "Greatest Generation"—a transnational history of military-industrial labor struggles, black soldiers' civil rights activism against criminal-justice racism, and veterans' protest of U.S. foreign policy.

Pedro Noguera is distinguished professor of education at the Graduate School of Education and Information Studies and faculty director for the Center for the Transformation of Schools at the University of California, Los Angeles. A sociologist and the author of multiple books, Dr. Noguera focuses his scholarship and research on the ways in which schools are influenced by social and economic conditions as well as by demographic trends in local, regional, and global contexts.

Dorothy Roberts is the George A. Weiss University Professor of Law and Sociology, the Raymond Pace and Sadie Tanner Mossell Alexander Professor of Civil Rights, and professor of Africana studies at the University of Pennsylvania. Her major books include *Fatal Invention: How Science, Politics, and Big Business Re-create Race in the Twenty-first Century* (The New Press); *Shattered Bonds: The Color of Child Welfare*; and *Killing the Black Body: Race, Reproduction, and the Meaning of Liberty*.

Aviva Stahl is a Brooklyn-based investigative journalist who writes about prisons and national security issues. She also reviews books, plays, and other works that engage with the issue of interpersonal violence. Her work has been published by a broad array of outlets, including *The Intercept*, *Harper's*, *The Guardian*, *Vice* magazine, and the *Columbia Journalism Review*. Stahl's deep dive into the Manhattan Correctional Center, published by *Gothamist*, won the 2018 James Aronson Award for Social Justice Journalism.

Thomas J. Sugrue is professor of social and cultural analysis and history at New York University. A specialist in twentieth-century American politics, urban history, civil rights, and race, Sugrue is author of *Not Even Past: Barack Obama and the Burden of Race*, *Sweet Land of Liberty: The Forgotten Struggle for Civil Rights in the North*, and

The Origins of the Urban Crisis. Sugrue's newest book, co-authored with Glenda Gilmore of Yale University, is *These United States: A Nation in the Making, 1890 to the Present.*

Michael Walzer is professor emeritus at the Institute for Advanced Study in Princeton, New Jersey, and an editor emeritus of *Dissent.* He has written about a wide variety of topics in political theory and moral philosophy, including political obligation, just and unjust war, nationalism and ethnicity, economic justice, and the welfare state.

Dorian Warren is president of Community Change and Community Change Action. He is also co-chair of the Economic Security Project. A progressive scholar, organizer, and media personality, Warren is co-author of *The Hidden Rules of Race: Barriers to an Inclusive Economy* and co-editor of *Race and American Political Development.* He has appeared regularly on television and radio including NBC Nightly News, ABC, MSNBC, and CNN and has written for *The Nation*, *HuffPost*, *Newsweek*, *Salon*, the *Washington Post*, and the *New York Times*, among other outlets.

Felicia Wong is the president and CEO of the Roosevelt Institute, which seeks to re-imagine the social and economic policies of Franklin and Eleanor Roosevelt for the twenty-first century. She is the co-author of *The Hidden Rules of Race: Barriers to an Inclusive Economy* and her work has appeared in the *New York Times*, the *Washington Post*, *Time*, *Democracy: A Journal of Ideas*, and the *Boston Review.*

David Zirin, *The Nation*'s sports editor, is the author of ten books on the politics of sports, most recently *Jim Brown: Last Man Standing.* Named one of UTNE Reader's "50 Visionaries Who Are Changing Our World," Zirin is a frequent guest on ESPN, MSNBC, and Democracy Now! He also hosts *The Nation*'s *Edge of Sports* podcast.

Publishing in the Public Interest

Thank you for reading this book published by The New Press. The New Press is a nonprofit, public interest publisher. New Press books and authors play a crucial role in sparking conversations about the key political and social issues of our day.

We hope you enjoyed this book and that you will stay in touch with The New Press. Here are a few ways to stay up to date with our books, events, and the issues we cover:

- Sign up at www.thenewpress.com/subscribe to receive updates on New Press authors and issues and to be notified about local events
- Like us on Facebook: www.facebook.com/newpressbooks
- Follow us on Twitter: www.twitter.com/thenewpress

Please consider buying New Press books for yourself; for friends and family; or to donate to schools, libraries, community centers, prison libraries, and other organizations involved with the issues our authors write about.

The New Press is a 501(c)(3) nonprofit organization. You can also support our work with a tax-deductible gift by visiting www.thenewpress.com/donate.